Song Sung True

Song Sung True
A Memoir

Malka Pukhraj

Edited and Translated by
SALEEM KIDWAI

A SISTER IMPRINT OF KALI FOR WOMEN

Song Sung True: A Memoir
First published in 2003 by Kali for Women

Reprinted in 2003 by

Zubaan
K-92, 1st Floor, Hauz Khas Enclave
New Delhi - 110 016

ISBN 81 86706 60 7 (Hb)

Typeset at Print Services, B-17, Lajpat Nagar, Part II
New Delhi - 110 024
Printed at Raj Press, R 3, Inder Puri, New Delhi 110 012

Dedicated to the memory of
my husband
Syed Shabbir Hussain Shah
and
Maharaja Hari Singh
the last ruler of
Jammu and Kashmir

Translator's Note

As I read the first few pages Malka Pukhraj's hand-written memoirs, I realized how lucky I was to be in a position to play a part, albeit a minor one, in conveying her powerful voice to the world of print. I also became aware of the tremendous responsibility that this task carried. Malka Pukhraj's memoirs were hand written in nine notebooks. It was clear that they would have to be edited, even in the original version, before they could be translated. I would also need many clarifications given that she wrote them in her eighties. Though written in fluent Urdu, with colourful Punjabi deflections, they contained a fascinating mixture of words and phrases from her mothertongue Dogri, and from Punjabi and English with even the odd term in pidgin French.

To ensure that I did not misread words, I spent many hours with Malka Pukhraj in Lahore. I sought her permission to make some changes though I omitted nothing of any significance. I removed repetitions and often rearranged the text in certain places for the sake of continuity. Though she had organized the initial part of her memoirs into chapters, the latter half was one long paragraph! The breaks in the text that you now see have been introduced by me. Many questions are bound to be raised about what has not been included here. The choice of what to include belongs undeniably to the author. I considered it an audacity suggest that she change anything.

I have been very careful in ensuring that I was able to convey what she wanted to tell the world about her remarkable life.

I owe gratitude to many. First, to Raza Qasim who handed the manuscript to me, and to Radha Kumar for suggesting me as translator. In the course of the work I would not have been able to manage without the help of Farazeh Syed, Malka Pukhraj's grand daughter who arranged and assisted in my sessions with the author. Her help in typing manuscript into Urdu and her deflection of other pressures was invaluable. She should be proud of her contribution in preserving this valuable history. Carla Petievich commented on parts of the first draft. Babli Moitra-Saraf, with her experience in translating, and S. Kalidas, with his knowledge of music and Indian music traditions, made valuable suggestions on the final draft.

Finally, it was Malka Pukhraj's music that helped most. I often played it while working so that her voice, so enchanting musically, was in no way deprived of its power once translated into words.

Saleem Kidwai

Contents

Part I

Part I

1. My Birth

I was born in a small village called Hamirpur Sidhdhar in the princely kingdom of Jammu and Kashmir. Hamirpur, which is about nine miles from Akhnur, lies alongside the river Chenab. My birth was nothing short of a miracle.

In the village lived an old man, Baba Roti Ram, whom everyone considered a saint. So involved was the Baba in his mystic quest that no matter what the weather, he wore no clothes at all, not even in Hamirpur's freezing winter. I remember sleeping out in the open in the month of June and needing a heavy quilt. From across the icy waters of the river blew a cold wind that would make our teeth chatter even under the heavy quilts. As it came close to the village, the river widened as though it were an ocean—standing on one side, you could not see the other shore.

It was believed that Baba had emerged from a rubbish dump. The villagers used to dig huge ditches to collect dead leaves, branches and cow dung; these dumps provided them the manure for their fields. People say that once when the manure was being taken out, a shovel hit the Baba's leg. When the rest of the manure was removed, they found Baba. God knows if this is true or not, but this was the version most people believed. In fact, no one knew who he was, where he had come from, whose son he was, whether he was a Hindu, a Musalman, a Sikh or a Christian. He even refused to tell people his name. And that was why the villagers decided to give him a name—Baba Roti Ram.

Baba never approached anyone. When supplicants came, he already knew what they wanted. Baba would not look at a supplicant. Directing himself at a third person, he would tell him all about the supplicant's problems. For instance, if a man came to him because his wife had eloped, Baba would turn to someone else and in his sweet Dogri, say: 'Look, brother, think about this matter and tell me honestly. Do I look like someone who goes around looking for wives willing to elope? If these pimps cannot look after their own wives, why should others risk getting their faces blackened? Am I a pimp or a whore-trader, that I should know about these matters?' Yet if he knew that the wife would eventually come back, he would add: 'She is not going to spend the rest of her life there. Let the fat one relax and indulge herself for a few days. Her appetite satisfied, she will be back in a few days. She will return.' Similarly, Baba knew what was on the minds of those who crowded around him for blessings and grace.

Baba often used foul language and did not hesitate to get into violent physical fights. Yet, the people worshipped him and had trementous respect for him. Baba was famous in all the surrounding villages. People would come from afar just to offer their respects. Baba never asked for anything, nor was he ever polite. Since people believed that anything he said would come true, they referred to his tongue as 'the naked sword'.

Baba's presence made our village, Hamirpur Sidhdhar, very famous. When they came to see him people brought offerings of food, fruit and sweets, but the Baba touched nothing. He liked only *pakoras* and dry tobacco. Four or five times a day he would eat a few pakoras and sometimes massage his gums with tobacco.

The village had no fruit trees except a couple of guava trees and one mango tree. In those days Jammu and Kashmir was ruled by Pratap Singh. The Maharaja had great faith in holy men of all types. Every winter, he would send Baba two sets of *bhengis*: large wicker baskets hung at both ends of a sturdy bamboo and carried across the shoulders. In these baskets as offerings were sweets, a velvet mattress and quilt, pillows and bolsters, a *pashmina* robe, *a dhussa*, an 'eared' pashmina cap, woollen socks and gold-embroidered shoes. The Maharaja was aware that the Baba was so intoxicated with divine ecstasy that these things did not mean anything to him, and he would therefore send four men along with the gifts to ensure that the Baba accepted them.

These men had an unenviable job. It was not easy to overcome Baba's resistance, no matter how hard they tried. First there was the awe that Baba inspired in everyone and then there was the huge stick in his hands. They also knew that one curse from Baba would be the end of their happiness. On the other hand, they feared the Maharaja. They might lose their jobs, even their lives, if they did not dress the Baba, and make him accept the royal gifts. After trying for a few days, they would somehow manage to dress and seat Baba against a bolster on the velvet mattress. An eared cap on his head, and wrapped in a dhussa, Baba looked like a doll. The villagers young and old, male and female, would gather around him to look. Baba would look at them with the hint of a smile and there would be a naughty, childlike twinkle in his eyes. All the sweets would be distributed among the people. The royal employees, having discharged their duty, would leave.

When the next day dawned, Baba would again be as naked as a plucked chicken, sitting like a crow on a mound of mud. The cotton stuffing from the beautiful mattress and pillows would be scattered all over and dogs would be running around with pieces of cloth in their mouths. Baba, as always, would be sitting quietly on the mound, head in hands, deep in thought. His body would be covered with a sheet of ice. Small crystals of ice that had formed in his hair and brows sparkled like pearls while Baba casually warmed himself in the sun.

When he was in a good mood, he would sing some couplets from the mystic poet, Kabir. He sang beautifully. His voice conveyed so much emotion that listeners were left stunned. If he joked, everyone rolled with laughter. And when he abused, he used words and phrases no one had heard till then. He was an amazing man. There were countless tales about his miracles. Anyone who had a problem would head straight for Baba.

At the time I was born, doctors were hard to find even in the cities, let alone the villages. Any woman who had six or seven children was considered experienced and capable of helping others deliver children. The more children she had, the more experienced the woman was believed to be. Two or three such women would work as midwives in each village. In the sixth month the midwife would begin massaging the expectant mother. Forty days after the birth, these midwives departed, having received gifts of clothes, food, and money. Some families even gave them a small piece of jewellery. As long as the midwife lived, every spring, on *baisakhi* day, she would thread a necklace of raisins, coconut and dried dates for the child she had delivered and would visit him. The child would be placed on her lap and the parents would gift her money.

When my grandmother found that mother had gone into labour, she ran out and called a few women. In those days it was a tradition that irrespective of the weather, there would always be a stove of burning coal next to the woman in labour. All the windows and skylights were closed to save the mother from the draught. My grandmother, too, lit a stove and placed it near mother. Mud houses had very few windows and even these she now closed. Every ten minutes or so she would throw some fragrant gum resin into the fire. This would cause so much smoke that it became impossible to breathe. When the pain increased, the mother was made to squat on two bricks placed on the floor. To support the patient, the *Dai* (midwife) would sit behind her charge. The expectant mother was constantly encouraged to 'push hard—the harder you push the sooner this will be over.' If the woman made too much noise or wailed too loudly, the older women would joke 'Daughter, you should have thought of this earlier,' and all of them would giggle through their toothless mouths.

Mother too had to go through the same ritual. Matters were not helped by the concoction of milk, *ghee*, almonds, and pistachio nuts which she was made to drink from time to time. Sometimes they would lay her on the bed and sometimes make her squat on the bricks. They tried all the tricks they had learnt delivering babies in the village but none of them worked.

Mother was in labour for three days and was almost dead from the pain she was going through. My grandmother went to my grandfather, who loved his daughter very much, and pleaded: 'Gulzar's father, if there is anything you can do, please do it immediately. Otherwise there is no hope.' Sobbing uncontrollably, she described mother's state: 'Nothing is working. She does not even have the strength left to speak. She looks at me in a strange way ... .'

My Nana ran to Baba. Fortunately he found him alone sitting on his *charpai*. Nana pleaded: 'Baba, I am in great trouble, please pray for me. God might help me. Today you must pray for me because I have never asked this favour of you before. Pray that the child is born safely.'

Baba, who was holding a *pakori* in his hand, stared at my grandfather. Then, offering him the pakori he told my grandfather softly, in Dogri, 'Go. Make her eat this.' Nana rushed home and sent the pakori inside. It was nothing but Allah's grace, for the moment the pakori was put in mother's mouth, the worst was over. When my Nana first heard the child's cry, he said: 'Wrap up the baby well and bring it outside.' I was wrapped up and handed over to my grandfather who took me straight to Baba. Nana was just about to enter when Baba said: 'Gobinda, (Baba always called my Nana Gobinda and my grandmother, Parvati) I do not know if it is a boy or a girl. But she is a *malka i-muazamma*—"the great empress." She will reign one day.' What surprises me today is that in a village where only a handful of people knew the first few of letters of the Urdu alphabet, Baba, who spoke only Dogri, gave me a name in such refined Urdu.

A childless cousin of mother's, too, had her hopes pinned on me. Before I was born she had kept insisting that be it a boy or a girl, the child would be hers. 'If it is a girl, I will call her Pukhraj— a topaz' she had already declared. The poor lady had pondered over names for months. Baba, however, had already named me on his own. Thus efforts had to be made not to hurt my aunt. After much thought, it was decided to let Baba's name be my first name and my aunt's, the second. This is how I became Malka Pukhraj.

2. Childhood

I was brought up in a home where I had all the love a child could want. There was the aunt who had named me. Then there was my grandfather's sister who had never married. She was simple, innocent, affable and generous. She managed to keep herself constantly happy. The third member of this family was mother's younger sister, about twelve years of age. The fourth was my grandmother. She loved me as though I was the greatest gift she had ever been given. So frantic was she in her love that if mother ever punished me, Nani would start banging her head against a wall. Everyone called my grandfather's sister Phupho Nikki. Once I arrived, she was interested in no one other than me. She never left me alone. I was her life and her faith. She would address me with great respect and, like a child, pretend to be afraid of me. For fear of upsetting me she never went against my wishes.

My grandfather was a poor, hard-working man. He had a small piece of land, which he and his two brothers cultivated. All three were tall, well-built and impressive. There was a buffalo in the house for milk and butter and a pair of bullocks for cultivation. There was also a horse for riding or carting fodder. In those days a good horse cost five or six rupees and a good, milk-yielding buffalo could be had for eight rupees. Land was very cheap. Good arable land cost three rupees an acre. Nana worked in his fields during the day, and in the evening he hand-stitched muslin *kurtas* for which he earned six *annas* per piece. For machine stitching, the charges were two annas for a kurta and four *paise* for a *shalwar*. In a day he earned eight to ten annas. Rice, wheat, sugarcane and lentils were produced in our fields and so we were comfortably off. My grandfather also managed to produce 30 to 40 *maunds* of cotton, which was used for quilts, mattresses and weaving cloth and sheets. These handloom sheets were warm enough, even for the winter. My Nani and Nana's younger brother's wife did all the housework.

Lord knows what steel these women were made of! I still cannot fathom how they managed to do so much in a day. In summer, Nani would get up at four and carry the milk pot to the river where, by holding it in the ice cold water, she ensured a better yield of butter from it. Then, she and my aunt would come home and feed the animals. They got baskets of husk, drew water from the wells, and then used it to wash the husk. Then they mixed it with fodder and put it in troughs for the animals. After this they would make *parathas* with very little ghee for everyone, young or old. Everyone got a breakfast of parathas, pickle and *lassi*. After breakfast both of them would start cooking lunch. They would put the pots on a fire of cow-dung cakes and then sit across from each other at the grinding stone. The pots, made of clay, would cook on the slow heat of the burning cow-dung and there was never any fear of the food getting burnt. After the grinding they would go out to collect more cow-dung and set about patting it into cakes. They would then move the animals to another spot while they cleaned the area where they had been tied. If the place got too wet, they would dry it by bringing in basketfuls of dry mud and sprinkling it over the dampness, which otherwise destroyed the hooves of the animals.

The courtyard of the house was very large and around it were mud rooms. On one side was the room for the animals. Next to it was a very long room, the godown, in which a year's supply of husk for the animals and grain for the family was kept. There was also a bamboo-framed, straw-thatched animal enclosure. All the other rooms were for the family. In one corner of the courtyard was a small well with a wooden wheel. It was rotated to let the empty bucket down and rotated in reverse to bring up a full one. In the middle of the courtyard was a slightly raised platform, which was edged by a low mud wall. On it were a few mud hearths. These were for cooking in the day in winter. Cooking here kept the smoke out of the living room. The platform on which they cooked was regularly plastered with a paste of cow dung and mud. It was so smooth and clean that we all used to sit on it to eat. There were also three or four hearths inside a room and a huge chimney so that dinner could be cooked there and the room also kept warm. Today people spend hundreds of thousands to build themselves fireplaces. Some use marble and others use wood. Yet those mud fireplaces of the village had their unique and unforgettable beauty.

Everyone in the family would help themselves to generous helpings of curry, and wheat *phulkas* were served straight from the iron *tavas* on which they were cooked right there in the room. They would be so hot that you had to blow on each morsel before putting it into your mouth. Only God can describe the taste of that food. Today, no matter how hard one tries, it is impossible to find those flavours again.

Looking after the mud roofs was also the responsibility of my Nani. The roofs of mud houses were made of reeds laid across wooden beams. Over this matting of reed was plastered a mixture of cow-dung and husk. And presto, the roof was ready! Whenever it rained, be it summer or winter, the roof would begin to drip. These poor women would then take the ashes from the *tandoor* and sprinkle them over the rooftop. When it stopped raining, they would plaster the roof all over again.

In the heat of the summer they would bake *rotis* in a tandoor for the entire clan. After dinner, by the light of oil lamps, they would spin cotton on their spinning wheels. They also kept the floors of the rooms clean and smooth by regularly plastering them with a mixture of white clay, regular clay and cow-dung. They polished it so clean that you could sit on the floor instead of on a low stool or a *binna*. In any case, there was no furniture in those days. Soft mats made of woven sugarcane fibre called binnas were offered immediately to every guest as a part of village etiquette. Otherwise the guests would be offended and complain: 'they did not even offer us a binna to sit on.'

My Nani and her sister-in-law would sit on either side of a mortar and pound the husk off the rice for dinner. They would winnow the grain. They would remove the seeds from the cotton. With their spindles they drew thread from the cotton and then spun the yarn on their spinning wheels. In those days a good housewife was one who had a dozen or two extra sets of bedding. Flse she was branded as good for nothing. Apart from this, they had to knead Nana's tired limbs while he fell off to sleep, henna his hair, draw water from the well to bathe him, oil his hair and massage his scalp, and wash his clothes. They looked after Nana as a mother cares for a child. And in spite of doing all this work, they were beaten a couple of times every month.

My Nana was a courageous man, hard working and large-hearted. He was completely illiterate, yet unafraid of any challenge. He made sure there was no shortage of anything in the house. Even if he had to borrow money on interest from the Hindu moneylender, no one at home ever found out. Whenever he shopped, he bought enough for everyone. For example, in the summer mangoes from other villages would come to our village. Each mule had a sackful hung on each side. Each sack cost five or six annas. At most, the price would rise by another two annas. My Nana always bargained for an entire mule load. For three or four days the whole family ate as many mangoes as they could.

The juice of the local mango was very watery. These mangoes could not be peeled or sliced. Every season he would buy a few mule loads. In the evening we would take the mangoes to the river, wrap them in a cloth and hold them in the water for fifteen or twenty minutes. By then they would be ice cold. We would sit on the bank of the river and suck the juice out of these mangoes. I remember each of those moments vividly. Till today I thoroughly dislike the hybrid grafted varieties of mango that have now become common. I taste a few slices of the *langda* every season. How I would love to have those sweet-sour, watery, yellow-juiced mangoes if I could find them again. Now, only occasionally do I find those mangoes in Lahore.

One of my Nana's brothers had studied Urdu and Persian. He did not share in the work in the fields. For him, it was only books— of fiction and books on traditional medicine. Fiction in those days usually consisted of stories of demons and fairies, djinns, or of Shah Bahram, Gul i-Bakkawali, the prophet Solomon, Saif ul muluk and the like. All the books were hand-written and some had pictures painted in gold. Since he practised as a physician, my grand-uncle had many books on medicine. Syphilis and gonorrhea were widespread all over the mountains. If one person had a hole in his throat, the nose of another would be about to fall off; some were unable even to move. He would treat them for six months or so and they would be hale and hearty. In gratitude they would offer money or clothes, and often even a buffalo or a horse. Therefore, he too was able to live very comfortably. He did not speak much. The family believed he had lost touch with reality because of all his reading.

The aunt who had named me was my Nana's niece. She was soft tempered, kind, pleasant and given to extreme cleanliness. She would scrub every coin with sand before she handled it, re-wash a clean dish before she used it and would not let anyone sit on her bed. She always wanted to have her way and would often burst into tears.

Mother was strict, hot-tempered and stubborn. She prayed five times a day and read the Quran daily. Minor illnesses never deterred her from fasting. She had also read five or six books in Urdu. Everyone was afraid of her, including Nana, Nani and my aunt. Nana would consult her on important matters. She loved me to the point of madness. She was restless if I was out of her sight for a moment but she would never express her love. I do not remember her ever hugging me, or kissing me on the forehead—I don't know why. Was she shy? Or did she think expressing her emotions was frivolous? There was not a single moment in my life when I felt she loved me. This has affected me. I have six children. I never embraced any of them, or kissed their faces. If they ever expressed their love I was as startled with embarrassment and shame as if I had been caught stealing. I would stand as stiff as a statue.

For the entire family, male or female, I was a plaything. They would dress me in silk even if they had to wear coarse handloom. They talked about how I had started talking when I was eight months old, perhaps because everyone had spoken to me at such great length. Whether I understood a thing or not, they babbled on endlessly like mad people. They would fight over me: 'You have had her for an hour, you cannot have her for the whole day. After all, I have claims too.' I have also heard that I was very fat and very dark. A child appearing in the family after so many years had driven them all crazy. My whim was their command.

Yet, I was not a spoilt child. I was not allowed to play with other children and never let out of sight. Since I spent all my time with adults I started behaving like one. I was not mischievous or bad mannered. If I spoke a few words, mother immediately scolded me. Mother's younger sister, who was twelve or thirteen, was crazy about me. She wanted me to be with her all the time. She was more like a friend than an aunt.

I turned three. Mother wanted to begin my education. She wanted me to master all the skills the world had to offer and to become famous. These dreams were meaningless in the village. Mother therefore reconciled with my father.

3. My Father

My father was a Pathan. He and mother were as different as the earth is from the sky. Mother was pious and given to praying through the night. When ill, she would pray in her bed. She fasted regularly. On the other hand, my father drank every day, except during the month of Ramzan and during the forty days of Muharram. Otherwise, come what may, he did not let a day go by without getting drunk. He was also known as the king among gamblers. He was so famous that people would come from far to fetch him for his skills. From Jammu to Bombay, gamblers acknowledged him as an *ustad*. His name was Abdullah Khan but no one referred to him by his name. They all called him Ustad.

Gambling was his profession. In the Urdu Bazaar he had rented a small vestibule. It was referred to as 'the ustad's assembly.' He had three or four other similar dens in Jammu. Wherever there was gambling, and whatever the bid, the winner put aside four annas from each winning for the Ustad. This was called the *naal*. No one could cheat on this. If someone tried, the loser would tell on him. In any case no one had the courage to cheat because they were all afraid of the Ustad. He was a courageous and strong man. If there was a fight, he would not be deterred even by ten men. He was famous for hitting the heads of his opponents with his own head. One knock with it and the challenger would faint and fall to the ground. Father was not tall but he was broad, strong and stocky. He kept the hair on his head short. Every evening he visited all his dens and collected his earnings. From there he would head straight to the liquor shops and buy a bottle for seven or eight annas. Drunk, he would step out into the bazaar.

In summer he dressed in a short sleeved shirt and wrapped a *tahmad* of coarse cotton around his waist and wore locally embroidered slippers. From the money he had earned as naal he would fold the two, four, eight anna and rupee coins into the knot of his tahmad. He always held on to the knot with one hand so that the weight of the coins would not undo it. His tahmad always trailed on the ground. A procession of fifteen to twenty children followed him chanting loudly, 'Baba give us a paisa.' Drunk, my father would say, 'In the name of God and his Prophet' and put his hand in the knot and give whatever coin came into his hand. Some got two annas, others a rupee, all depending on what fate had willed for them. He distributed all the money and never refused a beggar or an old person. For himself he saved four annas for lassi and breakfast in the morning. These he clutched in his fist while he fell asleep. Often, thinking that he was asleep, I tried to prise the fist open but could not. Once I bit the fist till it was wounded and bleeding yet it did not open.

Many people came from Lahore to see my father and take him away with them. They would dress him in expensive clothes and keep him in comfortable hotels. They would introduce him as a rich *Seth* to the rich gamblers they had picked for the sting operation. For the first two days my father would lose some and win some. He would bid in thousands. Eventually he would win thousands.

He was also considered the emperor of *sauli* and *dane*. Every day he practised for a few hours. Sauli is played with cowries. With his thumb he could manipulate the cowries as he threw them and he always got the spread he wanted. If he wanted, he could also make a few cowries disappear and still get what he wanted. Dane was a game played with ivory tiles with black dots on them. Fortune-tellers too keep such tiles. They are thrown like dice. Lord knows how this game is played but my father was considered a master of this game too. The third game was cards. He would mark the cards with his nails so that he knew who had which cards. Even if there were six people playing he would be able to keep track of every card. He could deal himself a good hand and win whenever he wanted. In short, he was a master at all forms of gambling. Those who took him with them to gamble for them would keep their honest share and return his winnings to him.

He always wanted, and tried for, reconciliation with mother but she hated everything about him. However, when I turned three, mother had no other option. My education was not possible in the village. There was also no other way she could stay in Jammu so for my sake she agreed to return. My father rented a large double storey house for eight rupees a month for us.

The house had a large entrance. On the ground floor were five or six rooms. There were three rooms upstairs, a huge kitchen, and three large courtyards. We only used the rooms upstairs. In summer it was so easy to drag out our charpais into the courtyard. Mother, the aunt who had named me, my Nana's sister Phupho Nikki and I moved to Jammu. The others stayed back in the village. Father handed over enough money in advance to take care of our expenses for a few months. He knew how undependable his profession was and that he might not have money when it was needed. He also used to pay the butcher in advance.

He had another wife too. She was an intelligent woman. She knew what her husband's profession was so she ensured that there was a year's supply of all necessities in the house. These necessities included jewellery, clothes, quilts and mattresses—in fact anything one might need. The house was full of things. She and mother did not interact with one another. I also had a stepsister. She was five or six years older than I. Her name was Iqbal but she was called Bali. My stepmother was a good woman. She was abstemious and prayed and fasted regularly. She died suddenly. She was doing her ritual wash before praying, when her heart failed. In those day people did not know about heart failure so Jammu was abuzz with rumours that a djinn who was in love with her had murdered her.

Bali was nine when her mother died. Her uncle lived with them. He had been orphaned at the age of two and Bali's mother had brought him up as a son. She had him trained as a mason and he became a good craftsman and began getting contracts. After her mother's death Bali was left alone in the house. My father realised that he could neither keep her with him nor look after her. He decided that it would be a good idea if her uncle got married. There would then be another woman in the house who could keep an eye on Bali and help her get over the loss of her mother. The parents of the chosen bride said they were agreeable, provided the ownership of the house was transferred to their daughter's name. My father thought about how much her uncle loved Bali and how he treated her as if she were his daughter. His own sister had brought him up as if he were her son. What was wrong with transferring the property to the girl, my father wondered? He went ahead and did so.

When his late wife was alive, father came to our home occasionally. On principle he did not step into the *mohalla* if he was drunk. For fear of him, no young man in the mohalla dared to act smart or take liberties with any girl. He would visit all the old, widowed and helpless women of the vicinity and distribute six or seven rupees among them. In those days when wheat cost ten annas a maund and for ten to twelve rupees you could get a canister of ghee, six or seven rupees easily took care of one's needs for food and clothing for a month. This was the sort of man he was. He did not think twice before transferring the deed of that house, full of things, to the bride. He assumed that Bali would now be her uncle's responsibility and when the time came he would get her married and willingly give her her due.

The uncle and the aunt turned out to be cruel and selfish. One can explain the aunt's behaviour because she was not related by blood, but the uncle had so many reasons to be indebted to Bali's mother. She had reared him like her own son since he was two yet he now became indifferent towards Bali, as though she were not even related to him. My father realised what was happening but he was helpless. How could he keep such a young girl himself? Nor could he complain now. He would visit her sometimes. He would be affectionate to Bali. He gave her spending money, but the moment he left, the aunt would take it away saying, 'You will lose this, give it to me. When you need something, just tell me.' Poor Bali! Although her father was alive, she was like an orphan.

I felt nothing for my father—neither affection nor hate. It was as if it did not matter to me that he was my father and I did not show him any respect. All my life I had heard only ill of him from mother. However, his few virtues were very rare ones. I was a child and was not capable of getting to the truth. I believed everything I was told. I never saw mother behaving with regard or civility towards him. He was very affectionate to me, but I was totally indifferent to him. I would demand money from him with authority as if it were my right, yet I behaved rudely to him. He, however, always fulfilled all my demands without showing any resentment.

There was one incident that I still think about. It is that one incident that has made me realize what a great and rare man he was and how unlucky I am that I never thought of him as a father and that I did nothing for him. The incident took place one winter.

In Jammu, whatever the season, between eight in the evening and ten in the morning there is a strong breeze that the people called *tedu*. When the tedu blew in summer, it seemed as if Allah *mian* had opened the doors of paradise. The same breeze was unbearable in winter. Jammu is surrounded by ice-covered mountains and the wind, when it bounced off these icy peaks, was killing in its chill and bite.

It was December and my father was going to his den to sleep. Even though he bore all the expenses, mother would stay away from him. She would not even speak to him courteously. Those days, matters were worse than usual so he often slept in the den. Usually he had his dinner at eight and left, but at one point, he had suddenly started to sleep at home. He would eat his dinner, and then fold the sheet spread on the floor into four, put a bolster under his head, unfold his warm shawl, cover himself with it, and go to sleep. In the morning he was gone before any one of us was up. It was so cold that I wonder if he slept at all. I was very young but neither my aunt nor my mother ever offered him a blanket or a quilt to cover himself. He was too self-respecting a man to even complain. Every night he went to sleep on the floor, covered with his shawl.

In those days there were no sofas or chairs. Whether the house was rich or poor, the floor was always covered. The poor spread a white sheet over a *durrie* and placed a few bolsters on it. The rich spread carpets on their durries. Or they would have a wooden settee called *takht* almost as large as the room. Durries and sheets were spread on this takht. This room served both as a drawing and a dining room. In our house there was only a white sheet on a durrie. Below it was the floor, cold as ice but father never once complained. Mother however, would often tell my aunt, 'I am sure he has now even gambled away his bedding.' We soon found out the truth.

One night on his way to his den to sleep, he heard strange human sounds coming from a shop with a *tandoor*. The workers at the tandoor would leave by eight but the tandoor stayed warm all night. Father stopped to look. He found an almost naked man, the thin cloth around his waist barely reaching his knees. He was lying there, his knees under his chin. In the icy wind and killing cold this almost naked man was trying to cling to the tandoor to keep warm and was making weird sounds. My father went straight to his den, wrapped up his entire bedding, brought it back, and gave it to the man. He was left with only his shawl. He could have kept some of the bedding for himself but he did not keep even a pillow. This happened when I was four but I still remember this incident. Today, even if I have visited a house hundreds of times, I still do not remember the directions and get lost. However, there are events, which happened when I was three or four that are permanently etched in my memory.

4. My Education

When I turned three mother began to worry about my education, and she entrusted it to the husband of a distant cousin. His name was Syed Gulzar Hussain Shah. He knew only Urdu and Persian and had a shop where he sold *paan*, cigarettes and syrups. He also used to dispense medicine for minor ailments. Poorer people, who could not afford to spend much on medicine, came to him.

There was no school for little children in the kingdom of Jammu and Kashmir. In any case, in those days, mothers did not consider their children ready for education till they were eight or nine years old. Then they were sent to sit on jute matting with a teacher who always had a stick in his hand and who thrashed the students regularly. Mother thought it best that I be taught by Gulzar Hussain. He had no BA or MA degree but he was very good at Urdu and Persian. A few other children studied with him. I began to hang around his shop, which was very close to where we lived, from eight in the morning till noon, and then from two in afternoon till the evening. After a year or two, by the age of five or six, I was able to read the most difficult of books in Urdu. I was smarter and more intelligent than the boys, who were all between eight and ten.

Since I was related to him, my ustad trusted me. In his absence, I would manage the affairs of the shop with quick efficiency, which pleased him a great deal. When he left the shop he would leave the key of the store with me. I became good at preparing paan. It was my job to send provisions to the ustad's house. And if patients appeared in his absence, I would also treat them. If someone said he had a stomach-ache, I would give him a dose of *panj arqa*, a mixture of five different extracts, and if he was constipated, I'd give him syrup of violets. There were tablets in labelled boxes, and I would also hand out those. Moreover, I would charge twice as much as the ustad did. All the bottles of syrup and boxes of pills were labelled. The ustad's wife made all the syrups herself at home. The tablets were ground and made at the shop. Four or five of the boys who came to study had to put the ingredients into a mortar and grind them with a pestle. I soon stopped drinking water. Even when I went home for lunch I still did not drink any water. 'Why should I ruin the taste of my mouth with tasteless water?' I would tell myself. Instead, I would run to the shop and when the ustad was not looking, I would have a drink of some syrup.

Ustad had two wives. He had ten children by his first wife, and her brother also lived with them. The second wife was related to mother. She lived in the Dalpatiyan mohalla in her own house. She rented out half of her house and could therefore live decently. She had no children. Ustad was very poor hence provisions for every meal had to be sent home to his other family. One of the boys who came to study would deliver the stuff.

It is hard to comprehend the world of difference between the prices of those days and those of today. Things were even cheaper in the kingdom. In Lahore, ghee cost fourteen annas a seer while in the kingdom it cost ten. Everything was cheaper there. The Maharaja had ordered that nothing produced in the kingdom should leave its boundaries, so prices were lower. This might have been the reason that people, in spite of being poor, felt content. Their needs, too, were very limited. No one lamented his or her poverty.

The boys who studied with me were all at least four or five years older than I was, yet I ruled over them. They would not dare sneak on me. In the ustad's absence I would take a few annas from the cash box and get *barfis* and pakoris for myself, though I would give them some too. I was very careful not to let them know that I had taken money from the cash box. But I would drink the syrups in front of them. Sometimes I would let them have a glass or half a glass.

Five or six annas were needed for each meal for the ustad's family. Three annas went for a *pao* of ghee and flour cost three paise. If they ate meat, it would cost six paise for a seer and another paisa or two for spices. The vegetables for dinner cost a few paise.

The rice they would eat was the cheap broken variety, ten seers
of which could be bought for four paise and which would easily
last for two or three days.

Gujjariyas, the women of the Gujjar community, sold milk and
dung-cakes in Jammu. They would pick dry firewood from the
jungles and make them into small bundles. These they placed
over the containers of milk. Over them, would be fifty or sixty
bundles of cow-dung cakes. All held in place with a rope. Carrying
these mountains in baskets on their heads, they sold four cow-
dung cakes for a paisa.

The Gujjariyas were an interesting gift of Jammu. The area
around Jammu was mostly populated by Gujjars. The men stayed
in their villages looking after their buffaloes, goats and land. The
wives, daughters-in-law and daughters would leave early in the
morning and walk nine or ten miles to the city to sell milk, dung-
cakes and firewood.

They all dressed alike: black shirt, a red striped shalwar and a
printed muslin dupatta. Their features were well defined and very
attractive; their complexion was wheatish but clear and sparkled
like gold. They were of athletic build, had thin waists, and walked
beautifully. Their men were mostly ugly and weak. All they wanted
to do was collect money and not spend it. The women looked
naïve and innocent but were extremely smart. They had one aim
in life—that their earnings increase each day and that they not
have to spend on anything.

In spite of the money they had, the Gujjars were very reluctant
to spend even a penny on their food. They would drink buffalo
milk and eat their rotis dipped in goat's milk. If they wanted
something sweet, they put some rice and sugar into milk to make
a *kheer*. During the day they ate their rotis with a chutney of onions,
chilly and salt. They bought one set of clothes every year. When
these tore or got worn out, they had to be patched and worn for
the rest of the year. They bathed and washed very rarely.

The young women came to the cities with dung-cakes and
milk. These women had no sense of modesty, and no matter what
people said to them in jest, they did not seem to care. In fact they
would partake fully in the repartee. They happily accepted small
gifts of bangles, *parandas* for their braids, bronze earrings, and

teeth whitener. A few of the city's young rakes would wait for them to come so that they could have a look at them. But this was the limit at which the fun stopped, for nothing went beyond frivolity. In these matters they were smart and firm. The following couplet of a mountain song seems to have been written about them:

Naughty people of the mountains,
With hearts as hard as stone.
They seldom let their bodies go
Their glances always roam.

On their way back from Jammu, they did their shopping. We would buy milk and dung-cakes for the ustad's house from them, for they sold them at less than the market price. Onions and garlic were so cheap that a few paise worth would easily last a month. The expenditure on the ustad's home was ten to twelve annas a day and with this thirteen people ate to their heart's content. He owned the house, which had a small garden.

Ustad was involved in the activities of the Sewa Samiti, a committee constituted for social service. This was his way of serving 'God's creatures'. Sewa Samiti was a government organization. If there was an unclaimed corpse at the mortuary, it was their responsibility to arrange for the final rites. The samiti consisted of four Muslims and four Hindus. If a Hindu died, the Hindu members went to collect the body, and if the dead peron was a Muslim, the Muslims went. The ustad considered this activity productive of religious merit so he joined the organization. He would leave for the hospital the moment he heard that there was an unclaimed dead Muslim. The corpse was handed over to him. The hospital also gave four rupees towards the burial expenses, which was the rate fixed per corpse. He would buy six or seven yards of coarse handloom, bathe the corpse and take it to the cemetery. He would pay a few annas to the gravedigger, get a grave dug and bury the corpse. In all, he did not spend more than a rupee and a half on the burial. He scrimped a bit on the cloth for the shroud so that sometimes there was not enough cloth to cover both the head and the feet of the corpse! From the money saved, one of the four Muslim members of the Samiti would go to the liquor shop and buy two bottles of liquor as well as pakoris, oranges, naans and kebabs. The graveyard was close to the river Tawi and they would wait amidst the wild undergrowth there. When the liquor and the food arrived, the four 'servers of God's creatures' would mourn the dead one. A summons from the hospital meant freedom for us. At first we did not know that he spent the day drinking, but we soon found out the truth. On such days I would lock up the shop and take the keys home. All the students prayed that there be a death every day to keep the ustad busy.

The ustad's wife was a fine woman, pretty and as good-humoured as the ustad was bad tempered. She spent the entire day working at home. She washed the clothes of their ten children, cooked for the family, and stitched clothes for them. She prepared all sorts of syrups and preserves for the shop and drew out the various extracts. All this was her responsibility.

Ustad was also very fond of chess and of playing the sitar, on which he could play just one tune. Whenever he felt like it, he played the same tune. Otherwise he catered to the educated and young men of Jammu. They would come to the shop, buy cigarettes and paan and recite poetry to each other. One got to hear some very good Urdu poetry from them. The ones who were employed came in the evening. Those who had time would come in the morning. They would start playing chess in the small room behind the shop. Some games were so long and involved that the players would forget about eating or drinking, yet the game would not end till the evening. Yes, they did however want a paan in their mouths all the time. I would take charge of the shop. If some one came for a paan, I prepared one. If someone wanted a drink of syrup, I would sell him some. And ustad continued to play chess with nothing to bother him. He trusted me so much that I was in control of everything.

The shop was very near father's main gambling den. I ran into him at least four or five times a day. Every day I would collect five or six annas from him. If he did not have the money I went with him to one of his dens and took the money from his earnings. I had a cash box in which I put all my savings. My daily needs were met from the cash box at the shop. I only liked pakoris and barfi and I would get so many for two or three paise that I had to give some to the others. Sometimes in the evening I would buy two paise worth of apples. In summer you could also get two ounces of ice cream, which was made only of milk and sugar. The milk was cooked till it was as thick as *khoya* and then frozen. It was wrapped in a warm cloth and then placed in a box, and sold around Jammu. It used to be so delicious that no ice cream of today can match it. I still do not like modern ice cream.

I was the richest one in our home. I kept my cash box on the top shelf of the cupboard. I counted its contents at least once or twice a day. Everyone knew that I collected money in it. Since there was no servant in the house there was no fear of theft. When I came home at noon, the first thing I did was to climb onto a charpai, get the cash box and count what I had. Only then would I have my lunch.

One day, very early in the morning my father came to me and said, 'Are you my daughter?'

I answered 'Yes.'

'Then give me the money you have saved and in three or four days I will return twice the amount. Some friends of mine have just arrived from Lahore and I have to arrange food for them.'

I said, 'Definitely not. Do not touch my money. I do not want twice the amount.'

He begged and pleaded but I was adamant. Disappointed, he left. I too left for the shop. He knew where the box was and took all that was in it. That day when I came home at noon I went to check on my treasure as usual. There was not a single paisa in there. I felt like killing him. I forgot about lunch and ran straight to his den. I climbed the stairs, and just as I put my foot on the last step, he saw me and realized what was coming. Before I could reach the top he ran and picked me up, carried me down and put me on the ground. He then placed his hands on my feet and began: 'I am at your feet for my honour is now in your hands. For God's sake do not humiliate me in front of my guests or else I will lose face completely. You know that I always give you whatever you ask. I promise and I swear that I will reimburse you with four times the amount. From tomorrow come and start collecting the naal for yourself. Look, I am begging you, come and have something to eat upstairs. I have cooked everything myself. The *pulau* is very delicious.'

This was a major shock for no one had ever hurt me in my life before. First I had to deal with my anger, and then with my helplessness. I began sobbing and all I said was: 'I am not starving that I need to eat your food. If from tomorrow I do not get the naal money then I will tell the world that you stole money from me.' I was so sad that I refused to eat. My father was very scared of me for he knew very well how persistent and stubborn I was. I do not know why, but I felt sorry for him.

So, from the next day I went at noon and took whatever money he had. I made a similar trip in the evening. Though he had other gambling dens, it was only the one that he spent most time in, and which was very close to our home, that I went to. It became a part of my routine. I would go there every day and demand money. He would smile and dutifully hand over the money to me. I have a feeling I collected not four times but a hundred times more than the original amount. Yet, I pursued him till he died.

I remember him laughing and pleading, 'You have collected a thousand times the amount. For God's sake, forgive me now.'

My usual retort would be, 'That's not true.'

He would laugh again and say, 'Your mother is a miser but you have the soul of a Pathan moneylender.' Every day he would gladly give me the money but he would also say, 'Take this and leave me alone from now on.'

I am sure he loved me and constantly tried to make me love him. But then, if the parents have no love for each other, how can the children learn to love? Mother always spoke ill of him. Hence I neither loved nor treated him with respect. I feel sorry now that in the atmosphere I grew up in, I could not get close to him.

5. My First Singing Teacher

Ali Baksh was the father of Bade Ghulam Ali Khan and lived in Jammu. Once a year he visited Lahore or Sindh, but he preferred to stay in Jammu. Mother enrolled me as his disciple. God had given him a voice that had no parallel. When he strummed the tanpura and began singing, his tunefulness would have his listeners in raptures. He would never go off-key. Great musicians have said that if the voice and instrument become one, their power can move mountains. There was no one to match him in singing the Sindhi *kafi* or *khayal*. He was a master of the Sindhi *bhairavi* too. He sang the *todi* khayal *'Sain Allah jane Maula jane'* very well. The general opinion about him was that he lacked learning. However, as a singer he was superb. There was a relative of his called Allah Baksh who also lived in Jammu. His voice and singing were much better than my ustad's, but he had gone insane.

My ustad, Ali Baksh, was penniless. He was, however, ready to teach me for two meals a day rather than leave Jammu. Lord knows what attractions, what magic, Jammu had that he did not want to leave even though he was on the verge of starvation. Ali Baksh was very happy with me. He always said, 'She will sing in tune. The musical articulation of her voice will be correct.' Often he would explain to me: 'Listen child, no matter what you sing, even if it is a *jugni,* sing in tune for only then will it reach the heart. You can stretch a tuneless phrase till the earth shatters, but that will not matter a jot to the ear. Music is only that which is in tune. You should know how to articulate musically. If one does not know how to articulate, one should not sing.' Till I was five, all he taught me was to travel back and forth between the note *sa.* For two years I was just practising the notes. It was only after that, that he began teaching me the todi *'Sain Allah jane.'*

I have not heard voices like those of Ali Baksh, Mian Maula Baksh Talwandiwale, who was to teach me later, and the mad

Allah Baksh. When any one of them started strumming the tanpura, in the lower octaves, it seemed as if the entire music of the world had contracted into their music. You felt that tanpuras were playing all around and every nook echoed with music. When they sang a khayal their music was so eloquent that the listener was transported into another world.

In those days I was not interested in music and was learning only because I was made to. Ali Baksh was keen that I learn more. He himself did not know more than five or ten ragas even though he was famous as a singer. Maula Baksh was very learned and his knowledge was like an endless ocean. Both my ustads—the one who taught me to read and write and the one who taught me to sing—were very pleased with me. I was intelligent and quick in picking up what they taught. I never had to be punished for anything and was only praised.

If I was ever beaten, it was for smoking the *huqqa*. I began smoking it when I was four. Mother used to smoke but she did not want me to start smoking too. She was right, for it is not very wise to start at that age. Phupho Nikki, who loved me to the point of madness, smoked too. She would gently try and discourage me.

'Please do not smoke. She will hit you.'

'No I will,' I would insist.

She would give in, 'All right, go ahead,' she would say gently.

If mother caught me smoking, she would beat me mercilessly and would also insult poor Phupho Nikki. My smoking reached such a point that I started to collect the cigarette stubs I found on the road and secretly smoke them at the shop. Sometimes in my eagerness to take advantage of an opportunity, I would quickly take so many drags from the huqqa that I would almost faint. The vice did not leave me.

The fathers of Ali Baksh and Allah Baksh were brothers. As I have mentioned, Allah Baksh sang much better than Ali Baksh and his voice, too, was better but he had lost his sanity and never left Jammu. Everyone had the same story to tell about him. On one occasion, the Maharaja of Jammu had invited the best known singers from all over. Allah Baksh's ustad was a well-recognized master. All the ustads assembled at the court sang in turn, offered their *salaams* to the Maharaja and returned to their places. Then it was the turn of Allah Baksh and his ustad and the ustad began to sing. The ustad and the pupil would perform together and it was the duty of the pupil to only imitate the ustad. If the ustad sang a note or indicated his musical intentions, the pupil was to repeat it, just as it had been sung, and not add anything new to it.

The ustad was very old and weak by then. Allah Baksh, on the other hand, was young and strong. It was the court of the Maharaja and all the best-known musicians were present. In this atmosphere Allah Baksh forgot etiquette and got carried away. Instead of mimicking his ustad, he sang such a complicated arpeggio that the entire durbar broke out in applause. The ustad could not match him and was terribly embarrassed. The ustad's heart broke. The note Allah Baksh had sung had been so difficult that he looked back helplessly. He looked at Allah Baksh and all he said was 'You mad man. Shut up.'

In those days the ustads were paternal and had the student's best intentions at heart. In return for obedience and service, they taught their students their art night and day. In fact, it was commonly believed that music could not be bought for money. There were some students who not only ate with their ustad but also served him unflinchingly, even if they had to stay up nights. Allah Baksh's ustad must have really felt humiliated for his words turned into a curse. For the next two months Allah Baksh fell silent. Then he went insane. He would sit quietly and never say a word to anyone. Nor did he ever wash. His nails were long. His unwashed hair fell in matted braids. There was a thick layer of dirt and grime on his neck, which was nauseating. He never spoke to anyone, so he never asked for anything. On one of the terraces in our house there was a balcony. He would come and sit on it. With his stoned, bloodshot eyes he would stare into space. Everyone requested him to sing but he never did. Sometimes he would make me sit in his lap and start singing on his own. I was very scared of him. When I turned five he constantly tried to get me to sit in his lap; as a result, when he came to the house, I would run away and hide. His clothes were so dirty that the dirt on them would shine as if it was charcoal. The colour of his hair, face and body seemed almost identical. He always wanted to play with me like a child.

By the age of five I had learnt a bit about music. One day while sitting he suddenly started singing. The words of the song were, 'What indifference my beloved! Your ignorance of my state.' What a voice! What pathos! What a song! It seemed that everything in the universe had come to a standstill. I did not know much but the others there—mother, aunt and ustad—were all sobbing like children. For one, the words of the kafi described his state so well. And then the way he sang! I started crying even though I did not understand anything. He sang the full kafi and then fell silent. People tried very hard to make him sing again for them. Some gave him milk to drink and some fed him. Others pleaded and begged. But he was indifferent to everything. He was his own master.

He came to our house every day. I was no longer scared of him. Like a child, he would sometimes play with my feet or my fingers. When I learnt music he would sit and listen. Sometimes he would begin to sing with the tablas. One day he sang a khayal in *bhairavi*. What style! His singing was so moving that whether you understood music or not, you forgot about the world. He never taught me, but I learnt a great deal from just listening to him. I could never inderstand why he loved me so much. Sometimes he would even sing when I asked him to. Listening to good singing is a lesson in itself, and he was the emperor of singing. God had given him music but snatched away his senses.

6. My Love for Music

There were very few Shias in the kingdom: at the outside, there may have been fifty or sixty. Ustad Ghulam Hussain was responsible for the Muharram arrangements. For the first ten days he would work so hard that he forgot about everything else. He would collect people for the *majlis* to commemorate the martyrdom of Imam Hussain and would prepare those who could do so, to read aloud the travails of the Prophet's family. There was no money so there was no question of inviting an orator or a *maulvi*. People would read to each other to remind themselves of the tragic events. Some would recite dirges and others would sing lamentations, and after the mourning and praying, the majlis would end.

It was because of the efforts of ustad that the numbers of Shias grew. I watched the numbers increase day by day and grow into thousands. From small neighbouring villages the women and children would come, thinking a fair was being held. Ustad began collecting donations and was able to pay a maulvi and a professional 'reminder'. Every year a beautiful tableau was made. The people who came from the villages would join in the procession. The route of the tableau would be lined with both Hindus and Muslims who would put up booths for water or *sharbat*. Indeed, the Hindus put up more booths for they were given to praying for miracles. Those whose prayers had been granted, would offer gifts of money. People would fling garlands of dried fruits and flowers at the tableau. Every year fifteen or twenty 'lamenters' came from Lahore and would flagellate themselves and lacerate their bodies with knives in public.

My father was very respectful of the months of Muharram and Ramzan. He did not touch liquor for the forty days of Muharram. Similarly during Ramzan he would announce that people were welcome to come to his den, not to gamble but to begin or end their fasts. He fasted for the entire month and also cooked for everyone himself.

Ustad had many books of *marsiyas* and *nohas*. He did not know how to sing but he would explain the tune of the dirges to me. He also taught me how to deliver these marsiyas. I have mentioned how in the early years there were so few people that they would arrange a majlis for themselves. Now, with the increase in numbers, the events of Muharram were recalled far more elaborately. On the seventh day there would be *mehndi* and on the tenth, a small procession would wind its way through the bazaars. Ustad taught me the nohas and the marsiyas so that I could recite them during the majlis' and the procession. On the seventh day he would put me on a stool, and make me recite. The 'lamenters' would stop beating their breasts while I recited the marsiyas in a full voice; people often wept at my recitation. The marsiyas over, the mourners would start lamenting again, loudly.

I often travelled with the procession the whole night. Wherever it stopped, I would recite the marsiyas and the nohas. The procession visited four or five houses on the day of the mehndi. There would be prayers in each house, and they would wait for me at all of them. Everyone wanted me to be the one to recite the marsiyas. My voice was good. I had learnt a bit of music. Since I was so young, people liked my recitations even more. Men and women would shower me with blessings and offer me treats of all kinds. The women would gather around me and say: 'May God add what's left of our lives to yours.' I became a daughter to all of them. Their offerings too, grew to ten times what they used to be. These people started referring to me as 'their little reciter.'

I would also participate in the final procession on the tenth day. My share of the offerings was sent to me at home, this went on for two or three years. One good thing that came out of all this was that I became interested in music. I began to appreciate music for because of it I received warmth and hospitality, love, flattery and blessings; not to mention a five-fold rise in my share of the offerings! I now began learning from Ali Baksh in right earnest.

7. My Aunt

My mother's younger sister was very pretty, even-tempered, kind and good-humoured. My Nana, Nani and my aunt all migrated to Jammu. My aunt too began to learn music, but that was a short-lived attempt, and did not lead to anything.

There was a *chaudhary* from Gujarat who was a disciple of my ustad. He too was a Shia, and he had proclaimed the ustad's wife to be his sister. On one of his visits to Jammu, he saw my aunt at my ustad's house. She must have been fifteen or sixteen at the time and he was perhaps over forty. He fell in love with her instantly. He belonged to the Gujjar caste, but he was educated and very charming. He was over six feet tall, dark, and had beautiful features. He had a pleasant manner and was well-spoken. So besotted was he with my aunt, that he began to find excuses to come to Jammu. His wife was alive but they had been separated for quite a while. He had a son who was five or six years older than me. My aunt become very fond of the child and began to treat him as if he were her own.

The chaudhary had the benevolent airs of a big landlord. He was a contractor for the dining cars that were attached to all trains running between Lahore and Delhi, and he had hotels at all the railway stations where western and Indian food was always available for passengers. In summer, after he sent orders from Lahore, we began getting huge slabs of ice at a special discounted price to cool our rooms. Those were the days of the British and if they were pleased with you, they allowed you everything.

In those days, all trains had four categories of compartments: the third, inter, second and first classes. The Europeans travelled mostly in the first and second class compartments. Here, there would be a huge tub of ice, water in earthen goblets and soda bottles lay cooling in the tubs. Passengers used to place other things in them as well to cool them. The breeze from the ceiling

fan alone cooled the entire compartment. Apart from this, the tub
also served as a protection against dust. The chaudhary was in
charge of arranging for these tubs of ice on the trains. When high
ranking British officials travelled by train, they were very pleased
at these arrangements and left him with glowing certificates. He
was an influential and powerful man and was always distributing
largesse. At Christmas he would buy cakes and turkeys by the
hundreds and, effortlessly, his contracts were renewed the
following year.

My ustad's wife was called Allah Ditti and we called her aunt
Ditto. The chaudhary was soon acquainted not only with my aunt
but also with mother and the rest of the family. He would stay at
aunt Ditto's and would sometimes drop in at our place. Aunt Ditto
was the one who arranged the meetings between the chaudhary
and my aunt. After nearly two years, the chaudhary said to mother:
'I want to marry her.' Mother refused. From then on, when the
chaudhary was in Jammu, my aunt was forbidden to visit the
ustad's home.

The chaudhary panicked at this. He pleaded and begged aunt
Ditto for help and one day, without telling anyone he took my
aunt with him to Lahore. Aunt Ditto was now in real trouble but
she denied any knowledge of their plans. I missed my aunt because
I loved her more than I loved mother. In fact, I considered her my
real mother. My aunt too had loved me as if I were her life.

Aunt Ditto's cousin was sent to Lahore. After a few days he
returned with the information that my aunt had married the
chaudhary and that she had no intention of returning. The house
was filled with loud lamentation. Mother and Nana were so angry
that if they had had their way they would not have hesitated to
kill her. Their constant refrain was: 'If we could only get our hands
on her, we would thrash her till her bones and ribs are turned
into pulp.'

Mother prepared herself to go to Lahore. I pleaded hard to be
taken to meet my aunt. Mother curtly dismissed my pleas with,
'Which aunt? Whose aunt? Had she been your aunt would she
have abandoned you? She has forgotten all of us. She is now
possessed by the demon called love. For us she is as good as
dead.' Nana and mother never stopped cursing her.

However, Nani loved my aunt a great deal. Her only son had died at the age of four during a plague epidemic. She would remember him every day and weep. Now she had only her two daughters. My aunt was the sort of person who was always ready to share in people's joys and sorrows. She was so gullible that she believed any tale of misfortune that anyone told her and would cheerfully give away whatever she had. She was God-fearing, and loving to all. My Nani loved mother too but she feared her more for mother exercised great authority over her. She shared no troubles with her nor did she consult her about anything. Naturally, my Nani's love was focussed on my aunt who was always ready to spend time with her and say a few kind words to her. Mother, on the other hand, considered Nani a fool and never had a conversation with her. With my aunt leaving, Nani's world became sombre. She did not say a word of complaint to anybody, but she wept all the time.

Mother returned from Lahore to report that my aunt had turned 'parrot-eyed' in her treachery, and no longer cared for any one. Now Nani began insisting that she wanted to go to Lahore to see her daughter. Finally Nana agreed and decided that an uncle would go with her. I wanted to go as well. I wept so much and so loudly that it was as if I'd brought the sky down. Then Nani decided that if I did not go, neither would she. Both Nana and mother strongly opposed my going. They knew how much my aunt loved me and were afraid that she might feel compelled to return home if she met me. For my part, I threatened that if I was not allowed to go, I'd stop eating and drinking. The threat worked and they agreed and we reached Lahore safely.

My aunt wept with joy when she saw me. 'May I be sacrificed for you,' she said when she ran to hug me. She wept for a long time. So did Nani, who cleansed the grief in her heart with her tears. Nani finally said, 'Sardaro, you know that I cannot live without you.'

My aunt said immediately, 'Come and live with me now.'

'How can I leave home?' Nani asked.

'Then come to Lahore whenever you want,' my aunt insisted. 'Daughters the world over leave their homes and go to their own homes. You too once left your parents' home. This is my home now and I have done nothing that is unusual. Tell me the truth, do you not want me to have a home of my own?'

My Nani was a simple woman who coveted nothing. She wanted her daughter to have her own home but she could not help how she felt. She was so simple that she never learnt how to count money. When I would see that she had small change worth two or two and half rupees, I would go to her and say that I needed change for a rupee. She would put all the small change in front of me. I would take all of it and give her a rupee, and she would be tremendously pleased that she now had a full rupee! I did this as long as I was young and she never caught on.

After five or six days we began preparing for our return to Jammu. The chaudhary and my aunt pleaded that we extend our stay but Nani was afraid that Nana and mother would get angrier if she lingered. They might even get angry enough to forbid further visits. My Nana, like other men of the village, respected women as much as he respected his shoes. Mother, too, did not have any special respect for her mother. As for me, I wanted to stay there permanently, but was forced to return. When we were leaving, my aunt gave Nani and me a lot of money so that we could come to Lahore whenever we wanted. The chaudhary too was very solicitous.

His son, who was four or five years older than me, was also quite sad at our leaving. We had played together all the time we were there. He would tell me stories or we would play hide and seek, or with a ball or cards. He told me stories that were so funny that I would roll with laughter. For me this was a totally new experience. I had never played with someone close to my own age. Those days passed as though in a dream. I could sleep whenever I wanted and get up when I pleased. I did what I wanted and no one ordered me around. The chaudhary was called Amanat Ali. It was typical of him to make the most serious matters sound like jokes.

8. A Second Meeting with Baba Roti Ram

We returned to Jammu. Nana and mother decided that we should go and pay our respects to Baba Roti Ram. 'We have not taken her to the Baba since we came to Jammu. After all she was born only after he had prayed,' they said. Hearing all the praises of Baba, one Hindu and one Muslim wanted to come along with us. The Hindu was called Shanak and the Muslim chaudhary was called Muhammad Ali. Both worked in Jammu. They were insistent about going with us so that they could ask Baba to intercede and get their wishes granted.

That year pumpkins had appeared in Jammu, out of season. We bought some thinking we would cook them with meat for Baba. We hired horses and reached Akhnur by the evening. We spent the night with some distant relatives, and in the morning we reached Hamirpur Sidhdhar. We cooked the pumpkin and meat and made paranthas. We put these over the meat, wrapped it all in a table cloth and took it to Baba. We had not even reached his doorstep when the Baba said, 'Gobinda has brought the *malka i-muazamma* with him.' As usual, he was sitting on his charpai and talking to those around him. He was in a good mood and was half-smiling. He went on talking and then suddenly started to sing couplets by Kabir, extremely tunefully. His voice had feeling and his notes were clear. It seemed that the Baba himself had been transported into another world. After the song died down, Baba was quiet for about five minutes.

Nana said to him, 'Baba, we have brought food for you. Please eat it.' Baba did not answer and instead turned to someone else. A little later Nana again said, 'Baba please eat something.' Baba again pretended that he had not heard. The Muslim chaudhary who had come with us from Jammu said, 'Baba, please see to it that I get heavy gold bangles.' The Baba smiled. Nana reminded Baba again, 'Eat a little at least.' The Baba was now irritated: 'I will eat, after all it is only pumpkin and meat. Why are you so concerned?' This was not the season for pumpkins and the food was wrapped in a cloth. Yet the Baba knew!

Baba's eyesight had begun to fail. In spite of this he had recognized us before we had appeared in the doorway. He called Nana by the same name he had always used for him; he remembered mine; he knew that there was pumpkin-meat wrapped in the cloth; we were all impressed. We laid the food out before Baba. Slowly he began to eat. The chaudhary began once again, 'Baba I have to wear bracelets of gold.'

'Why not, why not' retorted Baba immediately, 'I will put those around your wrist.' However the Dogri word he used meant iron, not gold. The Hindu who had gone with us began, 'I..' and Baba reacted with an explicitly abusive term involving one's own daughter, and called him one of those. The poor men, both fell silent. Baba continued to talk for a long time about this and that. I heard abuses that I had never heard before.

Then he began to talk to Nana, 'Gobinda, only dogs will be left to bark in Jammu. When the black-faced witch wanders around the streets of the city, only dogs will wail. She will leave, but only after the mounds of embers she carries die out. Till the fire burns she will be all over the town. The dogs will continue to wail. Gobinda, you are intelligent. There is nothing I can do. That black-faced witch is really evil. She moves around with a mound of fire on her head.' These were his predictions to my grandfather.

9. Baba Charas Sahib

We returned to Jammu the next day. In a month or two the chaudhary who had gone with us to Baba, and who Baba had predicted would wear iron bracelets, was arrested for forgery. The daughter of the second, the Hindu, eloped.

Soon Jammu was visited by a plague so severe that a family of sixteen members would have six funerals in one morning. No one was left to offer even water to the sick. With dusk, the wailing of dogs would begin. Terror settled over the city. There was such panic that even the healthy appeared dead. No one visited a house where there might be a case of the plague, even to ask after the dying. If they found a dead rat in their homes, people fled. Many forgot about their property, jewellery, and money, and camped out in the open. Death was all around and all anyone wanted was to survive. Families would come back after burying one dead and would find another ready to be buried. People spent their entire day preparing and burying the dead. Everyone was terrified. Sounds of mourning came from every home. The dogs' wails were so eerie that even the hearts of the brave shuddered. Vaccinations were not available then, so people were totally helpless.

There was a doctor called Radha Krishan, who was well liked in Jammu. He charged two rupees for each home visit. Another doctor, who had just returned with a degree from England, charged ten; so people rarely called him. His name was Dr Bhalla.

Dr Radha Krishan however, was a doctor for both the rich and the poor. God had blessed him with the power to heal. In the days of the plague, if he was called to visit one house he invariably had to visit another twenty. The moment he arrived at one place, people would turn up to take him elsewhere in town, where there would be many more sick. People waited for him round the clock. I wonder if he ever got time to sleep. And even though he charged only two rupees as fees, he earned enough money to send his son to study medicine in England!

Father too fell a victim to the plague. A huge lump appeared in his armpit. His fever rose so high that he became unconscious. When he regained consciousness, he told his men: 'Go, bring Baba Charas Sahib.'

They suggested, 'Let us bring Dr Radha Krishan instead.'

'You dare not bring a doctor to me,' father fumed. 'Just bring Baba Charas.'

Baba Charas was a *faqir*. He was always dressed in the same way: khaki trousers, a khaki shirt and a khaki hat. Summer or winter, he spent the entire night standing under an electricity pole in front of our house. He was constantly mumbling and counting something on his fingers.

People call Jammu the city of stone—it's extremely hot in the day and cold at night. When the tedu began to blow at eight, it would suddenly become very cold. In the monsoon the clouds would make things so dark that it was difficult to tell one hand from the other. The road to Kashmir began from Jammu. When it snowed in Kashmir, the wind turned icy cold in Jammu, but this made no difference to Baba Charas. He never wore anything warm, nor did he ever fall ill.

No one knew anything about Baba Charas or where he had come from. He spoke to no one nor did he answer anyone's questions. He never asked for anything. Sometimes he would say a few words, which no one understood. If people wished to, they could feed him. He never asked anyone for food.

Sometimes he visited us. He would knock gently on the door. When my mother or aunt opened the door, he would head straight for my aunt's charpai—she was the one who was so obsessed with cleanliness that she never let any one sit on her bed! If a guest happened to sit on it, the moment he or she left she would change not only the sheets but also the pillowcases! Charas Sahib carried with him hundreds of thousands of lice, each as big as a bed bug. Even if he sat on my aunt's bed for only ten minutes, columns of lice would march out. On the other hand, if he sat on mother's bed for an hour, we would not find even a single louse.

The day Baba visited, aunt spent the entire night killing lice. Since she was terrified of pirs and faqirs, she would not complain. Sometimes his shirt would be so ragged that its sleeves would drop off, leaving only the front and the back hanging around his neck. For fear of God, someone would give him another shirt, for he wore nothing but a bush shirt and trousers. He stayed away from those who tried to get him to wear shalwar and kameez. At first, people suspected him of being a spy or an army man. They'd named him Charas Sahib though he used no intoxicants.

Whenever my father's fever receded and he regained consciousness he asked for Baba Charas. People went out and after much searching they found him and brought him home. It took considerable effort to get father conscious enough to tell him that Baba was there. When he recovered a bit he clutched at Baba with all his might and forcibly made him lie with him on the charpai. Helplessly Baba pleaded, 'leave me, please leave me.' Instead of listening to him, my father tightened his grip and hugged him closer to himself. He held him so tight that the Baba could not move. For about two hours he lay there silently. Finally, he left because father felt better. The lump in his armpit began to recede. Baba was brought home a few more times. Within a fortnight father was healthy again.

He had taken no medicine, nor had he seen a doctor. When mother insisted that he see a doctor he would respond that Allah was his doctor. Or that Baba Charas was. Allah saved my father from the very jaws of death. He left his bed and things returned to normal. The fear of the plague started receding. Baba Roti Ram had predicted that dogs would wail in Jammu, that a witch would roam the streets with fire on her head and would only leave when the fire died—all these predictions came true.

10. Delhi

When ustad Gulzar Hussain saw that I had finished reading two or three books of Persian, and six or seven of Urdu, he came to mother and said: 'I have taught her all the Urdu and Persian I know. If you want her educated further, you had better employ another ustad.'

I had not studied mathematics or geography but I would write down the difficult words of Urdu and Persian and memorize them. Whenever I could, I studied. My Urdu was so good that there was no book I could not read. I had also become quite an expert in poetry. All the intelligentsia of Jammu gathered at the ustad's shop to eat paan. They would hang around and recite poetry. In those days the poetry of Ghalib, Mir, Minai, Zauq and Bahadur Shah Zafar was very popular. Every evening, for an hour or so, animated discussions took place. I too began to understand some of the poetry.

When mother realized that my education at the shop was over, she stopped me from going there and started music lessons twice a day. She ensured that I wasted no time. In order not to forget what I had learnt, I would also read and write every day. Since my aunt's husband had the contract for providing ice on trains between Lahore and Delhi and had to spend a fair amount of time in Delhi, my aunt moved there. It was easy to visit her in Lahore but visiting her in Delhi was more difficult. Nana and mother consulted each other. Since aunt had moved to Delhi, we should do the same, they decided. 'There she can learn classical dance and singing,' they reasoned. Mother had always desired that I learn all the arts of the world. In those days there was no one teaching classical dance in Lahore. Mother's ambitions live with me till the present. Even now, in spite of all the years that have gone by, I cannot spend a minute without doing something or the other.

Mother was severely pockmarked. Some marks were so deep that it seemed her skin had been scorched. She had good features but her skin was really horrible. Perhaps that is why she wanted to achieve through me, all that she had not been able to achieve herself. She would never joke, laugh or express her love for me. I too did not love her in any special way. If she had to go away for a few days I would be most pleased, and would pray that she did not have to return in a hurry. Her only obsession was to see that I did not neglect either my studies or my singing.

We began to prepare for the move to Delhi. Nana went ahead first, and my aunt's husband helped him rent a small, cheap house in Chitli Qabar. After making all the arrangements, he wrote to Jammu, asking us to join him. Nani, a maternal uncle, the tabla and sarangi players with whom I practised, all got ready to leave. Phupho Nikki and Nana's niece decided to stay on in Jammu. Both wept a lot, for this was the first time I was really being separated from them.

We arrived in Delhi without any problems. I was pleased because my aunt's stepson was in Delhi. His humour, my aunt's affection—everything seemed so wonderful. I had missed my aunt a lot during this separation and had hated the time I spent away from her in Jammu. She indulged me a great deal and was more of a friend than an aunt. If I said, 'I do not know how to play cards, so teach me,' she would patiently deal cards for hours. I had missed occasions like these. If I ever made a mistake she never got angry and would pass the matter off with a laugh. I went to see her the morning after we reached Delhi. She hugged me with all her might and kept kissing me for we were meeting after four months. Amanat Ali, my uncle's son, was also very pleased to see me.

My uncle was very fond of reading magazines, books, and religious literature. There were dozens of good books in their house. There were four large, thick volumes of the *Fasana' i-Azad* written by Rattan Nath Sarshar. These were different from the other books—the print was large and clear, and I read six or seven pages. When I was leaving, I asked uncle if I could borrow the *Fasana' i-Azad*. He said that I could take whatever I wanted as long as I took good care of the books. I brought all four volumes home. Till now I had only read dreary books and had never read tales or stories before. I enjoyed *Fasana' i-Azad* so much that I did not want to put it down. Sometimes, while eating, I placed the book before me and because the print was so large and clear, there was no problem reading while I ate. I did not know this then, but today I think that rarely has the Urdu idiom been used better than in this book. The book painted such a vivid picture of past times that it seemed you were there and watching everything yourself. The description of Eid was so real that it seemed I was part of the festivities of that time.

I have searched hard but have not found such a fine edition again. The ones I found were printed so badly that I did not feel like reading them. Mother was very annoyed by my absorption in the book. In Jammu the entire household was illiterate. I had not even seen a novel or a magazine till then. My world changed after I read *Fasana' i-Azad*. According to mother, however, I was just wasting my time. I was supposed to spend my time in song and dance or in reading poetry. Folk wisdom of the time said that if you read stories and novels it gave you inappropriate ideas. People used to say that whoever read the story of Shah Bahram went mad. Mother too worried that I would get ideas if I read a novel. So I had to read on the sly. When she slept in the afternoon, I would read as much as I could of the *Fasana' i-Azad*.

I had had no friends in Jammu, but I had Phupho Nikki, my other aunt, and the familiar faces in the neighbourhood. Here, in Delhi, the dress, the language, everything was different, and we knew nobody. I would sometimes go to my aunt's to spend the night there and come back in the morning to start my training. There was no entertainment at home except for reading the *Fasana i-Azad* but even that was hard because I was fearful of mother.

The people of Delhi were very lively and fun loving. Even if at the end of a hard day's work a man earned two rupees, he would go home, have a bath, oil his hair, line his eyes with collyrium, wear an embroidered kurta and a churidar pyjama and a crinkled muslin cap. Thus dressed, the men, their wives and children came to the Jama Masjid. Small shopkeepers spread their wares out on the steps of the mosque: toys, little things for the house, bangles, brass and silver jewellery for the women, cheap chinaware, readymade clothes, shoes, and all kinds of low priced cotton and silk cloth. Also on sale were animals and birds—parakeets *mynahs*, and *baya* birds. Often one would even find a blackbuck fawn for sale. There were all sorts of things to eat: *puris, kachoris,* potato *tikyas, samosas,* sweets, and *shami* kebabs. There was nothing you could not find there.

Every shopkeeper had a gas lamp at his shop. The stairs of the mosque looked as if they were covered with stars. Poor people, who lived in homes with very little space or ventilation, came here to spend a few hours in the open amidst the hustle and bustle. They would get to meet their friends and acquaintances, and the fatigue from the day's hard labour would disappear. The cool breeze would breathe new life into them for it was forbidden to build houses close to the masjid. In the home of every worker, all waited for the father to return so that they could go for their outing to the masjid. Many would cook rotis at home and buy a few annas worth of some spicy, tasty stuff to eat with them. The wife did not have to spend her evening with her face buried in the stove. Instead, they had a picnic and the family was happy. Close to the steps of the mosque was the shrine of Hare Bhare Shah. Everyone said the *fatiha* when they reached the mosque. Every day I waited for the evening so that I could go there. Sometimes I would buy myself a toy or a bird.

The food cooked in Delhi used to be quite delicious. Among the established families, so many kinds of food were cooked that the table spread would be covered with dishes. They added delicate touches to recipes so that the look of the dish changed. For instance *maash* lentils were boiled and then beautifully garnished with fried whole chillies, coriander and *garam masala*, white and red chillies. It was then ready to decorate the large circular food trays already covered with food. There would be many types of chutneys and *raitas*. These accompaniments only added to the splendour of the spread. Then there were the desserts, some with names which I had never heard before.

The elite had large houses with separate women's and men's sections. According to established traditions, when the master of the house was about to enter the women's section, the senior maidservant would call out to everyone in the women's section,

'The senior master is bringing his auspicious presence.' For quite a while they maintained the traditions, eminence and dignity of their ancestors. They also kept up their grand lifestyles. Many of the aristocrats were heavily in debt and their supposed fortunes were hollow, but they did their best to keep everyone from finding out. They maintained such formality and respect for older people that they would not look them in the eye while speaking to them.

Their style of living resembled that of Lucknow. The summer attire was beautiful: an *achkan* or *angarkha* embroidered with *chikan*, a white pyjama, a crinkled muslin cap, and *Salim Shahi* shoes. When they appeared in the men's sections dressed like this, they really looked like the progeny of nawabs or aristocrats. Their appearance, the way they walked and carried themselves, the way they spoke—everything set them apart from the rest. Attendants would lift the hems of their cloaks and place them next to them or in their hands when they sat down on the *masnad*. Many lazy, pleasure-loving young men, experts at flattery, would linger from morning to night. They would eat both meals with the hosts. Sometimes they could be so intrusive that they started behaving like members of the family. They never tired of being yes-men. The sons of the aristocrats, too, could not do without them for a minute, for they had been fed on flattery since infancy. If any of these hangers-on was late in making an appearance, messengers would be sent to summon him.

To maintain their social eminence, the elite would organize *mushairas, qawwalis* and *mujra* gatherings where the primary concern was that not one kind of food should be missing from the table. All the arrangements would be in royal style. Then there would be the kite flying contests, quail fighting, displays of fencing skills, pigeon racing and cockfights. When I went to Delhi as a child these were amusements for both the rich and the poor. The average man preferred to be called a *pehalwan*, the strong one, so that the other 'strong ones' would be in fear of him. You had to laugh when you looked at these pehalwans; the poor things were dried up, frail and tiny, yet they wanted to be called pehalwans.

The people were full of life. They were fond of going out and amusing themselves. They would celebrate all seasons and all festivals. During the monsoon, whenever heavy dark clouds appeared, or a light drizzle began, they would collect friends and food according to their means, and head for a picnic to the Qutab Minar or the Okhla barrage on the Jamuna. The month of Basant was devoted to kite flying and fencing contests. Experts at the art of fencing would lead a procession; accompanying the procession would be huge candelabras ablaze with light, gas lamps, drums, trumpets and shehnais. The musicians played well and everyone applauded.

God knows where all these people have disappeared. The fencers would confront each other and, to the rhythmic beat of the drums, show skilful manoeuvres with their naked swords. People very impressed by their suppleness and speed, would applaud so hard that they carried on with the display for hours. Many troops of these *gutka wallahs* would appear by turn and parade through the bazaars.

I remember one such parade. When an ustad of gutka had taught his pupil all his skills and tricks, there would be a ritual where the student tied a turban on the head of his ustad. The day would be fixed and all the gutka ustads were invited. When all arrived, the pupil would put clothes, a turban, sweets, and if he could afford it, a gold necklace, on a tray and place it before the ustad and then everyone else would garland the ustad. All the experts would walk in a procession carrying the clothes and sweets for the ustad. Drums and shehnai too, accompanied the procession. One such procession came our way and stopped below our house. Crowds gathered and formed a large circle. They spread a sheet and made the ustad, who was old and skinny, lie on it. Then they stuck a lemon on his forehead. The ustad wanted to demonstrate how cleanly his student could cut the lemon in two as a part of his routine.

The student began his gutka exercise to the fast beat of the drums. He was lithe and agile and he showed such moves that the ustad watched with pride. Every ten minutes or so the student would come around to his ustad and touch the lemon with his sword, and he continued his demonstration for nearly an hour. Then he moved to his ustad and took a full swing at the lemon, the fate of which no longer interested any one. Instead, blood spurted in a fountain from the ustad's forehead. Within seconds, everyone, including the drumbeaters and the candelabra carriers, had disappeared. The gifts and sweets were nowhere to be seen. Lord knows if the ustad survived or not, what is certain is that he arrived at the hospital wearing garlands!

People of all classes, whether poor or aristocrats, were given to boasting. Sons of the elite would begin each conversation by recalling the names of their fathers and grandfathers, the size of their grandfather's estates, or how their great grandfather had killed an elephant with a sword. All those listening would know that none of this was true, but they would listen silently because they were waiting to tell their own tall tales. Chatting with each other in this way was a part of their culture.

The airs, graces and ways of the women from elite families were also very amusing. Strict purdah was enforced in their homes. When I first went to Delhi, some remains of Mughal culture still survived. The same rites and rituals, the same style of clothing, the same magnificence and abundance—things seemed to have changed very little. If their daughters or daughters-in-law wanted to visit a neighbour, they were carried there in palanquins. In those days there were three common ways of transport in Delhi— the *ekkas*, the palanquins and the horse carriage. There were very few cars, and trams only ran along the main bazaars. The advantage of the palanquins was that the carriers would bring it into the women's section and leave it there. When the begum or the girl had settled in, the servant would call out to the men, who would then come in and carry it out. A maid would walk along with it. If long distances were involved, the maids followed in another palanquin. Their life-style included the carrying of their own *paandaans*, with all the ingredients needed for making paans, the *khaasdaan* to store and serve the paans, and their own personal spittoons.

Their dresses were very beautiful, particularly the ones they wore for wedding festivities. Satin *lehngas* with wide borders were embroidered with slanting golden creepers, crinkled gauze dupattas were trimmed with fine lace, and the net kurtas had tight sleeves. The way they held the hems of their heavy lehngas and the edges of their dupattas and still managed to walk delicately, made them appear like real princesses. Even at home, if any of

the younger women wore dupattas without lace, the older ones
would scold them severely. Wearing a plain dupatta was
considered unlucky for married women.

The women would get ready in the morning and then come
and sit on the takhts, and lean on the bolsters. Maids would place
a silver paandaan and a spittoon close to them. The whole day
they would talk to each other or to visitors, with a rolled up paan
stuffed in their cheeks. They had nothing to do with any of the
housework. The airs they put on were also strange. Completely
healthy women were obsessed with convincing others that they
were ill. It was fashionable to have palpitations or get headaches
for the slightest of reasons. They felt proud if the *hakim* had to
visit them at home at least twice a month.

The most famous hakim of that time was Hakim Ajmal Khan.
He was a man of traditional culture, dignified and regal. He also
dressed the part in a whiter than milk chikan angarkha, pyjama, a
muslin cap and Salim Shahi shoes. When he came to his clinic
from home, half one's ills were cured by the very sight of him. I
too went to him a few times to get a cold treated.

Another very amusing custom of the aristocratic women was
that if they were invited out for a meal, they would have a big
meal at home before they left. At the dinner they would take eight
or ten grains of rice and delicately put each one of them into their
mouths with their fingertips. When they tore rotis, it was into twig
like strips. All the women did this.

For me the custom of *aftar* at the end of the fast was also new.
I had never heard of it at home. The whole month of Ramzan was
so festive! Every day in some home or the other, some child was
fasting for the first time, and there would be grand feasts with
many kinds of sharbats. At other times people brought along their
own food and collected in a garden. The month would pass as if
it were a week.

The grand ways of the elite lasted as long as the rule of the
British lasted. After that, their traditions vanished without a trace.
Their way of dressing, their grand lifestyles and their rituals
disappeared so effectively that today it is difficult to recreate them
even in our imagination. When I returned to Delhi after Partition,
I looked everywhere to find one person who wore clothes in the

old Delhi style I remembered. I swear that I did not see a single man or woman who reminded me of the culture of old times: none of those grand *nawabi* horse carriages, none of the fashions of those times or those thousands of palanquins. Where had they all disappeared? Now you could not even make out a Hindu from a Muslim.

I had returned to Delhi after fifty years. I felt like crying when I saw the Jama Masjid with all the filth and squalor around it. I could not believe that this was the same place I had known. There were shops but no cleanliness; the grounds were filled with rubbish, and all around were slums and filth. I did not want to look at it. In fact, I wept in memory of those days of long ago.

I had visited Delhi many times before Partition for recordings; at that time Delhi used to be alive. Jama Masjid, too, was a place where one could go for a stroll. People used to boast how Delhi had been destroyed seven times and yet had always survived. But I think that if it has been destroyed, it has been destroyed now, after Partition. I had seen a living Delhi as a child. I think the pace of change has been faster there than anywhere else. I used to go to Lucknow every month for concerts. On that trip, after Delhi, I eagerly looked forward to revisiting Lucknow. I found it more devastated than Delhi.

11. Ustad Mamman Khan

Ustad Mamman Khan was very famous for the way he expressed emotion through classical dance. He had spent his entire life employed in various kingdoms and it took a lot of effort to make him come to our house. I sang for him and he was very pleased with my singing. I was young but sang in perfect tune and kept to rhythm. He agreed to teach me once he was reassured that if I came to any good, I would serve him for the rest of his life. There was also the prospect that if I learnt the art from him, I would make him famous as my teacher throughout Punjab. He accepted me as a student and agreed to teach me for a modest fee.

He came regularly at ten and would give me lessons till one. He would leave after having lunch. In the evening I would practise my singing. I was constantly learning something or the other from morning to night. There was no one of my age with whom I could play or have any fun, no real entertainment except the *Fasana' i-Azad* which I had to read in hiding. Mamman Khan started teaching me in right earnest. He made me do the work of months in a few days, and the work of many years in a few months.

Mamman Khan was between seventy to seventy-five years of age. He was dark, had large eyes, grand moustaches and large bushes of hair on his cheeks on which there were also black marks. He was bespectacled, fat, had a big round stomach which hung loose, yet when he moved his feet to a composition on the tabla during a lesson, it seemed as if an angel had descended from heaven. At the time dances were not vulgar as they are today. People appreciated a dancer who looked as if he or she were walking on water.

The hard work lay in learning how not to move one's torso even when the feet moved to the fastest of beats. If the torso moved, spectators referred to it as the dance of an elephant. Good dancers would dance to such fast beats that the *tabla wallahs* would tire but the dancers would not lose control over their bodies. They continued to dance, with smiling faces and expressive movements of the eyes and the hands, bodies light as if floating on water, and no indication on the face of the tremendous effort the dancer had to put in. After the dance I had to practise the expressive movements of a *thumri* for another two hours.

For instance there was the thumri '*sab din howat na ek samaan*', that is, 'each day is different from every other.' The weather came first: If you wanted to demonstrate that it was cold, you had to do so by shivering, warming your hands over a fire, pulling your clothes tight around you. 'Perspiration' marked the heat of summer. For the monsoon the clothes had to seem to be wet, you had show that you were terrified of the sudden flashes of lightning that accompany thunderstorms. We had to learn to depict every emotion. The birth of a child and maternal love; the mother bathing and dressing the child joyfully and with tenderness; combing his hair; holding him in her lap and singing a lullaby; swaddling him in blankets and putting him to sleep; taking him out to play, smiling and being indulgent of his mischief; blessing him every time she set eyes on him.

Then we had to learn to show the arrogance of the young male. This was done by adopting a strutting walk, showing him dressing up, admiring himself in the mirror while he tied his turban, and twirled his moustaches, adorning himself with jewels in the ears and around the neck; looking proud with a sword hanging from his waist. Young men riding in horse carriages, drinking with friends, listening to music, distributing money, all these were shown as if they were their pride and strength. All sorts of decadence had to be depicted, including drunkenness, as well as profligacy, wastefulness, gambling and getting into brawls, and finally, old age with the body becoming weak and shaky, the person having to struggle to walk with a walking stick, bent at the waist, exhausted with the effort.

Wealth and poverty also had to be shown. Wealth was expressed by distributing money while you walked, a *kalghi* crest pinned to the turban, a locket around the neck, and a sword at the waist. After evoking this picture one had to move on to show poverty—the torn clothes, homelessness and starvation; the contempt of people; the shivering in the winter for lack of clothes or warmth; the loss of sight; both palms spread out for alms. All this had to be expressed with just the eyes and the hands. The expressions on one's face had to make the audience feel as if they too were living through these emotions. When it came showing poverty and beggars, you had to do so in such a way that the audience actually had tears in their eyes.

You have to practise very hard to learn dancing. Just as all music consists of the notes *sa re ga ma pa dha ni,* dance is based on the beat *ta thai thai tat.* In the beginning I had to keep time to this beat at a fast pace for nearly an hour every day so that I would gain control over my entire body. When the ustad saw that I had acquired the requisite control over my feet and body, he started to teach me *todas*—compositions on the tabla—and songs. Every morning after getting up and learning a melody, I would have to practise the *ta thai* beat on one foot, holding my breath, for nearly fifteen or twenty minutes. Dancing on your feet is easy but dancing while holding your breath and also holding on to one foot is not. That half-hour was pure torture. At the end of it every muscle in my body ached. However, within a few months it became easier. I now began to practise so much that I would tire out the tabla player! I would write down the longer todas and memorise their words and the ustad would just have to teach me how to express them with his feet. We would then start on the dance expressions for the thumri. Thus I trained for four hours every day under the ustad's guidance.

The ustad was very talkative and told us such unbelievable tales that even the most foolish person knew these were blatant lies. However, the accompanists and I had to listen respectfully, and make the appropriate sounds of appreciation. He began every story with '*Assalamat beta,* May you live long my child, this is something I myself have seen with these sinful eyes.' His stories went something like this: '*Asslamat beta,* I once went to a village in the month of June. It was noon and the heat was killing till I saw a tree that provided deep shade and I stood under it. I then looked at the tree carefully and saw that its branches spread far in all directions. As far as I could see I saw the roots which supported these branches. I was amazed and muttered, O Allah, what miracle

is this? Is such a thing possible? *Assalamat beta,* this is something
that these sinful eyes have seen. Can you believe my stupidity? In
spite of the heat I became bull-headed and without giving it a
thought, decided that I would find out where the branches ended.
I was young then and youth is blind. I began to walk holding the
branches. *Asalamat beta,* just guess how many miles I walked?'
I would have to shake my head to indicate that I had no idea.
'Then listen, I walked four miles. It was very hot and I was
drenched in sweat. In spite of being young I gave up because I
feared I might faint. I swear on the Quran that those wretched
branches had not even ended after four miles.' He told tales such
as this every day.

He had spent his entire life serving rajas and maharajas. Most
of his time had been spent in the courts of Gwalior, Jaipur and
Udaipur. Gauhar Jaipurwali had been his student. In Delhi, there
were two sisters, Duanni and Chawanni, named after two and
four anna coins. It was said that elephants stood and swayed at
their gates. This metaphor was thought appropriate because
elephants were actually tied to those gates during Mughal times.
Chawanni was ugly and Duanni was very beautiful. Duanni's
daughter also learnt from my ustad. He took me to their house
and told them, 'See how young she is, and how well she dances.'
Duanni and Chawanni were then in their seventies. The daughter
must have been around forty. I had seen her dance on a few
occasions. She was slightly overweight but she was superb at
expressing emotion. Ustad made me sing and dance for them and
they were very pleased: 'Ustad, she is a human being after all.
You can convert stone into gold.' Duanni and Chawanni also had
a son who has been mentioned by Diwan Singh Maftun in his
book [probably his memoir *Nagabil-i-Faramosh*]. He married a
singing woman from Amritsar. This woman already had two
daughters. The Maharaja of Gwalior employed the older of the
two. The younger one spent some time at music but gave it up
when she met a man who had fallen in love with her the moment
he saw her.

Before the Partition she lived with her sister in Gwalior, and
was married there. The Maharaja may have given a *lakh* or two
for the wedding. Her husband, who worked in films, was a fine

and decent man, and together with him, they moved to Lahore. After the Partition, the sister from Gwalior also moved to Lahore. The younger sister's children too had grown up. Even though they lived in the same city, the daughters were very careful about meeting their mother. They sometimes went to meet her after dark so that no one would find out who they were. Both were married into good families. Lord alone knows what lineage they invented for themselves. I do not think they ever came to visit their parents in the daytime.

Apart from the hospitality and flattery, Mamman Khan was not paid much. But the ustads of that time were as different as the earth is from the sky when compared to ustads of today. If they found an intelligent student they would try their best to pass on their art as quickly as they could. 'Our fame will spread far and wide. People will be amazed that we have been able to teach so much in such a short time,' this is how they looked at things. The ustads of today are often quite ignorant. They have learnt nothing from any ustad. If asked what they have learned and from where, their immediate answer is, 'I have learnt from my father.' To be able to sing well is one thing. Learning is another. People like Khan Sahib Tawakkul Hussain or Wahid Khan had the knowledge even though their singing was not attractive. They were emperors of musical learning. Today, those who know something do not want to teach others. They are all avaricious and miserly. They do not realize that unless they pass on their art, classical music will die and people will start to dance to foreign tunes.

In Lahore there are institutions which have not produced an artist in forty years, and large amounts of government money has been spent on keeping them functioning. Mamman Khan was about seventy-five. He walked to our place every day. He would tire himself out teaching me: he toiled night and day to ensure that I learnt so much that people would be amazed, and no one would be good enough to challenge me. My aunt and uncle did their bit to help. Soon people began to drop in to listen to me. We managed to live comfortably.

Whenever uncle went to Lahore, my aunt would come to stay with us for a few days. We moved into a larger house with three or four rooms because the rents of houses in the area were low.

My aunt loved my singing. Whenever she liked a song, she would reward me with a rupee or two. Amanat Ali would come with her. My days turned wonderful and festive. My aunt would get beautiful clothes stitched for me and she bought me the toys that I wanted.

12. The Addition of Another Ustad

I have mentioned how beautiful my aunt was. In winter, when my singing lessons began at five, a man wrapped in a quilted sheet would come and sit on the stairs. He would stare at my aunt and keep repeating 'Allah, Allah,' and weep copiously. His tears would pour out of him like water from rainwater drains. He was assumed to be a faqir, and was invited in. He sat where people kept their shoes, at the threshold of the house, and cried while I sang. One day he gave me a *naat* in praise of the Prophet which he had written and asked me to sing it for him. I sang it as best I could, but he was not happy with my rendering and found countless errors in my diction. He would often make requests for naats or ghazals, yet he always found fault with my rendering. I used to seethe with anger. 'If he does not like my singing', I'd say to myself, 'what is his problem? Why does he have to be so kind to me every evening? Why does he not go and ask someone else to sing for him?'

A while later we found out that he was a professor in a well-known college and also an initiate in the 'Warsi' order. Near Lucknow there is a village called Dewa Sharif where Hazrat Syed Waris Ali is buried. He was a well educated and a saintly man. Lengthy, thick books have been written about him in which his life—from childhood to old age—is described in detail. Thousands of believers in the Warsi order collect for his *urs* annually. The Warsis were usually well educated with BA and MA degrees, and were litterateurs or poets. Bedam Warsi, many of whose ghazals were sung by Akhtari Bai, was one of them.

For those who just wanted to attach themselves to the order, the message was simple: 'Love others for it is in love that God is to be found.' But to become a part of the order was far more difficult and there were many stages through which seekers had to pass. In the first stage, they were ordered to love small children, then little girls and after that, young unmarried girls. Then came the turn of married women. The rules were that the seeker had to look at them from afar, love them unquestioningly, and never touch them. Anyone who passed through these challenging phases with his purity intact could become a faqir. He would have to wear unstitched clothes for the rest of his life. Wearing of shirts or shoes was forbidden and they were only allowed to wrap themselves in sheets of coarse cloth. However they had a choice of colours—yellow or orange. They would tie these sheets around their waists and drape them like a sari. Throughout their lives, no matter what they did, they had to wear only the colour they had chosen.

They were also forbidden to sleep on beds or use pillows. They could not ask for anything, nor could they carry any money except when they went on the *hajj*. They had to trust God to take care of their needs. They were required to pray five times a day, fast regularly, and read the Quran daily. They were not allowed to ride on any living thing and had to stay single. All this was necessary to be a faqir of the order. Those who could not meet these demands were barred from this status.

The man who came wrapped in a quilted sheet to hear me learning music was a professor in a renowned college, as I have mentioned. He could not only speak Urdu, Persian, Arabic, English and Turkish fluently but also could also read and write these languages. He had gone abroad twice as part of a delegation, which included Dr Ansari. Very well educated, he was in the first stages of initiation into the Warsi order. He came to hear me sing every day and also fell in love with my aunt. He had found out where she lived and would turn up there every day and would sit and stare at her. If it was hot, he would fan her. My uncle came to respect him. Their son, Amanat Ali, however, had a lot of fun at his expense. He would ask him, 'Maulana, tell me about the machine you have inside you, the one that produces these endless tears.'

When my aunt visited us, he would hang around our house till late at night. His name was Tafazzul Hussain Warsi. He was a good looking, well-born person. He usually came in the evening after college was over. During the vacations he would spend the entire day at our house, though he would eat nothing. In spite of our insistence he would not touch the sweets, fruit or sharbat offered to him. There were days when he would not eat or drink anything between nine in the morning and ten at night because he did not want to let my aunt out of his sight. If she asked for water, he would rush and get it for her; if she indicated that she was about to get up he would place her slippers at her feet so that she could step into them. When she slept in the afternoon, he sat with a fan in his hand, fanning her.

Matters were the same at her own house. My uncle tried very hard to force him to eat or drink, but in vain. He did not touch anything there either. We were all amazed at how he survived without eating from morning to night. My aunt was really irritated by all this attention. She wanted him out of her sight and wished that she need never see him. Others would try and calm her. 'What does it matter to you? He is involved in his own quest.' However, she was right to feel that way, for when she had to see the same face everywhere she went, she was bound to feel agitated.

When mother found out how well educated he was, she became very respectful of him. Maulana liked my voice very much, but was critical of my singing. Once, irked by this, mother asked, 'Why do you not teach her for an hour or two?'

So he agreed to teach me Urdu and Arabic. I categorically refused to learn Arabic. 'I do not understand Arabic nor do I feel like learning it,' I told them. He had wanted to teach me Arabic through translations. Now I regret my obduracy and wish I had learnt Arabic. I lost such a good opportunity because of my stubbornness. But, how can one recapture time?

But he did teach me some things. The first of these was the meaning of each couplet of the naat. He would correct every word, particularly the sounds of the letters *qaaf* and *kaaf*. If I did not get the qaaf right he would place his thumb on my throat, press it hard, and say, 'Now say qaaf.' I hated this and felt like killing him for doing it. He also used to emphasize the letters *ayn*, *he* and *se*. When he was satisfied with my reading, he would order, 'Sing it now.' When I sang, he would say the same thing. 'If you pronounce the word correctly when you read it, why do you ruin it when you sing it?' He would listen to the same couplet over and over

again. Gently, he would say,'*Hai*, how beautifully you destroy
the word in that wonderful voice of yours!' When this was not
enough, he would try and imitate me even though he could not
sing, and was never in tune or rhythm. I would get tired of
repetition but he would not be satisfied. All he would ask was,
'Do words change when they are sung?'

I began to hate him. I constantly wondered and prayed, 'Allah,
why has this curse attached itself to me? O God, free me from it.'
But there he was, without fail, every day. I was making fewer
mistakes now, but sometimes I would still mispronounce a few
words. If I made a mistake, he would wail, 'Hai,' as if he had been
stung by a snake, 'my heart is broken.' I would say to myself,
'May God really rupture your heart.' I used to be so furious that
every day I would pray that he would fall ill, break a leg or be
bitten by a rabid dog, and not appear at our house again! In the
morning there were three hours of learning from Mamman Khan,
then another hour or two of singing lessons. In the evening it was
ghazals and naats. Instead of praise, he only found fault, 'Do not
deliver it like that, do not pronounce it like this.' For fear of my
mother I could do nothing but curse him silently even though I
hated him so much that I could not look at him for more than five
minutes at a time. Often I prayed at the shrine of Hare Bhare Shah
and Hazrat Nizamuddin to be rid of him, but he would turn up
hale and hearty and on the dot, every day.

Sometimes I missed Jammu. What wonderful times those were.
I missed Phupo Nikki, my aunt, my father, even my first ustad. I
would think lovingly of my father. In Jammu, too, I used to sing
the whole day but it did not seem as hard as things did in Delhi.
The jokes, stories and gossip made Mamman Khan's training easy
and it did not seem like a strain. But Maulana Sahib was nothing
but trouble. He was about forty, but his constant weeping! God
alone knows where all the water came from. It seemed as if there
was plumbing at the back of his head and a tap just had to be
turned on. When his nose ran while he was crying, he would
wipe it with his sleeve, which I found disgusting. I had to put up
with all this, and also listen to his unending criticism, only because
I was afraid of mother.

We had lived in Delhi for two full years. Then aunt and uncle moved to Lahore. I had become quite proficient in singing, expressive dance gestures and dancing. My skills and talent impressed the more experienced women and good singers. I had practised so hard at dancing to a fast beat that the tabla players had a difficult time keeping up with me. I could dance for two hours and not feel the strain. Maulana Sahib had taught me correct diction. I remembered the dance gestures of the thumris well. Famous singers began to get nervous because of me. I was nine years old and they were in their thirties. When they sang and danced after me at functions, the audience was not pleased. They began making excuses to back out of commitments when they found out that I had also been invited to perform.

Phupho Nikki and my older aunt wrote from Jammu, 'The coronation of the Maharaja of Kashmir is being planned and preparations have begun at a hectic pace. Jammu is being decorated and everything looks splendid. People are coming from far away to attend the coronation. You have been away for two years and we miss you sorely. Come back. Come for a few months and watch the fun.'

13. Our Return from Delhi

Mother too had been missing her family, so everyone agreed that we should go back to Jammu for two or three months. 'We will get to meet everyone again and also see the celebrations,' was the argument that clinched the matter. When I heard this, I went crazy with joy. I wanted to fly to Jammu immediately. It took a few days to make preparations for the journey. Maulana came to see us off at the station. He blessed me profusely, 'May God protect you and your voice.' With tears in his eyes he continued, 'You crazy one, I know you hate me but I loved you. Teachers always love good and intelligent students. I wanted to make you as accomplished as possible, and that was the reason why I behaved the way I did; why I spent more and more time with you. Otherwise, we are at such different stages in our lives. I have initiated you as a Warsi and by this token, you are my spiritual sister from now on.'

His words had no effect on me. To myself I said, 'I did not need your education, nor do I need your love.' I was thanking God for ridding me of him. It was time for the train to leave. Maulana bid farewell to everyone and left. We changed trains at a few places and finally reached Jammu safely. We loaded our luggage on *tongas* and reached home. Phupho Nikki and my other aunt were delighted beyond belief: their eyes held both laughter and tears. Phupho Nikki kept saying, 'Hussain ji you have finally come. Thank you Hussain ji for coming.' In her joy she seemed to have taken leave of her senses.

I felt that I had stepped straight from hell into heaven, the way a prisoner must feel when he is set free. In Delhi Nani was the only one who was affectionate to me but I met her only at mealtimes or at bedtime because she observed strict purdah. All the housework, including cooking and washing the clothes, was her responsibility. Because of purdah, she was confined to just one room while I was busy training the whole day. In Jammu, things came back to normal – the familiar love, the same laughter. My father too, met me with great warmth.

'How much do I owe you now?' he asked.

'Nothing' I assured him.

'No,' he laughed, 'I am heavily indebted to you. Return to your daily duties and come and take your share of naal again.'

Nearly a week was spent in catching up with everybody. I would lie with my head in Phupho Nikki's lap and listen to stories till I fell asleep and she lived in constant fear that a witch would emerge from under the bed and take me away. She was always scared and even in the day she would not go into a room alone. I began practising both in the morning and in the evening. In Jammu you could rent novels from a lending library. Every evening I would go with Phupho Nikki and bring home a few which I went through in a day or two. Most of these were translations of English novels. First I went through several Sherlock Holmes novels. Then I read the forty volumes of *Fasana i-Landan* (*Tales of London*) and the historical novels of Abdul Halim Sharar. Soon I had gone through the entire stock in the library. When mother was elsewhere, I spent the whole day reading. I had no friends, nor was there anyone my age at home to play with. Reading novels was my only indulgence and I became an obsessive reader.

We must have been in Jammu for about twelve days when one day, at ten in the night, a royal orderly appeared.

'The Maharaja's secretary Abdul Qaiyyum Khan wants you to come over,' he declared to no one in particular.

Mother replied, 'Surely, you are mistaken. There is no one so eminent here.' He drove away in the car. A little while later he was back, 'He wants to see you.'

'Who?' mother asked.

'The girl who has come from Delhi.'

'She is only a child,' mother said, 'She is only eight or nine.'

'I do not care if she is five, but it is she who has been summoned.'

To this mother said, 'She is asleep at the moment. Please apologise on our behalf and explain that she would be good for nothing if she were woken now. If they want to listen to her

singing, they can send the car tomorrow. We will be pleased to
present ourselves.'

The next evening, the car arrived at eight. We reached Qaiyyum
Sahib's house. A few ministers and other high officials were seated
in a room. In the next room, behind a screen, sat their wives.
When they heard my singing and saw my dance and my *nritya
bhav* they could not help but praise me with sounds of '*ash, ash,
ash* ... .' They were so pleased that Thakur Kartar Singh said,
'Victory will be Jammu's. No wretch from anywhere else can
compete with her.'

Their wives invited me inside and showed genuine affection.
They would repeatedly ask the same question, 'How did you
manage to learn all this at such a young age?' Qaiyyum Sahib
himself was not good-looking but his wife was very beautiful.
She dressed very fashionably and spoke refined Urdu. At the end
of the evening we came back to our home. Two days later the
Maharaja's special orderly came again and left the message, 'The
Maharaja has thought of you. Be ready at eight.'

I did not need any time to get ready. I wore a tight pajama and
a kurta. My hair was thick and long and mother now braided it
into a plait. I wore a dyed muslin dupatta, and the car arrived on
the dot at eight. I took my accompanists and went to the palace
where we were seated in a huge hall. Ten minutes later an orderly
appeared and said that only I was invited in. I followed him. We
passed a few very large rooms before he indicated the room His
Highness was seated in, and said, 'Go in.' I strode straight into the
room. The orderly panicked and ran after me, 'Will you please
leave your shoes outside.' I ran again. I used to walk as though I
was running, and was not used to walking slowly. When the
orderly told me to take off my shoes, instead of walking out, I ran
further into the room in panic, where I heard loud laughter. I
returned, took off my shoes outside the room, re-entered and stood
there. People were still smiling. I recognized the Maharaja from
his pictures. In any case, he was sitting on a chair in the centre.
With his hand he indicated that I should sit. I sat down on the
carpet. My accompanists soon joined me. One of them threw the
ghungroos to me.

I began to tie the string of bells around my ankles. Another ADC of the Maharaja rushed to me and said, 'Do not point your feet towards the Maharaja. It is disrespectful.' I moved my feet away in another direction but he returned and said, 'You are still being very disrespectful.' I was irritated and reacted loudly, 'If I cannot stretch my legs in either this direction or in that, where should I put my feet? On my head?' I heard the others laugh again. The Maharaja summoned his ADC and instructed him, 'Let her do what she wants.'

It must have been due to my anger at the humiliation that I danced so well that people were stunned. I then sang a bhajan-like thumri with the words, '*Arey Ram, kaise par utariye*,' (O Ram, how do I cross this river?) in which the dance gestures indicated faith and prayer, and I sang for nearly half an hour. Then I sang a ghazal. In those days very few people in the Punjab sang ghazals. And if they did, the tunes were very bad. I had learnt different tunes in Delhi, and Maulana Sahib had polished my diction. In the end I sang a *pahari*. My earlier awkward behaviour was forgiven. Everyone was silent for some time and then they started to talk among themselves: 'What an amazing child! So proficient in all the forms and that too at such a young age! She is unbelievable! Allah has given her a unique voice. She sings better then most of the famous singers.' Each was trying to outdo the other in praising me. After the singing, the Maharaja called me to him. I went and stood in front of him.

I had heard that when confronted by a Maharaja, out of awe and fear, one lost one's voice, the body started shivering, and one's hands and feet swelled up. For two years I had heard stories such as this from Mamman Khan, '*Assalamat beta*, one day the Maharaja had other maharajas as guests. The messenger who announced visitors came to fetch me. I respectfully stated that I had a severe headache, and asked to be excused. The messenger returned and said he had been ordered to present me no matter what state I was in. I went. When I looked at His Highness, I began to shiver and my hands and feet began to quiver. First a Maharaja, then an enraged one! I swear on the Quran my child; I did not have the courage to look at him. The Maharaja said, "*Arey* Mamman, how dare you?" I was speechless. All I could utter was,

"O my benefactor, spare my life this time. This slave has erred." I immediately tied the ghungroos to my ankles and danced so well that the Maharaja could not stop saying *wah wah* in delight. Finally he took off the emerald necklace he was wearing and threw it at me and said "Mamman, this belongs to you".'

Tales like these had left strange impressions about maharajas and nawabs on my mind. Yet, I neither lost my mind nor did I shiver, nor did my legs quiver. He looked like any other man to me and I did not feel any fear looking at him. The Maharaja said to me in Dogri, 'You have learnt everything at such a young age. You sing very well. It is really surprising how good you are at everything. Where did you learn all this?'

'In Delhi,' I replied. I kept listening to his compliments silently and never said a thank you, nor expressed gratitude in any other way. I just stood there, agreeing with him.

'Come at seven tomorrow,' he said.

I nodded my head and turned away. I was so happy that I forgot where I was. My accompanists were standing at a distance and I ran to them. Once again loud laughter followed my moves. From sheer embarrassment, I did not look back. I could not change my ways in a day. When I came out of the room, the orderly told me, 'First, you do not turn your back to the Maharaja in the court. Second, no one runs in the *durbar*, particularly the way you did. This is outrageous. Learn how to walk.'

I later learnt that the Maharaja had gifted me a thousand rupees in cash and sanctioned another thousand for a dress for me which he had ordered to be ready in two days. The tailor was already there. He took my measurements, cut the cloth and gave it to have floral creepers embroidered on it, and to be decorated with sequins. When the dress was ready, it would cost five hundred rupees at the most. This was typical of the way things were. If the Maharaja had ordered a thousand rupees, they would misappropriate seven hundred and only spend three hundred.

The news that I had been rewarded with a thousand rupees and a dress for the same amount soon became well-known in Jammu. A thousand rupees meant a lot those days for you could buy a house with that much money. Next day the car again arrived at seven. We reached the palace and I was summoned as soon as we arrived. I had firmly resolved that I would do nothing that day that would make them laugh at me. Before entering, I took off my shoes. Then, in slow motion and using steps used while dancing, I entered the room. I must have taken six or seven steps when they were all laughing uncontrollably again. They had even forgotten the etiquette of the court. The orderly, who always stood behind the Maharaja's chair waiting for his commands, was also giggling, his face cupped in his hands. I was surprised and looked at everyone. 'What sort of people are these? They should be pleased that I did not race in again, but that I walked in so gracefully.' I was not used to walking slowly but today I had measured each step. Yet what I had dreaded had happened again. After bringing his mirth under control, the Maharaja beckoned me to him, made me sit near him and began to speak to me in Dogri. He spoke beautiful Dogri. He would never address any one with the informal *tu* or *tum*. Whether they were his orderlies or his ministers, he addressed them all with the formal and respectful *aap*. His spoke so beautifully and sweetly that I wished he would go on speaking so that I could continue to listen.

At eight-thirty, dinner was served. In a large silver *thali* were bowls of chicken curry, a meat *qorma*, fried trout, a few kinds of vegetables, a *dal* of black beans and a few kinds of desserts. On one side of the thali there was a pulao and on the other there was plain rice. The Maharaja was the first to be served and later I was served too. This was the first time that I was eating such tasty food and that too out of sparkling silverware. More than the food, I enjoyed the experience of eating in separate bowls. I ate so much that all I wanted to do after eating was to return home and go to sleep.

Immediately after dinner, I was ordered to perform. I did not feel like singing or dancing, but could not refuse. Nor could I admit that I had eaten too much. So I did the best I could. We were allowed to leave at eleven. I got another reward of a thousand rupees. This became the regular pattern. The car would arrive at seven and the food would arrive in thalis. Singing followed dinner and the evening ended at eleven. Sometimes I returned home with five hundred, sometimes with seven hundred rupees. I was also given a few *peshwazes*—knee length dress-gowns decorated with silver and gold lace edgings and with small stars sewn on. The blouse was so heavily decorated with stars and mirror-work that you could not see the fabric under it. The circumference of the peshwaz used to be nine yards and the length of the dupatta three and a half yards. They weighed so much that it was difficult to dance in them. Sometimes I would feel as if I was about to drop. Some of the todas and movements were long and I had to take a few circles during them. Dressed thus, it was difficult to twirl at a fast beat. But with time, I got used to this too.

Two months remained for the coronation. The rulers of many states were to attend. The Maharaja knew well that I had neither good clothes nor jewellery. Maybe this was why he was rewarding me every day. Male and female singers were gathering from far and wide. Well-known lady singers were invited from Delhi, Lucknow, Jaipur, Calcutta, Banaras, Lahore and whereever else they were to be found. Each charged differently. One wanted two, another three and yet another five hundred rupees per day. They were paid the cost of travel, and were guests of the state while in Jammu.

Jammu was getting livelier by the day for there was ever increasing activity. People were getting their homes painted and decorated. Both the rich and the poor wanted their city to look as pretty as a bride. The elders were as thrilled as the children were. They were getting new clothes stitched for themselves and their children. The people of the state were as involved in the preparations as if the coronation was a personal matter for them. They were proud and wanted every visitor to say that there was no city prettier than Jammu. People were simple and naïve then. They loved their city and their rulers more than they loved their own families. It did not matter if they were Hindu or Muslim, they all prayed for their Maharaja. They sincerely believed that since Allah had appointed the rulers, it was their duty to love and respect them. They loved their land so much that they did not think of moving to another city. Our kingdom was clean, orderly and pretty. When it rained the houses and streets were washed so clean that it seemed as if a scrub brush had been used. Now, newer roads were being built. With all the houses repainted, Jammu really looked wonderful. Every house had guests coming to stay, for everyone's relatives, even from distant places, were coming to see the coronation.

I would go to His Highness' palace every evening. Along with money I now started getting rolls of brocade and jewellery—bangles for my arms, a *jhoomar* for my hair and forehead, a jewelled collar and long earrings, as gifts. Soon I had jewellery to wear from head to foot. I also learnt how to wear clothes. My posture and walk changed.

A new and difficult duty was imposed on me. The real palace of the Maharaja was known as Mandi. It was the tradition of the kingdom that the rulers lived there. Maharaja Hari Singh had built himself a palace in Ram Nagar outside the city. Even though Mandi was a brilliant example of Kashmiri craftsmanship, Hari Singh did not like to live there. Tourists came from far and wide to see it. The Maharaja however preferred simpler things. At Ram Nagar everything, from the carpets to the furniture, was imported from Europe. None of these was ornamented. My new duty was to go to the temple at Mandi every morning to sing, at five. I knew a lot of bhajans. I had sung some of these for His Highness too. I would return from Ram Nagar at eleven. It would be midnight before I could go to sleep. I would get up at four to get ready to go to Mandi where I stayed from five to seven. The pundits would recite something to themselves and blow into the fire. They would keep ringing the sixty bells while I sang bhajans. They did not listen to me and I did not understand what they were saying. Mandi too was being cleaned and painted by hundreds of people because all the official rituals were to be performed here.

This new routine continued for some time and I was not getting enough sleep. I would try and sleep in the day but could not. One night when I went to Ram Nagar at seven, I leaned against a chair and fell asleep. I was woken up at dinner. After we had eaten, His Highness let me go without making me perform. The next day when I went to Ram Nagar, something very funny happened. After dinner an orderly appeared with something in a very beautiful box and first served His Highness from it. Since I was sitting next him, it was offered to me next. I looked at what was in the box. In it were glittering round, triangular, and flat pieces, placed in different compartments. Quickly, I picked a couple of pieces from each section and put two of them together into my mouth. When I bit into them they were horrible—sweet and bitter at the same time. This bittersweet stuff I swallowed but it was impossible to swallow the other stuff left in my mouth. I looked around and saw everyone unwrap the glittering covers before they put the pieces in their mouths. I made a small ball out of the foil in my mouth and then hid it in my hand. I was later to find out that this was chocolate, which I had seen and tasted for the first time!

The entire staff of the Maharaja was very considerate towards me. The head bearer would often give me toffees, dry fruits, chocolates and fruits to take home. The ADCs and orderlies would say 'You will be the "number one" amongst all of them, and the kingdom will be proud of you.' The day after the chocolates, when I went, I felt so sleepy after dinner that I found it difficult to sit up, or stay awake. When the accompanists arrived I told them I was feeling very sleepy and that I did not feel like singing at all. His Highness asked, 'What is the matter with you? You seem to be asleep most of the time.'

'I am not getting enough sleep' I answered truthfully.

'Why?' the Maharaja wanted to know.

I told him, 'I reach home, and by the time I sleep it is midnight. Then, at four, I have to get up to go and sing bhajans at Mandi. I cannot sleep in the day because I have never done so. In the evenings I come here.'

'Who has asked you to perform this duty at Mandi?' His Highness wanted to know.

'I do not know,' I said. 'The car just appears at four.'

To this he said, 'From now on do not go anywhere, no matter who comes. Just be here at seven.'

There was only a month left for the coronation. The preparations were now being completed at double speed. The *qalandari* had been put up. The qalandari was a huge encampment in which there were many rooms and thousands could live there. The walls and roofs of the qalandari were covered with the same embroidery that is found on Kashmiri shawls. Maharaja Pratap Singh gave half of this qalandari away to the Prince of Wales. In those days the splendour and honour of all the rulers was at the mercy of the British. When the Prince of Wales came, each tried to outdo the other in giving him precious gifts. That is where half the qalandari had gone. The Prince later abandoned the throne for a woman. I think she was called Mrs Simpson.

The qalandari was one of the unique treasures of the world. It was not easy to put up, and this one was being used for the first time. It took three months to put up. The plans were to accommodate all the visiting royalty in this qalandari and use the main room for dance and music sessions.

14. Guests at the Coronation

The guests for the coronation began to arrive. The first was the Nawab of Palanpur. He was a good friend of His Highness and they behaved as if they were brothers. Nawab Sahib was very serious, sober, dignified. He was good-hearted and interested in practising medicine. He was between forty and fifty, darkish, handsome and well groomed. In his youth, Nawab Sahib had been very close to Gauhar Jan Jaipurwali. Keeping this in mind, Gauhar Jan had been invited earlier than the others. She had stopped dancing by then. But her singing and *nritya bhav* were still excellent. She was between forty and forty-five, dark, very good-looking and well-kept. Her conversation was sophisticated. She fasted and prayed regularly. She had spent her life employed at various royal courts and even now, she was invited to every important function in every kingdom. Gauhar had also learnt dancing from my teacher, Mamman Khan.

Every day, a few more female singers would arrive. They would be invited to Ram Nagar in the evenings. Only one or two of them could perform each evening. I went every day, but only heard others sing. Many uninvited female and male singers had also arrived in Jammu, although His Highness did not like listening to male singers. Each one of them was desperate for that one opportunity to perform for the Maharaja for they were convinced, they would please him so much that they would be wealthy forever. All were disappointed. Many came to me to plead their case. Mother would tell them, 'How can she help you? She is still a child, and does not even know how to speak for herself as yet.'

Every day the maharajas of other states arrived with ceremony and splendour, in their own special trains. When a maharaja's train reached the station, he was given a gun salute befitting his stature and as defined by protocol. Each state had a different number of gunshots assigned as salute. Some got eleven and others had fourteen cannons going off when they arrived. The larger the kingdom, the longer the salute. When these salutes were given, people would know that a maharaja had arrived. They would come and stand by the roadside to watch the procession. The rajas and nawabs arrived in such large numbers that every two hours the cannons would go '*dhana dhan*'.

The special trains carried the complete staff of the maharajas—orderlies, a troop of cooks, furnishers, security staff, male and female singers, wrestlers, cars and drivers. All the private servants were there too. Each maharaja had at least a thousand to fifteen hundred attendants with him. Their lodging, food and drink, were the responsibility of the host. All kinds of liquor, meat, fish, grain, dry fruit, vegetables, fresh fruit, milk, ghee, sugar, fine and granular flour, were provided to them. The lower paid employees collected enough of these to take home where they lived off them for more than six months.

A hundred to hundred and fifty maharajas arrived. Goats, fowl and eggs were collected from all the nearby villages. Waterfowl, mallards, trout, fruit and vegetables came from Kashmir in buses. Big landlords and ministers waited to receive all the maharajas at the station with elephants, horses and cars. They would seat the maharaja on an elephant, and bring him through the city to his living quarters. Something or other was happening the whole day. People from all around Jammu had come to the city to watch the spectacle. Every home had visitors staying in it. Anyone, who had relatives or friends in Lahore, Sialkot or Kashmir, had invited them to watch the coronation. There were some other enthusiasts who had come without even having a place to stay. They would sleep out on the platforms of shops and the moment the day dawned, they would begin to watch the parade of the maharajas. As if this were not enough, the Maharaja had also arranged elaborate firework displays to entertain the people.

Every second or third day, the fireworks would make wondrous patterns in the sky. Once up there, they would sketch gardens, streets and flowers, made up of sparkling, twinkling lights. The pyrotechnic experts who had come from abroad actually wrote the Maharaja's name, and messages of congratulations to him in the sky. All these things were so entertaining and rare that people stayed on even if they had to sleep on the streets. They were kept busy the whole day: they would watch the Maharajas being brought in a procession. Everyone would offer their salaams. Since the elephants swayed when they walked, the heads of the Maharajas nodded automatically, and the people took this to be an acknowledgement of their greetings. I too would watch the processions because they had to pass our house to enter the city. Everything we were watching was totally new to me.

15. The Eve of the Coronation

Finally, there were just two or three days left for the coronation. Nearly all the guests had arrived. The Maharaja and his staff would make an appearance at the qalandari after dinner every day. All the women singers who had been invited from all over would be present there. There were well over a hundred such singers. Whichever woman was ordered to, would perform. The Maharaja would listen to a couple of them and leave. Some maharajas would stay to listen till three in the morning. Others would only show up at eleven p.m. They did as they wished, and came and left at will. The Maharaja of Jammu and the Nawab of Palanpur stayed only till eleven. His Highness had also ordered that I be sent home at eleven. All the others were ordered to stay till the durbar was adjourned.

The Maharaja of Patiala never appeared before eleven. Everything about him was different from the other maharajas. He was always drunk, and used to arrive with a glass of liquor in his hand. His eyes were the colour of blood. He was seven feet tall, fat and extremely imposing. He had lovely eyes, a beautiful nose and a wheatish complexion, yet his countenance was frightening. The demonic look in his eyes sent shivers down my spine. His ADCs and secretaries were as tall and well-built as he was. When they entered the qalandari, a hush would descend on the gathering.

The other maharajas dressed casually when they came to the qalandari after dinner—each wore a kurta and pajama with a shawl draped around him. The Maharaja of Patiala, even at eleven at night, would be in full courtly regalia: a brocade achkan, a Chinese silk shalwar with voluminous folds, and finely embroidered gold shoes. His beard was well-groomed and his hair hidden in his turban. Later I heard that he wore his achkan only out of necessity. Apparently his stomach was so large and flabby that it hung to his knees. In the morning after his bath, two servants held it up, and girdled it firmly in place with muslin wraps so that it would stay where it should be. They would then robe him in his achkan and button it down. He then wore the achkan till he went to bed.

He also had the reputation of being extremely cruel and tyrannical. He would order the execution of people for the smallest of mistakes. For minor offences he had girls thrown out of the window of his palace.

He was the best looking among the maharajas. Because of his height, he looked good in the large gathered shalwars, coloured muslin turbans and the large diamonds in his ears. In fact he looked good in whatever he wore. I had heard so many stories about him, and now I had the opportunity to actually set eyes on him. As Mamman Khan would have said, it sent a shiver through me. When he came into the qalandari, the singing ladies of Patiala followed him: old, young and very young—all very badly dressed. If one was cross-eyed, another was pockmarked. Some were dark and some fat. Lord knows why he had brought them with him for they were neither good looking nor could they sing.

Many of the maharajas had brought the women singers employed by them. None of them however, came into the qalandari accompanied by them. Maybe the Maharaja of Patiala wanted to show what a benefactor of the poor and the helpless he was. Most of the maharajas drank very little. Some never even touched liquor. The ones who did drink usually nursed their drink for hours. The Maharaja of Patiala drank liquor as if it were water, peg after peg, *ghataghat*. Till today the Patiala peg is famous. If someone pours a large drink, others will say, 'Oh no, you have poured us a Patiala peg.' One ADC constantly kept a bottle with him. When he emptied one glass, another full one immediately replaced it. I saw him for about ten minutes because I was only allowed to stay till eleven.

Since the singing sessions had started at the qalandari, I had not sung there even once, though I was expected to be in attendance every day. Some maharajas were still to arrive. One very strange looking maharaja arrived. He was dark, weedy as a twig, tall as a pole and with no hair growing on his face. He was young, but his face had wrinkles instead of hair on it. There were also dark marks on his cheeks. On his head was a turban, which looked as if it was made up of rope. He wore a brocade achkan and, on his stick-like legs a churidar pajama, and gold embroidered shoes.

Following him were twenty or twenty-five hijras. They wore expensive peshwazes and were loaded with jewellery and they followed the Maharaja with their mincing gait. This was the Maharaja of Alwar. He and his staff sat down on the chairs. Scornful, sarcastic smiles appeared on the faces of the other maharajas. After fifteen minutes, the Maharaja of Alwar ordered the singing to stop. He then gestured to his hijras who, after blessing him a few times, began to sing. Within five minutes other maharajas began to leave. Our Maharaja, being a good host, stayed for fifteen minutes and then left, saying he had to go to bed. By the time it turned eleven, only one or two hijras had performed when an orderly came to inform me that the car was ready. I was enjoying myself so much that I did not want to leave this strange and interesting session.

Till then I had only seen hijras when one or two badly dressed ones appeared with a *dholak* around their neck at the birth of a boy. They would accept a few rupees, bless the child and leave. But these hijras! Bedecked in gold and dressed in silver embroidered peshwazes, they had enough airs and graces to beat any woman hollow. Their faces were those of men but they behaved like women. Their voices were off-key. They danced to thumris and dadras, which they sang in their grating voices. It had been such an interesting evening, I'd never experienced anything like this before. But because of the eleven o'clock curfew, I had had to leave.

The next day it was only nine when the Maharaja of Alwar arrived with his troop of hijras. No one had begun singing, so he grabbed the opportunity and indicated to his hijras to start. They in turn, sought the Maharaja's blessing and then wriggling their bottoms, they began to sing and dance to music as well as the sound of their own loud clapping. The few maharajas who were there watched with disdain and scorn. However, on the face of the Maharaja of Alwar was a look of pure pleasure. His beady eyes twinkled like those of a small innocent child who had been

given his favourite toy. Gradually the other maharajas disappeared.
Our ruler too, after yawing a few times, left. I however had my fill
of listening and watching them from nine to eleven. I was thrilled.

The next evening the driver turned the car towards Ram Nagar.
I asked where we were going. The driver answered that he had
been ordered that I be delivered to Ram Nagar. When I reached
there, I found about a dozen maharajas, the Nawab of Palanpur
and about half a dozen other women singers, already there. Each
one heard their favourite singers. When all had sung, I was asked
to perform. I first danced. Then, with dance gestures, I sang a
bhajan-like thumri. All the maharajas were very pleased and our
Maharaja had a hard time hiding his joy. It seemed as if he was the
one who had taught me all that I knew. With great pride he
informed them that I was from his kingdom. He made me sing all
the pieces he liked. The session lasted till three in the morning.

Once again I was ordered to start singing bhajans at Mandi.
Singing bhajans there was considered a great honour. First there
was no one else around who could sing bhajans. Second, the
Maharaja did not want to entrust this privilege to anyone else. He
was doing me a special favour. I was still a child and belonged to
him.

The old palace at Mandi was very beautiful and full of exquisite
treasures. The large rooms and their high ceilings, the walls—all
were adorned with gold and silver Kashmiri craftsmanship. In the
central room, there was a huge chandelier, and its colour matched
the colour of the room. The decorations on the walls were so
beautiful they took your breath away. The doors were covered
with such superb work in gold that you had to wonder who these
craftsmen were who not only had so much skill, but also so much
time. The rooms were so large that the durbar hall could
accommodate two or three thousand chairs. Every room had a
name.

In the centre of Mandi there was a large courtyard. In the middle
of this courtyard was a marble platform seven or eight feet high
with stairs leading to it from all sides. All the durbars were held
there. The circumference of the courtyard was so large that after
accommodating the army, a troop of horsemen, the police,
elephants, mules, the army and police bands, there was still enough

space left for the subjects of the kingdom to watch the ceremony comfortably. The platform had deliberately been built so high that all the people, who crowded around to watch, could participate in the joyous occasion.

In those days murder and violence were not common. The Maharaja did not surround himself with guards. Nor was he afraid when he slept, unprotected by either the army or the police. The other maharajas too moved around freely.

Around the courtyard were the palaces of the maharajas and the maharanis. Every maharani, when she had been married, had brought with her forty to fifty young unmarried girls. These girls spent their entire lives locked up in the palace. They stayed unmarried, and served the maharanis all their lives. Poor people, greedy for rewards, would offer their young daughters for the privilege of being part of a royal household. They ate and dressed well, but they would never have husbands or homes. The purdah in the palace was so severe and the guardians so efficient that even a bird would find it difficult to sneak in.

On one side of the courtyard were the offices. There were so many rooms around the courtyard that it looked like a small township. Each maharaja had his own set of rooms: the room with green walls was decorated with real jade. In the yellow room, the ceilings, walls and doors were decorated in gold. Similarly, the white room was full of things made of ivory. In this room there were also two trees carved out of ivory. The tusks out of which these were carved were said to have been the largest tusks in anyone's possession in the world. These were priceless and rare things. This room also had a white chandelier that was unique because of its size. The palace was full of exquisite and unique artifacts.

The gate of Mandi was as large and strong as that of any fortress. It was opened only on the days that the durbar was held. Besides the main gate there were two smaller gates which were large enough for cars and horse carriages to pass through easily. These gates were kept open. The main gate itself was a fine example of the ironsmith's craft and was well worth seeing. If the gates were closed, there was no way of entering Mandi. Ever since the kingdom had been created, all the rulers had lived here.

Maharaja Hari Singh had been educated in England from his childhood. He preferred simplicity in everything. At Ram Nagar, he used nothing from the palace at Mandi. Nor did he spend any length of time in the palace. He constantly repeated that he felt uneasy with all the priceless things around him. He made it clear that he wanted to live with plain walls and ceilings, which had no embellishments on them. 'I cannot bear to have these floral motifs and creepers all around me,' he said.

Every one of his well-wishers advised him that while it had been all right for him as a prince to live at Ram Nagar, now that he was the Maharaja, it was only appropriate that he shift to Mandi. The Ram Nagar palace, they strongly felt, did not befit his status anymore. The Maharaja refused to succumb to this pressure. He made it clear that he did not believe in following every custom of his ancestors. He said he found peace at Ram Nagar, which he did not find at Mandi. In fact, he asserted, he felt suffocated at Mandi. He made his preference very clear, 'I want to live in a home, not in an antique shop. I do not care what my forebears preferred and what they did not. I will live here in Ram Nagar all my life.'

16. The Coronation Procession

The day of the coronation arrived. All the rajahs and nawabs reached Mandi. Elephants, cavalry, infantry, and the police and army bands were lined up on one side. All the maharajas were dressed formally in their court regalia—brocade achkans, turbans of Banarsi silk with kalghis of diamonds and pearls pinned on them; necklaces of large emeralds, rubies and pearls; huge diamond studs in their ears – in fact all that they had inherited from their ancestors. Their achkans had diamond buttons whose lustre blinded the eyes. Each maharaja was bedecked according to his means. An elephant would appear next to the marble platform for each maharaja. The mahout would bend down and whisper something in its ear and it would raise its trunk in salute. The mahout would then order it to sit down which the elephant would do awkwardly. Each *howdah* had a ladder attached to it, and the maharajas used these to climb on. One by one all the maharajas were seated. Finally, an elephant appeared for Maharaja Hari Singh. It was bigger than all the other elephants and covered with a silver embroidered caparison that shone so brightly that one could not look at it for long. The elephant was loaded with jewellery from head to foot—a necklace around its neck, thick anklets on its feet and thick bracelet-like bands at three places on its trunk. The howdah was made of gold; so was the chair in it as well as the sunshade over it.

His Highness mounted the elephant. The bands struck up a musical salute, which was followed by a twenty-one gun salute. The procession began: first the army with its riders and the infantry, the police and army bands, then the Maharaja's elephant. The rest of the maharajas followed as the procession left Mandi. People lined both sides of the roads. Others had been waiting for hours on the roofs of houses and shops for the procession to appear. The crowd was so thick that there was no place left to accommodate any more people. Some of the maharajas, in their brocade achkans and jewellery, looked like real kings. Others looked like the 'Khan Sahibs' whom they employed to sing for them. For instance the Maharaja of Jaipur—thin, weedy, short, and with a wheatish complexion which tended towards being dark; the Maharaja of Bikaner—dark, fat and short; the Maharaja of Alwar—thin, tall and with no hair on his face. The nawab of Palanpur was good-looking despite his wheatish complexion, yet he looked awful in brocade and jewels. Of the maharajas, it was only our Maharaja and the Maharaja of Patiala who could carry off their grand costumes and jewellery and who looked like real maharajas. A few others could have passed muster. The rest looked like timid jackals. When the procession appeared, people raised slogans wishing Maharaja Hari Singh a long life. All the maharajas acknowledged the people's greetings by waving their arms.

During the procession there was an amusing accident that involved the Maharaja of Chanaini. The kingdom of Chanaini was about ten or twelve miles from Jammu. When people travelled to Kashmir on horses or mules, this was the first halting place after Jammu. This small kingdom was a feudatory of the kingdom of Kashmir. The Maharaja of Chanaini had a small palace which was the only brick-built building in Chanaini, which otherwise consisted of about a hundred and fifty mud houses. These were built one above the other as is done on mountain slopes. The palace looked like an ordinary house in a city. One of Hari Singh's cousins was married to the Maharaja.

In the time of Maharaja Pratap Singh, people still travelled to Kashmir by horse or mule. In summer when Maharaja Pratap Singh travelled, he would be carried in a palanquin while the rest of his retinue accompanied him on horses and mules. Since the time of the Mughals, resting-places had been created at intervals of ten or twelve miles along the route. The Maharaja would stop at each such place and if he felt like it, would spend the night there. In the time of Maharaja Pratap Singh, however, cars had come into the picture. Most people still asked for forgiveness of their sins before they set out for Kashmir in case they did not return. It snowed so much at Banihal that people, along with their mounts, would turn into ice. Naturally, all kinds of arrangements were made for the Maharaja's travel. A thousand or twelve hundred people accompanied him. For the ordinary man however, going to Kashmir meant a serious risk to his life.

Those who stopped at Chanaini were greeted very warmly, and hospitality was lavished on them. This was the Maharani's wish. She felt that anyone who had come from her hometown should have no reason to complain. Lodging, bedding and food were all free. The people of Chanaini were simple and poor, untouched by the changes in the rest of the world. They were innocent of fraud, deception and dishonesty. They had not even been as far as Jammu. Their world was limited to Chanaini and its small jungle. The ruler too, was uneducated and simple.

The man who accompanied me on the *sarangi* had once travelled to Kashmir on a mule. He related how very cold it had become by the time he reached Chanaini. He was given a room warmed by a fire, a comfortable bed and a very good dinner. He slept very soundly that night. In the morning there was a sumptuous breakfast of milk, paranthas and eggs. He decided he was going to spend a few days there. Where else will I get these comforts, he reasoned. After breakfast he went out for a stroll and found that the Maharaja was holding court and dispensing justice in one room. The Maharaja would listen to all matters himself, before he made his decision. 'I decided to watch,' my sarangi-wallah told us.

The accused was presented. The Maharaja, with great authority, asked him in Dogri: 'Oye, you were supposed to appear yesterday. Why were you not present?'

'Your Highness, I had work to do,' explained the accused.

'All right. Come day after tomorrow,' the Maharaja ordered.

'Day after tomorrow again, I have work to do,' said the accused.

'Then come when you want,' the Maharaja said, and the court was adjourned!

In my time the punishment for prisoners in Chanaini was that they could do what they liked during the day as long as they returned to the jailhouse in the evening to sleep. They had to bring with them them ten seers of firewood back from the jungles. The next morning they were sent out again. There were no restrictions on them, and therefore the prisoners broke no rules.

The Maharaja had called photographers from England for the coronation, and some of the photos they took had interesting stories behind them. Like all the others, the Maharaja of Chanaini also came to the coronation on an elephant. As the crowds greeted him and cheered, he acknowledged their greetings with a salute. He was using his right hand and then, perhaps he got tired, he started using his left hand instead—an entirely inappropriate thing to do. By pure chance, each time someone photographed him, they caught him waving with his left hand!

Having wound its way through the town, the procession returned to Mandi. The mahouts led the elephants to the platform, made them sit down, and helped the maharajas get off. The maharajas then went and took their places on the platform, along with their staff. The Maharaja of Kashmir was the last to alight. Preceding him were a herald and hereditary panegyrist carrying thick silver staffs in their hands. They walked, taking turns to bang their staffs on the ground. The panegyrist was reciting the Maharaja's genealogy at the top of his voice and the herald was warning those present, in his heavy voice, to be prepared for the impending auspicious presence of the Maharaja. He said many other things that I did not understand. A number of people were doing their different aural duties at the same time, and it was difficult to figure out who was saying what. However the sounds created an atmosphere of majesty and dignity, and everyone else fell silent. Behind the Maharaja marched the ADCs, respectful, and elegant in their turbans which were adorned with small ornamental kalghis.

In the middle of the platform there was a smaller platform of gold. On it was a gold chair. Over these had been erected an awning of red velvet heavily embroidered with gold. The awning was held in place with gold-plated poles. The Maharaja seated himself on the gold chair and his ADCs sat down on the chairs below the gold platform. The two mace-bearers stood on either side of the Maharaja. The gold crown of diamonds, emeralds, rubies and pearls was carried on a red velvet covered silver tray.

The crown was placed on the Maharaja's head. Naturally he was a good-looking man, and at that moment he had the glow of a bridegroom on his face—almost radiant. The panegyrist who stood up and repeated the genealogy of the Maharaja wore heavy gold anklets on his feet. Wearing gold on one's feet was considered inauspicious. However, it was considered extremely lucky if a ruler had gifted you these ornaments. Maharaja Pratap Singh had rewarded this panegyrist with them, and he proudly wore them to every durbar.

When he had finished, it was the turn of the onlookers. The large landowners of the kingdom, aristocrats, government servants, generals and colonels from the army, presented the Maharaja with *nazar*, a gift of a golden coin placed on a handkerchief. There was a ritual prescribed for the offering of the nazar. First the sword was drawn from the scabbard, one foot was banged against the other and the sword was put back. The banging of one foot against the other made a loud sound. The person would then go to the Maharaja, bend down and offer the gold coin with both his hands stretched out. The Maharaja would touch each coin and the person would return to his seat without turning his back to the Maharaja. All the courtiers were dressed alike in Banarsi turbans, gold-embroidered achkans and a Banarsi silk dupatta tied around their waists, a gold sash, gold scabbards, black pump shoes and white churidar pajamas. The generals and the colonels were in their military uniforms.

I had been told to start singing the moment the offering of the nazars began. There was a minister of the Maharaja who was also a poet and had a written a poem for the occasion. I think he was called Khushi Muhammad or perhaps Nazir Ahmad. I had to begin with this poem. I still remember a couplet from it. The Maharaja was by caste a Suryavanshi – a descendant of the sun. This one couplet indicates that he was a good poet:

A son of the Suryavanshis, wearing a golden crown,
One sun shining over another sun's crown.

While offering their nazar, many made mistakes. One would salute before he lifted his foot and another would topple over while trying to bang one foot against the other. When this happened, a brief half-smile would appear on the Maharaja's face, but he would instantly regain his composure. After the poem, I sang something else. The offering of nazars ended. When the durbar ended, everyone congratulated me, 'The Maharaja has

honoured you immensely for you are the only one he chose to
sing at the durbar. You should thank him for this honour,' I was
told. The moment the durbar ended, the Maharaja's subjects, who
had been standing below the platform, began raising slogans
willing him a long life. With a gun salute, the durbar was formally
ended. I waited with my accompanists. The visiting maharajas
congratulated the Maharaja and left in their cars. The people who
had gathered continued to raise slogans. A car arrived for us. Many
families from the small villages around Jammu had come to watch
the celebrations. They saw me, a nine year old, dressed in dazzling
silver-embroidered peshwaz, a dupatta embroidered in gold,
wearing huge earrings, a jhoomar on my head, bangles on my
arms and a jewelled collar, along with pearl and other jewelled
necklaces around my neck. Seeing me dressed like this, the village
folk were convinced that I must be a goddess.

These simple and innocent people had not even seen a train
in their lives. My own Nani was like them for she, too, had first
seen a train when we went to Delhi. When they saw a train, the
villagers would fold their hands, even prostrate themselves before
the railway engine. Something as powerful as the engine had to
be a god, they felt.

When I began to come down the steps from the platform,
people closed in around me, women started touching my feet,
placing their children on them, rubbing the dust from my feet on
to their children's faces. I tried hard to stop them from doing all
this but there were so many of them that I could not move. The
crowd seemed to close in around me and I was terrified. With
much difficulty the driver honked his way in, and brought the car
up and rescued me from the crowd. He made me get in the car
and we moved. The women who had not been able to touch my
feet ran after the car, their children in their arms.

The Maharaja had invited all the other maharajas for dinner
that night. Before dinner, the pyrotechnic experts who had been
invited from England put up their display. The singing women,
who had come from all over, sang. People sat up till three at night.
The guest maharajas offered expensive gifts to His Highness. The
evening ended after this.

The guest maharajas began leaving the next day. The gun salutes continued for two days and we grew tired of the sounds of cannons. Every household in the kingdom was sent two seers of sweets. Both Hindus and Muslims were happy. In Mandi, every individual was given a quarter-seer of sweets so that those who had come from outside the city to join the celebrations, returned home happy as well. To mark the occasion, many prisoners were granted clemency and released, and many who had been condemned to death had their sentences commuted. Prisoners were given special food and sweets. The poor and the helpless were given charity. Hari Singh was praised all over the kingdom.

17. Maharaja Pratap Singh

Maharaja Pratap Singh had been like a god. He was very generous towards the poor and the weak. In the morning he would not have his breakfast till two hundred rupees had been distributed amongst the needy. He himself used opium and was often in a stupor so he'd go off to sleep while seated. The people around him took advantage of this and embezzled the money meant for charity and the Maharaja never got to know.

For instance there was the case of a widowed woman. She thought she would put her case before the Maharaja. She had no one to support her and her two daughters who were both of marriageable age. She came and stayed in Mandi for a few days but no one informed the Maharaja of her plight. Some people advised her, 'There is only one way for you if you are up to it. The Maharaja goes to the temple. Step forward and catch the bridle of the horse and bring his carriage to a halt. That will be your chance to tell him of your need.' The temple was very close to where we lived. The Maharaja went there regularly every week. On the day that he was expected, the woman found a place a little distance away from the temple because he did not like anyone near him when he got out of his carriage which was pulled by six horses. The woman's desperate plight made her indifferent to her own safety and she jumped and caught hold of the bridle of one of the horses. Naturally, the horses were startled and the carriage jerked. Concerned, the Maharaja inquired what the matter was. The woman came running and pleaded, 'My lord, I am poor and alone. My husband is dead. I have two grown-up daughters whom I have to marry off.' The Maharaja ordered that five hundred rupees be given to her. Five hundred in those days was the equivalent of fifty thousand today. The woman was grateful and blessed him a thousand times.

She reached Mandi first thing next morning. But the officials there put a mere five rupees in her hand. The woman cried, pleaded, and shouted, but to no avail. All they said was, 'We were ordered to give you only five rupees.' The poor woman went around the city telling people about the injustice—how instead of five hundred she was given only five rupees. People advised her to stop the Maharaja's carriage again in the coming week, and tell him about what had happened, so that the frauds around him got the punishment they deserved. So she did so. The Maharaja emerged from his stupor because the carriage jerked to a halt. The woman showed him the five rupees and told him that this was all that she had been given. The Maharaja, emerging from his opiated sleep, asked, 'What is she talking about?' In one voice the people around him said, 'She is alleging that the five rupees she has received are counterfeit.' The Maharaja was angry, 'How can there be counterfeit money in my treasury?' The carriage moved on.

They did not let the woman come near him again, and her money went into the pockets of the corrupt ones. Each one's share was fixed. They made poor illiterate people put their thumbprints on receipts for fifty rupees when they had only been given three. Even though the Maharaja wanted no one to go to bed hungry in his kingdom, his corrupt retainers would distribute only fifteen or twenty rupees out of the two hundred meant for distribution.

Maharaja Pratap Singh was good-hearted, generous, a true benefactor of the poor, simple and soft-hearted. One winter day he was sitting in the sun near the kitchen. In the kitchen they were slaughtering a goat. When they struck its neck with a sword they failed to sever it completely. The goat bolted and came and collapsed near the Maharaja while it writhed in pain in its last moments. The Maharaja looked at the goat sadly and sighed, 'What a pity! You have come to me when I cannot do a thing to save you.'

He summoned the cook and ordered that from then on, as long as he was alive, no meat would be cooked in the kitchen. For the rest of his life he never ate meat again. If his generosity had actually been converted into charity, there would have been no poverty in the kingdom. But the Maharaja was not to blame. It was the bastards around him who had woven such a web of

intrigue that he never found out what they were up to. It would
not be surprising if they had encouraged his addiction to opium
too. Wherever rajas, nawabs or even emperors existed, there were
always corrupt and venal people. Every king's reign was the same
story. Even if the ruler was intelligent, capable and just, these
base people would manage to deceive him. The Mughals had
ruled over such a huge empire. Their splendour and grandeur is
well-known and they were held in great awe. Even they could
not protect themselves from these frauds. Maharaja Pratap Singh
did not stand a chance against them.

Indeed he was so simple that some pundits had convinced
him that if he set eyes on a Muslim before breakfast, his faith
would be destroyed. Hence the Maharaja never faced a Muslim
before he had his breakfast. In general, things were so bad in
those days that if a Muslim in the bazaar touched a tray of sweets
by mistake, the *halwai* would fling the entire contents of the tray
into the gutter and then demand compensation from the Muslim.
The halwai would accuse the Muslim of polluting the sweets with
his touch. If a Hindu sold a Muslim something to eat, he would
place the goods in a cup made of dry leaves and toss it at the
Muslim, so that he would not have to touch the Muslim and
become unclean. If by chance he did touch a Muslim, he would
wail 'Ram Ram' till he got his hand purified again.

All this influenced the Maharaja. The pundits had put the fear
of God into him so that he would not go near a Muslim. There
was a certain Mian Lal Din who held an important official position.
The Maharaja was very fond of him and listened carefully to his
advice, yet he would not see him before breakfast. The poor
Maharaja did his best to please God. As far as charity was
concerned, he ordered that no difference be made between poor
Hindus and poor Muslims. In the end, though, neither Hindus
nor Muslims benefited from his generosity.

The Muslims had been born in this atmosphere, and had
learned to live in it. They were largely illiterate and unaware of
anything except their small worlds. Nor did they try to change
anything. They were happy and satisfied with the little they had.
Such things did not hurt them. Their sensitivities had been
deadened.

18. Maharaja Hari Singh

Maharaja Hari Singh had spent much of his life in England. He was very well educated and it was said that he spoke better English than many educated Englishmen. He was not interested in religious rituals and he did not believe in untouchability. The Muslims were happy about this.

A day after the coronation all the women who had come to sing were sent away. I presumed that my duties were over as well, but the car appeared as usual at seven in the evening. I had not been expecting it and therefore was not ready. I dressed in a hurry and left for Ram Nagar. When I was leaving that night, the Maharaja gifted me seven hundred rupees. From then on I was summoned every evening; on some days I got seven hundred, and on others five hundred rupees.

The Maharaja employed both Hindus and Muslims without any discrimination. There was Khusrau Jung who belonged to the royal family of Hyderabad in the Deccan. There were ADCs Nur Muhammad and Malik. Malik was a good polo player and the Maharaja was very fond of polo too. The Maharaja's head cook and headwaiter were also Muslims as were three or four of the orderlies. He would often say, 'Faiths should not be so weak that they be threatened by touch. Every one's God is the same and the differences have been fabricated by us.'

In his kitchen, only *halal* meat was cooked so that the Muslims could eat as well, even though Rajputs did not eat halal meat. His Highness did not care about what the Rajputs ate and what they did not. Nor did anyone have the courage to tell him what to do, or what not to do.

The festival of Baisakhi arrived. This was the first festival after the coronation and it was celebrated with special enthusiasm. All the Rajputs were invited for a meal so that even the poorer ones could participate. The arrangement for the durbar was made in the large hall at Mandi. I have described how beautifully the walls and doors of the hall were decorated with the finest examples of Kashmiri craftsmanship. The four large chandeliers illuminated the room brightly. As during the coronation, a golden chair was placed in the centre of the room. As soon as the Maharaja was seated, the *bhaat*, the hereditary panegyrist, began to recite the illustrious ancestry of the Maharaja. Nazars began to be offered and I began to sing. First it was the turn of the large landowners to present their offerings. Then came the high government officials, generals and colonels and after them, the elite of the city.

Among them was a wealthy moneylender from the city. He was so fat that he could not see his feet when he walked. He could not even dress himself. His stomach was so rotund that he could not see anything within a radius of two or three feet from his shoes. He could also not move his head sideways. When it was his turn, he tried to bend down to offer his nazar but his legs could not support his weight and he lost his balance. Like the others, he wanted to bang his feet against each other but stumbled instead. Only Allah's grace stopped him from toppling over.

Watching all this, I forgot about singing, music and court etiquette, and started laughing uncontrollably. It had been explained to me that laughing at a durbar was considered unforgivably rude, but I could not stop myself. I had a laughing fit. I tried hard to stop, but the more I tried to stop, the more I laughed. I had to stop singing. The durbar ended and His Highness left.

Janak Singh called me over and told me, 'His Highness is furious at you. You have behaved disgracefully. Your behaviour today was an outrage of protocol. Did you think you were watching a puppet show? Have you no respect for the dignity of the court?' I heard all this in silence. I was very frightened and told no one about what had happened when I returned home. The next evening I went to Ram Nagar. His Highness had invited his relatives and officers for dinner.

Carpets and chairs were laid out on the grounds of the palace. There were a few people who were very close to His Highness and whom he respected and honoured. These were Janak Singh,

Kartar Singh and the minister Sobha Ram. The latter was very aged, and His Highness always referred to him as *tau ji* or older uncle. Actually, he treated him as if he were his father. His help had been crucial in getting His Highness the throne.

When Maharaja Pratap Singh was dying, Maharaja Hari Singh was in Gulmarg and was deliberately kept ignorant of his uncle's condition. The wife of Maharaja Pratap Singh, Maharani Chadak, was Hari Singh's arch enemy. Chadak is also the name of a sub-caste of the Rajputs. Because of her hatred for Maharaja Hari Singh, she had brought up the son of the Raja of Poonch as an adopted son. The kingdom of Poonch too, was a feudatory of the kingdom of Jammu. Maharani Chadak had decided that after Maharaja Pratap Singh she would place her adopted son on the throne. She now tried to ensure that before he died, Maharaja Pratap Singh anointed him as his successor by putting a *tikka* on his forehead. Even though Maharaja Pratap Singh was like a puppet in her hands he was totally opposed to appointing her adopted son as his successor.

He was extremely anxious about this during his last days. He told everyone to send for Hari Singh immediately. The Maharani however, had won over everyone around the Maharaja, with promises of grand favours. So they all assured him that Hari Singh was on his way and would be arriving any moment. Yet, none of them even informed Hari Singh. If Maharani Chadak had succeeded in her plans, there would have been a dispute for succession after Maharaja Pratap Singh. The matter would have been referred to England. Since she was in control of everything, Chadak would then have argued that the last wishes of the late Maharaja be respected. The people around the Maharaja too, were in league with her. It is possible that she might have succeeded if she had bribed the British.

However, the minister Sobha Singh saw to it that the Maharani's plans did not succeed. He sent a trusted aide in his own car to Gulmarg. Hari Singh was able to see his uncle before he died, and the late Maharaja anointed him as his successor. There was a salute of twenty guns. The news spread that the dying Maharaja had applied a tikka to his nephew's forehead. Along with Sobha Singh, Janak Singh and Kartar Singh were also involved in this manoeuvre. His Highness respected all three of them. The first time I had sung at the Maharaja's secretary Abdul Qaiyyum's house, Thakur Kartar Singh and Janak Singh had been present. They both thought they had a claim on me because it was they who had brought me to His Highness.

That evening they told me that when I went to His Highness, I should tell him that I was very eager to see Kashmir and wanted to go there. I was amazed. A few hours ago they were scolding me for being ill-mannered and telling me how angry His Highness was with me and now they were suggesting this new trick. I listened to them as though I would do as they said.

Dinner ended and His Highness came and took his place. He asked me to sit near his chair and said, 'You lost control of yourself and I am partly to blame for this. It was when I laughed and looked at you that you lost control. After all, it was very funny. Laughter is one thing that cannot be controlled, even at the scaffold. I have ordered that in future, all civilians offer their nazar in a simple manner. They should not be made to behave as if they were at a military parade.' Bewildered, I stared at him. Janak Singh had told me that His Highness was enraged at me. And here was his Highness reassuring rather than scolding me! He knew how embarrassed I was at my behaviour, so he was being kind. For a few minutes we talked of various things and then he asked:

'Have you seen Kashmir?'

I told him I had not.

'Do you want to do so?'

'Yes, I do want to,' I answered, 'however, I have to go to Delhi, so I will not be able to go.'

His Highness was annoyed. 'You idiot, Delhi be damned. You are going nowhere. Get ready for Kashmir. The arrangements for your travel have been made.'

Janak Singh and Kartar Singh were listening to this in anger and surprise and with frowns on their faces. 'What sort of person is she?' they must have been thinking. Nothing they had said had affected me nor had I done what they had said. I was thrilled. They had humiliated me, and I had defied them. It was then from that moment that I began to like His Highness a lot.

For Baisakhi, I got a thousand rupees, two rolls of brocade, four bangles studded with diamonds and emeralds, a diamond and emerald ring, and a gem-encrusted bracelet. When the evening ended, Abdul Qaiyyum who was the Maharaja's secretary, told me that he would send the car at ten the next morning to bring me to his office. The driver said that I should take mother and my accompanists along.

The next day we went to Qaiyyum's office. There, Qaiyyum informed me that the Maharaja had employed me since the day he had first invited me, and that my salary would be six hundred and fifty rupees per month, 'At this age you are ranked as a Gazetted Officer. You will get a yearly increment of a hundred rupees though, since the Maharaja is the lord, he can raise the increments if he wishes.' All three of my accompanists were also employed at two hundred rupees a month with a promised annual increase of fifty rupees. We would have to spend six months in Jammu and six in Kashmir. According to the rules of the kingdom, anyone whose salary was five hundred, automatically became a gazetted officer. I was paid four months salary, on the spot and was told, 'You will be informed when you have to go to Kashmir.' Many came forward to congratulate me, including the orderlies and the other members of the Maharaja's staff.

The festival of Eid followed the Baisakhi festival. His Highness wanted to show that he considered the Muslim festival as his own too, and that he respected Islam. A day before Eid, it was announced that the Maharaja would go to the mosque at the time of prayer. The Nawab of Palanpur said his Eid prayers with the Muslims of Jammu. To show his respect, the Maharaja stood throughout the prayer. After the prayer, he offered the Imam who had led the prayers, five hundred rupees and a pashmina robe.

This was the first time that any Maharaja of Jammu had done this. The Hindus and the Rajputs were very angry. On the one hand, there had been Maharaja Pratap Singh who would not see the face of a Muslim till a quarter of the day had passed. Then there were those who threw away a tray full of sweets into the gutter if they had been accidentally touched by a Muslim. There were Hindus who would not shake hands with a Muslim, and Hindu women who, when bathing at a river, would make a row if they saw Muslim women approaching. How could Hindus like these tolerate that the Maharaja stand in a mosque for two hours? They seethed in anger.

They started spreading strange rumours. Wherever five or ten people gathered, the conversation would be something like this, 'On the sly, he has converted to Islam but he will not admit it for fear of losing the throne. What sort of a Maharaja is he? We have not seen him going to a temple, but he is happy to stand, like a slave, for two hours during *their* prayers. Muslims surround him and he only wants to employ them. He has no faith or religion. He has run away to Ram Nagar to escape the sound of the temple bells at Mandi.' His going to the Eid prayer had displeased many people. There were more Hindus than Muslims in the kingdom.

In the few Muslim villages around Jammu, the Muslims did not even know the *kalima*, the basic tenet of their faith, not to speak of their prayers. The Rajputs considered it below their dignity to touch a plough. In fact, they were forbidden to do so. In every village there were Muslim barbers, ironsmiths, carpenters, weavers, whom they called menials. Muslims also ploughed the fields owned by Rajputs. Yet, no village had a school or a mosque in it. My Nana's brother, Miran Bakhsh, the one who practised medicine and who was fond of reading Urdu and Persian books, had also read the Quran. My grandfather and his brothers had built a mud platform and a small arch too—a symbolic mosque on their own land. There was a small courtyard in front of this and around it, they built a low mud wall and created a space for praying. In two or three *canals* they planted fruit trees and installed a faqir there. The faqir, in turn, planted coriander, onion, green chilies and other out of season vegetables. Anyone in the village, who needed any of these, would buy them from him.

In the morning he would call out the *azan* to summon people to prayer and not a single Muslim would turn up. In the evening when the peasants returned from the fields with their bullocks, they would be called and told, 'You are Muslims. You should at least know the kalima. If you learn a word a day, you will eventually even be able to say your prayers.' Sometimes a few men would turn up, but most refused. However the efforts continued, and whenever they got an opportunity, they would try and convince them, 'If you do not even know the kalima, your are neither a Hindu nor a Muslim.' Sain Rahima continued to call out the azan but except for my Nana and Miran Bakhsh, no one turned up for prayers.

In any case, the majority of the families in the villages were Rajputs and Hindus. There were very few Muslims. One day Nana called all the Muslims together and said, 'Please come for just ten or fifteen minutes a day so that you can learn something about God and his Prophet. You will learn how to pray and God will be very pleased.' They listened to him and left unconvinced. There were a few who would come to the mosque but only to amuse themselves. They would stand at the back and imitate the worshippers.

Some others got together and went to the local revenue official. I remember that his name was Mangtu. The people put forward their complaints, 'Nambardar Sir, we have grown old under your kind protection and our life has passed without incident. Now, Karim Bakhsh and Miran Bakhsh insist that we go the mosque every day and contort ourselves into different postures. Should we work for you, our master, or should we go and perform those antics in the mosque? What do we have to with all this? We are all involved with our families and what is the need for all this useless stuff? He has become arrogant just because he has given four canals of land to Sain. He wants us to serve him five times a day! Does he expect us to begin working for him from five in the morning and work till it is time to sleep? Tell us, what is there to learn at our age? Can an old parrot learn how to speak? It seems we will no longer be able to live in this village.'

The next morning the azan was called. All the Hindus collected and came forward, 'This has never happened in the village before. This is something new that you have started,' they said.

Nana replied, 'You perform your rituals and prayers which is worship for you. If we call out the azan, it is a part of our worship. We cannot stop you from worshipping nor can you stop us from praying.'

Mangtu was a vicious, prejudiced and low man. He was also a coward. He began, 'I will go to the court of law.'

'Sure, go ahead,' said Nana, 'But keep in mind that both of us have to live in this village. Think of all the consequences.' Nana and his brother were tall, strong and courageous men and Mangtu did not want to court danger. He did not go to court but he kept instigating the villagers, 'No one can bully you. I am here for you. No one can force you to pray.'

There were also some who began to stop at the mosque on their way home. The garden began to come alive too. They would sit with Sain and learn to pray a word at a time. No one came for the morning prayers but there began to be quite a gathering in the evening.

Something very funny happened at this mosque. At the time of the sunset prayers, two brothers were returning home after work. One of them held the bullocks while the other stood with others to pray. The bullocks were strong and restive. When the brother holding them managed to get one under control, the other would start tugging in the other direction. With all this pulling and tugging, his arms started going numb. In Dogri he called out to his brother, urging him to hurry through his prayer, 'Bend, you pig, bend.' The other brother, who was in the middle of his prayer, answered, 'How can I till the pig ahead of me bends?' That is how simple those poor folk were.

19. The People of Jammu

There is an Urdu Bazaar in Jammu from which a few streets branch off. The Muslims lived in these areas. One other mohalla where Muslims lived was called, 'the mohalla of the Ustad,' but that was far away. The rest of Jammu was populated with Hindus. Literacy was not very high amongst the few Muslims who were there. Those who had a little education ended up a clerks or as assistants to lawyers, at best. Even these were very few in number. In the kingdom there might have been five or six Muslim families who were educated and whose members held high offices. They were all Pathans. They lived in Talab Khatikan near the Urdu Bazaar. Among them was one who had been the governor of Gilgit, and now had a few sons who were generals and colonels in the army. The sons of another family related to them had returned after studying in England and had also found favourable postings. There were a few other families like these who had access to the Maharaja and the court. These families were held in great respect.

The police or the army recruited many of the young men. A police constable earned between eight to ten rupees a month. All his life he stayed a constable because to be promoted you had to be educated. Some other unemployed young men would set up stalls selling *qahwa, baqar khani* bread, paan or cigarettes. However, most of the young men of the mohalla were ironsmiths, carpenters, or masons. Milk was only sold by the Muslim Gujjars and Hindus too bought milk from them. Surprisingly, the buying of milk did not threaten the faith of the Hindus! Only when the milk was poured into the boiling pan or made into sweets, would it become impure by a Muslim's touch!

Maharaja Hari Singh was a liberal man. He did not want to convert to Islam or to condemn his own religion. He wanted the Muslims to be treated as human beings and wanted that they find employment. He felt strongly it was his duty to see that justice was done. When he came to the throne, most of the Muslims were uneducated. Even those who went to school studied only till the tenth grade. Apart from the few educated Muslim families that I have mentioned there were no other Muslims in high positions.

In Maharaja Pratap Singh's time there was so much prejudice that even the few poor Muslim students who had managed to earn a Master's degree had little hope of finding a job. By the time Hari Singh came to the throne, this group of educated Muslims had already become old. The educated sons of the poor had roamed around unemployed, with nothing to do. In fact, their sorry fate became an example for others. People would argue: 'Look at what they have gained from all their education. Would it not have been better if they had stuck to their parents' trade, and been happy? At least they would not have been a burden on their parents.' They had to borrow every rupee from their families and they would spend their days playing chess, smoking cigarettes and eating paan. What could they do? With their education they were no longer fit to work as ironsmiths, carpenters or masons.

The Muslim children would spend their days bathing in the Khatikan Lake, playing *gulli* or marbles. They would fight and abuse each other. Even when they gained admission into schools, the children preferred to spend their days at the lake rather than go to school. After a few days, when their absence was noticed, other children would be sent to fetch the truants. Ten or fifteen children would run happily to the lake and drag the screaming truants back to school. There the teacher would thrash them mercilessly with a cane. The children would cry their hearts out and from then on it would be impossible to get them go to school again. The parents would try to use their powers of persuasion, and when those failed, they'd try to beat the children into submission. But the children would often say: 'You can chop me up into little pieces if you want, but I won't go back to school.' Parents were left with no option so they'd often console themselves by saying, 'Well, what is the point of education anyway. He would have been unemployed for the rest of his life.'

Most of the time, parents only sent their children to study when they were eight or nine. They argued that the child had to mature a bit before being sent to school. I remember a man, his hair gone white, still studying in the twelfth class! Even if he were to graduate, what job would he have found at forty? His parents who were already old would lament: 'We should have made him learn a skill. At least he could have supported us in our old age instead of our having to support him.' This gentleman now considered it below his dignity to take up any ordinary job. Poor man, he became an example for others to learn from. People would say, 'Look how they ruined his life by getting him educated.'

The old, the young and the children, all spent their days on the sidewalks of Urdu Bazaar playing cards or chess. Sometimes a single game of chess lasted the whole day. When they finished with this, they would begin gossiping and running down those who were better off than them. In the evening the young would get ready, oil and comb their hair till it was gleaming, and then go out into the bazaar. They would put a paan into their mouths, light a cigarette and buy a few strands of jasmine flowers strung on a thread. The flower sellers were usually pretty women. The men would place their hands on their hearts, flirt with the women and thus give expression to their pent-up emotions. Satisfied, they'd come home where food was always provided. The fathers of some of the men were ironsmiths, carpenters or masons. These educated unemployed young men were not willing to soil their hands with the trade of their forefathers. They would bully or beg their parents into giving them whatever they could. No matter how firmly the father might resist, the mother would always give in. The young ones boasted that they were not ready to do base, manual work. All they cared about was keeping their fathers' professions secret. This was the condition of the Muslims at the time of Maharaja Hari Singh's coronation. In spite of his best intentions, there was nothing His Highness could do about this.

Hindu children worked with their fathers—they'd learn how to run their shops, they picked up Hindi and Gurmukhi, and they quickly became proficient at handling the accounts. By the time they were sixteen or seventeen, they'd be ready to become partners in the business or to set up on their own. Overnight they went from being Amar to Lala Amar Nath. In the whole kingdom there were perhaps half a dozen large shops owned by Muslims. The Hindus controlled all the trade.

Before I went to Delhi, Chaudhary Ghulam Abbas, Allah Rakha Sagar, and Abdul Majid Karshi were regulars at my ustad's shop. By the time I came back, Ghulam Abbas had earned a BA and an LLB degree. But Allah Rakha and Abdul Majid had not even completed ten grades.

Ghulam Abbas' father worked for the chief judge, who had found him a job as a peon in the court, so that he would get a government salary. The judge was very generous toward Ghulam Abbas' father. Every day, when he returned from the court, the father would take the judge's children out horseback riding, help with the housework, and do the shopping. He was a good, honest and hardworking man. The judge, who did not trust any one else, came to trust him completely. He stood by his employee through thick and thin. Ghulam Abbas' father was as intelligent as he was hardworking. With the help of the judge he managed an education for his three sons. Ghulam Abbas got a law degree. The second son was appointed as the SDO (Sub-Divisional Officer) in the irrigation department where he earned a great deal of money and lived in style and comfort. The third son was my brother's friend. I have only one brother who is nine years older than I.

Ghulam Abbas' law practice was only a formality: normally, it took at least four or five years for lawyers to establish themselves and because ours was a Hindu kingdom, very few cases came his way. He earned nothing, and they could not afford a servant. So his poor wife, a courageous woman, was burdened with all the work. Just the washing alone—for everyone's clothes had to be kept clean—took half her day. My ustad had given up his shop to become Ghulam Abbas' clerk. He had calculated that he would have to work only half a day and he could rest for the other half, and still earn a lot more money. He was wrong though—he got all the rest he wanted, but no money! Since Ghulam Abbas had no earnings, at all, there was nothing to be shared! Both of them experienced hard times. We found out all this from ustad's wife when we came back to Jammu.

Ghulam Abbas was very intelligent and wanted to become a political leader. At the slightest pretext he would organize a demonstration of sorts and give a small speech. Allah Rakha and Abdul Majeed Karshi hung around him all the time. Neither was educated but both were very clever. Abdul Majeed's parents were poor but Allah Rakha was the son of a rich man. Hukm Din Patoti, Allah Rakha's father, owned many shops and houses in Urdu Bazaar and elsewhere. Hindus did not like purchasing property in areas where Muslims lived, and the few who still owned property in these areas, were eager to sell and move out. Hukm Din thus bought a lot of property at throwaway prices. In those days you could buy a shop for a hundred rupees and a fairly large house for two thousand rupees. People seemed to have no attachment to property. If there was unused land around their house, they would beg their friends: 'Please build a house on this land so that we can live close to each other. Then we will live and die together.' If the friend agreed, they would help him with the construction of the house, and still feel as if they had been obliged!

Hukm Din was smart and greedy. He acquired a great deal of property by giving out loans of ten or twenty rupees. When he saw someone in need, he would approach them with an offer of a loan: 'Take this for now. Return it whenever you can. Just mortgage your shop to me for the time being. It's very simple.' With a couple more loans of ten or twenty rupees, the shop would be his. If he spotted a house owner in trouble, he would reassure him: 'Why are you worried? Take these thirty rupees and just write off one eighth of the rent to me. Whenever you have the money, you can return it. You carry on with your work and do not have to worry, for we are family.' The man would put his thumbprint on the stamped paper. Hukm Din managed to acquire huge amounts of property by such devices.

Hukm Din was one-eyed. He was fat, dark, had a huge stomach, and was a widower. He was notorious throughout the kingdom as a miser. It seemed Allah had willed that he enjoy nothing of his wealth. He had two sons. Once a week he would cook a quarter of a seer of meat even though meat was only two annas a seer. In the summer he would buy mangoes only when they were at their cheapest even though his children longed for them all the time. He would not give his children any money to spend. I never saw Hukm Din wearing new clothes, not even on Eid. He was always dressed in a long waistcoat with deep pockets and wrapped in a dirty shawl. The shoes he wore would be so worn down that they had become slippers. He managed even to make these 'slippers' last for a year!

His house abutted the back wall of ours. It was a large house, and apart from two rooms, he had rented it all out. In those days the rent he earned could not have been more than two or three rupees. Apart from money, there was little else he cared for— even his children, or he himself, did not count. He would get the children one suit of clothes and one pair of boots every year. He would give them a bar of locally made detergent soap and tell them to use it to wash their clothes as well as to bathe with. He also ordered them to make that bar last for a full month. He never bought whole rice but only the discarded, broken rice that cost four paise for ten seers. He would cook himself, once a day. In Jammu it was widely believed that if you saw Hukm Din's face in the morning, you would starve for the rest of the day. And curiously, Allah Rakha, who had added 'Sagar' to his name, was the son of a rich man, but he was worse off than the poor, for he neither ate nor dressed well.

The third was Abdul Majid who had added 'Karshi' to his name. He had studied till the fifth grade. He was uneducated, good-for-nothing but crafty and totally indifferent to honest labour. He would impose his help on some simple unfortunate person who might have got entangled in a legal case, and extract five to seven rupees from the poor man. He would also help, for five or ten rupees, those who needed false testimonies. He would a find a client for his services every three or four days, which helped him maintain a façade of work. He got to know a lot of people this way. When Allah Rakha and Abdul Majid saw that Chaudhary Ghulam Abbas had become a leader, they added 'Sagar' and 'Karshi' to their names and also stepped into the hallowed circle of leaders. Jammu now had three new leaders. Among the things they did was to collect funds for *Eid milad un nabi*, erect a canvas awning on the road, and give short speeches. They were constantly on the lookout for excuses to organize demonstrations. During the demonstrations these three would be in the forefront of organizing the event and then they would stand on a stool and give a short speech each. Gradually people got to know of them.

Actually it was Abdul Majid who brought legal business to Ghulam Abbas. Anyone who came from the villages with a legal problem would go to Abdul Majid for advice, and he would then redirect them to Chaudhary Ghulam Abbas and thus both would end up making money. However, Allah Rakha's fate did not change, not even with the Partition. All his property was left behind in Jammu. Poor man, he was unfortunate from beginning to end. He got nothing from being a leader or from the property he inherited.

Because of these men's leadership, some Muslims became conscious of the fact that Hindus considered them base and untouchable and started to question their right to do so. Before I went to Delhi, no one had felt this way, nor had anyone complained about it. Now they were considering demanding reservation of jobs for Muslims. The truth was that educated Muslims were like a pinch of salt in a bag of flour. A few parents were in favour of education but most of them still opposed it. They still believed that education would reduce their child to a good-for-nothing!

The little that I understood, on my return from Delhi, was that the new generations were becoming conscious of their dignity and self-esteem. However, they were all sneaks and were quite selfish, lazy and disloyal. They constantly boasted, spent their days on the sidewalk playing cards and chess, and commenting on passers-by. They were envious of others and low enough to stoop to anything. For five rupees they would place their hands on the Quran and swear to a lie. For ten rupees, they would sell themselves. I began to hate the people of Jammu as much as I loved the city.

As far as Maharaja Hari Singh was concerned, he (unlike Pratap Singh) was not a puppet in the hands of the pundits. He realized that the Hindus did not like him. However, he did not care but continued to do what he thought was right. He was clean-hearted and he treated neither Hindus nor Muslims badly. He constantly tried to be fair to both. In spite of ruling such a large kingdom he considered himself an ordinary human being. He was very well behaved and never scolded anyone. When angered he kept quiet, but let the culprits know, through others, how he felt so that they could make amends. He did not use politics to suit himself. If he had wanted, he could have quietly favoured the Muslims, and no one would have been any the wiser. There was no duplicity in him. He never hid matters nor was he unjust. I worked for him for nearly ten years but not once did I see him being unfair to anyone or calling any one names.

20. My First Visit to Kashmir

The rent on our house in Jammu was six rupees for a month. It was the largest, double storey house in Urdu Bazaar. The entrance was so large that cars or horse carriages could easily be accommodated. Around the courtyard were four or five large rooms. Not a ray of light entered these and they were so dark that even in the day I felt afraid in them. On the upper floor were three courtyards. Two rooms faced the Urdu Bazaar and two the back courtyard. On the ground floor there were four shops. We stayed on the upper floor. The house belonged to a Hindu and Nana asked him if he wanted to sell it. The house owner, who did not relish owning property in an area populated by Muslims, agreed immediately. We had saved quite a large sum of money by then, and Nana bought the house which was worth six thousand rupees, for seven thousand rupees.

I would visit His Highness every day at seven o'clock. One day I was told that we had to leave for Kashmir within two days. A bus arrived for our luggage and a car for us. The route was so scenic that it is difficult to find words to describe its beauty. At short distances were natural waterfalls; slopes covered with all kinds of wild flowers which looked as if they had been dropped from an altitude of thousands of feet; the mountains were covered with huge trees. God's omnipotence was visible all around. We spent the night at Banihal and reached Kashmir the next afternoon. A large house in Gagribal was allotted to us. It had a drawing room, a dining room and four large bedrooms. There were wide verandahs all around the house and it had four acres of grounds attached to it, filled with pear trees. We were all very impressed.

The rooms were furnished with big beds, chairs, tables, sofas, in fact with everything. Like happy, crazed people, we roamed the rooms in a daze for it was difficult to believe that this was going to be our home. Everyone felt the same—disconcerted as though we had entered a house of mirrors. The house was at the foot of the Shankaracharya Hill. The Hindus called it the Shankaracharya Hill and the Muslims the throne of Solomon. After revelling in our fortune for a few hours, suddenly sadness descended on us. We had been used to living in small rooms, in which three charpais could only be accommodated if they were placed almost on top of each other. And once we had them in there, there would be no space left to move in the room. At night, we used to be able to tell when the person sleeping on the next charpai rolled over because the vibration would be transferred from one charpai to the other. In these rooms in Kashmir, you could lay out twenty charpais and it would make little difference. All around us were gardens, lawns, and complete silence. There were no sounds of honking cars or the shouts of *tangewallahs,* no rioting or squabbling. We heard no vendors shouting out and advertising their wares. It seemed as if we were living in the middle of a wilderness. Each day seemed to stretch and become as long as ten.

Even here, His Highness had built himself his own palace at Gupkar. Like Ram Nagar, it was furnished with modern European furniture. Gagribal was close to Gupkar. My time between seven and eleven in the evening passed pleasantly. When I returned, I would spend the entire night awake in my room, imagining ghosts and witches everywhere. I would recite all the invocations to Allah that I could remember, yet I could not sleep out of fear. After two such nights, I told mother, 'I do not want my own room. I want to sleep in a room where my bed is surrounded by other charpais.' The floors and ceiling of the house were built of wood. All night we heard sounds that seemed as if an army was marching. We later learnt that these sounds were made by rats running around in the ceiling. The rats were as large as mongooses.

Apart from the rats, there were the fleas called *pissu*. We could not move the beds—they were too heavy—so I had mattresses spread on the floor so that someone could sleep next to me. We could do nothing about the fleas. Their bites were painful and left marks on us. Our fingers got tired from scratching these bites all night. Pissus were smaller than ants and almost invisible, so were impossible to either catch or kill. When the carpets at Gupkar were hoovered, these fleas filled the entire bag. It was surprising that even in the houseboats that stood in the middle of the water, there were more fleas than on land. There was no place in Kashmir that was not full of them.

I would often cry in Kashmir. There was no hustle-bustle, no one to socialise with. I travelled back and forth between home and Gupkar. Kashmir was the image of paradise, but I was sad in the new house and new environment. I was not used to living in large empty rooms or to sitting on chairs. It seemed as if the house had swallowed me up. After five or six days, His Highness asked me if I had ever watched polo. I said I had not. He told me to come at four the next day. The car arrived at four the following day and took me to the polo ground. Horses were running around and the riders were hitting the ball in different directions. Sometimes all the horses would gather at one place. One rider would take the ball forward. I had never seen a game like this and did not understand it at all. All I saw were horses running around. When I came home after the match, I had no idea who had won and who had lost.

That evening when I went to Gupkar, Malik came to me in the drawing room and said: 'When you go to His Highness today, he will ask you who you thought was the best player. You should tell him that you only saw him wherever you looked.'

Malik was a good polo player. So were Kishen Singh and Anup Singh, relatives of the Jodhpur royal family, who were also His Highness' ADCs. I had heard that among them, Malik was the best. Malik instructed me repeatedly that I should name no one else. Perhaps, he was afraid that if I named him, it would offend His Highness, who might also get displeased with me. He also told me that if I was asked which horse was the best, I should say 'the black one.' When I went in, His Highness made me sit close to his chair. After a while he asked, 'Did you watch the game?'

'Yes,' I answered.

'What did you think of it?' he wanted to know.

'I enjoyed it very much,' I said.

'Who played the best?' he asked.

I told him the truth. 'This is the first time I saw the game being played. How can I judge who was the best?' Malik, who was standing behind His Highness' chair, was constantly gesturing at me to say that His Highness was the best player. I just ignored him. I hated to have to say: 'all I could see was you.' Till today I cannot figure out whom my lies would have benefited, him or me.

His Highness later asked: 'All right, tell me which horse did you like most?'

I immediately named the horse named by Malik. The room resounded with applause. Those present commented, 'She knows everything but is pretending to be innocent. She is intelligent and smart.' From then on, the car took me to watch polo two or three times a week. I went only to please His Highness. I did not understand the game and did not try to. Perhaps he summoned me to these games thinking that I enjoyed them. It was Allah's grace—whatever happened was for the best. Maybe the adage that 'man makes mistakes and the Lord rectifies them' is correct. Even if I had said something stupid they would have said it was smart. I was totally inexperienced, innocent of intrigues and not a sycophant like the rest. Nor was I afraid of His Highness.

One day His Highness asked, 'What have you seen in Kashmir? Which places have you visited till now?'

'Gupkar and the polo grounds,' I replied.

'This is completely unacceptable,' he said, 'In all these days you have only seen the polo ground! Come on, let me show you Nishat Bagh. I will show you Nishat Bagh the way Nur Jahan must have seen it once. Now it will be your turn.'

21. Nishat Bagh

His Highness immediately summoned his secretary Abdul Qaiyyum and gave him some instructions. He also told him to see that I reached Nishat Bagh before sunset, on Saturday. He told others to decorate each leaf with strings of light. Dinner was to be served on the topmost terrace.

I was very happy at the prospect of an outing in the garden. I was ready at six that evening. The car had not arrived till seven and there were still no signs of the car at eight. I began wondering if the plans had been cancelled. I was tired of staring at the road by eight-thirty. It was that day I discovered how long the 'moments of waiting' could be. The car arrived at a quarter to nine. We rushed into the car and headed to Nishat Bagh. We were not even halfway there when we saw His Highness' Rolls Royce. The driver stopped our car and asked the driver why we were so late. I told him I had been ready since six and had left the moment the car arrived. His Highness' driver asked me to get into his car and asked the others to follow. At breakneck speed he drove me the entrance of Nishat Bagh. I got out of the car and entered. There I saw His Highness waiting with five or six other people. He asked me the reason for this delay. I told him that I had been ready since six and had left the moment the car arrived.

Nishat Bagh is laid out in seven terraces. Each terrace was ten to twelve feet higher than the preceding one. These terraces were very large and there was a fountain in the centre of each. Beside these fountains were pathways hemmed by large flowerbeds. What made these gardens special was that on each terrace were planted flowers of the same colour. The terraces ended in a waterfall on either side of the fountains. If you stood on the lowest terrace and looked up, you could see the seven fountains and seven waterfalls all rise up in a row. The water sparkled like silver as it cascaded down the waterfalls. When we climbed up to each terrace, flowers of another colour awaited us. The whole garden was glittering with lights. There was a bulb at the tip of each fountain and oil lamps lined the pathways. The huge trees were covered with lights. I do not have words to describe how beautiful everything looked. The terrace with yellow flowers looked like a beautiful woman bedecked in jewellery. All the terraces had twelve arched *baradaris* which sparkled with bulbs and oil lamps. As it is, Nishat Bagh is unique, and the lights turned it into an unbelievable vision. I had never seen such a sight nor can I even conjure it up in my dreams. His Highness had done what he had promised. He was the ruler and could have had this done whenever he wished. Nishat Bagh was not decorated like this again for ten years after this.

Later, I went back to Kashmir after sixty years. What a pity that Nishat Bagh was no longer what it used to be! The terraces were no longer planted with flowers of the same colour nor was the grass green. The trees looked devastated. I told Farooq Abdullah Sahib how each terrace used to have flowers of the same colour, and asked why they could not plant the garden in the same way or pay attention to the grass. He promised to do something about it but his government did not last.

His Highness had come to the gate because he was convinced that the car had had an accident. Why else would I have been two and a half-hours late, he must have wondered. The first words he said when he saw me were: 'Thank God you are alive.' There were a few ADCs, and Khusrau Jung and Qaiyyum Sahib with us. Qaiyyum Sahib had had too much to drink but the others seemed fine. His Highness told me that he was sure that something had happened to me. Qaiyyum Sahib took the opportunity to add, 'How sad that you put His Highness through so much worry. This is unforgiveable.'

'I was ready at six,' I retorted. 'How could I come when there was no car. How am I to blame?'

His Highness was silent. We had to climb up to the seventh terrace. A short while later, Qaiyyum Sahib started again.

'You are completely inconsiderate and do not care how His Highness feels. You were late by two and half-hours! You should never have done this for His Highness was really worried. Look how far he had to walk down.' I repeated my defense. His Highness was not paying attention to what Qaiyyum was saying and kept walking in silence. Five or ten minutes later, Qaiyyum began his speech again and I was close to tears. I was shocked by his hostility and could not understand the reason for it, for I had done nothing to harm him. In fact, six months ago he had been telling the Maharaja, 'Look at the unmatchable gift I have found for you.'

It was a long way to the top. All the arrangements had been made on the seventh terrace. Everyone was admiring the lights and garden as they climbed. Qaiyyum started again. 'I am surprised that you behaved this way. His Highness arranged all this for you and you have broken his heart.' Both his legs and his tongue were unsteady, yet, every couple of minutes he would start on the subject again. I must have explained at least twenty times that I too had been very excited about coming here and had been ready since six, but he would not leave me alone. I was about to cry. His Highness tried a few times to talk about other things but Qaiyyum did not give up. Finally His Highness lost patience and showed his anger.

'First, tell me who gave you the right to ask for any explanations? How are you concerned with any of this? You are in charge of the garage, so why did you not send the car on time? Should she have walked here? You have to answer for this for I am convinced that it was done deliberately. You are dying of jealousy. And who are you jealous of? A ten year old child! At forty you are competing with a ten year old? I demand an explanation from you. Tell me, how all this happened! It was your duty so why did you not ensure that the car was on time? I have been listening to you prattle for two hours and you will still not leave her alone. She has not bothered me but you have. She is not your employee and you have nothing to do with her, nor should you have anything to do with her in the future.'

I now realized that all the attention His Highness directed at me had made many people jealous of me even though I could not have replaced them or they me. Yet they could not tolerate royal kindness towards me. I began to learn ways of protecting

myself. I had to be careful about the smallest of things. Except for
Sahabzada Nur Muhammad, Khusrau Jung and Malik, the rest of
the private staff resented the royal favours shown to me. They
wanted to know why His Highness was so kind to me, why he
cared for me so much and they all wanted to see me fall from
grace. In any case, the entire staff was jealous of each other, and
was constantly stabbing each other in the back. Every one tried to
replace those in proximity to the Maharaja. When His Highness
was angry, all he would do was call them sycophantic mules. He
hated flatterers.

His Highness loved the Nawab of Palanpur so much that he
had a house called Talah Manzil built for him on the top of a
mountain in Gupkar. Whenever the Nawab came, he would stay
at Talah Manzil for a month or two. Another regular visitor was
the Maharani of Cooch Behar who came to Kashmir three or four
times a season. I was innocent of such things originally but
gradually learnt that the Maharani came only because of Nawab
Khusrau Jung. She rarely came to Jammu but visited Kashmir three
or four times each summer. On each visit, after ten or twelve days
we would hear that she was leaving the next day. The next day,
we would find out that she had postponed her departure by a
few days. Often her plans changed two or three times before she
actually left and it was obvious that she did not want to leave. She
was so stunningly attractive that I wanted her to keep sitting so
that I might gaze at her.

22. Maharani Dharamkot

The second wife of Maharaja Hari Singh was the daughter of the Maharaja of Dharamkot. The Maharaja had given his daughter so much dowry that the kingdom had been left stunned. Before this, all the Maharajas of Jammu had married the daughters of large landowners of their kingdoms. Maharaja Hari Singh was the first to marry the daughter of a Maharaja.

I heard tales that when they were married, the length of the procession carrying her dowry had stretched to five or six miles. In this procession, each person carried one thing on his head: silver vessels, silver *thaals* for eating, *lotas*, paandaan, khaasdaan, gold vessels, gold bed posts, a gold chair for the bridegroom, gold jewellery arranged in sets on silver trays. Apparently the procession stretched from the railway station to the palace at Mandi. There was jewellery of diamonds and other gems; in fact there was nothing that was not there. The palanquin for the Maharani was also made of gold.

Along with the Maharani had come maidservants, staff for the kitchen, security guards and a doctor. Since these people were meant to be a part of the dowry, their salaries were paid from Dharamkot. When they were married, Hari Singh was a prince and she a princess. Neither as a princess nor later as a Maharani did she and Hari Singh have a relationship. He would visit her a couple of times in a year and that was usually on a festival, or some other special occasion. According to a tradition among the royalty, once married, a princess never returned to her natal home. The Maharani of Dharamkot spent all her time in Mandi. Occasionally, she went out for a ride in the car. She spent half the year in Jammu and the other half in Kashmir.

A woman's life is centered on her husband. Lord knows how she survived—without parents or husband. I feel that nothing in her life made her happy. When she became very unhappy, she would invite her younger brother, whom she loved a lot, to come and visit her. He was young, simple, short, and wore thick spectacles. His eyesight was so weak that he could see nothing without his glasses. He was quite ugly. Since he was his brother-in-law, His Highness had the right to play all sorts of practical jokes on him. Sometimes he would hide his spectacles. Or he would ask some singer to come and sit next to his chair. The lady had already been instructed to talk to him and tell him how much she liked him, that she had fallen in love with him, and how she wanted to spend her life sitting next to him. The poor man would be so embarrassed that even in winter, beads of perspiration would appear on his forehead. He would escape to his room and His Highness would tell the girl to follow him. Soon he would come running right back to his chair. Such ragging was common but out of respect for the Maharaja, that poor man never took offence, or protested.

The Maharani of Dharamkot sent a servant to my house with a harmonium and with instructions that I learn how to play it so that I could give her singing lessons. She had earlier asked me whether I knew how to play the harmonium and I had told her that I did not. She said that I should learn as fast as I could, and inform her when I was ready. Two months later she sent a servant to ask if I had learnt how to play and I sent word saying that I still had not. Her eagerness was due to the seclusion that the maharanis were kept in, where they were accessible to neither man nor bird. Obviously there was no question of male accompanists being allowed into their quarters. It was my misfortune that all this did not matter to me then. Learning how to play the harmonium was very easy. Yet I did not learn, nor did I try to. I wish I had had the maturity and had used the opportunity to learn.

The Maharani was very innocent and kind, almost angelic. Perhaps I could have brought some brightness into her life. She might have enjoyed my singing. I had heard that she did not understand a word of Urdu or Punjabi—this had discouraged me. I wondered whether she would understand anything when she did not even know the language. I never learnt to play the harmonium and never visited her. She continued to live in her gilded cage.

23. The Birthday and the Basant Durbars

The Maharaja's birthday was always celebrated in Kashmir. The old palace in Kashmir was also called Mandi and its plan was similar to its namesake in Jammu. The walls and ceilings were decorated like those in the Jammu palace and there were large chandeliers. One advantage it had over the Jammu palace was that a river ran along one side of the palace. A few three or four storey houseboats were anchored in the river. People came from afar to see these, for they were fine specimens of the craftsmanship of Kashmir.

For the birthday, a few other lady singers from elsewhere were invited. The Nawab of Palanpur was also there for the celebration. The musical soirées started two or three days earlier. Ministers and the large landowners whom the Maharaja liked, were invited to these private *mehfils* before the durbar. Since the possibility of others hearing the singing at these soirées did not arise, they would begin offering nazars the moment the durbar was assembled. And I would begin to sing the moment people started presenting nazars. At each durbar I was the first one to sing. Others would get about ten minutes each to sing.

After the durbar, there would be a rowing competition between college students. All the students would be dressed alike in yellow shirts, white socks and black pump shoes. The boats, eight feet long and three feet wide, were also painted yellow as were the oars. Fifteen or sixteen boys sat, two to a seat, next to thick iron rings that kept the oars in place. The boys would move their oars to the same rhythm. When they bent forward and then flung their heads back as they moved their torsos backwards, their black hair would fly. This looked so beautiful that those watching would involuntarily utter 'asshh ... asshh'. The team that won was given a prize by His Highness—he would come to the river to watch the race the moment the durbar ended and the cannon salutes had begun to be fired. Each boat had the name of a college on it. People collected on the shores of the river. When the race began some people ran beside the boats, clapping their hands, leaping and shouting encouragements. All this was very spirited and cheerful. After awarding the prizes, His Highness would return to Gupkar. In the evening, the Rajput fraternity was invited for dinner at Mandi. There, the singing continued until well past two at night. Nazars were offered only on two occasions in a year—on the birthdays and at Basant.

His Highness had built a residence for himself next to the Dal Lake. Its grounds were surrounded by water. The beauty of the place lay in that the grounds looked like a plate, with a beautiful offering on it. Every year, His Highness who loved sitting under the open sky, spent about two months here. Every evening he would sit in the grounds and even dine there. I will not even dare to describe how beautiful it looked on moonlit nights when the Dal Lake shimmered like a sheet of silver. To reach this residence, there were always a dozen or so *shikaras* on duty. Though there was a land access to it, I too preferred to go there in a shikara because the Dal Lake was close to Gagribal, and whether I came by car or shikara, it took two minutes.

The official shikaras were very beautiful and comfortable with soft cushions delicately embroidered in wool, and with four rowers who moved in tandem. They were such experts that they knew many different ways of rowing. Most of those who came for a visit to Kashmir would use shikaras. They were cheap and one got to see the river, the houseboats, and the people living in these houseboats. People came to Kashmir from everywhere—England, Marwar and Punjab. There was no place from which people did not come to see Kashmir.

Basant, the festival of spring, was celebrated with great enthusiasm in the kingdom. The rich, the poor, Hindus, Muslims— all wore yellow turbans. The women dressed in yellow from head to foot whether they were young or old and all you saw was yellow in every direction. It was not as if this was done on royal orders. People did so because they wanted to celebrate this festival. There was a lot of poverty but for some reason there was also hope in every heart. Everyone looked for reasons to celebrate and you could see the happiness on people's faces. Everyone considered each festival to be his or her own.

The Basant durbar was organized with a great deal of grandeur and splendour in Jammu. All the roads of Mandi were covered with yellow powder. The stairs His Highness climbed to the platform were yellow and so was the carpet on the platform. On it was the golden chair and on it a canopy of yellow velvet embroidered in gold. The courtiers were dressed in yellow brocade achkans, yellow cummerbunds, and scabbards of yellow velvet, embroidered with gold.

Of the six dresses that His Highness ordered for me from Poona, one was yellow. It was made of tissue in which a strand of silk alternated with a strand of gold. The colour of the silk decided the colour of the fabric. When this fabric wore off, goldsmiths would buy the dress and recover the gold. My dress was heavily decorated with embroidered stars and sequins. In all the other durbars and in the private *mehfils,* you could wear whatever colour you pleased, but it was ordered that at the Basant durbar, everyone dress in yellow. The sight at the Basant durbar had to be seen to be believed. Durbars were held practically every month for some festival or the other but the Basant durbar had its own special magnificence.

24. His Highness' Visit to England

We returned to Jammu in September. A few days later we found out that His Highness was going to England. 'Good,' I said to myself, 'let him go to England and I will go to Lahore and have some fun and do some shopping.' Two days before he left, His Highness called me to him and instructed me: 'In my absence do not visit any one employed by me, even if they are my ministers or their wives, at home. And also do not leave the kingdom.'

'May I visit Lahore for a few days?' I murmured.

'Definitely not.' He was firm.

His Highness left for England and despondency set in. It seemed as if Jammu had been abandoned. I had nothing to do and nowhere to go. When His Highness was here, I would have to get ready in the evening, go to the palace, and listen to interesting conversation till eleven every night and I did not notice time passing. After his departure, my heart felt desolate. I could not think of anything to do. In the morning I would practice my singing for an hour or two and that was it.

There was a girl of my age in the neighbourhood. I asked her if she would come out for a walk with me in the evenings. She readily agreed. We went out the next evening. On the way, next to the Nanda Bus Service, there was a cycle repair shop and close by there was a man selling parched gram and roasted maize. In the middle of the gram was a small earthen pot with burning coals and steam was rising from the gram which made them look very tempting. My friend asked me if I had any money. Pretending to sound like an adult, I joked, 'Money—I do not even have money if I need to buy poison for myself.' We moved on.

The next evening when we passed the shop we heard someone say, 'Do you have any money,' and from across the road, someone answered, 'I swear, I do not even have money to buy myself poison.' Surprised, my friend and I looked at each other. A little

while later we realized that that was what we had said yesterday.
We wondered if it was just a coincidence. The same thing was
repeated the next time we passed the shop. We heard someone
asking, '*Yaar*, do you have any money?' Again the response came
from across the road and was the same. We were now convinced
that they were imitating us. The boys who were doing this did not
even look at us. All they did was stand across from each other on
the road and ask and answer a question.

We decided we would not walk this way again even though
this was the way to a very beautiful park meant only for women.
In it there were swings and benches. We could sit, run and jump
for as long as we liked because there were only women there.
We just cursed the boys and decided not to come this way again.

The other direction led to Residency Road and there were no
gardens or parks in that area. We soon returned from that walk.
Just as I was about to climb the stairs of our house, I heard someone
say 'yaar, do you have any money?' From across the road another
boy shouted back the same answer. My blood boiled. I
immediately turned around and looked at them but they left
without looking at me. From now on, from within the house, I
heard these words once or twice a day. I thought to myself, 'What
was the point of changing direction when these frustrated guys
send their mocking voices right into the house? At least there are
swings in the garden.' We started going back to the garden. When
we reached their shop we would lower our eyes and walk past
silently.

Things reached such a pass that I was alert every moment even
when I was at home. At most, my house was ten or twelve feet
high. The terraces had two balconies and we would often sit on
these in the evening to watch the happenings in the bazaar. Those
wretched boys found this out and would pass by the house at
least a couple of times a day. Now there were no longer two of
them. The boys who came to get their bicycles repaired at the
shop were all told about it. They were all Hindus. God alone knows
how many of them there were. A few times a day I regularly heard
them. A few times when I heard them while I was walking I thought
of confronting them and giving them a piece of my mind. Then I
would wonder what I could say. They were not saying anything

unpleasant, nor did they laugh at us nor did they look at me. What could I be angry about? Helpless, I decided that I would let them bark because they could do me no harm.

His Highness had been away for months. Lachchu, a favorite orderly, came one day with a parcel, saying that His Highness had sent it for me. Excited, I opened it. There were a dozen skin-coloured stockings in it. I thought to myself, what is the point of wearing socks that others do not even notice? I called the dyer and told him to dye them to match twelve different saris. When he brought them back they looked very strange. They were double-layered at the bottom and therefore the colour there was different from the rest. I was very angry with him and told him off for destroying them and ordered him to remove the dyes. He tried to but instead they ended up with bizarre spots all over. Later I found out that these were very expensive stockings. They were made of silk, and in those inexpensive days they cost eighty rupees a pair! In my ignorance I had made a mess of them.

Six weeks later His Highness returned. I found out that he had arrived the moment the cannons were fired. At seven that evening I was driven to Ram Nagar. The moment I arrived, His Highness called me over. He asked, 'How have you been?' I felt like saying 'Your Highness, I was sad without you. Jammu seemed deserted,' but could not say this. Instead I said, 'I have been very well.' A few minutes later Highness summoned Lachchu and he brought three small boxes. I opened the long one first. In it was a platinum bracelet studded with diamonds and some black stone. The strips were joined as if by a spring. The second box contained a platinum watch the cover of which was studded with diamonds and rubies. Even its chain was of platinum and elastic. You could pull it as wide as you wanted and it always returned to its original size. In the third box was a platinum ring with three rubies surrounded by diamonds. Without thanking him and without even praising them, I put the bracelet on one arm and the watch on the other. Neither through words nor demeanor did I indicate whether I was pleased or not. Instead I was thinking why His Highness had had such beautiful things made out of silver. Not only had I never seen platinum, but even my father and grandfather had never heard of it!

I always tried to ensure that His Highness knew that material things really did not matter to me. His Highness too, never mentioned anything he gave me or did for me. After some time he asked if I had visited anyone's home in his absence.

'Never,' I said.

'Good,' he was pleased.

Dinner was served. After dinner there was singing for an hour or two. After that we talked about this and that and then I came home.

25. His Highness Cooks

His Highness loved to cook. Three or four times a week he would cook along with his private staff. Sahabzada Nur Muhammad always cooked the pulau. His Highness would cook the chicken. Everyone cooked something or the other. The servants placed all the meat, chicken, ingredients and spices near them. They would also light the stoves and place them next to chairs. A servant was present next to each stove to hand over whatever was needed. I had to assist His Highness who would sit on a chair and give orders: 'Check whether the chicken is tender enough or not. Stir it. Taste it for salt. Now dry the excess water.' I did whatever he said. When the food was ready, they would judge whose cooking tasted best. They would discuss and argue for hours. Often either Khusrau Jung or Nawab Sahib was made to judge. It was not essential that everyone praise only what had been cooked by His Highness.

Every day I would leave home and come to Ram Nagar at seven. I would dine here every night. One day while I was stirring the chicken, His Highness said, 'Is there no food at home that you eat here every night?' The words hit me like an arrow. They hurt so much that I immediately decided that even if I was to die of hunger, I would never eat here again. 'He calls me at seven and keeps me here till eleven. When am I supposed to eat? And then he taunts me!' I fumed to myself. I had always been very careful that he should never think I needed anything. I never gazed at the clothes and jewellery he presented me. 'He thinks this is a joke but for me eating here is forbidden from now on,' I decided. I remember clearly that as a child even if a neighbour invited me to eat, I would refuse even if I had wanted to eat. I never ever wanted to indicate to anyone that I was hungry.

When His Highness said this, tears appeared in my eyes. Ten minutes later His Highness said, 'The chicken is ready, taste it for salt, and take it off the fire.' I answered, 'You will have to taste it for salt yourself because from now on, eating anything here is forbidden to me.' His Highness laughed aloud and for so long that tears started flowing from his eyes. He said, 'Have you gone mad? I was only joking.'

'Whether it was a joke or not, I have vowed that everything here is *haram* for me. I have eaten what I was to eat. From now on, eating anything here is akin to eating pig. My vow is firm.' I made myself clear. While I was saying this I had also started to cry because I was feeling very hungry.

He fell silent. The servants were setting out the plates. His Highness made me sit near him and said, 'Come on, be a good girl, have your dinner and tell us who has cooked the best.'

Very reluctantly I said, 'I cannot eat.'

His Highness said, 'I place you under oath to eat for my sake.'

'I have taken an oath already,' I said.

To this he said, 'I will place you under a more powerful oath and see how you defy that. May you eat my flesh if you do not eat your dinner.'

'No one is ever going to eat your flesh,' I dismissed his attempts. 'For me eating here would be as if I was eating pig,' I reasserted.

Defeated, he said, 'If you do not eat, then neither will I.'

I am glad that no one else was listening to this conversation because I was sitting very close to His Highness. If Mamman Khan had been there he would have said, 'Any other Maharaja would have said "You trollop, how dare you."' His Highness however was so kind that he kept trying to reassure someone as badly behaved as I, that he was only teasing me. Perhaps this is what he liked about me. Perhaps he was tired of all the yes-men. He again said, 'Come on, do not behave as if you are crazy. Go get the food.' I was dying of hunger. My anger was like a storm that appeared one second and passed the next. After ten minutes I felt I should ask his forgiveness. But that was not going to happen. Nor would I admit that I regretted my stubbornness. I held all my regrets inside me.

Having had to cook every second or third day, I had become quite an expert and therefore the curry that His Highness was supposed to have cooked was always the best. Nani used to cook very well. At home she had a few hearths built in one of the courtyards. Whatever was cooked was thus always done in full view. In winter I would happily sit and stir the pots. I would cook His Highness' curry, as they did at home. I knew all the tricks and therefore whatever His Highness cooked was the tastiest. Sometimes while cooking, His Highness would request me to sing and I would, without any accompanying music. It was easy for me because I had had a lot of practice reciting marsiyas. In fact His Highness used to say that I sang better without my accompanists. And he was not the only one who said this. There were those who said they preferred listening to me sing without any other music.

April arrived and preparations began again for the migration to Kashmir. As usual we were given a car. In Jammu there was only one petrol station, next to the Nanda Bus Service, where all the cars and buses had their tanks filled. In fact they would even fill a few drums and carry them along in case they ran out of fuel on the way. Our driver, too, stopped there to get petrol. Immediately, from the bicycle shop, came the words, 'Yaar do you have any money.' I thanked my stars that I was leaving and would not have to hear these boys for another six months. Eight or ten days after reaching Kashmir His Highness decided to go hunting.

26. Lachchigam

Everyone was informed about the plan to go hunting. There was a place close to Kashmir which some people called Lachchigam while others referred to it as Darapa. All kinds of game was available there. There were countless bears as well as deer, blue bulls, twelve-antlered *sambhars* and wild fowl. There was a huge rest house in Darapa where the Maharaja could stay.

His Highness was a bit worried about taking me with him. He was afraid that my accompanying him on the hunt was bound to invite comment that he could now not even hunt without me. After much consultation it was decided that since taking my accompanists was out of the question, I should go disguised as one of his orderlies. As an orderly it would be easy for me to go anywhere that His Highness went.

Once the decision was taken, the tailor was there in a flash. He measured me up and my uniform was ready: a short buttoned-up coat, breeches, a coloured muslin turban and black boots. It was very difficult to get into the breeches, and I only managed to do so after a lot of effort. I wore the short coat and the boots but the real problem was the turban. My hair was so thick and long that it was almost impossible to even plait a paranda along with my hair. I wanted to wear the beautiful parandas made in Patiala. The royal ladies all got their parandas and draw-strings from there. But whenever I did manage to get a paranda in my hair, it dragged on the ground.

An orderly, who was an expert in winding turbans, was ordered to hide my hair in a turban. My hair was tied into a knot the way the Sikhs tie their hair, and a turban was wound over it. When I looked into the mirror I looked so ugly that I hated the sight of myself. As it was, I was dark and also slightly plump. His Highness had coined two epithets for me. When he wanted to tease me he called me a *bhatiyaran*, the woman roaster of grains, who had faced the fire all day and thus had a blackened face. When he was angry he would call me the 'Offspring of Muharram,' implying that I was born in the dark month of mourning. With my hair up, and since I rarely smiled, I looked frightening. His Highness took a few photographs. Often he used to show them to me and say, 'Look carefully, this is what you look like.'

We had to drive to Dachigam. In the royal car, His Highness and Khusrau Jung sat at the back and in the front were the driver and me in my role as an orderly. All the cars stopped where the path to Dachigam began. As an orderly I should have jumped out and opened the door for His Highness. Instead, as soon the car stopped, he quickly opened the door and stepped out. The grooms were standing with horses. A horse was led to each one. When it was my turn, two orderlies helped me into the saddle. The horses moved off in a row. The trek up was so dangerous that I wanted to keep my eyes closed. The rocky path was, at most, three feet wide. It was strewn with odd shaped rocks and the climb was very steep. On both sides were sharp slopes.

The horses, however, were well used to this climb. They would first plant one foot on the slippery rock before they lifted the others. If both their front legs slipped, they would manage to balance themselves with their hind legs. Often in panic, I would jump off the horse and start to walk. But the path was impossibly steep and in a couple of minutes I would be panting. The climb was so long that it seemed it would never end. But on the way I saw beautiful sights, which I will never forget. On both sides I saw herds of black buck and blue bulls. They would appear wherever there was flat land, and would fearlessly stand at a distance of two or three feet from us. When the horses approached them, the does would form a circle around the male deer and continue grazing.

His Highness had forbidden the shooting of female animals. Only those who came from abroad, or His Highness' friends, were permitted to hunt here in any case. And those who were given a 'permit' were not allowed to shoot more than two animals. This jungle was meant only for His Highness. Pistachio trees grew in abundance in the forest. On the way I also saw a female bear suckling her five cubs in the sun. She was so deeply asleep that she did not open her eyes even when we passed. All the female animals seemed to know that they were in no danger.

I, on the other hand, was in extreme discomfort. The breeches were tight, the saddle hard, the ascent steep. Having to sit in the same position for six or seven hours at a stretch had made my legs completely stiff; my waist had folded over. I had grazed the skin off my legs at several places. Mercifully, the journey ended and we reached the *dak* bungalow. There was a large uneven plot of ground in front of the bungalow that was surrounded by a deep gorge. God forbid, if anyone were to fall into it, it would be difficult to find any trace of them. Iron wire fenced the grounds.

When I dismounted I was so stiff I could barely walk. At the spots where the skin had come off, my flesh was burning. There were chairs on the ground and soon everyone was sitting. We were immediately served tea and things to eat. After having eaten and drunk, I had a hard time getting out of the breeches; the wretched things seemed to be stuck. There was a small room attached to His Highness' room and this was assigned to me. Before we left I had asked him whether I should take someone from the family with me. He had teased me and said, 'Do not worry. No man, not even a wolf would be able to carry away this *bhatiyaran*. You will be in no danger.' Actually my complexion was wheatish. When he constantly referred to me as dark, I would get so angry that I would be on the point of crying. He would be very amused by this.

I was not used to sleeping alone. I was very scared but so tired that I fell asleep easily the first night. I slept so well that I only woke at nine or ten when they knocked to announce breakfast. His Highness was sitting on the ground. They competed at hitting targets and after lunch he played cards. In the evening His Highness suggested that it was time to go to the waterfall.

At sunset, the waterfall was a dazzling sight. I have seen the Niagara Falls. They are huge and are decorated with red and blue lights. However, this little waterfall, without the help of lights, had a beauty that was completely natural. God had created this Himself: once you have seen such a sight, you want to see it again and again. I still find myself longing to do so. When the water fell over the edge, thousands of trout jumped out into the air before the water hit the rocks. In the rays of the setting sun, they would glisten in their myriad colours. Like lightning, they would be out of the waterfall and into the flowing water again.

Though this was happening around the clock, at sunset when the rays of the fading sun fell on the trout they looked like sapphire, emerald and ruby fairies dancing. The scales of trout have thousands of colours on them. The fish would jump a few feet into the air and somersault before falling back into the water. His Highness would sit with his staff and watch this sight till it was dark. One evening he asked me to sing a *pahari*. I started to sing. Lord knows what happened because I felt strange. I forgot who I was, where I was, and that there were people all around me. The sound of the water was like music. I think the others also were in a similar state. When the song ended, there was silence, and then His Highness spoke, as if he could not control himself any longer. 'May God give my years to you. May you live for ever.' It could not have been my singing. Perhaps it was the atmosphere.

My singing teachers often said of me, 'She sings in tune. Her articulation is superb. The voice is steeped in feeling. God rarely gives such a voice to someone.' At that moment, though, all this praise was as nothing. It was that sound of the waterfall, the glow of the sunset, the dance of the fish, and the song that blended with them. The hills came alive. That day I also saw tears in His Highness' eyes. I wanted to tell him how much I liked him but could not. I gazed at him intently and kept silent.

While there were so many beautiful things there, there were also frightening ones. Everyone kept their guns with them all the time. There was danger from bears at every step. Anyone who stepped out of the bungalow took his gun with him. After three or four days, when everyone was asleep, a female wolf appeared at the bungalow and started howling. The voice was loud and scary. I was so scared that I almost stopped breathing. I had never slept alone in a room, but here I had hardened my heart to do so. Now there was this new nuisance! People stepped out with their guns but the wolf disappeared in the dark so they returned to their rooms. Half an hour later she was back and howling again. Guns, torches and men appeared again but the wolf was so clever that she melted into the dark and no one could spot her. That night, I did not sleep.

The next night we were still awake when she arrived, quite furious because she scratched at the windowpanes. When she appeared under my window and hit the glass with her paws I was afraid the glass would break and she would leap in. My heart was hammering so hard that I had to try to calm it with my hands. Again and again people would go out with guns, but the wolf would disappear the moment a door opened, only to return in fifteen minutes. In this way, we managed to pass the night somehow. There I was—the one who always insisted that people sleep on both sides of me—all alone in a room with these fearsome sounds and the animal at the window. Thankfully the windows had thick iron bars on them else she would surely have managed to get in.

The cursed one made an appearance every night, as regularly as a guard appears for duty. The whole day I thought of what would happen that night and I prayed that the night would never come. The third night she was even more furious. She hit the widow panes so hard that the windows and doors began to shake. I could bear it no longer. It was two at night. One door of His Highness' room opened into my room. I knocked hard on it. The door opened. I was trembling with fear.

His Highness asked, 'What is the matter? Why are you shivering?' I could hardly speak. All I managed to say was, 'I am alone. If I am left alone, I will die. Please let me sleep in your room. I will sleep on the floor or I will sit through the night but I will not go back to my room to sleep.'

He reassured me. 'I will keep the door of my room open and you need no longer be afraid. The windows are made of iron. Not even a tiger—let alone a wolf—will be able to break through. Relax and sleep without any fear.'

'No,' I said, 'I will sit in your room but will not stay alone in my room.'

After thinking for a moment he called his ADC, 'Bring in yours as well as her charpai into my room. She is very frightened.' The orderlies came and made the beds. I spent that night very peacefully. I slept soundly till ten the next morning.

The days passed very pleasantly. In the morning around ten, His Highness would sit in the grounds. The entire staff and I were blindfolded and had to search for whatever he flung at us. Like blind men we would be on all fours, crawling around and searching for it with our hands. Whoever found whatever His Highness had flung would get a hundred rupees. Sahabzada Nur Muhammad was very fat. It would take him a long time to get down on to the ground and start searching. He would try to cheat by trying to sneak a look. We used to laugh a lot at him. There were two or three orderlies of my age. His Highness would tell us to race and touch a particular tree and the winner would get twenty rupees. I never won the race, nor won the prize though I had to compete a few times. Sometimes we would play cards. I only knew how to play 'trump-piece'. Sometimes, while playing, His Highness would try to cheat. My partner would keep quiet but I would confront him. 'You have played your card. You cannot change it now. You will have to play the same card.'

The whole day we played something or other. A few times they also went to hunt and killed some deer and two or three bears. When they went out to hunt, I would stay inside the bungalow. In the evenings, wood was arranged in a huge pile and lit. When it turned into coal, skewered pieces of venison were roasted on it. We would sit on chairs around the hot coals and eat the meat off the skewers in turn. A barbecued piece of venison is unlike any other meat. That is why there are so many tales about kings chasing deer. Their meat is extremely tender. The kings would barbecue it, add salt and chillies and eat it there and then.

We had had a lot of fun on the trip. On the way back, I again dressed as a man and returned to Kashmir. It was the second of September when we came back to Kashmir.

27. Mian Maula Bakhsh Talwandiwale

Back in Jammu His Highness ordered that I learn music from some good 'Khan Sahib'. He said that the state would pay his salary, but the Khan Sahib had to be very good. After much inquiry it was found that Maula Bakhsh was the best ustad around—there was no one who could match him far and wide. My Nana went to Talwandi where the ustad lived and told him that he would be paid by the state if he agreed to teach me. Maula Bakhsh said: 'Neither my forefathers nor I have ever taught a woman. You say that I will be employed by the state. So, I will teach her.'

A few days later he arrived in Jammu with his nephew. He must have been around fifty. He was respectable, affable, pious, and a regular worshipper. He was a wise man: he had none of the habits of other 'Khan Sahibs'. Ordinary ustads were greedy, shrewd, addicted to intoxicants. Their demands were endless. Maula Bakhsh was a contented man. He did not laugh or joke and was businesslike. He did not believe in asking for more than his due. God had given him such a voice that when he began the note *Sa*, it would seem that tanpuras had begun to be strummed all over the room—the room would echo with the sound. Allah had concentrated as much sweetness as possible, into his voice.

He asked me which ragas I liked. 'I like *Jaijaiwant* and *Shankhara* a lot,' I told him. He started me on these two ragas. His voice had so much feeling that I often forgot that I was supposed to be learning and should be singing with him. Only when he stopped and waited for me to join him, would I realize what I was supposed to be doing. I would get completely absorbed in his singing and forget to copy him. This was not music. It was worship. I have never again heard voices like those of Khan Sahib Ali Bakhsh (the mad one), Allah Bakhsh and Mian Maula Bakhsh. Their voices were steeped in passion and had the magical power to make listeners forget themselves. They were icons of *Sur*, the note, experts at musical articulation. Whether they uttered a word or not, the moment they uttered the first sound the audience was bewitched. I enjoyed listening to them more than learning from them. Their singing was not dependent on words because they did not sing thumri, dadras or ghazals.

I was at an age when I did not really understand their music, nor what good music was. Yet, listening to Maula Bakhsh had a profound effect on me. It took a great deal of persuasion to make him stay with us for six months. He had never left Talwandi before, and he missed his wife and children. Maula Bakhsh was not educated but he knew all there was to know about music. Learning from him improved my singing. His Highness, who was a discriminating listener, also noticed the difference. His Highness himself, however, did not like listening to male singers and never invited them to the palace.

28. Maulana Sahib

A Maulana sahib said to be connected to some royal family used to visit His Highness from Lucknow. He was dark, had a long beard, and was fat and unbecoming. His dressed differently from everyone else. His pyjamas of long cloth were so wide at the bottom that they looked like women's pleated *ghararas*. Over these he wore a long kurta and either a short coat or an achkan over that. His red cap had a tassel on it. He worshipped regularly and spoke in the typical style of Lucknow. He spoke his refined Urdu so softly that you invariably had to ask him to repeat himself. He used such difficult words that His Highness would have to ask for their meaning. There was a delicacy in the way he ate, drank or moved. His Highness would never let Maulana sahib leave before he had spent two or three months with him. Whenever he asked for permission to leave, His Highness would angrily refuse and make him stay on.

I was not the least interested in him; actually, I disliked him. When His Highness referred to him as naïve, simple and innocent, it made me very angry. I was convinced that his behaviour was a performance. I was sure that his act of innocence was meant to earn him a few months of royal hospitality. He got to spend the whole season in Kashmir in luxury by convincing people that he was as innocent as a five year old child! His Highness would end up rolling with laughter at Maulana's remarks, and would later repeat them to others. The sycophants would laugh so loudly that they almost tore their mouths open.

Sahabzada Nur Muhammad, however, found a funny side to everything. His Highness would affectionately address him as Nuri. He was always in good humour and would laugh and joke with everyone. He was cultured and a connoisseur of poetry. His mother tongue was Persian and he had a sharp, intelligent and shrewd mind. One day when I went to Ram Nagar, an orderly informed me that His Highness was at the poolside. This pool whose depth went from three to eight feet had been built near the palace for His Highness to bathe in. Around the pool were twelve arched pavilions, the marble lattice work of which was carved in the Mughal style. Carpets were spread on the marble floors and chairs were placed on them. At the deep end of the pool were steps which people climbed up to dive. The water of the pool could be heated.

I found His Highness and his staff there. He was in his bathing costume and talking to Maulana. Khusrau Jung dived into the pool a couple of times. Some swam like fish and others went underwater for long periods of time. Some floated as still as a corpse. The water was clear as glass and even a twig could be spotted in it. The Maulana was sitting on a chair and watching the fun. When someone dived he would delightedly praise God by uttering 'Subhan Allah.' When someone went underwater, Maulana would stop breathing. He would look worried. When the person emerged from the water, Maulana would clap his hands like a happy child. Watching him having so much fun, His Highness asked him if he knew how to swim. 'Yes,' Maulana said casually. An orderly was immediately asked to fetch a bathing costume but since Maulana was so fat, they could not find a costume that would fit him. A tailor was called and he had one ready in ten or fifteen minutes by cutting off the legs of a pair of trousers. With difficulty, Maulana got into it. He looked very strange in this garb, more animal than human. Actually he looked like a small gorilla. A small head, a bizarre shaped stomach, fat ugly arms. He looked both amusing and repulsive.

When Maulana was ready, His Highness politely said, 'Go ahead, go into the water.'

'If that is your pleasure,' Maulana answered.

In a flash he had climbed the ladder and was at the top. Everyone was looking at him. Maulana asked, 'Shall I jump?'

Happily, every one said, 'Yes, yes, go ahead.'

He jumped into the water and for a minute or two, no one knew what had happened. When the water became still again, Maulana was seen lying spread-eagled, his face on the floor of the pool, making a '*budd*... *budd*' sound. It took a while for people to realize that Maulana had drowned. Soon there was panic, for the Maulana showed no sign of moving. Everyone jumped into the water. They brought him up but it was difficult to get him out of the pool. The orderlies and the staff tried hard to lift him out but they would slip. Finally they had to drag him out. They laid him face down on the floor. Maulana was unconscious. The doctor arrived in a short while. He put something hard under his stomach and then climbed on his back and pressed his stomach hard. *Gudh* ... *gudh* ... *gudh*, the water began pouring out of his mouth. The doctor also kept moving his limbs. Others helped in different ways. He must have banged his head when he jumped and that is why he must have stayed at the bottom. Everyone was worried, even praying for him to recover.

His Highness was particularly worried. After about ten minutes Maulana's arms and legs began to move. His dark face had acquired a strange colour with the rush of blood into it. His colour began to return to normal and finally he was fully conscious. He was helped to a chair.

His Highness asked, "When you dived why did you not come up?"

'I dived when you told me to dive. I remember nothing after that,' replied Maulana.

His Highness asked again, 'Do you know how to swim?'

'No' he said, 'I thought I would do exactly what you were doing. It did not seem difficult.'

That convinced me that Maulana really was a simple and innocent man and not a fraud and deceitful as I had believed him to be. The doctor said that he had been saved in the nick of time. For the next few days this became a joke. His Highness would tease him by repeating: 'All of you said jump, so I jumped.' His Highness continued to respect him a great deal and was considerate towards him in all matters. If Maulana was late for dinner, His Highness would wait for him.

29. Holi

New dresses were made for everyone for the holi durbar. My accompanists and I were given the dresses a few days before the festival. I got a white muslin peshwaz robe and a white muslin dupatta. The accompanists were to wear white achkans, white pyjamas and white turbans. His Highness and his courtiers too were dressed similarly. Buckets of coloured water and large metal syringes for spraying colours were kept on the platform in Mandi. There were also mounds of coloured powder for everybody's use.

After His Highness was seated, I sang for about ten minutes before some courtier threw colour at His Highness and the commotion of colour began. All the courtiers now started throwing colours at each other. So much colour was thrown around that it seemed that a coloured cloud had descended and enveloped everything. I stood in one place.

I sang *holis* at the durbar. The bandishes of these holis were very beautiful. Holi is sung like a thumri. I had not even finished singing before people started playing holi. I was still singing when someone squirted colour at me. I covered my face with my hands. Anyone who wanted, came and threw coloured water or powder at me. The only thing that I disliked about all this was my hair getting wet. My hair was thick and long, reaching almost to my feet. I hated wet hair. So many colours were used that people's faces became blue, yellow, red or black. People could not recognize each other and everyone looked frightening. His Highness was a total mess because every courtier wanted to squirt colour at him.

The celebrations for the festival usually began a month ahead. Hindus and Muslims would celebrate the festival together and splash colour on each other. Celebrations went on the whole day in every street and lane. If any one appeared in clean clothes, children would immediately pour buckets of coloured water over their heads. At this festival, people even stopped caring about untouchability. And this was not just true of Maharaja Hari Singh's time. Holi had been celebrated in the same way even in Maharaja Pratap Singh's reign. The whole bazaar enjoyed the sight of the boys bathing people in colour. Sometimes the person in clean clothes would realize what he was in for and would run with the boys giving chase. The people in the bazaar would shout encouragements to the pursuers and the whole thing would become a game. Everyone sided with the boy with the colour and did not want the other to escape without being dyed blue or yellow. For if he escaped, he would surely go and boast elsewhere that he managed to escape clean from that particular mohalla.

The colours smeared on the face were mixed in such a way that they took at least a couple of days to wash off. Some venerable old men with long beards were not spared either. When the children threw colour on them they would begin cursing the children. The entire bazaar came to the defense of the children: 'It is not the end of the world. The festival comes once a year and the children enjoy it. Why don't you join in too? Your life will become longer.' The whole month of Holi passed in fun and games. The old, young, Hindus, Muslims, all celebrated Holi together. And after it was over, everyone would begin planning for next year's Holi.

As long as the weather was good, His Highness would sleep out in the open. Nights in Jammu are very cold. The wind that blew between eight at night and ten in the morning was so strong that no mosquito could withstand it. As soon as the singing was over, an orderly would lay a bed on the carpet. The feet of the bed were made of silver and the milky white bed sheets were imported from England. The bed sheet was tied at the corners with red *sej bands*, strings that kept it in place. There was a special technique for tying these strings. Chamberlains employed in the *farrash khana* where all the carpets, durries and bed sheets were stored, were responsible for tying these sej bands. Because of these strings, the bed sheet would not crease while you slept. I had silver sej bands made for my bed and often thought I would ask one of the chamberlains to teach me how to tie the knots. I had tried to do them myself but they would come undone the moment I lay down. The farrashes lived close to where we did but I did not dare call them over to teach me the knots, thinking of the gossip that would start: 'So, she can no longer sleep without sej bands now? Look at where she was yesterday and the airs she puts on now.' Just the possibility of this happening, kept me from learning how to tie the sej bands though I still have the silver ones with me.

Once the bed was laid, His Highness would sit on it and would talk to us for an hour or two. When he felt sleepy, he would say. 'Go and get some sleep.' Usually he was asleep by eleven though sometimes he would stay up till midnight. He was not one to stay up late.

Something very amusing happened around this time. My accompanists were also employees of the state. His Highness decided that they should dress in the same colours as the saris I wore. The state gave them four sets of uniforms for summer and another four for winter. For summer they got four muslin turbans, four muslin angarkhas, four sashes for the waist, pyjamas, socks and black pump shoes.

In the beginning I wore only very light coloured saris so that the difference between the colour of my dress and those of my accompanists was not noticeable. Once, His Highness had some visitors from abroad. I wore a carnation red sari. This is the colour that results from mixing black with red. The tabla player was wheatish in complexion but the *sarangi-walla* was almost black. Carpets were laid out on the grounds on one side and dinner was laid out at the other. After dinner everyone took their places. The accompanists were summoned. They appeared, looking demonic, dressed in dark red from head to toe. His Highness called me to ask why they were dressed like clowns. Actually, they were only supposed to get their cummerbunds and turbans dyed to match my saris but they had their angarkhas and socks dyed too. His Highness ordered that they be given new dresses the next day and that from then on they should only stick to getting their turbans and cummerbunds dyed to match the colour of my saris.

In the end, the accompanists benefited from this affair. They got four new sets of uniforms along with shoes. The shoes had not been affected by this attempted colour coordination, but then, who cared about such small things in these princely kingdoms?

30. The Maharani of Cooch Behar

Preparations to leave for Kashmir began again. Within a week the Maharani of Cooch Behar arrived. I was always very happy when she came, for her presence embellished a gathering. My only desire was to get to look at her for as long as possible. She always sat with her feet up on the chair. Close to her would sit Khusrau Jung. Sometimes they would exchange a few words; otherwise they neither conversed nor laughed. They seemed to be immersed in deep thought and indifferent to the world, untouched by the atmosphere around them. As long as she was there, I always saw her in this mood. Sometimes she took out a small silver box from her brocade purse and put some betel nut and cardamom, with great style, into her mouth. Sometimes she would offer some to Khusrau Jung. They were so engrossed in each other that they did not know what anyone else was doing, or for that matter, singing. They only had eyes for each other. Khusrau Jung had good features and complexion but because he was so thin, he did not look attractive. He looked almost like a skeleton.

The Maharani was beautiful. Her movements, laughter, conversation, the half-smile on her face before she addressed somebody, combined to wreak havoc on those who saw her. She arranged her hair in the western way into an old style bun. She used makeup but very subtly. The rouge on her face looked like it was her natural colour. Her eyes were so beautiful that they immediately touched the heart and her hands looked as if an artist had sketched them. She was not the epitome of beauty but the way she draped her sari, the way she handled her *pallu* when she walked, the mixture of Indian and western cosmetics, her royal bearing, her height and her figure all made her stunning.

She paid attention to every detail of her appearance. At a time when no one in the country realized that hands and feet were important for appearance, she paid great attention to them. Her

hands were so well manicured that they added to her beauty by
their shape, length, and the light pink nail polish she used. There
was not a hint of artificiality in the way she made herself up. If she
placed her hand under her chin or on the arm of a chair, she
appeared to be a vision painted by some great artist. She was not
like the ladies of today whose nails remind you of Satan's fingers.
In my time if they depicted the devil in a theatre, he usually had
nails an inch long. The Maharani on the other hand was so good
at makeup that you did not even suspect that she had any on.
However, there was so much sadness in her eyes that I would
start feeling sad when I looked at her. I dearly wanted her to
speak to me, but she was not the least interested in me. I too, was
incapable of praising anyone or showing affection else I would
have gone and told her how much I liked her. It was because of
this personal inhibition that I never told her how I felt and
continued to admire her secretly in my heart.

She would visit three or four times a year. She was very
pleasant tempered. Sometimes I thought I saw tears in her eyes,
but then her eyes would quietly re-absorb them. One day I was
singing a ghazal by a very ordinary poet. One of the lines of this
ghazal was 'How was I to know that we were meant for
separation?' Khusrau Jung was in some other room and therefore
she was paying attention to my singing. She listened for a while
and then suddenly got up and disappeared. A little while later
she returned to her chair. She requested me to sing the ghazal I
had been singing, again. I sang it again and this time sang it even
better than the previous time. When it was over she said politely,
'You sing very well. There is such pathos in your voice.'

I suspect that that was the first time she had actually paid any
attention to my singing or tried to understand the music and
poetry. She left the next day. After she had gone His Highness
would tell Khusrau Jung 'Friend, what has happened to you?
Come on, smile.' Khusrau Jung would try hard, but in vain, to
smile. Then he asked His Highness for a month's leave and went
away to Hyderabad. He returned with his former good humour.
Perhaps he had found a way to deal with his sorrow.

31. The Royal Shikars

His Highness had been a keen hunter since he was a child. So, the moment we arrived in Kashmir, everyone got busy with hunting waterfowl. The Dal Lake in Kashmir is very large and deep. The water appears totally still but under the surface the currents are as strong as those of a river. From the banks, the lake looked like an ocean. Every year, teal and mallard arrived there in large numbers. The hunt was organized in a peculiar manner. Forty or fifty small boats were filled with branches and leaves. Two or three of the hunters would sit in them, hidden by the foliage, and the oar-less boats were pushed into the lake full of birds. His Highness too would be in one of these boats. The boats would slowly float towards the centre. The birds saw the foliage and did not suspect danger and continued to swim. Suddenly, guns would be fired from all directions and thousands of birds were hit. When the surviving ones rose into the air like a cloud, their sheer numbers hid the sun. The hunters would then fire at the birds in the air, and many would drop from the skies. Each of the hunters would bag around five thousand birds. It would take nearly two hours to gather all the dead birds from the lake, which were then piled on boats and brought to the banks. His Highness also had trained retriever dogs from England.

There would be mountains of teal and mallard on the side of the lake. This sight did not make me happy; instead, it saddened me. The feathers of the mallards were so beautiful that you saw the creator's own work in those colours. First, to deceive these innocent birds, and then for the sake of numbers, to slaughter hundreds of thousands of them, seemed so unnecessary. The birds were distributed amongst the entire staff. Everyone got countless birds as their share. Lord knows whether they ate them or just discarded them for there were no deep freezes then to store them in. I did not like eating the meat of these birds because I did not like their odour, or 'flavour' as it is referred to today. In our house, except for the musicians, no one else ate the meat. We would distribute our share. However, I loved the meat of the hill and Bartavelle partridges.

Often His Highness took me along when he went on a hunt for tiger, cheetah or bear. Big game is always shot from a *machan* built high up in the trees. These platforms were so high that no tiger or cheetah could leap up to them. Two or three hundred men with small sticks in their hands would form a circle and beat the bushes while making the sounds of *hu ... hu* with their mouths. As they moved in and the circle got smaller, the encircled animals were driven towards the machans. As the circle of the beaters got closer, the animals would begin to appear. The hunters, if their aim was good enough, would shoot the animal before it disappeared again.

At one such hunt something out of the ordinary happened. Twelve or thirteen machans had been built. On one of these were three ADCs: Devi Chand, Anchal Singh and Sahabzada Nur Muhammad. As soon as he was seated, the Sahabzadah declared that he did not know how to hunt, nor did he care about shikar, and that he had come only to watch. I was with His Highness, Khusrau Jung, and an orderly on another machan. The beat began, and soon the beaters driving in the animals were close to us. The Sahabzada had been sternly warned that he should not even breathe if that was going to make a sound. He was also told not to speak, and that if he did, he would never be included in a shikar again.

I think His Highness mistakenly believed that I actually enjoyed the hunt. I enjoyed the experience only up to this point—the preparations for the hunt, the climbing on to the machans, the hustle bustle, and the sound of the beaters—but I did not enjoy the killing that followed. Not a single animal appeared before our machan that day, but strange sounds began to emanate from the direction of the neighbouring machan. The beaters were now extremely close. There was total silence on our machan so as not to scare away any animal that might approach us. The sounds from the other machan however continued and none of us could figure out what was happening. No one could dismount from the machans till a ladder had been set up. For half an hour, the loud frightening sounds from the other machan continued. We held our breath in suspense: what was this sound? What was happening? The machan was so far that we had no way of finding out. Sometimes it seemed as though someone was groaning, at other times we heard sounds of conversation. We were clueless about what had happened. Soon the ladder and Sahabzada Nur Muhammad arrived, almost at the same time. We descended and Nur Muhammad told us what had happened.

'Devi Singh and Anchal Singh have been grievously injured by a bear. You know that I do not hunt myself and had only come to watch. During the beat, a bear appeared very close to us and I shouted "Fire" but the other two froze with fear. The bear then began climbing the tree. I kept screaming "O my saviours fire at him, pull the trigger." However, the other two sat silently as if they had been mesmerised. They could have fired twenty times in the time it took for the bear to reach the machan but it seemed they had sworn not to touch their triggers. The bear knocked both of them along with their guns from the machan. I only had a pistol with me and I aimed and shot at the animal. The bear was practically on top of them and luckily my shot found its target, for those two were destined to live. By then the beaters had arrived and they removed the bear from over them.'

They were put on charpais and taken to the hospital. Both had been seriously injured. After a fortnight they were moved from the hospital to an official houseboat anchored near his Highness' riverside residence. Two or three times I went with His Highness to call on them. The Sahabzada would be with us and he would always ask. 'O my protectors, was it because you were related to that bear that you did not fire? If you did not know how to shoot, why did you pretend to be hunters and get on to that machan?' The poor men hung their heads in shame and keep silent. Every morning, they had to hear all the details recounted by the Sahabzada. He would enact the whole event—how they held their guns as they watched the bear climb the tree; how they had sat as if they had been turned into stone and stared at the bear; how, like senseless people, they had stared wide-eyed at him when he shouted at them to fire. The Sahabzada would mimic them so well that every one had a good laugh.

The two injured hunters were confined to their beds for three months. Their progress was well monitored. It was some time before they could walk again, but they were never able to look others in the eye ever again.

Maharaja Hari Singh himself had escaped death a few times while hunting, particularly while hunting wild buffalo because these had to be shot while standing on the ground. In one totally unexpected attack by a buffalo, His Highness was lucky to have escaped alive. His Highness was a brave man.

During the duck hunt he would fire so many times that once there were wounds on his shoulder at the end of the day. The doctor dressed and bandaged the shoulder but the next day, His Highness was on the lake again, firing away. The wounds began to bleed again and the bandages, and then his shirt, soaked up the blood. In the evening when he tried to take off his shirt he found that it was stuck to his wounds.

The doctor tried to remove the shirt and worked as it from seven in the evening till one at night but without success. Swabs of warm water did no good. If the doctor tried to exert any force, the flesh would begin to come off with the bandages. Through all this the Maharaja did not make a sound. It was clear that His Highness was no coward because if he had been weak hearted, he would not have gone shooting the next day. I however could not stop myself from uttering *uuunhs* and *huuuns* and *hais* as I watched all this and His Highness asked me to go to another room. 'If you have to sit here, then do not look this way,' he added. Mercifully the wound was clean by two. The doctor dressed and bandaged it again. In spite of his luxurious upbringing and lifestyle, the Maharaja had not complained once the whole evening.

At the palace at Gupkar there was a huge room containing the Maharaja's trophies—tigers, wild buffaloes and bears. Expert taxidermists were summoned from abroad to preserve the animals. These stuffed animals were arranged in amazingly natural postures and sometimes it seemed as if the animal was just about to spring and attack. Each animal was set in a different pose. Young strong wild buffalo bulls, which are more dangerous than tigers, stood in a row as if about to charge. The taxidermists were so good that the sheen on the fur of the animals looked like that on a living creature. His Highness would bring those guests who were fond of hunting to this room, that was otherwise kept locked. The servants would spray chemicals on the stuffed animals to preserve them. I believe that even in those days it cost him lakhs of rupees to maintain those trophies.

32. The Exhibition

In order to encourage handicrafts in Kashmir, Maharaja Hari Singh announced the organization of an exhibition. He wanted to give the craftsmen of Kashmir an opportunity to show the best examples of their craft. The wood workers, the silversmiths, those who worked with papier-mâché, the ones who embroidered shawls, the stone carvers and others, were informed that awards would be given for the best work. The shopkeepers who stocked such pieces would be given certificates. The Maharaja knew that *seths*, rajas, maharajas and nawabs came from all over to visit Kashmir. At the exhibition they would place orders for various things. The farmers, too, were invited to bring their produce to compete for awards. The exhibition was interesting to the tourists and encouraged their interest in all things Kashmiri.

Truly, the exhibition was unique. Each thing on display was beautiful. There were beautiful and expensive shawls, the costs of which ranged from eight rupees to five hundred rupees. The double sized *doshalas* cost between five hundred and a thousand rupees. The *jamawar* shawls were so finely embroidered that it was impossible to distinguish one stitch from the other. You could buy a reversible embroidered shawl for a thousand or twelve hundred rupees. A ruffle shawl with an embroidered border could be bought for eight rupees. The poor could buy these for their wives and children. Silver cost two annas a tola then. All sorts of silver vessels were beautifully worked upon and the craftsmen charged two annas per tola as their labour. Their sketching was so fine that no craftsmen from anywhere else could match it. The rich ordered dinner sets, tea sets, paandaans, khaasdaans or whatever else they fancied. They would choose designs from books and the craftsmen spent the winter servicing these orders.

All sorts of furniture was made from the wood of walnut trees. The carving on wood too, was unparalleled. This furniture was even exported to England. Thousands of things were also made out of papier-mâché and decorated beautifully with colourful designs. The craftsmen created numerous beautiful things— penholders, bookcases, and book covers, tables, chairs—each thing unique because of the beautifully painted patterns on it, yet cheaper than anywhere else. Both the rich and poor could afford to buy things at the exhibition. The rich bought pashmina and the poor, ruffle. The richest or the poorest could buy hand embroidered tablecloths, bedspreads, bed sheets, dupattas and saris. The rich would buy them in *bafta*, tafetta or *shahtoosh*, the poor in ruffle or cheap pashmina.

Sapphires, topazes, onyx and carnelians were carved on small machines, made into earrings, necklaces and bracelets and sold by the hundreds. There was such variety at the exhibition that the entire day could be spent just looking at the things on display.

The farmers too worked hard all year round preparing for the exhibition. Every farmer wanted to be the one to win the first prize. Each vegetable at the exhibition was four times the normal size. It was difficult to believe that they were real and not monstrous fakes. For instance there was a gourd so long that it had to be carried on a *charpai*, a pumpkin so large that next to it was a board announcing that anyone who could lift it unassisted, would win fifty rupees. There were grains of corn the size of almonds. Even the pistachios, almonds and walnuts were so large that that their size had to be seen to be believed. There were French apples the size of small water pots. Every vegetable and fruit deserved a prize. Lord knows how they got them to grow so large.

Everything in the exhibition was one of a kind. The Kashmiris also began to innovate and create new things for each exhibition. The fame of the exhibition spread far and wide. People would come to Kashmir a couple of months in advance to submit applications to be permitted to put up swings and other amusements for children. Big merchants, carnival owners, organizers of gambling games, small theatre companies, magicians and troops of dancing girls would plead hard for permission to be allowed to participate, and if they succeeded in getting it, they would earn a lot of money at each exhibition. More and more people came each year. Arrangements for the exhibition began two months in advance. The exhibition ground was so large that one could not see the whole thing in one day.

Kashmiri food too was delicious and very different from food anywhere else. Different spices made each dish distinct in taste, unlike our cuisine today, in which the same spices are used for every recipe, making every dish taste the same. Tasting the food made by Kashmiri cooks, one realized that that this was food meant for Mughal royalty. They prided themselves on being able to use every part of a goat. They cooked offal in such a way that you mistook it for cooked greens. Other native cuisines or the western ones did not stand a chance in comparison to Kashmiri food.

Handicraft activity was given a boost by the exhibition and the people were very pleased.

33. The Houseboat Owners

Many Englishmen came to Kashmir for a holiday and they went crazy when they saw it. They liked living in houseboats. When they rented one of these, the owners would keep their own boats tied to the houseboat. One half of these boats served as a home for the family of the boatman while the other half was used as a kitchen for the larger houseboat. They would also hire out the shikara along with the houseboat for shopping. The boatman and his wife would become the servants of the memsahib and the sahib. If the sahib was single, that too had its benefits, but it was just as good if he had his wife and children with him. They cooked for them, took care of all their needs and were so obedient that their temporary employers would more or less fall in love with them. In England only a Lord or a Duke could afford servants. On a houseboat, even an ordinary person found a complete family of servants. The boatman's children would crowd around the memsahib the whole day. Wherever the memsahib or sahib wanted to go, they would seat them in a rickshaw and get them there.

Renting houseboats was the main source of income for the boatmen. They would rent their houseboats for the whole season, and live off what they earned for the rest of the year. They preferred to have 'English' tenants—they did not like letting out their boats to Indians because they knew they could not make fools of them the way they did with foreigners. They served the foreigners for the whole season in such a clever way that they ensured the guests lost touch with reality. If the memsahib had children they treated them so lovingly that soon the children began to relate to them better than they did to their own mothers. As the holiday neared its end, the memsahib's things would begin to disappear. The boatmen and their families stole watches, cameras, clocks and cash. There were such cleverly concealed spaces in their small boats that searches unearthed nothing. They constantly extracted money as *baksheesh*. Neither the baksheesh nor the pilfering deterred the English from returning to Kashmir and becoming the slaves of some other family. The next time round they would decide that the new couple they had found were angels. Yet the pattern of robberies repeated itself when they were about to leave. For the boatmen and their families money was the only thing that mattered.

They did not hesitate to do even the most terrible task provided if got them money. Nor did they have any honour or shame. When an Englishman was alone, they would ask politely, 'Sir do you want a woman?' If the Englishman said yes, they would present him with their wife, sister or even their daughter if she was old enough. And they would happily extract baksheesh from the sahib every day. Some of the boatmen had three or four wives. In those days girls were easily available for fifty or a hundred rupees, so they'd get these girls, marry them and bring them to Punjab to make them work as prostitutes.

In Jammu, there were a few Kashmiri houseboat owners who traded in girls. The houseboat owners would wait till they found an Englishman to rent their boats. If they were not fortunate enough to find one, they would sit and commiserate with each other over the loss of a season's earnings. They realized that it was only with the English that they could get away with all they did. If they did not find an Englishman, they wept at their fate for the rest of the year.

That was not all. These Kashmiris would marry a girl and take her from Jammu to places as far away as Calcutta and there divorce her and then sell her for many times the amount they had originally paid for her. These poor women then had to spend their lives exiled from Kashmir forever. Whether it was Madras, Calcutta or Bombay, Kashmiri girls fetched huge prices. One reason was that in these places everyone else was dark. The Kashmiris were fine-featured but it was their fair skin that made the women stand out. Once these men had married four times, they would take their wives to one of these cities and sell two of them to pimps at a premium. They kept the other two and made them prostitute at home in big cities. When it was time for them to leave the city to return to Kashmir, they would sell these two as well and use the money to buy another houseboat for themselves and set themselves up in business.

There were many such victims in Jammu also. Some would resist and fight back. They'd refuse to follow the men's bidding and even threaten to commit suicide rather than prostitute themselves. For this they were kept hungry and beaten black and blue. A Kashmiri had rented one of the shops in front of our house. He returned every two years with two fresh girls who could hardly have been more than fifteen or sixteen. The older girls he would sell in Lahore or some other city. The new ones were beaten like their predecessors, and often the older ones would explain things to the younger ones and advise them not to resist.

'You will really be sorry if you disobey him. Do as he tells you or he will skin you alive. Look at us. We also refused to do his bidding. He would starve us for three days at a time and not even give us water to drink. We were beaten. We screamed, shouted and pleaded. We wept and cried but no one came forward to help us. No one cared. If out of kindness someone even suggested that he not beat us so badly, he would answer, "Mind your own business. She is my wife to keep alive or kill and I can do as I wish with her. In any case, how does this matter involve you?"'

If any of these girls managed to escape with someone, the Kashmiri 'husband' would immediately file a case against her. He would lament and wail in court, 'Lord, he has stolen my wife. I am an outsider here.' The girl would cry and plead, 'He makes me do shameful things. Save me from him.' The law favoured the man, and the court would hand the girl over to him. He would now make her labour three times as much as before. The rate of a new girl would start at eight annas but would fall to six and then four annas. After winning his case in court he would treat the girl so pitilessly that she could only seek mercy from God. In our city the clients for these girls were usually soldiers from the Gorkha regiment.

I am still amazed that this was happening in the Urdu Bazaar where mostly Muslims lived. And all the leaders, those who claimed to be guardians of the community's future, the ones who talked the most, lived next to where all this was taking place.

They were witness to the barbarism and cruelty that these girls suffered and how they were forced to do things they did not want to do. Day and night the girl's plaints, 'Oh God, why have you willed this for me?' could be heard but they were always ignored and no one bothered to help them. If they were courageous enough to elope with someone, no one would dare accompany them to court. But there were many who were willing to become witnesses for the man and state on oath that the girl was his legally wedded wife. These girls neither had a voice nor a chance to get justice. They became living corpses. Within a year or two they would contract tuberculosis. The Kashmiri men would return to Kashmir, wear huge turbans, and join the ranks of the respectable. The respectable people of Kashmir did not really accept them, but money has such power that gradually they would become landlords, and then acceptability came easily.

These men became rich and socially established through the barbaric treatment and exploitation of innocent girls. The clientele of these girls were *bhangis, chamars,* Gorkha soldiers, or men from the villages. Many had tuberculosis, venereal disease or other infections and the girls would contract these. Several of the girls took to smoking and drink. All these innocent girls ended up in this manner. This is something that should have made the Muslims hang their heads in shame, for only they were involved in this business.

34. Dussehra

The Dussehra durbar was splendid. The *Ram Lila* was enacted every evening for a whole month. The whole story of Ram, Lakshman, Sita and Ravana was dramatized. The Muslims would watch it as theatre and for the Hindus it was a religious performance. Very beautiful bhajans were sung during the performances. Their tunes were based on ragas and they were wonderful. It was obvious that they had been composed by master ustads. The entire *Ramayana* was enacted as a play. Ram, Sita, Ravana and his sister Sarupnakha, dressed in beautiful costumes, would be paraded around the streets on platforms mounted on cars. Their colourful attire and the dialogue between them made even this seem like theatre.

In a large ground near the city three effigies, larger than life, were built of thin slivers of bamboo and held up with strings tied to pegs in the ground. The largest effigy was that of Ravana. These effigies would be about fifteen feet high, with long limbs and large heads. They were filled with fire crackers. Ravana had ten faces. The professional makers of fire crackers lived in the area called Darugar mohalla. It took two months of work by many people working night and day, to make these effigies, and they were expensive to make. Once the bamboo frames were ready, they were filled with firecrackers, and then beautifully dressed in clothes made of coloured paper. The 'dressing' of the effigies took a long time. Paper had to be glued on to each square of the bamboo frames.

On the day of Dussehra, the Maharaja arrived at four in the evening, riding an elephant and leading his army in regal splendour. He first shot a fire-arrow at Ravana. The moment the arrow touched his 'body', Ravana was set on fire. With this the fireworks started. Ear-splitting crackers resounded and fountains of fire erupted. The flames leapt so high that they seemed to touch the sky. Many people in the audience ran away in fear. They had nothing to fear though because the fire that rained down from these fountains was cool by the time it touched the ground. Even if a spark fell on someone, it did not do them any harm. This was a part of the art of the firework makers who worked the whole year to introduce innovations that would fetch them rewards. They worked for about two months constructing the effigies and made enough from that to live on for a year.

At the court, there was a festival to be clebrated almost every month. Hindus and Muslims participated equally in these. The rural folk were simple, innocent and fun loving. Even if they had to walk ten or fifteen miles to participate in the celebrations, they did not mind. There was a lot of poverty but there was also contentment and a glow on the faces of people. The one who earned two rupees was just as happy as the one who earned four. Even the one who earned four annas was content and got a good night's sleep. They neither chased wealth nor complained about their poverty. They were not like people today who might be millionaires but have wan faces, are constantly under stress, and are unable to sleep without swallowing pills. These are ones who are constantly trying to turn their one million into two. In those days, people lived peacefully in their world of poverty. Fashions, rituals and customs change in every age. Today it seems to me that even laughter has changed. When rich people laugh it sounds as if they are weeping within, and the laughter is merely a façade.

In Jammu there was no form of entertainment, neither cinema nor theatre. Sometimes a *raas* was arranged. In this, half a dozen boys would sing and dance. It took the organizers a couple of days to get one of these together. They would spread out a huge durrie in the bazaar. The boys would all be well dressed, some wearing female attire. A harmonium and a dholak formed their accompaniment. The raas would begin with a boy, a black cloth covering his face and bells wrapped around his ankles, beginning to sing and dance. The words would be 'Come O wild one.' I enjoyed watching the 'wild one' so much that I am sure that even the best theatres in England would not entertain me as much today. I would wait with eager anticipation for the black cloth to be removed and for the moment when we would see the face below it. When the heart is happy, the most insignificant things give pleasure.

I am talking about the time when I was still employed. Master Labhu Ram's theatre arrived in the kingdom for the first time. His Highness was away in England. Every day, a man in a tonga would beat his drum and announce all over town: 'Do not miss this wonderful opportunity. Master Labhu Ram's wonderful theatre is going to stage the famous story of Shirin and Farhad.'

We made all the arrangements in advance so that we got the best seats closest to the stage. Who knows where they had got the fifteen or twenty old sofas that we sat on!

35. Labhu Ram's Theatre

The seats on the old sofas cost three rupees each. The steel chairs at the back cost one rupee and it cost eight annas to sit on the durrie. After anxiously waiting for two or three days, we reached there early and took our seats on the rickety sofas.

The curtain rose and six or seven boys, who looked as if they had just emerged from sacks of flour, appeared. Their faces, plastered with cheap powder and cosmetics, were ghastly white and their clothes dirty. They sang the song that was usually sung at the beginning of theatre performances and retreated behind the curtains. We were so close to the stage that we could hear and see everything that was going on in the wings and behind the scenes. The boys were fighting amongst themselves over whose turn it was to go on stage next. Each was pointing at the other. In the course of the argument someone pushed the actor playing the role of the trouble-making *kutni* on to the stage. 'She' appeared, a basket on her head and a broom in her hand, and started wailing very loudly, '*Hai, hai* what a calamity! Shirin is dead.' In the script of the play, the king had arranged with the kutni to spread the false news that Shirin had died. This, he had hoped, would cause Farhad, her grieving lover to either commit suicide or leave the kingdom. With the appearance of the kutni the play was supposed to end. Naturally, the curtains came down.

Master Labhu Ram appeared on stage to apologize. The kutni had appeared by mistake, he explained. The play was going to begin all over again. Slowly the curtain rose again. Khusrau, the king, dressed in the uniform of a bandmaster, was sitting, proud and angry, on a chair. Next to him was a half-naked Farhad with a shovel in his hands. The curtain was only half way up when the king began, in tones meant to inspire awe: 'Do you not know who I am? I am the *Ba.*' He didn't manage to complete the sentence boasting that he was the *Badshah* of Iran. He had just uttered the syllable *ba* when the curtain came crashing down on his head. The *Badshah* fainted and fell, feet up in the air and head on the ground. They had to carry him off stage!

Master Labhu Ram appeared on the stage again to apologize for the unfortunate happenings. People could come back and see the show again the next day with the same tickets, he assured the audience.

Every season, half a dozen or so singing ladies would come to Kashmir. The weather was wonderful and they knew that rich people from Bombay, Calcutta, Marwar, and Bihar came to Kashmir for the summer and this was a good opportunity for them to earn a lot of money. This also provided occasions for them to get acquainted with rich merchants, rajas, *nawabs* and *zamindars*. Since there was no other entertainment available, these visitors would either invite the singers over to sing, or visit them in their houseboats. These ladies thus got introduced to many rich men.

Each of these singers, at one time or another came to visit me. They usually ended up saying: 'You are like a daughter to me. Put in a word for us. I long to pay my respects to His Highness.' I too would be very eager to hear them sing for I enjoyed listening to new singers. I had no diversions other than the palace. At home or at the palace, I met the same fifteen or so people all the time. Every day was routine. This seemed like an interesting diversion. I always tried to get His Highness to invite these women to sing, irrespective of whether they were good or bad singers. Whenever I sat near His Highness' chair, I would start: 'I have heard that a very good singer is visiting.'

His immediate reaction would be, 'Have you visited her?'

'No, my musicians tell me so,' I would answer.

'What do they say?'

'Only that she sings very well.'

'If I invite them and they are no good, how do I punish their teachers?'

Meekly I would say, 'Do not expect them to bring down stars from the skies. They are already here so we may as well hear them.'

In jest he would retort, 'So you think I have nothing better to do than try out new singers?'

'Forget it. Let them be good or bad. You do not have to listen to them.' When I visited him the next day the ladies would be present. Such evenings were fun.

There was a Kashmiri woman called Gilli. When she was advanced in years, she bought two girls and moved to Lahore. She called one girl Nanhi and the other Munni. Whatever she had earned, she spent on ustads to teach the two girls music. When the girls grew up, she moved back to Kashmir. Munni barely knew how to sing but she had a very sweet face. Nanhi looked like an albino rat. Having lived in Lahore they spoke Urdu well. Soon they had their own houseboat and decided to stay permanently in Kashmir. His Highness invited them to sing.

One of His Highness' ADCs was Kishen Singh, who was a close relative of the Maharaja of Jodhpur. He and his two nephews were famous players of polo and this was why His Highness had employed them. Kishen Singh must have been nearly sixty. All three of them wore the most glorious, coloured Jodhpuri turbans. All the styles of the turbans of Rajputana are very beautiful. The tie and dye designs on the material used for them were painstakingly made. Jaipur, Jodhpur and Radhanpur were particularly famous for their turbans. Kishen Singh was a sober gentleman. His Highness made Munni sit near his chair.

Munni must have been barely eighteen then and Kishen Singh must have heard that she was from Kashmir. When she sat next to him, Kishen Singh blushed deeply. He started sweating. His two nephews were sitting in front of him, which made his plight worse. His Highness enjoyed the evening so much that he invited the girls back the next day. He hired Munni at three hundred rupees a month and explained her duties to her. These were to follow Kishen Singh everywhere. Munni followed the orders diligently. She appeared wherever he sat and began to sweet-talk him. Within a fortnight this game turned real. Kishen Singh fell madly in love with Munni. There he was—a sixty-year-old man in love with an eighteen-year-old girl! It was clear that love had driven him insane.

When I would sit next to His Highness, he would say, 'Watch, how adoringly the old man is looking at Munni. Look at the eyes he is making at her. Notice how his complexion is glowing.' His Highness always found something new to entertain himself. This was a new distraction. I too spent the evenings watching them—the way he spoke to her, the faces he made, how lovingly he looked at her. He was no longer self-conscious and did not care what others thought. With great love and pride he spoke to her openly. He took no account of anything else, including his two grown-up nephews who were embarrassed by their uncle's behaviour. The uncle, however, could not have cared less about what people said or thought. He seemed to have taken leave of his senses.

This entertainment continued for a couple of months but then His Highness got bored with this diversion. Munni knew nothing about singing. She was relieved of her royal employment after five or six months. Lord knows what happened to Kishen Singh's passion for her. Maybe he continued to meet her secretly.

The wives of all these three men from Jodhpur were with them. They dressed in a peshwaz, a *choli* and a three and a half yard *chunri-dupatta*. The chunris were dyed in beautiful colours. They were very tall, had good figures, and beautiful features. Kishen Singh's wife, even though she was fairly old, was very beautiful. The women of Rajputana are beautiful. She was also from a royal family. Each of these women was prettier than the other. But no one knows what happened to the love affair. Kishen Singh's nephews were witnesses to everything and they were very unhappy about their uncle's behaviour. It's possible they managed to bring him under control by applying some pressure.

36. The Maharaja of Alwar

One day we heard that the Maharaja of Alwar was about to arrive to spend the summer in Kashmir. Though the Maharaja paid for his own food, drink and other living expenses, it was the duty of the state to look after all his comforts. For instance the right spot was found for him next to the water in Chinar Bagh, for you could only anchor a houseboat near Chinar Bagh with official permission. If rajas and maharajas were planning to come for a visit, they would write to His Highness informing him that they wanted to come and spend some time in Kashmir. The state would write back and say that the Maharaja would be pleased to welcome them.

Eight or ten days before the guest was due to arrive, a troop of kitchen staff, orderlies, some soldiers and furnishers, would begin to make preparations. They would put up a few tents and awnings in front of the houseboats and spread out durries. Electricity was made available and the grounds swept till they were as clean as glass. The trees were decorated with large electric bulbs. Awnings were used to fence off the area around the houseboat. In Chinar Bagh there were many old trees on the trunks of which people had carved their names and dates. From these it appeared that some of these trees were a hundred to a hundred and fifty years old.

The visitor's entourage, who had arrived in advance, would rent houseboats according to their needs, seek out the ideal spot and get a permit. They would anchor their houseboats, clear the grounds and put up their own awnings. After all this was done, the maharaja was informed that he could now come. He would arrive and would be greeted by an appropriate gun salute. The Maharaja of Kashmir would send a few officers to welcome him.

The Maharaja of Alwar arrived in Kashmir and His Highness sent him a message of welcome. He also ordered that as long as the guest was in the kingdom, he should not lack any comfort. A few days later His Highness told me that it was the Maharaja of Alwar's birthday and that I would have to attend for about three hours in court dress as an honour to the visiting dignitary. The next day, fully dressed and bejewelled, I arrived at the Maharaja's at the appointed time. A member of His Highness' staff was with us. There were tents on the grounds and on the water were five or six large houseboats. Between the smaller tents surrounded by awnings, a huge and beautiful tent had been constructed. The staff member accompanying us asked, 'Where is she to be seated? Where will the durbar be held?' Someone pointed in one direction and my accompanists and I followed him. We entered a huge hall with beautiful walls. In the centre was a carpet and on it, in a circle, were thick cotton mattresses covered in white sheets. The Maharaja of Alwar was sitting in the middle surrounded by his courtiers. In front of the mattress there was a white sheet that looked like a dining-spread. On it were many small cups and saucers. In the cups were cardamom, saffron, aniseed, and a few kinds of scented betel nut, which left the mouth perfumed for days. In the saucers were almonds, pistachios, walnuts, and every other kind of dry fruit. In beautiful khaasdaans were paans made with different spices. Each paan had its own name and taste. The betel nut used in them had been cut in different shapes. Everything had been arranged with great elegance and care.

All the courtiers wore turbans tied in the *marwari* style in which the width of the muslin is reduced by twisting it till it looks like a rope. There were hundreds of folds in these turbans. They were not easy to manage and I think it took a whole day to wind one of them. Once wound, these turbans could be used for a few years. Every turban, including the Maharaja's, was similar except for the colours. Except for white and black, there were turbans in every colour—red, blue, yellow, maroon, crimson, and turquoise. There were rich and light shades, and not a single colour was missing. Each courtier wore a brocade achkan. In front of them, were placed these glistening cups and saucers. It was a wonderful sight. Even though our durbars were matchless, this one had its own charm.

The faces of all the courtiers were similar; dark and small-eyed, and no one had a moustache or a beard. At first sight they appeared like statues made of iron and dressed up. Watching them and the small utensils in front of them, I was reminded of my childhood. As a child I too would place small cups and plates in front of me. In one would be parched gram and in another parched rice; sugar in one and pakoris in another. We called this game 'Come let us play house-house.' Our cups and plates were made of clay, not silver, but at the Maharaja of Alwar's durbar, I felt that they were playing their version of 'house-house.'

A silver pot with a very thin spout was being passed around from which everyone took a sip. This small *lutiya* looked like the ones used to feed infants milk. The nozzle was so thin that milk would trickle down in drops so as not to choke the child. When the lutiya was empty, another full one would arrive. They continued to sip from it as long as the durbar lasted. When I asked what this was, they told me it was called *chuski*. This was a potent and expensive liquor which only maharajas and rajas could afford to get distilled for no ordinary man could afford the ingredients that went into it. It was said that two pegs of this could intoxicate as much as two bottles of whiskey. By sipping from the same spout a feeling of camaraderie was fostered and the Rajputs referred to it as brotherhood. This was a custom prevalent all over Rajputana. This liquor was made of pearls, and beaten silver foil. The stock was made from partridges, quails, wild fowl, Kashmiri starlings and grape juice, among other things. Many other similar expensive concoctions were made. If any other Maharaja came for a visit, at least two bottles of this were presented to him.

In the durbar of Maharaja Alwar everyone was giggling from the effects of this drink. After sipping the chuski, they would take something from the cups, put it into their mouths and pass the pitcher on. The Maharaja of Alwar was quite ordinary looking. No hair grew on his face, which was dark and full of wrinkles. Hs voice was thin and high-pitched and he spoke so softly that he was hardly audible. Because it was his birthday, he was dressed in a glittering costume with a string of big pearls around his neck. On his turban was a kalghi brooch studded with diamonds and he wore large rings on his fingers. But because of his dark, ugly face, all the fancy clothes and jewels looked awful.

After the chuski had been passed around for about half an hour, a well-dressed hijra entered the tent. He greeted the Maharaja with three salutes, bending at the waist and swinging his hand from the ground to his forehead. He went close to the Maharaja and whispered to him. The Maharaja nodded and the hijra left the tent. Within a couple of minutes a young, pleasant faced hijra, wearing a peshwaz robe and a choli blouse and with ghungroo bells tied to his ankles entered. His head was covered with a beautiful golden laced dupatta; he wore bangles on his arms, a necklace and long earrings. His long hair had been styled, using a beautiful paranda, into a plait. Following him, were not one, two or three but fourteen other hijras. They greeted the Maharaja one by one and the Maharaja acknowledged them with a smile. One carried a harmonium, another a dholak, and many had tambourines in their hands. Two of them began to sing. The courtiers began to sway to the music to show their appreciation, and this pleased the Maharaja even though their bizarre, totally tuneless voices sounded like split drums.

Suddenly two hijras leapt in front of the Maharaja and began wriggling their waists. The ones who were dancing returned to their places. The Maharaja and his courtiers were in splits at the dance of these two hijras. Fifteen minutes later, two more hijras jumped into the centre to replace the earlier couple. They wiggled their buttocks and sang, 'My Maharaja is a man of pearls.' Soon another pair appeared. Each of these pairs made their appearance with an arrogance that suggested to those already dancing that they should go and watch them, the new couple, and they might learn how to really dance and sing. Each pair would bellow louder than the last. They would drive themselves into a frenzy with all their gyrating and jumping around. However, the Maharaja and his courtiers were enjoying themselves, and loudly encouraging the performers.

I could not for the life of me understand what pleased them so much, what they were praising, and whether they were serious or only mocking. Perhaps everyone there was making a fool of the Maharaja who appeared the happiest of all. Each pair tried to out-wriggle the last one and all made sure that the songs they

sang were about the Maharaja. For instance, 'I am devoted to my
Maharaja for there is no other like him.'

A very amusing incident took place involving one couple. There
was one song which went something like this: 'my Maharaja is
very naughty, very beautiful, and his eyes brim with mischief.'
When the qualities of the Maharaja were extolled, his courtiers
would tease the Maharaja who would blush appropriately. His
small eyes would contract further and look like serpent eyes, and
with these he looked around as if he was really the mischievous,
wrist-twisting, teaser. He would either double up in embarrassment
or look proudly at the others.

I enjoyed all this so much that I still remember it vividly. It was
all totally new to me. Our Maharaja vehemently discouraged
sycophancy. Nor was he so idiotic as not to recognize it when he
came across it. What was happening here was totally contrary to
what I was used to. The people around the Maharaja had made
such a fool of him that he did not even realize how silly all this
seemed. It was like those tales from history where the king was
kept ignorant of the real world by selfish courtiers and was never
allowed to find out how his subjects cursed him. Instead, he was
reassured that he was blessed by all. The Maharaja of Alwar too
had become a ruler of that type. What is really surprising is that
he himself believed that he was a youthful dandy!

I had been waiting, presuming that I would be asked to sing
when the hijras were done. But far from being invited to sing, no
one even looked at me when the hijras had finished their
performance. Nor did anyone even offer us anything to eat or
drink. The *pir* of the hijras would often go up to the Maharaja and
while blessing him with his hands would whisper something to
him. The Maharaja would answer with a nod of his head. The
ustad would then instruct his hijra students and they would begin
to sing something. The member of the royal staff who had
accompanied us was waiting for us in the cars. I told him that the
hijras had begun to sing and dance again and no one had noticed
me or asked me to sing or for that matter, even spoken to me. I
asked him what I should do because there seemed no point in
sitting around. The Maharaja was so besotted with his hijras that
they had begun all over again. The royal staff member advised

me to wait a bit more. I returned and took my seat in the durbar again.

After each pair of hijras had finished their number, the maharaja would summon the hijra who played the tambourine and say something to him. The hijra would acknowledge this with a salaam and return to his place. Perhaps he was the music director for these hijras for he would proudly return and announce to no one is particular, 'Look, the Maharaja was really pleased with your style.' All the hijras would then bless him. I could hear all that they were saying because the hijra with the tambourine was sitting right next to me.

Next to the Maharaja was a large round silver tray on which were bags of red cloth. Each of them was said to have two or five hundred rupees in it. One pair of hijras put up such an act that the Maharaja writhed with emotion and immediately flung a bag at the tambourine player who accepted it by swinging his arms and touching his forehead seven times and showering a thousand blessings on the Maharaja. He placed his hands on his hip and wriggled his buttocks in such a way that the entire audience broke out in applause while they also rolled around in laughter. The security guards heard the din and began peeping into the tent.

Once again I spoke to the royal staff member who was with me: 'We have been sitting here for four hours. No one has paid any attention to us. When they do not seem to want us, why should we hang around?' He agreed with me. My accompanists and I walked out of the hall and got into the car. The driver had started the car when a host courtier appeared running. We all thought that having realized their mistake, he was coming to apologize and tell me that I could not leave till I had sung and that the Maharaja had summoned us back. The driver quickly turned off the engine. The courtier innocently asked, 'Were you sent here to sing?' I was fuming by now and before I knew it I had said, 'No, I was sent here to give him a massage.' I looked carefully to see if he was really innocent or if he was making fun of me.

We returned to His Highness at the palace. I mimicked all the hijras for him and we had a good laugh. I recited the words of the songs sung for him. I was so amused by my own retelling that I did not look at His Highness. When I had finished recounting my stories I looked at him. His eyes were red with fury. His eyes were very beautiful and you could always see red threads within them. This was the first time I saw him so angry. It seemed as if blood was about to drip from his eyes. I was scared and fell silent.

His Highness called his secretary and told him to invite the Maharaja of Alwar and write to say that his entire staff was included in the invitation to dinner. The secretary said that it would be done and left the palace.

His Highness turned to me, 'Were you asked to dine?' With my head I indicated a negative. He immediately ordered dinner for me and I got busy eating. As I was doing so I heard His Highness telling an ADC, 'He has not insulted her, he has insulted me. I had sent her as an honour to him, for her participation would have represented my participation in the happy occasion. If he did not want to reward her with anything, at least he could have behaved politely to her.' When I heard this, I realized I had been humiliated. I pulled a long face and came home after eating.

The next evening when I arrived, everyone was eagerly awaiting the Maharaja of Alwar. All the arrangements had been made in the grounds. The chief guest arrived at eight and His Highness embraced him with visible enthusiasm and made him sit with him. Drinks were served. I think His Highness had instructed his orderlies that the guest's glass should never be empty. A new drink was offered the moment the last one finished. Dinner arrangements had been made in another area. His Highness nursed one drink while the Maharaja of Alwar downed one after another. Around ten, everyone proceeded to the dining tables. At the table too, the Maharaja of Alwar continued to drink instead of eating. He was knocking down a glass every five minutes.

Playing the role of a polite host, initially His Highness too continued to hold on to his glass. But soon the guest had lost his senses. There was no point in saying anything to him any more. He was drinking at his own will while His Highness was not fond of liquor and rarely drank. When he did, he drank a peg or two. The courtiers of Alwar were such sycophants that none of them had the guts to try to stop their ruler from drinking so much. He stood at the dining table and continued to drink. He was unsteady on his feet and his speech was slurred. Yet, he always had a glass in his hand. His Highness ignored him completely, not even inviting him to sit down. The two grounds where the party was spread were about five to seven feet apart and I could see everything very clearly from where I was.

His Highness ordered me to sing. He sat down and made himself comfortable while he listened. Meanwhile, the Maharaja of Alwar was tumbling around from one courtier to another, all of whom had to help him stay on his feet. His Highness was observing all this with a scornful smile on his face and seemed pleased at what was happening. I think the Maharaja of Alwar no longer knew where he was or how he was behaving. His Highness returned from the dining table within an hour. The Maharaja of Alwar and his retinue hung around the liquor table, and finally the Maharaja of Alwar sat down at that table. His Highness was watching all this keenly.

The Maharaja of Alwar continued to drink till midnight when he finally got up from his chair. He tried to stay upright and then *dharaam*! He lay spreadeagled on the carpet. His Highness hurried to the spot and commiserated with his staff. As it is, the Maharaja was ugly, but when senseless he looked frightening – the pallor of death on his face, froth emerging from his wide-open mouth. His Highness told the Maharaja's staff, 'The Maharaja seems to need some rest.' The courtiers tried to lift him. Someone held an arm and someone else his legs and he was carried to the car as if he were a corpse.

The next day we heard that the Maharaja of Alwar had departed. He never came back to either Jammu or Kashmir at least as long as I was employed there.

37. Kashmiri Food

My family decided to hire a *donga* boat and go to Nishat Bagh to spend the day there. Every Sunday, hundreds of people hired dongas for a ride on the lake. We sent for a professional cook, who in Kashmir is called a *waza,* and he was instructed to cook as he would at weddings or special occasions. The waza arrived with a goat, spices and his cooking vessels. I still remember all the details. The goat had cost two or three rupees; the rent of the donga was five or six rupees. The spices cost another few rupees. The day's picnic must have cost us at most, twenty-five rupees.

The donga is where the boat-owner's family lived. When he rented it out, they arranged carpets and bolsters in the large room and the family occupied itself in steering the boat. In the small kitchen there were a few wood-burning hearths. The waza cooked while the donga crawled on the water. People would feel totally at home in it—they would play the gramophone or play cards. They lay down when they felt like it, or got the donga to stop at any particular spot they wished. The waza served tea every hour for Kashmiris are very fond of tea. They have a huge samovar of tea brewing all the time and they continuously pour out tea from it. The samovar was constantly replenished with tea leaves, sugar, milk and water, and the tea never ran out.

If the donga could be rented out on a Sunday, it was good for the donga-owners. They earned money and their families got to share a good meal. All they had to do in return was to row gently. The entire family, including the children, took turns at the oars. When it was time to eat, we were close to Nishat Bagh. The waza laid out the food. He carried a portable *chilamchi* to every one and poured water from an *aftaba* so that we could wash our hands where we sat. Then, he served rice on plates and placed them before us. He had already poured small quantities of various kinds of curries onto the rice. He then went around serving out more curry from a small pot. There must have been fifteen or twenty different curries that he served us in turn. The wonderful thing about the food was the distinct flavour of each curry. The waza used every part of the goat to make a stock. In fact he even cleaned the intestines and put them in. They made *tabak maas* out of the ribs, which smelt only of aniseed. It was so good that we could even eat the ribs of the animal. The waza put the ash from the hearths on to a big tray and then spread the ribs, coated with a little oil and let them cook slowly in the light heat. When ready, even the bones would be soft. They minced the offal and cooked it with fresh fenugreek leaves in a way that you did not suspect what you were eating. Mustard oil was the cooking medium they used.

When I first went to Kashmir and was invited to a wedding, I heard that the Kashmiris were not very particular about cleanliness. I had also seen a few things myself which confirmed this. For instance, when the women used large pestles to pound grain, they would first collect spit in their mouths, spit it on their palms, and rub it all over their hands so as to soften their hands to be able to hold the pestle better. Then, I noticed that in spite of living by the river, the women would not wash their hair for six months at a stretch. They tied their hair in such thin braids that it took them a whole day to do or undo the braids, hence their reluctance to wash their hair. They kept their hair covered with a cap or scarf so no one could tell what state the hair was in.

The Kashmiris were also very loving and hospitable. They ensured that no guest left without at least drinking tea if not having a full meal. On occasions when they insisted that I eat, I once ate offal thinking I was eating a dish made of fresh greens and enjoyed it very much only to find out later what I had actually eaten! Fish was cooked with dried ginger and chili water. Another gravy was made with curd and red pepper and there were meatballs cooked in milk and spices. The meat was pounded so hard that it became a paste with no fibres left, and this was then made into balls and cooked. Of all the dishes prepared in milk, these *goshtabas* were the only thing that I could not bring myself to eat. They were so large that they looked like the head of a newborn child. My family members who ate the goshtaba often told me how tasty it was.

During weddings, they would serve rice in large round trays and four people would sit across each other and eat from the same tray. The pile of rice would be so high that it would normally need ten people to go through it but they would serve rice three or four times again before the meal was over. Every few minutes a waza would bring around a pot of a different curry and pour it over the rice. At some weddings there were no less than twenty or twenty-five curries. The Kashmiris ate rice at every meal. They also ate *kulcha* bread with tea. The kulchas were so hard that they were not easy to break with the hand. They would eat four times as much as I did, but I did not see a single fat man or woman. Perhaps it was something in the water they drank or the air they breathed that the food left no trace of weight on them.

Our waza cooked very good food. He kept serving out hot curries with a spoon and I ate everything except the goshtaba. That is when I discovered that Kashmiri cuisine was the best in the world. I ate a lot that day. When we reached Nishat Bagh, I immediately climbed to the seventh terrace and sat down with my feet in the fountain pool. I could see all seven terraces from where I sat and I could hear the sound of the waterfalls. I could also see the row of fountains. The pleasant, cloudy weather, the beautiful colours of the flowers on the various terraces combined with the stupor induced by the huge, good meal that I had eaten, had a wonderful effect on me. I began to admire everything that God had created. I saw the towering trees that had been planted by the Mughals and wondered how the princesses must have walked here, dressed in their beautiful ghararas. I also wondered where Nur Jahan might have sat. I was in a state where all this appeared to be real—I could even imagine her maids running hither and thither!

Then I began to wonder about Jahangir and Nur Jahan's love-talk. Did Nur Jahan have to be respectful when she spoke to him? Or would she have said, 'Jahangir, listen to me!' Would Jahangir have said, 'Why do you not stay quiet sometimes? Do you have to go on with your stupid chatter all the time?' I laughed at these thoughts. If anyone had seen me then, they would have presumed that I had taken leave of my senses. Suddenly I heard a voice, 'Arrey yaar, do you have any money?' It seemed as if I had been hit on the head with a hammer. The world my imagination had created disappeared in a flash. In panic I looked around. It was the same group of boys from Jammu who were talking, once again without looking at me.

I walked back to where the family was. Those accursed boys had ruined my dream. We came back to the donga. The waza served us rose-tinted salty tea. We rowed some more on the river and then came home. It was time to go the palace so I got ready and left.

38. Polo in Lahore

On the second of September we returned to Jammu. I had now been employed for two or three years. His Highness would go every year to Lahore to play polo. Every year I had insisted he take me along. 'You are better off here,' he would always say, 'If you go there, you will be corrupted by the ways of the city.' That year I tried harder and even though he refused at first, he finally gave in.

We went from Jammu in a special train. The staff—from the kitchen staff to the orderlies—travelled on the same train. The others had reached Lahore a day earlier to keep things ready. I was excited about being in Lahore and found it difficult to pass the time till we got there. I kept imagining the good times that I was going to have. I would window-shop, buy things and wander about the whole day. I was bound to have fun because I was alone; no family member or accompanist was travelling with us. I was also thankful that I did not have to dress like an orderly as I had done when I went to Lachchigam, to be able to travel with His Highness.

In Lahore a car, its windows curtained, drove right up to the train. It drove us straight to the Mall Road residence of the Maharaja. The retinue of servants who had arrived a day earlier had seen to it that we felt like we were back in the palace at Jammu. We lacked nothing.

The day we arrived, His Highness stayed at home. He planned to play polo the next morning at seven. Early in the morning, he came and sat in the round room. I was up, but I stayed in bed. When I heard noises around the house, I came and sat in the room to remind him about why I had wanted to come to Lahore. I was hoping that he would say, 'Take so and so orderly and go and see the city.'

The Maharaja's special orderly, Lachchu, who was also in charge of his wardrobe, brought his high boots and breeches into the room. On seeing them, the Maharaja said, 'Not these, bring me the other pair.' Lachchu returned with another pair and the Maharaja again described the particular ones he wanted. The orderly returned a fourth time with yet another pair. The Maharaja threw these on the ground and again described the ones he wanted. Lachchu went and returned with another pair.

The Maharaja was furious by now. He threw the breeches at Lachchu's face, and Lachchu immediately left the room. Ten minutes later an ADC appeared and said, in tones full of apology and fear, 'By mistake, Lachchu has given those breeches for washing, and they're still wet. I have a matching pair that Your Highness had gifted me before we came to Lahore. Why do you not wear those?'

His Highness summoned Lachchu. He entered, trembling, his skin the colour of turmeric. Even his lips were quivering with fear. He stood there like a culprit, his hand folded and his eyes bent. His Highness said, 'Distribute all my breeches amongst yourselves.'

In a shaky voice, the surprised Lachchu managed to say, 'We already have enough; everything we have is because of you. We are able to eat and have clothes to wear only because of you. For the sake of God, please forgive me. Please wear another pair and the one you want will be ready by tomorrow. It is only a matter of one day, so please wear any other pair that pleases you for one day.'

'I have told you that I will not play polo today,' His Highness was curt, 'Empty my cupboards and distribute everything in them. Take a few pairs yourself and give the rest to the ADCs.'

Lachchu stood there silently, his head bent and hands folded. After a while he managed to say, 'I am at fault but please do not punish me in this way. I will happily accept any other punishment you may want to give, but please, for God's sake, do not ask me to do this. Wear anything else today and please go and play polo.'

His Highness heard him through. 'Listen to me carefully,' he said, 'I will not play polo and I will not wear any other pair of breeches. If you do not empty my cupboards in ten minutes, I will set everything in them on fire. Go, distribute the clothes.'

The orders had to be obeyed. The clothes were piled on a carpet. His Highness himself distributed all the clothes to various people including Lachchu. One ADC mustered enough courage to ask, 'But Your Highness, what will you wear?'

'I do not need anything,' His Highness answered.

'Polo,' was all the ADC managed to utter.

'Cancelled,' said His Highness.

Till now no one had offered me either tea or breakfast. It was almost ten and I was sitting watching all this in silent amazement. I was afraid people would blame me for these developments. Perhaps they were thinking, 'Her presence is really inauspicious. Because this green-footed, ill-omened one has come, even polo has been cancelled.'

His Highness looked at me and something occurred to him. 'Give her breakfast. She is starving unnecessarily.'

Breakfast arrived. I very much wanted to say, 'Your Highness, why do you not also eat something?' But I did not dare. I looked at him with a look that said, 'Please eat.' I thought of the incident that had occurred a few years ago. Then, lovingly he had said, 'If you do not eat, neither will I.' I wanted to beg him to eat. Unfortunately I could not say a word and looked on helplessly. Perhaps he understood the meaning of my look and how I felt. However all he said was, 'Come on, eat something. Don't make a fuss for nothing.'

Even though I did not feel up to it, I did eat something and then I went back to my room. I do not know whether he ate anything or not because I next saw him at lunch. I thought I would seek his permission to visit the city but that was out of the question in these circumstances. The Maharaja was so fond of playing polo that he usually counted the days till he could play next. Now all his plans had been cancelled in one morning. At lunch the air was solemn and there was total silence. No one talked and there were no jokes or laughter. Even Sahabzada Nur Muhammad, who always had something funny to say, was so silent that it seemed that he had just lost his mother. Everyone felt there was nothing left to be said nor did any one have the courage to talk about what had happened.

I might as well have stayed on in Jammu. I had begged and pleaded to come to Lahore and all that I got to do was to spend time in my room. We were supposed to stay in Lahore for a fortnight and I had looked forward to having some fun. Now it was decided that we would return in six days. A day before our departure His Highness ordered, 'Go and see the city.' The evening had already turned dark and the windowpanes of the car had curtains on them. It was so dark that I could barely see anything. Nor did I get out of the car. For two hours I peeped into the darkness through the curtains and my eyes began to ache even though I could not see one god-forsaken thing. This is how my trip to Lahore turned out to be.

On the way back the cars once again drew up to the royal train. We got into the train. I had seen nothing from the car and saw nothing from the train. There is a Punjabi saying, 'I returned in the same torn shoes that I left in' which now applied to me. I returned as if I had not been away. Damn those breeches.

Within a couple of days of returning to Jammu, His Highness was his usual self.

39. Mehr Nigar

Mehr Nigar was from Jammu but had lived in Lahore most of her life. She knew a bit about singing. She was well-spoken and passable to look at, but she knew how to dress. She moved to Jammu and visited me. 'You are like a daughter to me and I am very fond of you. I feel like spending all my time with you and I am glad I have this opportunity. When you were little I used to come to your house every day just to see you.' She said many other affectionate things.

Mother confirmed that Mehr Nigar used to live in Jammu. She was the daughter of an oil-vendor who had sold her to a woman. The woman who bought her was nothing much to speak of even when she was in her prime. She had bought this baby girl and had taught her to sing, given her a bit of education and then she took her to Lahore. The girl was smart and they earned a lot of money which helped to raise their status considerably. Mehr Nigar's mother had become old. Mehr built herself a large beautiful house in Jammu where she came to live, and we started meeting often.

That summer Mehr Nigar arrived in Kashmir while I was there. There too, she behaved with great affection. She also expressed, for the first time, her great desire to sing for His Highness. The woman was very sly. She had not said a word about this lifelong wish of hers in Jammu, but once in Kashmir, she egged me on. 'If you were to request him, there is no way His Highness will refuse to invite me to sing,' she insisted. She was one of those who had camped in Jammu during the coronation, hoping to get a chance to sing at one of the ceremonies. She must have tried her best but had not succeeded. She now concentrated all her efforts on me. One day, very lovingly, she asked, 'Will you do this for me?'

'Yes I will,' I assured her with great confidence. The very next day I praised her highly to His Highness.

He smiled, 'Whenever I have invited anyone on your recommendation, she has never been any good.'

'Have all those you have invited from all over always been good?' I retorted. 'Perhaps two out of ten have been worth listening to. This lady is in the city at the moment. If she is no good, you do not have to invite her ever again. After all, she is from Jammu and has learnt in Lahore. You should listen to her at least once.'

His Highness invited Mehr. She could sing a bit. She was also presentable and very good at conversation. His Highness employed her after hearing her sing. To tease me, he was very generous towards her. He would talk to her intimately and he tried to make it appear as though I was a fool and she was very intelligent, beautiful and smart. He always called me *bhatyaran* when she was around.

The lady herself changed dramatically. Whenever His Highness addressed me as bhatyaran, she would smile, look at me, and smirk. At these moments I felt like scratching her face. I had never minded His Highness addressing me as bhatyaran earlier for I detected affection in his use of the word. Now, I felt he was calling me by that name because she had bewitched him with her charm. I was very unhappy about all this and I did not feel like singing when he asked me to. Through all this, His Highness always had that special half-smile on his face.

One evening, His Highness had a couple of pegs of whiskey. He lay down on the carpet with a cushion under his head and closed his eyes as though he had passed out. The crafty woman moved close to him immediately and began to fan him with the hem of her sari. She then moistened a cloth and placed it on his forehead. After that, she again began to wave her sari-end frantically over his face. She wanted every one to know that she was very worried about His Highness and did not know what she could do for him. She began massaging his hands and feet and then she lifted his head to her shoulder and began running her fingers through his hair. I sat there and silently watched the entire sham. So did some of the ADCs.

She turned to me, 'Come on, massage His Highness' feet.'

'Are you not already doing that?' I asked. She then asked me for a glass of water that she sprinkled on his face. She carried on in this manner for ten to fifteen minutes. Soon His Highness looked fine.

It was summer. A part of the palace was built on water. In the moonlit night, the water of the Dal Lake shone like silver. His Highness sat for a little while and then went to bed. Mehr Nigar had barely been in his employment for a few weeks. In this short time she had tried to create the impression that she was very close to His Highness. She had even begun to speak to me disdainfully.

Four or five days later, something happened involving one of His Highness' ministers. He was tall, skinny and ugly and was one of those who have no hair growing on their faces. He was also rich and from a well established family. I will not name him for I do not want to hurt anyone. His grandchildren might be around and they might get upset. One evening, His Highness told this minister and this woman, 'The weather is very good. Why do you not go for a drive?' The two readily agreed. Then His Highness said to me, 'It is a moonlit night, why do you not go too?'

We all got into the official car. An ADC who was around forty years of age was sent with us. I had never seen His Highness order anyone out for a drive before. The minister must have been no less than fifty. He was a decent man and had probably not looked at another woman before. The driver headed towards Nishat Bagh. It was a straight road and when we were close to the garden, the minister asked the driver to stop. There was a large open space next to the road. We alighted from the car. 'I am going for a walk and will be back in a little while,' the minister said. Both of them walked off together.

The ADC told the driver to bring out one of the seats of the car. The driver did that and the ADC and I sat down on it to wait. The moonlight began to fade and soon it was pitch dark but the couple had not returned. We had had the seat placed next to the car and facing away from the road so that no one in a passing car would see me for if they had, they were bound to wonder what I was doing sitting on a deserted road at eleven-thirty at night. I had taken this precaution even though there were very few cars then and it was very unlikely that anyone would be on the road to Nishat Bagh at that time of night.

I was beginning to feel afraid in the dark. We all called out in turns and we honked the horn of the car, but there was no response. We began to get worried. We wondered if an animal had attacked them. The sound of the car horn echoed deep into the dark quiet night, but there was no response from them. The driver and the ADC became really alarmed. We discussed whether they could be walking for so long and whether it was possible for anyone to stroll in the dark for an hour and a half.

We were debating whether we should return and report their disappearance when suddenly they appeared, strolling as if nothing had happened. The three of us spoke simultaneously, 'Thank God you are safe. We were afraid you had met with an accident.'

Casually, they explained, 'We just happened to walk too far. That is why it took us so long.' The driver hurriedly fixed the seat back into the car and we returned to our homes.

The next day at the palace, after dinner, His Highness began to converse as usual. Mehr Nigar on the other hand, began looking at the ADC who had been with us, or me, and started to titter. Soon she was doubling up with laughter. I was completely confused for I did not know the cause of this mirth. The ADC too was taken aback. The poor chap began to worry for His Highness seemed very fond of Mehr Nigar. His Highness called Mehr Nigar over to sit beside him and they began what seemed a good-humoured conversation.

Mehr Nigar became even bolder. She began to laugh so hysterically that she had difficulty catching her breath. His Highness asked her fondly, 'Come on Mahi. Tell us what is so funny that makes you laugh so much.'

'It's a joyous occasion,' she announced, 'We should ask these two for a treat.'

The ADC, a father of five, turned pale and his throat must have gone dry. I was shaking with fury. I wanted to get my nails on to her face and also smash her head. This was the same woman whom I had helped get here by praising her falsely and insistently pleading her case! I had never had any problems with her, nor had I ever badmouthed her. Why was she doing this to me?

Whenever I tried to say anything, His Highness would snub me into silence. Instead, he went on encouraging her.

In the state that I was in, I neither listened to what she was saying, nor comprehended what I heard. Instead, my ears buzzed with anger and sorrow. I wanted to start weeping, loudly, right there. I also wanted to throw something at her that would make her disappear from the face of the earth.

The minister who had accompanied us on the trip sat through all this silently and took no part in the conversation. Occasionally, he looked at her and smiled. For about an hour and a half His Highness encouraged her to carry on. I do not recollect any of the other rubbish she uttered. I was crying through all of this.

His Highness summoned me to him and said to her, 'So you want to be treated to sweets?'

She nodded her head.

'Then it is you, and not she who should be buying sweets for everybody,' he said. 'You also have to tell me where you disappeared to when you stopped the car to take a walk. Did you lose your mind while walking for you even forgot how much time that walk of yours took. I had sent her,' he said referring to me, 'to observe everything so that I could tease her about you. However, she has not uttered a word. And you! You did not even give me a chance to tease her. Do you think I do not know her? I have known her since she was a child. I have left her alone and tested her on many occasions and never caught her doing any wrong. Nor is she as sly as you are. You did your best to turn me against her, did you not? Now it is your turn to explain what you were doing for that one and a half-hour. She, I know was sitting on the car seat with the ADC. My driver was with them. They called and they honked but that did not have any effect on you. You think I do not recognize the likes of you? I know you well and you are not only crafty but also a base person. This, I learnt within a week. Remember the time I lay down on the carpet with my eyes closed? I just wanted to lie down for a while. But you dramatically started fanning me. I lay still on purpose to see how far you would go. I often lie down on the carpet but when I heard you going "*Hai hai*, look what has happened to His Highness," I decided to keep quiet. You pretended to be solicitous and I wanted to test your pretense so I kept still. That is the day I began to dislike you for I found out how false you were. I saw you play-act and realized how dangerous you could be. You disappeared for two hours and got the others worried yet none of them sneaked on you. Let us not talk of the fun that you have had. Since you have come, all you have wanted to do is make me suspicious of her to get her into trouble. She is neither a trickster, a sneak nor a flatterer. She had pleaded your case and within a week you want to compete with her? You are a sinister woman. Did you not know that I keep myself informed of everything that goes on?'

The way His Highness insulted her pleased me no end. I beamed with delight and blessed His Highness in my heart. The minister, who had been a pawn in this game, sat through all of this silently. The trick His Highness had played had ruined everything for him. He was plain looking, weak-willed and very rich. He must have felt that there was little harm in seducing her. Lord knows what games were played in those two hours that they were together.

In fact I too got my share of His Highness' ire, 'Have you seen the result of your recommendations?' She was fired within a month of being employed and His Highness presented me with a ring that day.

40. My Desire to Speak English

Whenever His Highness spoke in English, I did not understand a word of what he was saying. I stared at his face like a fool and felt terrible about it. I decided to learn English. I found a teacher in Kashmir, bought an English primer, and began to study with him. I learnt the A B C. When it came to words, my teacher started: 'I, T, is yit, T,H,I,S, is dhish.' That was the way the Kashmiris pronounced these words. When I returned to Jammu, I found a new tutor who laughed uproariously when he heard my pronunciation. I persisted in learning, and began to understand a bit.

There used to be a weekly journal published from Delhi called *Riyasat*. It was owned and edited by Diwan Singh Maftun. He concerned himself mostly with the affairs of the princely kingdoms. Rajas and Nawabs often paid him off because they were afraid of him and the sensational stories his weekly carried. A few times he published stories about His Highness. Nothing in these stories could have caused the Maharaja any concern for the articles were a mixture of fact and fiction. Actually, they were nothing but rubbish. For instance Maftun wrote that on his birthday, His Highness had invited 'only one or two' singers from outside. Playing on the metaphor of Agha Hasan Kashmiri's play about a mythical ruler and fairies named after precious stones, *Inder Sabha*, he wrote, 'At nine at night, Raja Inder holds court. He sits on his throne and then the *Neelam* fairy and the *Pukhraj* fairy sing in turns. The Raja is so flattered that he flings the necklace that he is wearing at them.' Editions carrying stories like these were sent to His Highness.

Inviting singers from outside the kingdom was of no great significance for the Princes. Even the smallest of principalities employed at least a dozen singers and wrestlers for they considered the numbers they employed to be an indicator of their stature. Many generations of a family worked for the same royal family.

When singers became too old to perform they were assigned a pension.

Similarly, when wrestlers became too old, they turned into *khalifas* or masters and they began to teach others. Phrases like, 'so and so khalifa has produced six *patthas*,' were commonly used to refer to the students. If one of the students turned out to be a good wrestler, it added to the fame of the khalifa and both he and the student, were rewarded. The student's fame formed part of the teacher's glory.

In those days people would watch wrestling bouts the way they watch cricket today, and there was a lot of money to be made in wrestling. The princely kingdoms were the only patrons of the singers and the wrestlers. If a singer or a wrestler found employment at a court, he and his children and grandchildren could be assured of a life of comfort.

However, the Maharaja of Jammu employed neither male singers nor any wrestlers. I was the only singer he had employed, and that too when I was only nine. So, what disparaging things could Maftun have written about me? And to what effect? The wishes of the Maharajas were all that mattered. Every department of administration and every court of justice was run according to their commands. A court could find someone guilty of murder and order him to be hanged. The guilty could appeal to the Maharaja for mercy, and if the ruler wanted, he could pardon him. If his pleas did not move the Maharaja, the accused did not stand a chance.

The Viceroy, through the British Resident, dealt with all matters concerning these kingdoms. If any Maharaja exceeded his authority, the Resident had the power to remove the Maharaja from the throne. This happened in the case of the Maharaja of Indore who was dethroned for the murder of Seth Bawla.

41. Maharajas and Their Affairs

Mumtaz Bawlewali was from Amritsar. The Maharaja of Indore invited her to his court and she stayed on. Living there, she got in touch with one Seth Bawla and arranged the time and place for a rendezvous. She left the palace dressed as a scavenger, and then escaped to Bombay with the Seth. The Maharaja had fallen in love with her and was enraged at her betrayal. He was humiliated to be abandoned for a Seth. Furious, he assigned many men to watch over the couple and to keep track of Seth Bawla's movements. He even bought over the Seth's own servants to work as his informants.

The situation was very embarrassing for the Maharaja for he had given Mumtaz the status of a Maharani and for about four years she had been known as the Maharani of Indore. Now, she had run away disguised as a scavenger, and was living with another man! Humiliation and rage made him take leave of his senses. He kept himself informed of all their movements. One day the Seth and Mumtaz went for a drive to Malabar Hill. The Maharaja's men fired at them. The Seth, poor man, died on the spot. Mumtaz was grievously injured but she survived.

The Resident sent a report to the Viceroy. The Viceroy, as was usually done, accepted the Resident's report and the Maharaja was dethroned. Lord knows what happened in Indore after that. In other cases, if the heir was a child, the Resident appointed the *diwan* or a minister as the regent so that the affairs of the state could continue to be dealt with. The child was sent to England to study and the Resident became the *de facto* ruler of the kingdom.

In spite of these powers, the Resident usually did not interfere in the affairs of the state except in extraordinary circumstances. If there was a conflict between a maharaja and his maharani, or between a maharaja and his uncles or brothers the Resident would step in as arbiter. If succession was an issue and there was more than one claimant to the throne, it took years to decide the matter. Every ruler tried to keep the Resident happy.

Though the rulers were free to do what they wanted, their acts of benevolence were far more than their acts of barbarity. Stories of their acts of cruelty spread fast so the rulers did their best to keep their subjects happy and not give them reason to complain. Also, at that time, people did not have the discernment to notice small acts of injustice and thus did not complain about small matters. In fact the logic they used to explain their resignation was simple, 'After all Allah has made him a ruler. It is his good fortune that that he is now able to do what he wants. He is the *anndaata*—our provider.'

The sycophants and the selfish, who hung around the maharajas and nawabs, naturally accepted whatever they did. They also hid the truth from the ruler and kept him ignorant. They did their best to ensure that others did not get close to the rulers. Yet, the rulers were kind to these very people and gave them gifts and lands. Most of the rulers were generous, kind and good people. Their excesses were usually due to the sycophants who surrounded them.

The rulers employed not just singers and wrestlers but also other artistes. If an artiste in royal employment died, his family was given a pension and even if the sons were incompetent, they were appointed to royal service. Many poor and helpless families were thus looked after. Even artistes not in royal employment could petition some ruler when they grew old, 'I am now too old and no longer capable of performing. I am in dire straits and have no other source of income. Nor do I know any other way of earning a livelihood.' A generous ruler would immediately sanction a stipend for them. Many rulers were known particularly for their kindness and generosity and many needy people would go to them with their difficulties and none returned empty handed.

But then, getting to meet the rulers was almost an impossibility because the sycophants surrounding the rulers did not want others gaining access to their generosity. These were the people who encouraged the rulers towards over indulgence and addiction and made them into puppets that they could control. Otherwise the rulers could be very kind and generous.

If, as often happened, someone saved the life of the Maharaja, the ruler gratefully instructed his heirs that the descendants of his saviour too had rights over the kingdom. The rulers were also conscious of their role as protectors of the honour of the women of their kingdom. The ruler of a small kingdom called Radhanpur did not step out of his palace between eight and ten in the morning, and between four and six in the evening, because that was when the women went out to fetch water from the wells. The ruler of Radhanpur was also very fond of music and wrestling and had many singers and wrestlers in his employ.

Certainly some rajas and nawabs did use their power and their resources to indulge in excesses of all sorts and no one could stop them from doing so. If they were infatuated with a singer, they would employ her for a couple of years and spend all they wanted on her. For instance the heir to the kingdom of Hyderabad and his son both employed many singers. The Nizam of Hyderabad was a miser so they were always short of cash though they possessed priceless jewellery. The middlemen informed the women that they would earn nothing in cash but would be paid in jewellery and the women readily agreed for they were gifted jewellery worth lakhs of rupees. There are a couple of women who now live in Karachi who own a lot of the jewellery gifted to them in Hyderabad. The Maharaja of Jammu was different from the rest. His personal income was equal to that of the state and spending it was his personal prerogative. Some of the other Maharajas, however, were heavily in debt.

There were a few princely kingdoms like Nabha, Patiala, Jind and Rampur, which were associated with all sorts of ignominies. In fact, people referred to Rampur as Harampur, *haram* meaning illegal. Thousands of stories did the rounds about the state and someone even wrote a novel called *Harampur*. We often heard rumours that the Nawab had been replaced but none of them was true and he continued to rule. His subjects were unhappy. No woman was safe in the kingdom. It was difficult to believe some of the stories—for example, there was one that described how people were taken in boats on the pretext of a boat ride, and then pushed into the water in mid-river. Among these people were many unfortunate women whom the Nawab had used and then discarded when he got bored with them. They were eliminated and so were the traces and proof of the injustices done to them. People with attractive daughters left Rampur to settle elsewhere.

Another ruler who was infamous for his misdeeds was the Maharaja of Patiala. Whenever he heard of a pretty girl, he sent his men to the girl's house to persuade the parents to send their daughter to the Maharaja. If they did not agree they were made to suffer. False accusations were levelled at them, they were imprisoned and the Maharaja had his way with the girl. He would tempt the parents of others to offer their daughter to him with promises of land and prospects of an increase in their status for they would have the Maharaja as a son-in-law. I heard that many parents voluntarily stepped forward to offer their daughters and pleaded with the Maharaja to accept them: 'Your Honour, we have waited for this day for fifteen years. Our daughter has now grown up. If it please you, we will bring her over to be your bride.'

Pleased, the Maharaja would accept their offer and in return give them some piece of arid land. If the girl were pretty he would enjoy her for a couple of months and then send her into the harem that already had a few hundred women in it, and forget all about her. The girl would become a prisoner and rot in the palace forever.

No man was allowed to enter the harem. The girls acquired the title of Maharani and their numbers added to the glory of the Maharaja. The Maharaja was very conscious of his honour and wanted nothing to sully it. The women's relatives were not allowed to meet them nor could the women ever step out of the palace. Armed men guarded the first entrance to the harem, and women guarded the second one. The male guards were changed every week to ensure that no contact or relationships developed between them and the women. Once or twice a year, on ceremonial occasions, the Maharaja would visit the harem and all the Maharanis got to look at him at the same time. That was the extent of their contact with him.

Sometimes the Maharaja was informed: 'Your Honour, so and so's girl is very pretty and is worthy of you.' The girl's parents or relatives were summoned. If they dared to say that the girl was already promised to someone else, their fate was sealed. A few days later, neither the father nor the fiancée of the girl would be alive and the Maharaja would have his way with the girl.

One incident was particularly well-known. The Maharaja was going from Patiala to Chail. On the way he passed a wedding procession. The bridegroom was taking his bride home in a palanquin. The Maharaja was completely inebriated and decided that the bride should spend the night with him. He ordered the driver to stop the car and demanded that the girl to be brought to him. The Maharaja's men dragged the bride from the palanquin into his car. The members of the wedding party wailed at the injustice and the bridegroom pleaded in vain. The bridegroom was a resident of the kingdom and there was no one he could go to for redress for no one would listen to him, or help him, for fear of the Maharaja. He had to accept what had happened and keep quiet. The Maharaja always acted on impulse. He considered his subjects, and everything that was theirs, as his property. According to him it was the privilege of the subjects to satisfy all his wishes. The Maharaja was also famous for his drinking. Till today the large 'Patiala peg' is well-known.

There were many shopkeepers in Lahore, Delhi and Bombay whom the Maharaja drove to bankruptcy. When Maharajas went to a shop, they usually emptied the establishment of half its stock. At sari shops they would buy dozens of saris. If they bought cloth, it was by the bale for to buy cloth by the yard would be beneath their dignity. But shopkeepers would also pray for a royal visit for that could sometimes change their fortunes. Many shopkeepers, for example, displayed the certificates given by the maharajas not just to impress their regular clientele but also other royalty. Every city had a few choice shops. These would either be shops selling jewellery or cloth. At the jewellery shops the maharajas bought jewellery studded with precious stones and also utensils of gold and silver. Traders also visited the kingdoms on their own initiative where they were paid the prices that they cited. Jewellers carried precious stones, which were beyond the means of ordinary people, to the royal courts. There they presented the gems and jewellery as something that was only worthy of being owned by royalty. If the maharajas liked them, they paid for them on the spot. The shopkeepers trusted the royal clients to the extent that if the princes liked something it was considered the same as having money in the bank. Of course they quoted double the price for everything they sold.

The Maharaja of Patiala was an extravagant shopper. When he had chosen the goods he liked, the shopkeepers would pack the merchandise and hand it over. However, often the bills were not cleared. The reminders they sent were ignored. The shopkeepers panicked and tried to see if they could personally recover their dues. They went to the kingdom and tried to see the Maharaja but they were never successful. They would visit Patiala a few times but always return empty-handed. In fact these trips would add to their losses, for apart from the expenditure incurred, they also had to leave their shops unattended for a fortnight or so while they were being given the runaround in Patiala. In their absence, their employees would cheat them. Finally they would give up and accept their fate.

And yet, the Maharaja of Patiala could also be generous and there were people who sang his praises all their lives, though his tyranny ruined many others. The behaviour of the rulers of Patiala and 'Harampur' was very similar.

Diwan Singh Maftun, the editor of *Riyasat*, never found much that he could use to write about our state. He tried to use satire but the Maharaja was not troubled by anything he wrote. He wrote about me too; that I was influencing the Maharaja against the Hindus; that this was the reason that he had appointed Muslims on his staff. The truth was that I had no say in such matters and there was no substance in what was written. The Maharaja told me not to bother about such allegations. As far as I knew, his Highness was a softhearted gentleman and very considerate of others. When angry he would hurt himself rather than others. He was also very naive. Sometimes he did not comprehend situations that were clear even to me.

For instance, he was never interested in tales of the supernatural, witches and ghosts. As I've said earlier, he preferred to sleep out in the open in the summer. Often he sat on his bed and talked to us for hours. Sometimes when he was wide-awake, Sahabzada Nur Muhammad would begin telling ghost stories—of haunted houses, of jungles where she-devils could be heard. The

Maharaja would begin to yawn, and would soon say, 'I think it is time to go to sleep.' The courtiers would exchange smiles and leave. I saw through the ploy but the Maharaja did not.

Sometimes His Highness told us stories about his own life, and these were always interesting. Here is one:

'In the reign of Maharaja Pratap Singh, I once went to call on my father's elder brother, whom I addressed as *Tau*. He had still not emerged from his chambers. It was summer and there was an orderly standing with a pitcher of water. I was very thirsty and asked for some. Five minutes passed and none was offered. I thought the man had not heard me so I raised my voice a little and said, "Give me some water."

"He is coming," the water carrier said.

"Who?" I asked.

"The water server," the carrier answered.

I was thirsty and now very angry. I summoned him and asked, "Can you not serve me water?"

He repeated, "The water server has gone somewhere. He will be back soon."

Hearing this I was even more irritated. "You have the water and there is the glass. Why can you not serve me water?"

The man explained, "My job is to hold the water-pitcher. Serving the water is another man's job."

That is when I decided that if God ever elevated me to the throne, this system would be the first that I would change.'

42. Rani Billauran

One evening, His Highness seemed to be sad. He had had a couple of pegs of whiskey with Khusrau Jung who was the only one, apart from me, who was present. He began telling us the sad story of Rani Billauran, his first wife whom he had not been able to forget.

'Billauran, my first wife, was a village girl. She was so pretty that I yet have to see someone as beautiful as her. She was so fair and her skin so clear that you could see water trickle down her throat. She looked as if she was made of glass, hence her name Billauran, which means glass.

'We loved each other. When she conceived, my *Tau ji*, the Maharaja Pratap Singh was thrilled. He donated a lot of money, a large number of hungry people were fed for a several of days and many bales of cloth were distributed. When Maharanis became pregnant, each month of their pregnancy was celebrated. Rani Billauran's first month too was celebrated with great fervour.

'My uncle's wife was from the *chadak* caste and therefore was known as Maharani Chadak. She hated me and if she had been able to have her way, she would have had me killed. She was obsessed with ensuring that I did not succeed her husband to the throne and she constantly tried to poison his mind against me. Every day she thought of new schemes by which she could ensure that I never sat on the throne. She had adopted the son of the Raja of Poonch, which was a kingdom subordinate to the kingdom of Jammu. Tau ji was aware of these plans of hers but she had such control over him that he was helpless and could not confront her. He did not want to displease her at any cost. If she decided that it was day, it was day for him too and if she decided that night had fallen, he agreed that indeed it was night.

'Tau ji was addicted to opium. He was a simple man and lived the life of a mendicant. Chadak watched over him as though he was a four-year-old child. She never left him alone for a minute and she ensured that we never spent even ten minutes alone. Thus my uncle and I could never have a conversation in private. The Maharaja was afraid of her and he was well aware that she was a deadly enemy of mine. He knew that she did not want me to succeed him, but he kept silent over the matter. She tried very hard to get him to publicly favour her adopted son, but he did not say a word. Chadak also had anonymous letters written against me to the Diwan.

'Maharanis were usually never allowed to speak to men but Maharani Chadak was in such control that she sat behind a screen and issued orders. She had bought over all the Maharaja's servants to her side. Since Tau ji listened to everything she said, they all tried their best to keep her pleased. Anyone she considered smart, she immediately won over with favours. She prepared the annual report that was sent to the Resident and was ready to do anything to stop me from succeeding her husband. She sent frequent gifts to the Resident so that he would help her in getting her adopted son accepted as the heir. Every one around the Maharaja was a part of her scheme and she spent thousands of rupees on it.

'The Maharaja loved me dearly and was kept unaware of her schemes. He was keen that I succeed him for after all, we had the same blood in our veins. Chadak mounted endless pressure on him to accept her adopted son as his successor but he did not give in. The Maharani had therefore been left with no other option but to scheme with the employees of the Maharaja.

'Whenever I went to see Tau ji I was told that he was resting. If I tried approaching him through the Maharani, she would tell a dozen lies to stop me from seeing him. She would ask me to wait, saying she had sent word to my uncle. Half an hour later she would return to tell me that Tau ji had said that he was too busy to see me. This game was repeated endlessly in the hope that I would get annoyed with Tau ji. On the other hand she tried to convince Tau ji of my lack of affection because I never came to see him.

'She wished me dead from the bottom of her heart and was capable of the vilest of tricks. With me dead, the obstacle to her

desires would be removed and she would have her way. The
Minister Sobha Singh, a well wisher of mine, constantly warned
me not to eat anything, which was offered by her. Actually, he
went further and asked me to have a taster taste my food even
when I ate at my own palace. I therefore tried to stay away from
the state as much as I could.

'Rani Billauran naturally could not accompany me. The
traditions of those days would not allow this. My uncle was a die-
hard traditionalist and Billauran accompanying me was impossible
while he was alive. Chadak knew how much I loved Billauran.
Till today I believe that God had created Rani Billauran especially
for me. I have liked no one else since her and am unlikely to ever
do so in future.

'The only attraction that kept me in Jammu was my wife for
there was nothing but fear and tension around me. I had to watch
what I ate or drank and worry about being safe when I slept. I
was tired of a life where I had to treat each employee of mine
with suspicion. Sometimes I felt like giving up everything and
becoming a mendicant.

'Even in this state of living, constantly surrounded by enemies,
life seemed bright because of Billauran. I felt secure with her.
When her pregnancy was approaching its end. Chadak managed
to manipulate Tau ji into playing a part in one of her most devious
schemes. She convinced him that Billauran and I should not be
allowed to meet till she had given birth. God, she had argued,
had been very merciful and no risks should be taken. Tau ji, a
simple man, fell for her argument. He called me and instructed
me severely. "You are a fool. I have been praying forever for this
occasion and your aunt is so delighted. She is concerned and does
not want anything to go wrong."

'Since it was the Maharani who actually ruled, Billauran and I
were forbidden to meet each other. I tried to meet her secretly
but Chadak was in such command that I failed even to bribe the
servants. Chadak knew that Billauran was my weakness. She
mounted such an efficient security that no servant could have
helped me even if he was ready to do so. She had made it clear to
every servant that if any of her orders were not followed they

would rot in prison for the rest of their lives. She fully used tradition to harass me.

'She maintained the immaculate façade of her concern for Billauran and the unborn child. The monthly ritual celebrations were duly held. She distributed charity to ensure the well-being of the unborn child but in secret she tortured me. If I was ever included in any of the rituals, she chaperoned Billauran so efficiently that we could not even talk and I left these occasions having not even spoken a word to my wife. Chadak convincingly displayed her delight at the prospect of childbirth. She told every one that she was convinced her home was going to be blessed with a son who was going to be as attractive as the full moon and she would ensure that nothing went wrong before his birth. Her implication was clear: that, by keeping me away from the mother, she was only ensuring the safety of my son. Often I wished I could take Billauran and escape from Jammu. Yet, I was helpless because there was nothing I could do. I could not complain to Tau ji because she had already convinced him that she was doing everything only to protect my unborn son.

'I was helpless and miserable. Fed up, I decided to go away to England. I wanted Billauran to be with me but since that was denied to me, I was going crazy in this situation and felt that there was no point in staying in Jammu.

'I requested that I be allowed to meet Billauran before I left. I went to the palace and Billauran appeared accompanied by Chadak who did not leave us alone for a moment. Instead, it was she who did all the talking. She told me about how I would come back to find a beautiful son awaiting me.

'Maharaja Pratap Singh was childless. There always had been a shortage of sons in the royal family. Pratap Singh was therefore eagerly awaiting the birth of my son and was thrilled that the nephew who was going to succeed him to the throne was about to have a child. Chadak, as she watched his delighted anticipation burnt within with fury. For her, this must have been akin to rolling on burning coal and being slowly reduced to cinders.

'I am such an unlucky man that I did not even get another glimpse of Billauran. Chadak poisoned her during labour and she and the child died. The child was a boy.'

His Highness' eyes were full of tears. After a few minutes of silence, he began again.

'I was married a second time but I was not attracted to my new wife. We spoke different languages. Whenever I went to her, all she said, in her language, was, "May I massage your head?" The new queen was the daughter of the Maharaja of Dharamkot. I have already mentioned how her father sent and paid for her entire staff including a doctor.'

By this time I had been employed at the court for three or four years and had never asked the Maharaja for a thing. When I liked something I avoided taking a good look at it. I wanted to impress His Highness that I was used to, and familiar with beautiful things. I did not want to give the impression that I was poor or that I was greedy. I refrained from praising anything for fear of it being mistaken for a hint.

One day an orderly offered paans in a large silver box with three layers, which when opened, looked like a flower. In the top section there were small compartments to keep cardamoms, betel nuts and other condiments for the paan. Below this was a section which contained the *catechu* and slaked lime. At the bottom was the space to keep the paan leaves.

I loved the box and wished that His Highness would immediately gift it to me. I do not know what attracted me so much to that box but I began of thinking of ways to acquire a box like that. I wanted it and yet did not want to ask for it. I thought I was being very clever when I said, 'Your Highness, where did you get this box made?'

His answer sounded like a severe reprimand. 'Do you think I bother to keep myself informed about such things?'

I was embarrassed but still mustered enough courage to carry on, 'Can you loan it to me for a week or so that I can get it copied?'

'Never,' he said curtly.

I fell silent for I was cursing myself for having brought this humiliation upon myself. Why had I let myself get insulted? What had I gained from this humiliation? I wanted to leave the room and cry. In those days silver cost two annas a tola and the box would, at most, have cost two or three hundred rupees. I was in tears and sat there silently. After a while His Highness called me to him and I went and stood near him.

'Sit down,' he said.

'I was very comfortable where I was sitting,' I answered and without waiting for his response, returned to where I had been seated. I thought of all that he had gifted me on his own. Now, when I liked something, he was not even ready to loan it to me. After about ten or fifteen minutes, His Highness left to go to bed. I returned home and on the way I continued to reproach myself for my own humiliation.

The sun was yet to rise the next morning when there was loud knocking at the door. The whole household was asleep. When the door was unlocked, Lachchu, His Highness' special orderly was standing there. 'Please call Malka,' he said. I went to the door. He handed me a brocade bag. When I opened it I found the silver box in it. Lachchu explained the reason why he was there at this time of the morning. His Highness, before he went to bed, had ordered that the khaasdaan be delivered to me before I woke up the next morning.

I was so pleased that I wanted to cry. Oh, the horrible things I had thought about him! I began to love him twice as much as I already did. Yet, when I went to the palace the next day, I was unable to say a word. I did not even say a 'thank you,' to him when I wanted to say, 'Your Highness, you are wonderful. I love you very much.' Instead, I did not say a word.

In the days when gold cost only eighteen rupees for a tola there was a time when there were not even two tolas of gold in the house. Nor was there cash, silver utensils nor such expensive clothes. But now, I owned so much, either because of the grace of Allah, or His Highness' generosity. Allah had given His Highness the gift of magnanimity and he never thought of me as ungrateful. When someone gives a gift, the least he expects is a token of thanks in return. If I were in his place, after the first gift, I would not have bothered to gift anything else.

I was never afraid of him. Quite the contrary; but many of my friends who were a part of his staff would advise me to fear him more. 'It's neither wise to be in front or right behind a horse,' they would tell me. I thought of him as a friend, even a girl friend. I knew how isolated he felt and I knew of the selfishness of those who surrounded him. Not one of them really cared for him.

All His Highness' close advisers—the minister Sobha Singh, Janak Singh and Thakur Singh—had been stressing the need for an heir to the kingdom. Finally, His Highness agreed to marry again. The astrologers however declared there would only be an heir from his fifth marriage. The mother of the child would also be from the chadak caste. His Highness had only been married twice. He therefore had to first wed a tree, and then a sword, before he was ready to marry his fifth wife, a woman. Because of the condition that his wife had to be from the chadak caste, he had delayed the matter for over a year. Finally a date was fixed.

The wedding was to be held at the Chasm i-shahi. Thousands of tents were put up and arrangements were made for guests to live there for a week. Finally, after wedding a tree and sword, he married a girl chosen by his well wishers. I heard that she was the daughter of a minor revenue official of some village. She was uneducated and soon it was known that she was pregnant. It had been widely believed that His Highness was unable to sire children. Mercifully, God made sure that his wife became pregnant so soon after the wedding and proved everyone wrong.

The Maharaja did not keep his new wife in purdah. Whenever he called me to sing, his wife would sit besides him. A girl, older than the Maharani, and perhaps from the same village, worked as her secretary. The Maharani was a presentable, simple woman who did not even know how to sustain a conversation. She was good natured, innocent, unaware of most things and understood little of what was going on. One evening, when I finished singing, she called me to her. In Dogri she asked, 'Are you well now?'

'Absolutely,' I answered.

The next day she asked again, 'Hope you are keeping well now?'

She only spoke Dogri, simply and politely. She had a pleasant voice and was still untouched by influences from outside. I wished that we could talk and that I get to hear her speak unadulterated Dogri.

A couple of months later the royal couple left for England. News arrived from there that they had had a son who had been named Karan Singh. His Highness returned with his wife and son. The senior employee of the state and the large landowners went to welcome him. His Highness entered Jammu riding an elephant.

The entire kingdom celebrated. People sang and danced. Many singers were invited from all over. Alms and sweets were distributed. The rejoicing lasted a fortnight. The incomes of the landowners were raised.

The time in England had changed His Highness completely. Before they left he would always look for excuses to talk to the Maharani. She invariably sat next to him when I sang. His Highness constantly sent her messages through his orderlies and they would carry back the Maharani's response. This went on even when performances were on.

All this had changed when he returned. She never came again to listen to music nor did the Maharaja invite her. One day when I had finished singing, an orderly came and told me that she wanted to see me. The Maharani was sitting in the verandah. In her beautiful voice she asked, 'Are you well now?' She had repeated the query from our very first meeting! It was then that I realized that that was her way of inquiring how I was. Till now I had mistakenly believed that she had heard some false rumours that I was ill.

I sat with her for about twenty minutes. She kept smiling pleasantly. She was well made-up and her long nails were beautifully painted. She wore huge diamond earrings; four diamond studded bangles on each arm and a huge ring. Made up, she looked very beautiful. But there were no signs of her earlier innocent charm and simplicity. She too, had changed completely. An orderly announced that dinner was served. I wished her and took my leave. After that I never saw her again nor did I ever hear that His Highness was going to visit her. Nor were there any more public messages exchanged between them. Before going to England, he would often interrupt a performance and send an orderly to inform her that he was on his way. Now, he was the person he used to be before his marriage. He would sit in the courtroom and chat to the ADCs till it was time to sleep.

His Highness was intelligent and sensitive. He put on no pretenses and was no politician. If he had been one he would not, so soon after his coronation, have stood while the Muslims said their Eid prayers. He could easily have found other ways of displaying that he made no distinction between Hindus and Muslims. The Rajputs turned against him. They spread countless false stories about him. Perhaps his mistake was that he was not very careful about the political fallout of his actions.

Then there were people like Ghulam Abbas who had now begun agitating. Changes were taking place in the kingdom. Every Muslim now began to demand his rights. Processions were being held every day in Jammu. The welfare of the Muslims was close to His Highness' heart. He summoned a minister. 'Go to Jammu and fix a day for the representatives of the people to come to Kashmir. Assure them that I will meet them and that I will be completely fair to them. Every legitimate demand of theirs will be accepted.' We were at the Dal Lake residence at that time. I was witness to him instructing a minister to fix a date with the leaders of the agitators. The minister returned with a date and he had also told the leaders of the Muslims to bring their demands in writing. They had been assured that His Highness would be happy to meet them.

43. Hindu Muslim Riots

I do not remember the exact date, but I do remember that it was just before the day fixed for the meeting between His Highness and the Muslim agitators that trouble began. As usual, I was walking along the embankment between Gagribal and Ameeran Kadal. Suddenly, I saw a Kashmiri pundit, bleeding from his head, running for his life, followed by a Kashmiri Muslim with a stick in his hands. I could not figure out what was happening, and I had no idea that a Hindu-Muslim riot had begun. I had presumed that this was just another fight.

I screamed at the sight of the blood flowing from the injured pundit's head. I called out to Nana to save him for it seemed he was about to be killed. Nana, who was tall and strong, stepped forward and held on to the pursuer giving the pundit a chance to escape. He told the man he had just stopped: 'Have you gone mad? Drop that stick. What if you had killed him?'

The man replied, 'Sir, you have made a great mistake. I wanted to kill him because he was a Hindu, a pig, and a bloodsucker. We have to get rid of these Hindus, these *kafirs*.'

It was soon clear that a religious riot had begun. Chaudhary Ghulam Abbas had instigated the riot. If His Highness had been informed of the genuine grievances of the people, all suspicions and grievances would have been dealt with. However, if the Muslims felt reassured, Ghulam Abbas' dreams of leadership would end. He had always wanted to be a political leader, an ambition which once acquired, is difficult to get rid of. For him, a political leader was one who was willing to lie and indulge in all sorts of deceits for his own benefit.

For political leadership he had to contend with Sheikh Abdullah who was greatly loved by the people of Kashmir at the time. Ghulam Abbas thought he could achieve the same status, but much more quickly. He had already failed as a lawyer and if he failed as a politician, there would be nothing left for him to do. Inciting communal riots between Muslims and Hindus, just before the Muslims were to meet the Maharaja, was a part of his politics.

During riots, people behave like sheep. Once the fighting begins, everyone is ready to kill or die. I still do not know how Ghulam Abbas was able to spread the rumour that the Maharaja was unwilling to accept the demands of the Muslims. I wish the minister concerned had summoned all the Muslims and spoken to them publicly instead of only speaking to their leaders. This is what His Highness had wanted him to do. No one except a few people knew the truth and it must have been easy to encourage a feeling of resentment against the Hindus in both Jammu and Kashmir.

His Highness was deeply shocked and hurt by what, to him, appeared to be a betrayal on the part of the Muslims. He kept repeating the same things, 'I had sent word that I would accept their genuine demands and that justice would be done. Why then did they break their word? Were their interests only confined to inciting violence? I have always wished the best for them and this is the result I get! I have never differentiated between the Hindus and the Muslims for the two communities are like my two eyes. I wanted to show them what justice meant. What a pity that they have destroyed all my plans!'

At the court everyone discussed the matter for a few days. The entire staff would listen to His Highness in silence. Khusrau Jung and all the other Muslim ADCs kept their eyes lowered and kept nodding their heads. They all knew very well that His Highness had decided to accept all the demands of the Muslims and that by doing this he had already greatly displeased many of the Hindus.

His Highness was so distracted that he even stopped sending for me every day. Often four or five days passed before I saw him. When I went there, I used to find an all-pervasive silence around him. There was no laughter and no light-heartedness. His Highness looked sad and stayed silent. He even stopped discussing the situation in any detail. He withdrew into himself as though all joy had vanished from his life. His eyes betrayed his deep sorrow and he was constantly lost in thought. Obviously, he was unprepared for a situation such as this. He gave the impression that all his hopes were now buried within his heart.

He was not particularly attached to the Maharani. If he had a companion to share his sorrows with, life might have been more bearable. The Maharani of Dharamkot too, had got upset and had gone home to her father. There was absolutely no question of His Highness confiding his private feelings to those whom he employed. The Nawab of Palanpur was a close friend and he came to meet His Highness after he heard of the recent developments. Yet it seemed as if His Highness had lost all hope.

My visits to the palace became infrequent. The cooking sessions, which were organized a couple of times a week, were abandoned. These used to be a lot of fun because not only did His Highness participate in the cooking but because it was an occasion for much laughter, frivolity and discussion. His world seemed to have changed. He stopped trusting any one and became totally isolated. He even stopped going out.

Those with whom he had earlier talked and joked freely, were now men before whom he was terribly embarrassed. For instance, in the past there used to be jokes about the cowardice, miserliness or shrewdness of a moneylender. The purpose had never been to laugh at the Hindus for he made no difference between the two communities. Amongst the generals and colonels of his own caste, he had talked of the honesty, simplicity and bravery of the Muslims. He had also told them what he thought about untouchability: 'I belong to everybody. Whether they be Hindu or Muslim, they are all my subjects,' he used to say. 'The Muslims have the same claim to the kingdom as the Hindus.' Many of those to whom he had said these things now said, 'Look, those you wanted to elevate are trying to bring you down. These people have never been a part of us and never will be. The correct way to treat them was the way our forefathers used to treat them. We are glad that they themselves have made you realize your mistake. Never trust them again, for they are nothing but scorpions who will sting you the moment they get a chance.'

His Highness had to listen this kind of thing all the time and soon he grew irritable. The silence at the court continued to grow deeper. I was only concerned about His Highness and was ready every evening to go the palace where there might be singing and some conversation. Sahabzada Nur Muhammad, never one to stay silent for long, was now completely quiet. The ADCs, be they Hindus or Muslims were now also mute. The atmosphere had changed so radically that even among the royal staff, there were now two camps. All the camaraderie and bonhomie now turned into suspicion.

I was deeply affected by all this and I now felt uneasy when I went to the palace. I wondered if His Highness enjoyed my singing any more or whether he only asked me to sing out of politeness, or to show others that nothing had changed.

I found I did not care for anything any longer. I was convinced that he no longer enjoyed listening to me sing. He continued to invite me to sit near him but he barely spoke. He seemed indifferent to everything. He might invite a minister or a landlord and have a drink with them, but he no longer indulged in light-hearted conversation. I have never seen anyone change as drastically as he did. At meal times he ate with little enthusiasm. Watching him in this frame of mind troubled me deeply. Often I felt like telling him: 'Your Highness, please take yourself in hand or you will fall ill.' However, what would the point of that have been? Who was I to offer him any advice?

Even in that state of mind he never once spoke to me in anger. In fact, he would always say a few kind words to me as if to stress that nothing had changed even though everything about him showed how much he had changed. All life seemed to have drained out of the Muslim staff and they behaved as if they were guilty even though they were in no way responsible for what had happened.

The atmosphere at the court was suffocating and I did not want to stay there a minute longer than necessary. His Highness had been the life of the court. Once he was so depressed, how could his staff have been happy? His Highness had nothing to blame himself for. The most ordinary people feel depressed when betrayed by people they love. Allah had blessed His Highness with everything—honour, wealth, and a kingdom. His ambition had been to do things that he would be remembered for, policies that would be held up as examples for other rulers.

However, after the recent developments, it seemed that he felt that he no longer had a role to play in the affairs of the kingdom. This was such a major disappointment that that he lost interest in life itself. All his dreams were destroyed in a day.

Riyasat and another publication called *Ranbir*, which was published from Jammu, were full of unconfirmed news reports about the court. *Riyasat* invented a story of how I had tried to poison the Maharaja. According to the weekly, the Maharaja had forgiven me for trying to assassinate him only because he had been my patron since I was a child. These papers carried such stories all the time. Many people in Jammu believed them and would ask me why I had tried to do such a thing. The newspapers were so relentless in spreading this calumny that many people came to believe that I had tried to kill the Maharaja and was in prison.

One evening when I went to sing at the palace, I took a copy of one these reports with me and read the news story out to His Highness. His response was, 'First he only barked like a mad dog. Now he has truly gone insane.' The things they printed about me hurt me but watching the state His Highness was in, worried me more. Gradually, matters improved a bit, but relations between the staff continued to be strained.

I now began to worry about myself. I would be an easy victim of someone's intrigue. What if I was set up by one of those envious of me? What if they planted poison on me and then reported it? What would happen to me if this happened? What if I was imprisoned? I spoke to mother and Nana about leaving royal employment. At first mother and Nana were against the idea of me withdrawing from the court, but soon they too began to understand my fears.

However, my courage failed me regularly and stopped me from taking that step. Every time His Highness summoned me to the palace, I would decide that this would be the time I would tell him of my decision. Yet, every time I set eyes on him, I would change my mind. I felt that he would feel that even I was abandoning him the way others had done. I was well aware that my leaving would make no difference to him, for I knew I mattered for nothing in the scheme of things. I often wondered if all that was happening around me was for real.

Things carried on as they were for some more time. In September we all returned to Jammu. After his return, His Highness did not send for me for six weeks. Eventually when I did go to the palace I was hoping that the atmosphere would have changed. I was disappointed. I found that the same silence and the same foreboding lingered in Jammu too.

As usual dinner was served and then with a gesture he summoned me and asked me to sing a pahari. I began to sing. The words of the pahari were 'Who are the ones who will have to leave, which are the ones who will stay with us.' Lord knows what was going on in my mind when I chose to sing that particular pahari. Perhaps it was the idea of leaving someone who had given me so much love, respect and wealth. I sang myself into a state where I began to cry. His Highness was sitting in the dark and I did not see how he reacted to this. When I had finished singing, he called me to him and I sat besides him. I had still not recovered from the emotions of that song. To make conversation, His Highness asked me if my journey back from Kashmir had been comfortable.

'Yes,' I answered. I had decided that this was going to be day when I told him of my decision to leave him and the court. Yet, when I looked at him, just the very idea of speaking to him about it made me break into a sweat. I could not say a word. I could not even tell him how uneasy I had been over the past six weeks when he had not invited me. I had been ready every evening at seven, expecting to be summoned. I wanted to complain about this and ask why he had ignored me. I wanted to grumble and tell him that even if he had not wanted to hear me sing, he could have just called me over.

I wish I had been able to say all these things to him, for then he would at least have found out how much I loved him and that I was no ingrate. But then, even till today I cannot give expression to my love, even to my children.

Affairs continued in this manner for some time. He would call for me every week or ten days. I would sing and then come home. The time for the annual migration to Kashmir arrived. Even there, he asked me over once or twice a month. I had nothing else to do but walk to kill time.

One day I was walking in Chinar Bagh. The waters of the lake adjoining the gardens were amongst the best places to anchor houseboats, and every tourist tried to find a place there. The advantage of anchoring there was that you could rent an area of the park adjoining the houseboat. Those with families could enclose the area with canvas awnings. Within the enclosure, they would spread carpets and durries and turn it into a private courtyard. If they felt warm inside the houseboat, they slept outside in the garden.

Walking in Chinar Bagh was always a great deal of fun. Each houseboat window presented a different sight—costumes of every country, pretty women, ugly women, fat women, fair and dark women. You saw other kinds of people too. This was one reason why so many people went for walks to the Chinar Bagh, for there was always so much going on there. Sometimes I went there too.

Once I chanced upon a group of young men sitting on a durrie in front of a houseboat. They were listening to a man who was singing a Sindhi Bhairavi very well. These eight or ten young men were generous in their applause. Listening to the man sing, I slowed down my pace. It was delightful listening to the *kafi* that he was singing. A couple of days later when I passed that way again, some other man was singing. The rest of the group was applauding with loud, appreciative *wah wahs*. They were so engrossed in the music and so oblivious of their surroundings that I stood there for nearly ten minutes listening to the man sing and no one even glanced my way.

I enjoyed listening to their music so much that I began to walk by that place every day—there was always music there. Every afternoon they heard someone sing and all of them sang very well. I felt sad that in those conditions I could not even try and convince His Highness to listen to these men. 'They are here,' I could have pleaded. 'If you do not like them, you can always ask them to stop whenever you have had enough.' In any case, in those days the Maharaja was indifferent to almost everything. I found out who these men were from my accompanists. One was Chhote Ghulam Ali, another was Tawakkul Hussain, and a third was Rafiq Ghazanvi. They were all in Kashmir together for a holiday.

One day, when I passed that way, there was no music or singing. One young man was sitting on the planks of the houseboat and I noticed him looking at me. I looked carefully at him and then walked passed him. I looked back to see if he was still watching and caught him smiling. Extremely embarrassed, I started walking faster and decided that I was never going to come this way again.

A few days later I convinced myself that the men would be so involved in their music that they would not notice me if I went there again. As usual, they were sitting on durries and applauding whoever was singing that day. The man from the other day was also among them. He noticed me immediately. I was disconcerted in case he presumed I had come there to see him again. I left immediately, and never went back to Chinar Bagh.

I was already fifteen or sixteen by then. Strange thoughts began to form in my mind. I felt like falling in love. I wanted someone to tell me that he was madly in love with me and could not live without me. I wanted a prince to appear and look longingly at me and I would gaze lovingly at him; I imagined us sitting by ourselves and talking and being able to do whatever I felt like doing; going wherever I wanted to go.

But there was no possibility of any of my fantasies becoming a reality. At the palace there were the same familiar, boring faces which I had been seeing for the last six or seven years. None of them was interested in me and neither was I in any of them. Sometimes I would imagine I was Heer and at other times that I was Sohni. But neither a Ranjha nor a Mahiwal ever appeared.

One day it occurred to me that I had not gone to Nishat Bagh for ages. It would be fun to ride in a donga and to eat Kashmiri food again. We rented a donga and arranged for a waza to come and cook for us. My family and I settled into the donga—some resting against the bolsters, others playing cards while I watched the river flow.

I sat at a window. Soon another donga pulled up alongside ours. Someone was singing in that donga. The donga rowed alongside ours for some time and we were parallel to each other briefly. Then, the other donga pulled ahead.

When we reached Nishat Bagh, they spread their sheets, whether accidentally or intentionally I do not know, close to where we had decided to sit. Soon the singing began again. The tourists from elsewhere did not recognize me but the ones from Jammu did. This group had found out who I was and was trying to take a good look at me. It was well-known that I was employed by the Maharaja and had been at the court for some time now. *Riyasat* had given me so much publicity that now everyone wanted to have a look at me. I used to dress plainly hoping that people in public would not recognize me. I also used no make-up. No one was allowed to visit me at home so few people had met me. However, it was clear that this group knew who I was from the way they constantly looked our way and the way they whispered to each other. I sat with my back to them and listened to the singing.

We left at four to return home while they were still involved with their singing. I did not go to Chinar Bagh again, so I never found out where they went and when.

44. The Lady from Amritsar

Festivals continued to be celebrated at the court as usual, but the joy had gone out of them. Instead, there was tension, bordering on hate, between the Hindus and Muslims. Celebrating festivals together was now a thing of the past. Something always went wrong at these celebrations.

On His Highness' birthday, a lady singer was invited from Amritsar. I do not want to mention her name. Everyone knew of her in Lahore for she had been famous and popular in her time. She had some sort of a relationship with Agha Hashar too, and in her theatrical style, would sing his poetry. A day after the birthday, a musical evening was arranged in the pavilion on the seventh terrace of the Shalimar Gardens. Mattresses and bolsters covered in white were laid out. Everyone including the Maharaja settled down.

The lady singer made an appearance with her father and her musicians. She looked like a Chinese or a Japanese woman—small eyes, thick nose and fair skin. She must have been thirty or thirty-two and she looked very attractive. She greeted me very warmly when she arrived. Out of respect, I greeted her as I would an aunt, and called her *khala*. The word hit her as though I had shot an arrow. She reacted immediately.

'I am not old enough to be your khala,' she snapped. 'you can call me by my name.'

Before I knew it I had repeated the offending word again, 'Khala, you are reacting as if I have abused you. Since you are older than me it is only out of regard that I addressed you as khala.'

'Abuse me!' She had found a new word to be upset about and was angrier now, 'Who do you think you are that you can even think of abusing me?'

I was stunned and I looked at her in silence. She carried on loudly, 'You dare abuse me. I will complain to the Maharaja.'

'Do as you wish,' I replied. It was stupid of me. I should have immediately reported the entire episode to His Highness. But I was not smart enough at the time.

The entire staff drank a toast to His Highness' health. Dinner was served. As soon as dinner was over, she went straight to His Highness. I was sitting at some distance from His Highness and did not hear what the devious woman said to him. He called me over.

'Apologize to her for insulting her.'

'I have not insulted her,' I said firmly, 'Nor will I apologize to her.'

'I am a guest here,' the horrible woman said, 'instead of being hospitable, she insults me!' She was so deceitful that she pretended to wipe her tears and placed a handkerchief over her face. Her father, who was always drunk, began to mumble and cry to keep her company.

His Highness again said to me, 'Come on, apologize.'

'I will never apologize to this fibber,' I insisted, 'I have not insulted her and she is lying about everything. I am ready to apologize to you, but not to her. She is not only cunning but also a fabricator.'

'She has some grudge against me,' the woman went on, 'She has humiliated me and I will never live it down for as long as I live.' Lord alone knows what story she had made up.

She wept copious tears and I saw that His Highness was not ready to believe me. Nor did he give me chance to say anything. He kept insisting that I apologize. After a while His Highness got up and went and sat at a distance. His staff followed him. He began to listen to her sing. After an hour two, the singing session ended.

This was another sign of His Highness' greatness. I had disobeyed him yet he did not admonish me publicly. Instead, he got up and went away. If it had been some other ruler, I would have been dismissed immediately. Or, if it had been Patiala or Rampur, I would have been executed. After His Highness left, I went home. I was sad as well as angry. When the incident with

Mehr Nigar had happened, he had assured me that in future he would believe my version of events. Yet he had not even let me speak this time.

As was customary, the rich and the poor of the Rajput community were invited for dinner a day after His Highness' birthday. Singing usually followed dinner. That day, when the food was brought to me on a tray, I returned it saying that I was not hungry. After dinner, an orderly came and told me to get ready to sing. I sent him back saying that my throat was sore. The orderly came back with orders that if I could not sing, I should at least dance. I told him that my body ached too.

When His Highness heard this, he was furious. Perhaps, if this had not been a durbar, he would have slapped me. Close to the bathroom where my mother was sitting, he was heard telling Khusrau Jung, 'Look at her arrogance now. It was only yesterday when she had came to court. She did not even know how to walk properly then. She used to run like a horse. I taught her how to behave, how to sing. I have protected her in every way. Now, she puts on airs. When I ask her to sing, her throat is sore, when asked to dance, her body starts aching. When food is served, she is not hungry.' Ten minutes later, he returned to his seat. I do not know whether he said all this deliberately within my mother's hearing or if it was meant only for Khusrau Jung.

He ordered the lady from Amritsar to sing. I was furious not only because I was not going to sing but also because I had not been given a chance to explain. I did not even know what lies the lady from Amritsar had told. Without checking with me, he had believed everything that she had said! I decided that as long as she was here, I would not sing. A few times I stole glances at him to find him looking very displeased. The next day the lady left.

For a week or so after that, he did not send for me. I knew he was very angry but I was not sorry. In fact I was hurt and heartbroken. I loved and respected His Highness. I had never imagined that he would believe a stranger whom he had just met instead of me, and hold me out to be a disobedient liar. I had spent my childhood with him. He also knew that I never lied nor had I ever been disloyal or deceitful. I had treated him like a god. Perhaps it was the atmosphere that made him behave in the way he did. It was true that it was his kindness and gentleness that had made me so bold; I was not afraid of him and therefore had stood my ground. If it had been any other maharaja but him, I would have been taught a lesson I would not have forgotten. Disobedience could have been meant death. He did not say a word and behaved magnanimously. May God give him a place in heaven.

A few days later he called me to sing again. I wished him, sat down and began singing. He did not look at me while I sang nor did he call me to him. He continued to ask me to sing but refused to speak to me. This went on for three months. It was now September and preparations for returning to Jammu began.

In Jammu when I went to the Palace, Khusrau Jung and Baldev Singh met me and took me with them to His Highness. There, they said to me: 'His Highness is displeased with you. Apologize.'

'I was ready to apologize to you that very day,' I said addressing the Maharaja, 'But not to that liar,' I added. He began to speak to me again. I told him the entire story. His Highness was depressed as usual but there was a slight improvement in his mood.

The tension between the Hindus and Muslims was still growing. *Riyasat* regularly exaggerated the developments in its reporting. The papers continued to write something or the other about me. I did not understand why they had chosen me as a target. Their constant refrain was that I was siding with the Muslims and that I wanted to poison the Maharaja. This was repeated so often that people began to believe it. Some people in Jammu were convinced that I was disloyal and ungrateful. Some even admonished me for behaving in this way after being indebted to him even for the salt I had eaten.

I went insane with rage when I heard this. 'What is all this?' I asked, 'You all live in Jammu you foolish people. If I had tried to poison him would I not be in prison? Or do you think he pardons me every evening to invite me to the court to sing?' How would the others who read these papers know how blatantly the papers were lying? His Highness would laugh when he read all this.

By now, my nervousness was increasing day by day. What if all that was being said and written, were to come true? What if a member of his staff placed a small packet of poison in my purse?

Or concocted allegations like that lady from Amritsar had done? What if I was imprisoned? His Highness was a simple man and some people envied those who were at the receiving end of his generosity. He had fallen for the play-acting of that woman and believed her story. What if a few others got together and set me up? I wanted to leave my job to save myself.

Yet, I could not find an excuse to do so even though I was in constant danger and I was afraid all the time. There was no peace in the kingdom as in earlier times. Earlier, his Highness used to be very fond of Muslims. Now he hated them as much. He had dismissed a few. There were times when I wanted to laugh. I had nothing to do with politics and I had nothing to do with the Hindu-Muslim riots. Nor did I understand any of these things. Yet, the Hindus had become my enemies. Leave alone those living outside the kingdom, even those living in the kingdom had started to believe the stories of me wanting to kill the Maharaja.

If I was guilty of any interference, it was when someone in trouble came to me with a tale of woe. I would try and help him for officials listened to me because His Highness was fond of me. I had been able to help some people in this way. Except for these small matters, I had nothing to do with matters of state. However, the campaign against me by these publications convinced many people that I was disloyal and an ingrate. I got into arguments with many but few believed me. The general opinion was, 'He employed her when she was nine, even appointed her a gazetted officer. He has given her so much wealth and such honour. And this is what she does in return!' Everyone had his or her own version of this story. I had had enough.

One day I decided I had to tell His Highness about it and I said it softly. 'My parents want me to go to Lahore.'

He looked at me intently. Signs of anger appeared on his face but only for an instant. He was soon back to his normal self.

'Do you really want to leave your employment?' he asked.

Just this one question and all my resolve collapsed again. I wanted to scream 'No.' A shiver ran through my body. I wanted to say loudly, 'Absolutely not. I cannot leave you for I remember all your kindness.' Instead I kept quiet and just nodded my head.

Perhaps he thought I wanted to earn more money, that I was an ungrateful and disloyal person and that I was not in the least sorry about leaving him. I wish I could have told him the truth about what made me take the decision and my wish to stay with him forever. How I wanted to tell him of my fear that what the newspapers were writing might actually come true. He did not speak to me after that. How I wished to retract that gesture of mine and say that all this had been a joke and that I wanted to spend my life with him. Again I did not say a word.

I sang that evening and this was the last chance I got to sing for him and I was aware that I might never sing for him again. I even thought of the possibility that we might never meet again. The first line of Ahmad Faraz's couplet, 'This time when we part, perhaps we will meet only in a dream,' seems appropriate to describe the state of my mind. I sang with emotions that I was unaware were within me. There was a request for a pahari. The way I sang the pahari that day, I doubt I will ever be able to sing again. I wept within my heart and my singing sounded like the wail of a *been*. His Highness left the moment I stopped singing. I did not even get the chance to wish him a final farewell. A year and a half later I met one of his ADCs in Lahore who told me that His Highness had been very sad that I had turned out to be disloyal and greedy.

If I had been avaricious, I would have asked for a raise. His Highness did not know that I had nothing to do even with my own money. I spent nothing and everything I earned went to mother and Nana. Yes, my signatures would surely be there on the financial transactions they conducted. I never felt the need to buy anything. I already had pretty clothes and jewellery. Since I was a child, I had lacked nothing and everything I owned was due to him. I wished to see him just once more because I thought of him all the time and for hours at a stretch I would think of the times we had spent together. Now, memories were all that were left. I could no longer see him, or meet him.

An early portrait of the author

A young Malka Pukhraj

Maharaja Hari Singh of Kashmir

The author's husband, Shabbir

With Roshanara Begum (left) on her Indian tour in 1977

Performing at a public concert sometime in the 80s

On holiday in the hills

Recording in a studio, probably for All India Radio

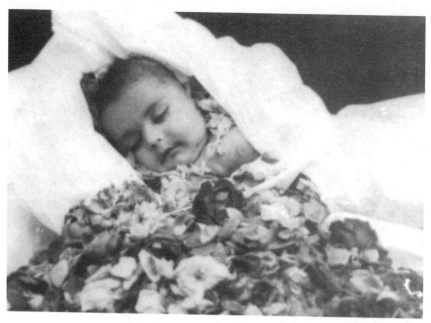

Chachu, the adopted child who died early

With her grand-daughter, Farazeh Syed

Malka Pukhraj's mother

A studio portrait of the author

*The family: Standing (l to r) son Tanvir, Sajda, Tanvir's mother-in-law,
son Tauqir, Malka Pukhraj, Maliha, Tanvir's wife, son Tasvir;
sitting (l to r) Nazi, Tauqir's wife, unknown, daughter Saifi, daughter Tahira*

45. How the Maharajahs Acquired the Kingdom

The people of Jammu often recounted how the family of the Maharaja had become rulers. Who knows how much truth there was in what they said, but all the old and venerable people of Jammu had the same story to tell.

In the reign of Maharaja Ranjit Singh, two poor brothers had set out on foot to find work. Near Wazirabad there is a village called Imanabad and it was dark when they got there. They decided to spend the night there before resuming their journey in the morning and began looking for a place to sleep. They spotted the shop of a Hindu moneylender and asked him if they could spend the night in front of his shop. The brothers were so attractive and comely that the shopkeeper could not stop staring at them. He asked them where they were going. They told him that they were going to the court of Maharaja Ranjit Singh. Lord knows what the shopkeeper saw in their future for he told them not to worry about a thing. He offered to take care of their food, lodging and everything else that they needed.

Beds were made for them and they slept in comfort. The next morning the shopkeeper asked them if they would spend a week with him before heading towards the Maharaja's court.

'Have a bath, put on clean clothes. I will buy you clothes, swords and good horses. You can then go to Maharaja Ranjit Singh in style,' he advised them. The immediate reaction of the brothers was that they could not accept such an obligation. 'We do not have a penny,' they told their host, 'If we had money to pay for all these things, would we not have stayed at home?' The shopkeeper dismissed their hesitation and said he would make all the necessary arrangements. He told them that all they had to do in return was to sign a promissory note that one-eighth of whatever they earned from Maharaja Ranjit Singh would be given to him as his share.

They agreed readily to this proposal. They were even ready to agree to give him half of what they might earn. The shopkeeper told them that he would be happy with just an eighth. He got their thumbprints on a paper and kept them with him for a few days. He bought them fine clothes and good horses. The brothers were good-looking and once clean and well dressed, they looked like princes. The shopkeeper also gave them sixty rupees as spending money for the rest of their journey.

The brothers reached Lahore and planted themselves in front of the court every morning hoping to be noticed. One day the Maharaja caught sight of them and inquired of a courtier who they were. He was told that they were brothers who wanted an opportunity to serve His Royal Highness. The Maharaja called them in. He liked the way they looked and he employed them as courtiers. They were to accompany the Maharaja at all times. The Maharaja grew fond of them and began lavishing favours on them. Naturally the other courtiers became jealous.

The Maharaja reached the stage where he did not want them to leave his side for a moment. The courtiers were amazed at the speed with which the brothers had got so close to the Maharaja and wondered what spell they had cast on him. The real secret, probably, was that God was kind to them.

The Maharaja liked to watch men fight tigers. A huge pit had been dug where tigers recently captured from the forest were put. Every year, two men armed only with swords had to take on the tiger. People would come from near and far to watch this contest. The two men confronted the tiger with their drawn swords and the tiger would charge at them. Often the tiger would kill or seriously injure the men. Those who managed to kill the tiger were rewarded liberally with gifts and lands. Sometimes the tiger killed both the men.

A tiger was captured from the jungle and a date for the confrontation was fixed. Inquiries were made about who would be willing to face the tiger. The courtiers who were jealous of the brothers had nicknamed them 'fairies' because of their beauty. They suggested to the Maharaja that he ask his two favourites to accept the challenge. The Maharaja was fond of them and wondered how these lean, delicate creatures would fight a tiger, which surely would kill them within minutes. So he said that they were still not ready for the challenge. The two brothers knew that others mocked them by calling them 'fairies.' They came forward and offered to fight. The Maharaja tried to dissuade them by telling them that their turn could be next. But they pleaded, 'Your Highness, if you do not give us the chance to challenge the tiger, we will be unable to show our faces around here and we will have to leave.'

The Maharaja was left with no option. The brothers drew their swords and faced the tiger. It is said that they were so swift that they fell on the tiger like lightning and killed it within a few minutes. Their narrow waists were spring-like, and when they moved, they seemed to fly in the air. The faces of their opponents fell almost by the yard while the Maharaja went wild with joy. He ordered that they be given the kingdom of Jammu as a reward. The area extended to the fort of Bahu. The illiterate moneylender however claimed that the Maharaja had ordered that the limit be at the Nile ki Tali, which is near Sialkot. The kingdom thus became a large one. The moneylender began to get his one-eighth share of the income from the state. The recipients of this percentage came to be known as the Diwans. This arrangement went on till the reign of Pratap Singh. The way it ended was a story in itself.

In the time of Maharaja Ranjit Singh, a group of mirasis had left their traditional role as singers and become mimics. Their profession was to make people laugh. They became so good at their art that they could find a funny aspect to every situation. The noblemen, the elite, the rajas and nawabs, all employed them and kept them around them at all times. These mimics lived well. They ate and dressed well, and they frequently got gifts or favours. These illiterate men were more intelligent and better at repartee than many well-respected scholars were. They would even joke about politics and were often able to convey important insights to the ruler.

Maharaja Pratap Singh employed one such *naqqal*, Thotha. He went to wish the Diwan, as was customary, on the occasion of a marriage in the Diwan's family. But instead of giving him a symbolic gift in return the Diwan insulted Thotha. Naturally Thotha was very unhappy about this.

A few days later he was called to entertain Maharaja Pratap Singh. Thotha began to mimic the deeds of a gang of thieves. The plot involved a gang, which had set out to rob. The gang arrived at a village and while they were consulting each other whether they should rob the village or not, a train of mules loaded with gold coins arrived. Two of the thieves thanked God for being so kind to them, 'Our fortunes have been made. Seven generations of our families will not be able to spend so much wealth.'

Thotha then stepped into the discussion, 'Yes, just the wealth on one mule would be enough for seven generations. But you better not touch any of it. If you even look at it with greed, your heads will be cut off and your families eliminated. Let us move on and find another place and please do not mention to anyone that you even contemplated looting this wealth.' The other thieves were now not only scared but also curious. 'Which place is this? What is it called? Whom does this wealth belong to?'

Thotha had all the answers. 'The place is called Imanabad and this is where the Diwans come from. From every rupee accruing to the kingdom, they get two annas. These gold coins have come from Jammu. I have heard said that one day there will be more wealth in this village than in the entire kingdom. Do not let yourselves be tempted. These people are cruel and if they catch you eyeing their wealth, there will be no sign of your family left. Let's run from this place and never think of it again.'

The gang moved on. They finally arrived at a large city. They were delighted. 'Ahhaa, ahhaa, just look at those lights. One can stare at them for ever.'

'Oyee you jackasses,' Thotha interrupted their reverie, 'Do you know what this city is? It is Jammu.'

'Should we rob in this city?' the thieves wanted to know.

'Go ahead, rob at will,' Thotha said confidently, 'No one will be bothered in the least. If you want, you can even rob the entire kingdom for no one cares. This is one of the best things about this kingdom.'

The Maharaja got the point. It struck him how much of the kingdom's wealth was being drained and so, he immediately abolished the share of the Diwans.

There were other famous stories about Thotha. He was expected to walk with the funeral processions of all royal relatives. The cremation grounds were next to the river Tawi and though they were not far, the route let through several narrow lanes. After one such funeral of a Maharani, the Maharaja sat down on the way to rest at a place close to where Thotha lived. The Maharaja had made a generous gift of money to Thotha so that he could build a house. A courtier who was jealous of Thotha, decided to used the occasion to settle scores. He pointed out to the Maharaja that Thotha could have built himself a palace with the money that had been gifted to him. 'Yet,' added the courtier, 'Thotha continues to live in this dilapidated mud house. The conditions he lives in reflect badly on Your Highness. People assume that you give him nothing when you give him gifts every second day. He should have built himself a house, which would have been a testament to your generosity. Instead he chooses to live in style worse than that of a *faqir*. If you had given so much money to anyone else, the fame of your benevolence would have spread far by now.'

Maharaja Pratap Singh was angry. He ordered that Thotha be presented before him immediately. An orderly ran and fetched him. Enraged, the Maharaja said,

'You Thotha! I had ordered you to build yourself a house. Why then do you live in these ruins? I have given you so much and you insult me by pretending that you have nothing. Why has the house not been built? Why have you been dishonest?'

'You are absolutely right,' Thotha admitted humbly, 'You are very generous and you have given me more than I need. Alas, there is this black-faced witch that gobbles up everything I get and leaves nothing for me. I have tried as hard as I could to get rid of her but she will not leave me alone.'

The Maharaja was angrier now, 'You mock us with your jokes?'

'God forbid that I dare do that,' Thotha replied, 'If you do not believe me I can bring the witch and show her to you. If I have your permission, I can present her to you right now.'

'All right,' said the Maharaja. 'Bring her immediately.'

Thotha ran home. Fifteen or twenty minutes later he returned with a bundle so large that he needed the help of a couple of other men to carry it. He dumped the bundle in front of the Maharaja.

'What is this?' the surprised Maharaja asked.

'Just wait and see,' Thotha said as he began unwrapping the bundle. He peeled off one quilt and then another and then one more. In short, every piece of cloth in the house had been wrapped around the witch: quilts, sheets, and mattresses. When all the layers had been unraveled, a small black earthen pot meant for holding fire emerged. Thotha respectfully presented this to the Maharaja.

'Your Highness, whatever I get, is consumed by this black witch. She has consumed so much ghee by now that this little thing is going to blaze like a beacon to your glory forever!'

There is another amusing incident relating to Thotha. Pratap Singh too, travelled to Kashmir every year. The entire entourage would be on horseback; the baggage on mules and the Maharaja travelled in a palanquin. Everyone was given an official mount. Thotha found himself stuck with an old, feeble horse. Since Thotha was technically only a mirasi, the officer-in-charge had simply gone through the formalities of providing him with just any mount.

The royal party reached the first encampment. Before they left again, Thotha hung two heavy stones across the neck of the horse and similarly, two across its lower back. He then held the reins and stood besides the road. When the Maharaja passed that way, he was surprised at the sight and asked for an explanation.

'Sir,' Thotha explained, 'if I had not hung these stones the horse would have either toppled on to its face or on its behind. With the stones, I have managed to restore the balance. At least the horse is safe from harm now.'

The Maharaja immediately ordered that the horse be changed. Thotha's horse was exchanged with the mount of the officer who had assigned Thotha his horse!

46. After My Employment

For many nights after I had withdrawn from the court, I thought of His Highness before I fell asleep. His kindness was what I recalled most. It was only after I had left him that I realized how attached I had become to him and how much I loved him. I felt like going to Jammu and seeing him, to tell him that I wanted to live with him; that I could not live without him. If he had forgiven me, I would have told him everything truthfully.

But I did not go to Jammu, nor did I try to meet him. He was very angry with me. After Partition when the kingdoms were abolished, His Highness moved to Bombay. I wrote him countless letters asking for permission to see him just once. I received no acknowledgement for any of those requests. He now hated me as much as he had once loved me. I think he did not even wish to set eyes on me. Till today, to this very moment, I love him.

Two days before His Highness died, I dreamt of him. I thought I saw him sitting in a durbar. In the dream, he called me to him and said, 'Jammu is beautiful, is it not?'

'Yes, it is very beautiful,' I had agreed.

'Did you know that I am now leaving for Jammu?' he had asked.

Two days later I learnt from the newspapers that His Highness was dead. I felt as if I had lost my closest friend and my greatest benefactor. I will always be sorry that I never got a chance to meet him again.

When I withdrew from the court, *Riyasat*, playing on the meaning of my name which meant empress, had headlined the story across its front pages in bold letters: 'The Raj of Malka Pukhraj ends.' I had achieved a lot of fame because of my employment at the court and also because of all the stories in the papers. Everyone now wanted to hear me sing. Or at least to see what I looked like. A few days after leaving the court, we decided to move to Lahore. We found a good, well ventilated house whose owner had recently married and hence her house was vacant. We fixed the terms for the place and moved to our new house.

We bought a car as soon as we arrived. Nana loved horses. In Jammu we had a beautiful Yarqandi mare and a tonga. We took these to Lahore too. It was widely believed that I was very rich and that money did not matter to me. I had laid down a strict rule that I would sing for no one after eleven at night. Often there were occasions when those who visited me brought along their whiskey and demanded glasses and soda water. In these situations I would clearly tell them: 'You have come here to hear me sing. You can listen to me and then drink afterwards. If you insist on drinking, please do so with pleasure. I will sing for you some other time. If we do both together, you will not enjoy the music nor will I enjoy singing.'

At first people were really offended by my attitude. Some even complained that they had came to listen to song, not to pray at a mosque. 'If she is so pious,' they said, 'why does she sing at all?'

To this my answer was categorical. 'It is true that I sing and that is not considered a good thing to do. Nor am I a pious person. Yet, I do not mix liquor with song. You can only do one thing at one time—either drink or hear me sing.' Within a few months this attitude of mine was known to all. Those who wanted a drink, would have one before they came to hear me sing.

Whenever I was invited to sing outside, I would check with the hosts the time when the function was to begin and end. I would promise to be on time and would make it clear that I would perform only for two hours. To those who invited me at nine, I stressed that I would leave at eleven no matter what time the performance began.

The custom was that whenever someone arranged a musical gathering, the singers were at the mercy of the hosts for the whole night. I had a run-in with many people over this, and was thus declared to be proud and bad-tempered. Some people also said that I was arrogant because of my wealth. My defence was always the same, 'I am neither arrogant nor temperamental. I had agreed to sing for you for two hours and if you cannot stick to your promises, why blame me?' A few times I left such gatherings without even collecting my payment. Since I had my own car, I did not need to depend on anyone for coming and going. Those who were genuinely fond of music did not complain. The others soon got used to my ways.

I did not know too much about singing but many people praised my singing. In fact I had created such an impact that when the other singing ladies from Lahore, including the best known ones, found out that I was to sing at the same function as them, they would plead bad health and withdraw. There was no one else in Lahore who danced or used dance gestures while singing like I did. I had been well trained in these arts. The audiences loved classical dance, and my singing, using dance-gestures, was a novelty for most. Sometimes people paid me twice what I asked so that they could ensure that I perform for them. Sometimes I was booked to perform at two venues on the same evening.

Since the impression that I did not care for money was widespread, people were willing to offer me four times my normal charges. Performing wasn't hard work for me. If I sang a thumri, it would take an hour to complete for I illustrated it with dance gestures. The dancing too was no drain on my energy.

Hindu pundits taught singers the art of using dance gestures. Every pundit had a few masterpieces in his repertoire. My first teacher had been a Muslim, but even he had learnt from a famous pundit. Each of these masters had worked so hard on a couple of thumris at least that they would express each *asthai* of a thumri in such detail and with such subtle variations that it could take an hour to complete it. I have already described the thumri that I learnt from Mamman Khan in Delhi, the words of which were, '*Are Ram, kaise paar utariye,*'—O Rama, how do I cross this river to get to you. In this thumri, I would depict a rainstorm, the problems of crossing a river during it, the fear, the prayers seeking God's help, the tears and many other emotions, that I had learnt to express from him. This bhajan-like thumri therefore lasted a full hour.

Whenever I liked a particular thumri of a pundit, I would employ him at a generous salary for a month or two and I would learn the thumri and the dance gestures from him. One thumri that I liked, I have mentioned before. It was, '*sab din howat nahin samaan*'—all days are not the same. The theme of the thumri

related to the changing fortunes of human beings. First, time had
to be indicated: morning, day or night; then the weather; then the
depiction of the phases of life from birth to death. The birth of the
child had to be shown and then his youth and and finally
decadence, old age and poverty. And then there was death, which
had to be evoked. At the stage when poverty was evoked, even
the eyes of those with brave hearts would begin to brim with
tears.

I had learnt about half a dozen such thumris, which made
performing very easy and effortless for me. Yet, they always had
a profound influence on the audience. Very few other singers
were able to do this. Those very people who once called me proud
and arrogant, now became my friends or my fans.

One friend who I would like to mention was the lawyer
Govardhan Lal. He was the brother of D.N. Madhok who then
ruled the film world. Every song he wrote became a hit. He
composed the tunes for his songs himself. At times he composed
the tune by playing the rhythm on a matchbox. His songs sound
wonderful even today. They were all simple and went straight to
the heart. The film *Rattan* for which he worked, ran in the same
movie theatre for three years. Film producers would chase him
for a year or two to get him to agree to work for them. '*Sawan ke
badalon, unse yeh jaa kaho*'—O monsoon clouds, will you carry
this message to him—is one song of his that is still remembered.

There was another song: '*Barsaat ki raat, kaali kaali re; koi
paas na ho, jawani kya kare?*'—this dark rainy night is wasted
when you are alone. The beauty of the opening phrases of his
songs astonished everyone. Both D.N. Madhok and Govardhan
Lal were ugly to look at. Govardhan was not a very skilled or
successful lawyer either, but he was a good conversationalist and
a great entertainer. No gathering was complete without him. He
would translate the lyrics of Punjabi folk songs into English and
then sing them in the original tunes. He translated well for there
was no difference of rhythm or metre when he sang these. Thus
the Punjabi folk songs were transformed without losing their
musicality or lyricism. People would often be in splits when he
sang these songs. He was popular amongst the lawyers and judges,
even of the High Court and had friends among both Indians and

Englishmen. All the judges respected him and tried to help him in any way that they could.

He became a close friend of mine. He might not have been good to look at but he carried joy and happiness wherever he went. All the lawyers would get together and throw a party every month. I was always invited to these. Everyone who came was educated and cultured and I enjoyed the parties immensely. Khwaja Firozuddin, the father of Khursid Anwar, was ofen there at these parties. He was about forty or forty-five, a sophisticated and sober man who was very fond of music. He liked my singing. After me, Govardahan would sing his translations. The words of one of these were: '*Mahi we main bhulke tarna, te chhad meri binni na maror, bhulke tarna*'. His translation went like this: 'Dear *Ammi*, tomorrow I shall go, do not break my wrist maiya bhulke tarna.' He held his cap in hands while he sang. The Englishmen were usually so pleased that his cap was soon full of money. Someone put in two hundred rupees, others five hundred and some even a thousand. He used to then come and overturn his cap in front of my accompanists and let them share the money he had collected. Everyone, including the Englishmen, had a good time at these parties.

A few days after one such party, I got a message from Khwaja Firozuddin inviting me to dinner at his 'humble abode' the next day at eight. I sent word that I was flattered that he had thought of me and if he were to send someone to guide me to his place, I would happily be there on time.

Singing followed dinner. A young man was sitting next to me. I was sure that somewhere in the past I had once taken a good look at him. He requested me to sing a *Sindhi Bhairavi*, which I did. Then he asked for a pahari and I sang that too. However, by this time, he had wept himself into a sorry state.

Everyone enjoyed the singing. All the guests seem to understand the nuances of both music and poetry. And I enjoyed singing for them. When the musical part of the evening was over, we ate a delicious dinner and talked and bantered and suddenly I realized it was three in the morning!.

Khwaja Sahib told the young man who'd shown an interest in my singing to accompany me home. I assured him that I would manage since I had my own car. But Khwaja Sahib insisted that it was too late at night and that his car would follow mine. He introduced me to the young man who was undergoing training and was posted as a *tehsildar* at the District Collectorate in Lahore.

The young man also introduced himself. 'My name is Syed Shabbir Hussain and I am a good friend of Khwaja Sahib's son, Khurshid Anwar, which is why Khwaja Sahib treats me like a son. And this is my friend Khurshid Anwar, who is learning how to sing though none of his friends has heard him sing. He practices in secret.' Khwaja Sahib had paid me by cheque. Shabbir offered to get the cheque encashed the next day and deliver the money to me. I gave the cheque to him—perhaps he was looking for another excuse to meet.

I began to wonder where I had seen him before. On the way back I asked him. 'I feel I have seen you before. Have you ever met me before today?'

'Yes,' he said.

'Where?'

'Kashmir,' is all he said

In a flash everything fell into place—how I had always walked in a particular direction in the Chinar Bagh to where the group of young men had sat listening to music. I felt a flush of embarrassment.

The next day, around noon, he came to deliver the money. He left after fifteen or twenty minutes. A few days later he visited me with five or six of his friends. All of them were cultured and interesting. They told jokes well and recited good poetry. My family and I got so engrossed in talking to them that we did not realize that by the time they left it was well past midnight.

Soon Shabbir and I became good friends. Often he would drop in during the day too. He liked to hunt. I had told him I only liked venison and partridge meat. He therefore brought over the partridges that he had shot.

Living a life of monotonous routine for nine years in Jammu had put me into a strange frame of mind. When I was fourteen or fifteen I had wished for my own 'hero' in my life, someone I could go out with, someone I could talk to. When I looked around, I saw no one who could fit the bill. Everyone I met was much older—often even older than my father. All of them were also nothing but sycophants of His Highness. They were also all envious men, jealous of me.

Lahore, on the other hand, was a completely different matter. Everyone who visited me wanted to impress me so that I would have eyes only for him. I had longed to be treated this way. I liked all those who came to visit. Yet, within a fortnight I would lose all interest in them and not want to see them ever again. Something they said or did gave them away as shallow and uncouth. The turmoil within me had subsided too after a year or two. Despite my efforts, I could not recreate those tides of feeling again.

Every man, young or old, who expressed his love, told me the same story. They were all unfortunate victims whom the world had picked on to be unfair to. I believed none of them. In fact, the sorrier their story, the more amused I felt. I wanted to laugh at some of them. Even if they were fifty or sixty, they expressed their love in the same way as the younger ones did, had similar stories of misery to tell, and I had to reassure them that their age did not matter to me.

I made it clear to all that I would marry a man who would be only mine; someone who gave no one else precedence over me. They amazed me at the readiness with which they agreed to this. Perhaps they were only fooling themselves. While expressing their love, some would pull a long face and look so stricken that even their cheeks quivered. Others, when they told me that they loved me, looked as if all the blood in the bodies had rushed to their face. There would be a sparkle in some eyes, terror in others. In short, each had his own way of telling me that he loved me. Some sober, well educated people would end up saying such foolish things which made my feeling of respect for them instantly turn into contempt.

There was one Rai Sahib who lived in Head Rasool. He had studied engineering in England and was now in charge of the canal network. He had dozens of official servants, and timber contractors followed him with folded hands looking for contracts. He lived in a fine bungalow belonging to the Irrigation Department. A couple of acres of land were attached to the house.

Vegetables, milk and ghee cost him nothing. He earned more than was reasonable.

I met him at some function. He liked my singing, and liked me too, very much. Every Saturday he would turn up in the evening and stay till nine or ten. He also spent Sundays in Lahore and returned to Head Rasool on Monday. Every week he brought a basket of vegetables, ghee, fowl, eggs, partridges, quails and butter with him. There were countless chicken and good buffaloes in the grounds around his house. So he did not have to spend a penny for these gifts. He set aside Saturday and Sunday for listening to music. He was plain looking, short, and dark with visible black marks on both his cheeks. His eyes were small and glinted like those of a serpent and his manner of speech was crude. His wife had died sixteen years ago from consumption and he was childless.

Listening to me sing was only an excuse for he talked more than I sang. He had memorized all of Shakespeare's plays. He quoted lines full of gloom and foreboding from them thinking that I understood English well (perhaps because I had employed an English woman to stay with me so that I could learn to speak English fluently).

Rai Sahib would tire himself out reciting Shakespeare to me even though the beauty of the lines escaped me completely. Yet, like an earnest student I listened to him carefully. When, during a recitation, his eyes would fill with tears, I would put on a solemn expression and applaud his declamation. Every week I had to listen to him for a few hours. Sometimes I would get so bored that I wanted to scream at him to stop mouthing this rubbish. But somehow, I did not want to shatter the illusion that I had created.

After visiting me regularly for two years, Rai Sahib lost all his reservations about expressing his love for me. I hated this even more than his recitations. Instead of referring to Shakespeare, he tried to describe his state himself, tried to tell me how difficult it was for him to go on living without me.

'*Oye* Malka, I swear by God, I am neither at peace in the day nor restful at night. In the morning, when I go the bathroom and sit on the commode, I think of you. The moment I conjure you in my thoughts, everything else comes to a standstill. What is down there stays there, and what is up there does not move.'

I hated him when he said things like this and never wanted to see him again. I started asking for expensive gifts hoping that he would not get them and that thus I would be rid of him. But he did whatever I asked for, and continued to spend his weekends regularly in Lahore. What I never understood was the connection between his love for me, and his constipation!

During this period, my friendship with Shabbir continued to grow. Shabbir's cousin Syed Salamatullah Shah was a well-known person in Lahore. His friends ranged from peons to High Court judges. He ran a huge Auction Mart on Macleod Road. He organized all the official auctions. The expatriates who were returning home would also hand over all their stuff to him to sell. In fact there were few people in Lahore who did not know Salamatullah.

Salamatulallah was also a generous man and helped anyone who asked. If someone had problems with a court case, Salamatullah would go with him to the courts. If someone was broke, he would help him with money. People then were very different from those of today: most people were selfless, concerned about those in trouble, and true friends.

Often all of Shabbir's friends would collect at the Auction Mart in the evening. The latest verses of Dr Iqbal would reach this gathering first. Amongst the people who gathered there were a couple who used to visit Doctor Sahib every day and in the evening recite his most recent poetry to the others. All sorts of people collected there: poets, actors, singers, hunters, music directors, the clowns, the educated and the illiterate.

Three people stayed permanently at the Auction Mart. The Mart was in a large house where all the goods waiting to be sold were displayed. People would come and select things. The auction was held every Saturday and the highest bidder got each item. Of the three who lived there, one was *Haji* Rasheed. The second, an elderly man called Haq. The third was Shaikh Asghar who belonged to a well-known family and was the son of rich father. However his father, annoyed at this ways, had disinherited him. His father had also remarried in his old age.

A few days after his remarriage, Asghar's father said that he had not been feeling well and was thinking of going to Delhi to consult a *hakim*. Asghar immediately caught on that it was actually his new mother who wanted a holiday in Delhi, so all three went to Delhi. They booked two rooms at a hotel and later in the day Asghar developed a fever. At about seven in the evening his father's new wife came and sat by his bed.

'Bless you son, may you get well. Why do you not eat something? Why do you not cover yourself with this blanket and go to sleep.'

'Do not worry,' Asghar told her, 'It is only a slight fever and I will be all right soon.'

'No,' she insisted. 'I will sit here till you go to sleep.'

Asghar again realized she was up to something for such concern was unlike her. He pulled the blanket over his face and after ten or fifteen minutes he began to pretend to snore. The mother rose and softly left the room. As soon as she was out of the room she called a bearer and mumbled something to him. The bearer headed for the bazaar. Asghar too went out to the bazaar and stood among the crowds. Soon the bearer arrived with a horse carriage, which waited while he went up to inform Asghar's parents. The parents came down and got into the carriage. Asghar too, quietly and with his face covered, climbed on to the foot-board at the back of the carriage. The carriage took them to the theatre where the play *Indra Sabha* was being staged. Before the show ended, Asghar left and was back in his bed by the time his parents returned to the hotel.

His parents came to his room in the morning. His mother sounded extremely concerned, 'How are you now son? I have been very worried because of you. May Allah see to it that you get well soon.'

'*Amma*, I had a very bad night,' Asghar said.

'*Hai* may I die,' exclaimed his stepmother, 'What happened?'

Asghar began to draw upon the plot of *Indra Sabha*, 'I dreamt I was in the court of an emperor. First, a black demon attacked me with a club. When I managed to save myself from him, a white one attacked me. I spent the whole night screaming.'

His parents were stunned, and silent.

It was pranks like this that had made his father disinherit him. He now lived in Lahore permanently, sometimes at Auction Mart and sometimes at Shabbir's house.

Salamatullah was not rich but he was influential and had contacts. He was also a very elegant man. They kept the Auction Mart alive. Anyone, who attended even one of the gatherings, began to come back to them regularly. I too came to Auction Mart in the evenings. Salamatullah and I became very good friends and we saw each other regularly. I got to hear all the new jokes at these meetings. Because of Khurshid Anwar's contact with musicians, many of the masters of music also visited the Mart in the evening. Often, the evenings were devoted entirely to music and one got to see the masters arguing and quarreling amongst themselves. Sometimes these arguments came close to becoming physical. Asghar would add fuel to the fire to get them to attack each other more bitterly.

Asghar was very familiar with the finer points of music. He even knew which notes were used in which raga. Since he was not educated, people often thought that he belonged to a family of mirasis. He was intelligent, skilled at sizing up situations, and very quick-witted. I have never met anyone else like him. When two singers would be arguing he would so dexterously and innocently lead them into a quarrel which lasted till they could quarrel no more. It took him no time to react to any situation. On the spur of the moment he would say something that would make people laugh even ten days later. He was different from everyone else. Even on occasions as serious as death, he would say things that would cause a twitter in the midst of grief.

An example of this was when Haji Rasheed's father passed away, I went with Asghar, Salamatullah and Shabbir to pay a condolence visit. Wiping his tears, Haji Rasheed joined us. We said how sorry we were and we asked about his father's last moments. Haji Rasheed began to describe those in detail. 'There were no signs that this was about to happen. When I got up in the morning, my wife gave me a cloth and asked me to go and get some meat. When I returned with the meat ... .'

Asghar interrupted, his face sad and the fingers of both his hands clenched between his teeth, '*Hai hai*, poor you! How were you to know that there was already meat in the house.' Everyone tried to ignore the remark and not to laugh, but the way Asghar had said this, none of us could keep from laughing. Every other day he came up with something so funny that everyone remembered it for a long time.

Shabbir continued to visit me every day. We would talk about this or that for the hour or two he spent at my place. I had frequently been invited to perform by people from the kingdom of Patiala. The state was so infamous and I had heard such hair-raising stories about it that I often invented excuses to refuse. I did go to sing in the other princely states but I was scared of going to Patiala.

Close to our home there was a famous perfume shop owned by Sikhs. Apart from the perfumes from Lucknow, they also stocked various condiments for paan as well as tobacco. The shop was known as *Bhaiyon ki dukan*—the brothers' shop. Some people would amuse themselves by calling the shop and asking, '*Sardarji*, what is the price of tobacco today?' [Perhaps because the use of tobacco is forbidden to Sikhs.] Every morning the owners fed a hundred hungry people before they opened their shop. They were rich, honourable, generous, kind and honest. Because I had consistently refused invitations from Patiala, the people from Patiala approached me through these Sikh brothers. The gentlemen came to my house to plead that I accept an invitation.

I told them what I was worried about straightaway, 'I have no objection to going there but I am sure you are aware of what goes on there.'

'We stand guarantee that nothing like that will happen to offend you,' they promised. 'You just have to go for one night.'

They were so persistent that I agreed. Then they showed me the telegram they had received from Patiala: 'Please reassure her that we have deep respect for her. I have invited the heir and some *jagirdars* for dinner at the club.'

I did go and I sang for two hours. After dinner I was immediately taken to the place where arrangements for my stay had been made. I was back safely in Lahore the next day.

I was told that Shabbir had come by while I was away. He had left a note: 'I am very disappointed that you are not here. *Inshallah*, I will come again to pay my respects.' He came the next day and greeted me with such joy and enthusiasm that it seemed as if we were meeting after years.

Often we talked of staying the best of friends forever. 'It does not matter that you are a woman and I, a man,' Shabbir would say. I, however, was aware of what was happening. We had been friends for nearly two years but on no occasion had he indicated by word or deed that he considered us to be anything other than the closest of friends. To me it was clear that he was completely smitten and did not want me out of his sight for a moment. I was also sure that everything about me attracted him for he did not let a day pass without seeing me. He was reluctant to leave even after having chatted for hours. Sometimes he would find excuses to come over more than once a day. Sometimes he came with his friends to hear me sing and when I sang, he would begin to cry. He would weep so copiously that I am sure he would have had to wring his handkerchief out afterwards. Yet he continued to insist that we were only the best of friends and that my being a woman was irrelevant. He would also repeatedly tell me how dearly he loved me, but only as a friend would love another friend.

I wondered if this was just love between friends. Was it only that? I was also forced to wonder what sort of a man he was. As far as my limited understanding went, it was clear that he had crossed the point of no return in our relationship. Did he lack the courage to express his love? Often while talking to him, I led the conversation into directions where he might unwittingly reveal his true feelings. Instead, he put forward reasoning that was beyond my comprehension.

Finally, I concluded that he was either very clever or so innocent that he had no idea how far he had let his feelings develop. If, by chance, I ran into him in the bazaar, his face would light up as though he had finally found the treasure he had been looking for. He would forget where we were or that people were watching us. He would run to where I was and in a single breath ask scores of questions, 'What have you come for? How have you come?

What do you have to buy? When will you return home?' Just running into me by accident would throw him off balance.

Days passed and things continued to be the same between us. I now began to visit Patiala a couple of times a month. I came face to face with the senior Maharaja only a few times. Otherwise it was the heir, the Maharaja's younger brother, who had been appointed guardian to the heir, and their staff who used to listen to me sing. The heir was almost a teetotaler. He was a sensible, well-mannered and quiet young man. Where his looks were concerned, he was one in a million. Even the staff of the senior Maharaja could not dare misbehave in his presence though they were free to drink, joke and laugh as much as they wanted.

Sometimes, when they particularly enjoyed the singing, they would come and sit down on the carpets. Each one was nearly six and a half feet tall, all had long dark beards and strange faces, and suddenly it seemed as if the audience was made up of supernatural beings. When they felt particularly affectionate towards someone, they would hit him so hard that the sound would resound across the room. They would think of things that no one else thought about.

Once a jagirdar invited the heir to dinner. He invited me to sing for the chief guest. When the singing was over, the heir left. Among those who stayed behind was a general who had had too much to drink.

'You sing so well,' he said to me, 'I loved it. And since I have never had such pleasure in my life before, I am going to end my life under the wheels of your car.' Turning to the others, he added, 'At least she will be sure that she had one true admirer.'

He came and lay down in front of my car. The others had to pull him away. Just when I thought I could move, there he was on the ground again!. It took half a dozen soldiers to hold him back so that I could leave.

Such incidents happened all the time and I enjoyed them. In fact I would miss Patiala if a month went by without me being invited. The people in Patiala both liked and respected me and were very mindful of my comforts. Nothing was done against my wishes. If someone was drunk and tried to be cheeky, the others firmly put him in his place. I became friendly with so many people there that all my apprehensions about Patiala disappeared.

The dialect spoken in Patiala was different from the one that I was used to. It was neither all Punjabi nor all Urdu. I loved listening to the local people speak. The Patiala style of singing a pahari was also different though it did not compare at all with the Jammu style. The people of Patiala often asked me to sing paharis and they liked my rendition more than their own local style.

Once I was invited to sing with two or three other women. They sang first. When the first one had finished, the host asked her to come and sit beside him on the sofa, which she did. The others, when they had finished, also accepted his invitation to join him on the sofa.

When I had finished singing, he asked me too, to come and sit on the sofa with him. I politely told him that I was already very comfortable where I was sitting.

'What is this?' he asked, 'Come, do not hesitate. Come and sit here.'

'I have great respect for you,' I told him, 'How then can I sit next to you?'

'*Tauba, tauba,*' he exclaimed, 'God save us. What is this that you are saying?'

A gentleman who had been listening to this exchange, joined in. '*Oye*, what illusions are you under?' he wanted to know of his host. 'If she agrees to sit besides you, I will give you five hundred rupees in cash on the spot.'

The host was now in a spot. He changed tack. He turned to me, 'Look, in front of everyone here, I declare that I consider you my sister. Now, as a sister, come and sit next to your brother so that he can extract those five hundred rupees.'

'God is very kind and I am very happy that he has gifted me with a brother,' I told him, 'As far as the money is concerned, I am sorry I do not have five hundred on me. I will write you a promissory note and you can go and collect it from the money that is due to me for singing tonight. For me, five hundred rupees is a very small price to pay for a brother.' No one was offended by this attitude of mine. In fact, my friendship with the people of Patiala increased.

47. Futile Dreams of Love

One day a man appeared bearing an invitation. He told me the host had invited about twenty people for dinner and wanted me to join them. He assured me that they were all well-known and well-respected people and left the host's address behind.

The host was a very good looking, tall and attractive man. In his well-cut trousers and jacket, he looked very handsome. He sat next to me at the dining table and we made small talk. Clearly, he had been greatly influenced by western culture. The dinner comprised mainly western dishes. Everyone used knives and forks to eat. The half a dozen or so women who were there were also dressed and made up in the western fashion. When they spoke they preferred English to Punjabi or Urdu. If they used Urdu or Punjabi words, they made sure they used an accent to show that they did not use the words often.

I had worn a French brocade sari. In those days good saris were made in Paris, Bombay and Poona. I had a large range of expensive saris, each more beautiful than the other. His Highness had ordered all these saris for me from abroad. I was not beautiful nor did I consider myself attractive but I did have exceptional hair. When I wore a sari, my thick plait snaked down my back till it reached my feet. Unlike the women at the party, I had neither concocted a bird's nest on my head nor did I have devilishly long fingernails. I was dark and used no make-up. In fact, I was clueless about using makeup. A few times I had tried to make myself look fair by powdering my face, but I had ended up looking so awful that I had to immediately wash everything off.

I was very fond of glass bangles. I wore bangles that matched all the colours of my sari. I covered my arms, from my wrist to my elbow, with these coloured glass bangles. My hair was done plainly unlike the other women whose hairdressers had teased their hair so high that their faces looked disproportionately small, like those of monkeys.

The men and women there praised my sari and my hair. I sang after dinner. They listened to me in rapt attention. Before I left, I spent ten or fifteen minutes talking to the host. He had a huge factory that manufactured goods for export. His was the only factory in Lahore making those particular goods. He was young and rich. Every year he imported a new and very fancy car. He wore the finest suits and shoes and even used the best quality handkerchiefs.

Apart from his looks, Allah had also blessed him with a fine physique. He spoke well and that first day, when he spoke to me, he set off a turmoil within me. He looked into my eyes and placed a small handkerchief into my hand saying, 'Please put this in your purse. Perhaps, when you look at it, you will think of me.'

I did look at the handkerchief frequently when I got home, and recalled everything about him. This was the first time that someone had overpowered me in just one meeting. I kept thinking about him for a long time. I had always been very careful in following my head rather than my heart in whatever I did. I was also fully aware of the strange desires within me. I knew well what happened when resolve faltered. For a couple of hours of pleasure, the woman would find herself permanently in the well of infamy. Men stopped respecting her and the woman herself would turn into the slave of her male master.

I prided myself for my self-respect and hence knew how to bring such temptations under control. Two days went by. On the third day he arrived with a few friends to hear me sing. That day too, he was very well dressed. In fact I began liking him even more. When he was leaving after spending a few hours, he quietly asked me, 'Did you look at the handkerchief?'

'Once or twice,' I lied

'Did you think of me?'

'Yes,' I answered truthfully.

A few days later he invited me again to his home. Five or six of his friends were there. We sat and talked at the dining table for more than an hour. The conversation consisted mostly of him telling me how he thought of me every moment, how he wished he could spend all his time talking to me, and how he wanted to spend his life with me. He asked me how I felt. I told him that I still had to reach the stage that he had reached, though I admitted to thinking about him.

I sang for a short time that night.

A couple of days later he sent a message asking me out to a film. He assured me the film was very good and he would drop me home immediately after it was over. Mother firmly refused to let me go, 'No, you are going to no picture-*wickchar.*' I sent back word that mother had refused me permission to go. Two days later, he appeared himself and listened to me sing. After that he hung around for an hour. My family too, stayed so close that we got no chance to speak privately. He was very agitated about this. When he was leaving he came close to me and in a whisper asked if we could meet somewhere else.

'I have no answer to that. I also don't know what to do,' I told him. He left very disappointed. He tried to invite me out to dinner a few times but my mother would have none of that either. He then invited me again to his house to sing. I sent back word that I would be there between eight and eight thirty. In the evening when I was getting ready to go, mother asked me where I was going. I told her that he had invited me to sing.

'I do not approve of these constant invitations,' she made herself clear about how she felt about him.

'Why?' I asked, 'Does he not pay me my fee? Or is he paying me less than the others do? When I can perform elsewhere, why can I not do so at his home?'

Mother fumed but kept quiet. I was ready at eight and went and sat in the car. Mother was forced to come along with me. Dinner was served some time after we reached there. Dinner was the only occasion when he could talk to me. He was very upset. He constantly said the same things, 'Tell me what to do? I want to meet you every day. How can I arrange this? Your family treats me as though I am a dangerous criminal. Their foreheads crease into frowns the moment they see me. No one even offers me a glass of water, not to speak of a cup of tea. What have I done to displease them? At least you can ask them this; make them change their attitude towards me.'

Again, I made it clear that I was helpless

'Why,' he wanted to know, 'Why are you so helpless? Do you not have the right to see whoever you want to in your own house?'

I had also been seething with resentment at these developments. But then, since I was relatively young, I was completely in awe of mother and did not have the courage to confront her. I was even surprised that mother had discovered that I was attracted to him. Surely, something about me had changed to give me away.

I hated the idea of anyone else finding out that I was in love. Just the thought of it embarrassed me as much as if I had been caught committing a grave sin. I had definitely fallen in love with him, and if I had any doubts earlier, the attitude of my family, made me more adamant about it. I had nothing to do with my property, money, jewellery or anything else. I did not care for any of these things nor did I spend any time thinking about them.

However, who I liked and who I did not was my personal affair. Did my family have the right to make these decisions for me? Did I always have to do exactly what they wanted? Was I supposed to run after the people they liked and if I liked someone, they would not even let him into the house! I wondered what it was about him that made them oppose him so much. I had been meeting him for about four months and that too, always in their presence. In fact, I still had to make up my mind about what sort of a man he was.

I had been meeting people that my family approved of for twenty years. After twenty years, when they got the slightest of hints that I liked someone, they had all become his deadly enemies. My family became even more adamant as far as he was concerned. It almost seemed that they wanted to ensure that I would never like anyone in the world. I grappled with my anger and turned irritable. I stopped meeting everybody. If someone visited me, I would excuse myself and disappear into my room. I did continue to see a little of Shabbir, and he frequently commented that he had noticed a change in me. I denied this.

Then one day, he came to visit me. I greeted him warmly, asked him to tea and ignored everyone else around. I went and sat close to him and kept him there for a long time. My family did not say a word to him. When he was leaving, I asked loudly when he was going to come again.

'Whenever you want,' was his immediate response.

'Drop in whenever you want to,' I told him

I do not know how I had become so fearless. There was a great deal of tension in the house. Mother stopped speaking to me. I ignored her. I spoke sharply to all visitors but when he dropped in every second or third day, I greeted him with enthusiasm. We usually spoke to each other in soft voices.

One day Shabbir arrived soon after him. He sat down at some distance. I was not happy that Shabbir had dropped in at that particular time. I felt as if he had caught me stealing. I was tongue-tied and sat there like a stone. Ten minutes later Shabbir left saying he would come back some other time.

Left alone, he asked me, 'How long are we going to go on meeting like this?'

'Why, have you run out of patience already?' I asked him.

'No, it is not that,' he reassured me, 'I just wonder where all this is going to lead.'

'Well, what do you think?' I wanted to know.

'Marriage.'

'That is fine,' I said, 'However, I cannot do that in a hurry.'

'I am desperate,' he pleaded, 'I cannot live without you for a minute. If there had been a possibility of us meeting regularly, I could have waited a lifetime. Your family hates me. I, like every other human being, have my self-respect. I feel humiliated every time I come to see you. If you want to marry me, marry me now.'

I told him that I did want to get married but not immediately. I said I would like to think carefully before I did. It was one step that I did not want to retrace.

The next day Shabbir visited me. 'Yesterday I found out why you have changed so much.'

'And what did you discover?' I wanted to know.

'Ask yourself and your heart that,' he shot back.

'Well, my heart tells me nothing. Nor am I the weak person you imagine me to be,' I told him. 'I do not know what conclusions you have drawn.'

'Well,' he said, 'that man is not a good man. He is well-known as a flirt. He is pushy and promotes himself on every occasion. His wealth is new, and he comes from a very ordinary family.'

'Why should I care what he is like when I have nothing to do with him?' And as far as his family is concerned, I am no Mughal princess either. I do not care what he is and what he is not.' I tried to make my position clear. I was not going to admit anything to anyone.

Things changed dramatically soon after. I did not know whether it was he who had been telling people or if people were drawing their own conclusions. Every acquaintance that I met would invariably bring up the subject of marriage, 'We have heard that you are planning to marry so and so?' they would ask. Some were even more blunt and asked when I was getting married. I would question them about the source of their information and invariably they would name him. I would tell everyone, 'He is lying. I have not accepted his proposal nor do I intend to.' Suddenly it seemed that everyone in the city had turned into my sympathiser and was trying to rescue me from the trap of a trickster. Yet, I wanted him. I continued to meet him regularly. I asked him how this matter about us getting married had become so well-known. He admitted that he had been telling people about our possible marriage. 'When my friends ask me why I meet you almost every day and why I waste so much money on you, I tell them it is because you will be marrying me. You tell me. Is there anything else that I can say?'

Worse was to come. There was an ordinary contractor whom I had met somewhere. He had declared that he considered me his sister. He was ugly, illiterate and given to bragging. This man showed up one day and came straight to the point. 'I have heard that you are planning to marry him. I treat you as if you were a sister and my self-respect will not allow that you marry a man who has been with me as my woman.'

I could not figure out why people disliked him so much. However, their attitude towards him had one effect on me. I began to become increasingly conscious of his shortcomings. I do not know if all of them were real or if I was imagining things. Yet my passion for him did subside.

A person who knew him well told me all about him. He had been married in his youth. His father had died when he was very young and his mother had spoilt him with her affection. He had also fathered a daughter while still very young. When Allah was kind to them and gave them all the wealth, the mother and son could no longer stomach his simple wife. They took away the daughter and he divorced her. Now they were waiting for him to get married again. He was about thirty or thirty-two. His daughter lived with his mother.

I became even more wary of him when I heard all his. I also began to be afraid of him. I continued to meet him as before, but I no longer pined for him. Now I did not believe half the things he said to me and usually found shallowness in everything he said.

Life soon returned to it normal routine. I began to become interested in all the things I had become indifferent to. There was a friend of Shabbir's who was from Gujrat. He was from a respected family, serious, well-spoken and a man of letters. He was neither attractive nor was he ugly. He was over six feet tall, well dressed and given to refinements. He always wore an achkan, a spotless white shalwar and exquisitely embroidered gold *khussas*. This attire suited him a great deal.

Soon he began to drop in on me without Shabbir. Sometimes he brought vegetables or *rewris* made of jaggery for which Gujrat was famous. I used to love those and would thank him profusely for them. He never came empty handed from Gujrat. Despite being from a well-off family, his financial condition was no longer good. He had an ordinary job. He too was only thirty or thirty-two but he had already sired eleven children. Lord knows how he managed to stay so well dressed or how he managed to maintain his elegant lifestyle and dignity. He owned a lot of land but he earned little from it. Yet with his skills, he managed to maintain an elegant lifestyle.

On one visit, in a sad voice, his eyes brimming with tears, he pulled a long face and said, 'There is something that I want to say to you. But you will have to promise that you will not mention this to anyone.'

I assured him that I would not. He then proceeded to tell me what was on his mind, 'I have been in love with you for a very long time but have not had the courage to tell you so. Now, every night at three, you appear in my dreams and ask me why I do not tell you of my love when I love you so much.'

I burst into laughter when I heard this. He started sobbing like a child when he heard me laugh. When he would not stop, I started to get concerned. Having laughed at him already, there was little I could say to soothe him. I was seething inside. Why did these men always blame me for the state they got themselves into? I began to hate him.

I did not tell Shabbir or Salamatullah anything about this. I had lost all respect for the man. Even the rewris he brought now tasted as though they were poisonous. He continued to come from Gujrat every week to see me. On every visit he told me of some new dream of his. Apparently, sometimes I looked very worried in his dreams which made him head straight for Lahore to check if everything was fine with me. He also cried for an hour or two whenever he visited. I had never seen so much water flow from anyone's eyes. I found I hated the sight of him weeping and felt very uneasy about it. Yet, every week he continued to indulge himself once or twice at my expense.

Finally, one day I offered him a solution. I told him: 'All you want is that I start loving you too, is it not? But then, there is no single way to love a person. There are many ways of loving. You know that you have eleven children. I can never love you in the way you want. Instead, why do you not look start looking upon me as a sister? Then, I will be able to see you as a brother and I will be able to tell you of all my joys and sorrows. This is one bond that cannot be broken.'

My words hit him as though they were bullets. The faucets in his eyes were turned on full blast. After weeping for a while, he left. He returned after a few days. He looked much better. First he told me of his latest dream. Then we spoke some more about inconsequential things. Finally, he said, 'From now on you are my sister and I your brother.' I really do not know if he meant what he was saying. To be truthful, he continued to love me forever. Whenever he came, he still told me about his dreams. He continued to keep himself informed of my welfare till he died.

I was invited to Patiala for the wedding of the heir and his younger brother. I was told that I would have to spend a month in

Patiala and I was also asked what my charges would be for the month. I made it clear to them that it did not matter whether I was invited for two days or two months for I would charge by the day. I told them that if they found this too much, they could only invite me for a day. I knew that these petty matters did not concern the Maharajas who ordered rather than bargained. It was the petty officials of the court who, to prove their concern, tried to be clever. A few days later the invitation bearer had returned and told me which day I was supposed to arrive in Patiala. He also informed me that my terms had been accepted.

I started preparing to go. Early that day, Shabbir arrived. I told him that I was going to be leaving in four days to spend a month in Patiala.

48. My Visit to Patiala

Shabbir fell silent when he heard of my plans. I had my saris, blouses and dresses ironed and started packing them into trunks. We talked while he helped me pack. He seemed to be a bit sad and asked me several times if I intended spending a full month in Patiala. Pleased, I answered, 'Yes, but then, as the Sikhs say, it only takes a moment for the month to pass.' Shabbir was not amused.

In the four days left before my departure, Shabbir came every day, in the morning and in the evening. But he had changed. He had lost his sense of humour and he seemed to have forgotten that there were such things as laughter or jokes. Instead, he looked distracted all the time. I tried hard, but in vain, to lighten his mood.

Finally the day for my departure arrived. The train for Patiala left in the evening. When I reached the railway station, Shabbir was already waiting for me there. He held an English magazine in his hand. I took it from him and began leafing through it. He stood on the platform by the window of the railway compartment while I sat inside and flipped the pages of the magazine. He looked so sad that I thought he would burst into tears at any moment.

I felt mischievous. I wrote 'I' on one page of the magazine. Seven or eight pages later, I scribbled 'love' on another page. Another fifteen or twenty pages later, I added 'you.' The guard of the train blew his whistle and the train began to move. Shabbir continued to walk along with the moving train. When the train started to pick up speed, I said 'Oh ho' and handed the magazine back to him.

When I reached Patiala I found that performing ladies from about fifteen or twenty other cities were already there, even though some of them were not particularly good or famous. It seemed that numbers were the only things that had mattered to the organizers. Tented residences had been put up for all of us. Each tent was supposed to be shared by two or three of these ladies. Mercifully, I was given a tent all to myself. The other women objected and said that they too wanted independent tents. They were told that this is the way the Maharaja had ordered things and the organizers were helpless to change anything. I am sure the Maharaja knew nothing about all this and it was his underlings who decided these matters. I knew all these people and many of them were friends.

Everyone was given the choice of opting for cooked food or provisions. All opted for the latter. Each one of them said they were concerned that the meat served to them might not come from animals slaughtered in the right way. This, when there was a huge troop of Muslim servants in the Maharaja's kitchens! In each kingdom they kept the dietary preferences of their guests in mind. Yet, no one accepted the offer of cooked meals.

I too had opted for provisions but two or three trays full of dry fruit, chocolates, ice cream and many kinds of *halwas* were delivered to my tent twice a day. Every day two durbars were held where singing took place. One was for special guests and the other was meant for the others. The heir, his staff, his uncles, and the son-in-law of the Maharaja, as well as the heir's younger brother who had a broken leg, attended the special durbar. I do not know if they were real brothers or stepbrothers. The Maharaja's younger son limped, was acceptable to look at and he was a good and honourable young man. I liked him a lot and had become good friends with him. I usually tend to forget names but I remember his—Bir Singh.

The jagirdars, generals, colonels, the nobility and the elite of the kingdom attended the other durbar. Huge electric bulbs lit up a large tent. Dinner was served between nine and ten. Then the singing would start.

I had now been to Patiala many times. All the state employees had heard me sing. Every day they sent requests that I be allowed to perform for them too. Therefore, I would sing at the second durbar for a short time. They all talked of me and they were not interested in hearing the others sing. They accused the other women of not knowing how to sing and not being very good performers.

In the first few days I was treated with great respect and honour. The groom had to go in a procession to Bahadurgarh where the bride lived. However, before the groom's party left, the Maharaja held a durbar where only I sang. The women who were employed by the state were very resentful of this, 'We have served the kingdom all our lives. We present ourselves wherever and whenever the Maharaja wishes us to. This is grave injustice to us that on this special occasion an outsider is given the privilege of performing. It is our right to sing at this durbar,' they complained.

No one paid any attention to them. Poor things, they were all employed at hundred or two hundred rupees a month. They were all very ordinary to look at and their clothes, as well as their singing, were pedestrian. They had neither good clothes, jewellery nor looks to compensate. Since many rulers of the other states had been invited to attend the wedding, only I performed at the durbar.

The groom's party left for Bahadurgarh. A large wooden platform with wheels had been built for the procession. This was to be pulled by two elephants. The heir and his brothers were dressed as grooms and made to sit on chairs on that platform. After the procession left the city, every one got off the platform and got into cars to go on to Bahadurgarh.

Tents had been put up in Bahadurgarh too, indeed the whole city seemed to consist only of tents. All the guests were accommodated in these. There was a palace but it looked like a large house. The heir and the Maharaja's son-in-law stayed there. Everyone else lived in the tents.

The army was on guard all the time and the soldiers patrolled everywhere. Some of the roads were covered with brick dust. Set against this brick red, the white tents looked stunning. Of course, Bahadurgarh was no match for the grandeur of Jammu but it did look as though a fairyland had been created out of a jungle.

People from Patiala came by the hundred to watch the wedding. Landless labourers with their families carrying bundles on their heads were walking towards Bahadurgarh. They hoped to find villages close by where they could spend the night. With their children on their shoulders, they looked happy.

I went to the tent allotted to me and rested for a while. Then I got ready and went to the palace. All the other performing ladies were already there. The gathering was very small: only the heir, Bir Singh, the Maharaja's brother who was the guardian of the heir and a few ADCs. The heir was looking very good. I had rarely seen such a handsome man in my life. He was lean, taller than six feet and was fair with a pinkish tinge to his complexion. The Maharaja himself was a good-looking man but there was an element of savagery in his looks. Because he drank so much liquor his wheatish complexion had now turned dark. In contrast, the heir's colour looked as if vermilion had been mixed with chalk. I had seen him scores of times but tonight, dressed as a groom, he looked so dazzling that it was difficult to look at him for long. There was nothing about him that belittled his dignity. Because he almost did not drink, he never did anything foolish that could have given others the opportunity to laugh at him behind his back. The rest of the staff however, drank liquor as though they were drinking water.

Singing began at ten. I sang after two or three others had performed. While the lady who followed me was singing, the Maharaja came in along with a few ministers and ADCs. This was the first time that he had appeared at a gathering arranged for the heir. I had never seen him in such a state before. He wore a turban of Banarsi brocade, emeralds and pearls around his neck; a large gathered shalwar of boski silk and gold-embroidered khussas on his feet. He was also frothing at the mouth and his hands hung in front of him as though he was a cripple. Silence descended on the gathering the moment he appeared. Everyone stood up in greeting.

The Maharaja asked after some son-in-law of his and the heir told him that he had just left to go to bed. Perhaps the Maharaja did not know the names of any of the other ladies present for he turned to me and said, 'Pukhraj, bring the others and follow me.' The Maharaja headed for the room of his son-in-law. I led the procession, in single file, of the singing ladies and all the others who had been there. We looked like an army platoon doing the drill for a parade.

We reached the room. The son-in-law was in deep sleep. I was immediately behind the Maharaja when we entered the room.

'Pukhraj,' he said.

'*Ji*,' I answered respectfully.

'Go and lie down beside him,' he ordered.

Lord knows whether the gentleman was really sleeping or only pretending to, for he still did not wake up even while all this was happening in the room. The Maharaja wanted to play a prank on his son-in-law by getting a woman into his bed.

'Your Highness,' I said, 'You have invited me here to sing. If you ask me to sing by the roadside, I am willing to do so. This, however, is not one of my duties.'

The Maharaja looked at the other woman standing in line behind me. He asked her to get into the bed and she also refused. All the women had heard me refuse. They must have reasoned, 'if she can refuse, so can we. After all, who does she think she is?' They all refused to get into the bed with the sleeping son-in-law.

The Maharaja was furious. 'Get lost,' he shouted. We filed out in a single file just as we had entered. The Maharaja followed me out of the room. He stood in the hallway and we stood facing him. The heir and his group stood silently to one side. There was terror and apprehension on their faces for they must have witnessed many similar incidents. Silently, they were signalling that I should ask the Maharaja to forgive me. Bir Singh, his own hands folded, was gesturing at us pleading with us to ask to be forgiven. Everyone knew the punishments the Maharaja meted out for disobedience, so they all tried disperately to indicate to me that I should apologize but I stood behind the others, silently.

The Maharaja's brother tried to defuse the situation, 'This is a very happy occasion. Your Highness, why do you not forgive them this one time? You are a lucky man. No previous ruler of Patiala has witnessed the marriage of his heir. These women are naïve and foolish for having disobeyed you. You are the ruler and you can do anything. Why do you not forgive them?'

He then turned to us, 'Come on now, kiss His Highness' feet.'

This surprised the Maharaja and he took a couple of steps backwards saying. 'No! I will not allow this.' A little while later he had changed his mind, 'All right, I forgive you,' he said as he put

a foot forward. It did not take the others long to decide what to
do. They all stepped forward and began kissing his foot.

Only I continued to stand where I was. It was not as if I was
fearless. I was thinking how I had never demeaned myself even
for the one for whom I had worked for nine years; one who had
given me love, respect and who had gifted me so many things. I
was not religious nor did I have any pretensions of being saintly.
All I knew was that you only prostrated yourself before God. That
I bend in front of the Maharaja and kiss his feet was out of the
question. Others could do what they wanted. All the women
exonerated themselves by doing as they had been asked. I was
the only one left.

The Maharaja spoke to me. 'So this is how arrogant you are!
That Hari Singh has spoilt you. But then, he was not even a man
but a eunuch. He gave you too much attention. You are so arrogant
because you have so many clothes, coats and jewellery.'

At that time I used to make sure that I had a coat to match each
sari. I would match the brocade with the coat and then have fur
added to the collar and the cuffs. I had about fifteen or twenty
very pretty coats. The Maharaja had not finished with my coats,
'So you are arrogant because of the number of coats you have?' I
was surprised that he noticed this kind of detail. He went on,
'You must realize that I am no eunuch like your Maharaja. I am a
man. If I want to, I can have you dumped into a well. I could have
you burnt alive. I could send you to a place where no one would
find you for the rest of your life.'

He then turned to his brother – the one he had appointed as
guardian to the heir. He began to abuse him, 'You bastard, why
did you invite her? I have appointed you to look after the interests
of my son. Do you not know that she has already destroyed one
kingdom? Do you want our kingdom to be destroyed too?'

Turning to me, he said, 'Get out of the kingdom at once.'

I left the palace immediately. I do not remember how I felt at
that moment. I do not know where my courage and strength came
from. I ran to my tent, which was at a fair distance. Briefly, and in
a hurry, I told mother what had happened and that we had to
leave everything and get away immediately. If we got out alive,
my accompanists could always bring our luggage back. I did not

waste a moment. I took off my jewellery, changed my sari, and wrapped myself in a handloom sheet that I borrowed from one of the accompanists. We took one accompanist with us and he, my mother and I left the tent without telling anyone.

It was one-thirty at night. The army was on guard everywhere. We crouched and walked silently behind the tents holding on to the ropes that held them in place. We managed to evade the guards and reached the road coming into Bahadurgarh. The closest railway station was twelve miles away. Allah was kind to us. Hundreds of people from Patiala were still walking to Bahadurgarh for the wedding. The road was full of bullock carts, tongas, horses and people on foot. A small dirt track ran alongside the main road. We took that road and started running. We were so scared that we did not even realize that we were running. We wanted to get out of the kingdom before daybreak and we ran as fast as we could. After a few miles, the road was suddenly lit with blinding, bright light. We immediately turned around and pretended to be among those heading for Bahadurgarh. A car passed us by. The Maharaja was sitting in the front seat along with the driver. I was wrapped in the cotton sheet and my mother and the musician too were dressed as plain folk. It was impossible to pick us out in the crowd.

The car turned around and drove back towards Bahadurgarh. We turned around and again started running towards the station. The Maharaja drove up and down three times looking for us. He might not have believed that we could have gotten this far in such a short time. The headlights of the car were shone in all directions to scan the crowds. The lights were powerful and lit up large areas. Thank God he did not find us and mecifully the fear of death made us run even faster.

We reached the railway station before daybreak, bought tickets and found a place in a third class compartment. The station was in British territory. The moment we sat down in the train, I started shivering so violently that my teeth began to chatter and I had to hold on to my face with both my hands. It could have been exhaustion, or fear, for we were still not out of danger. The Maharajas had such power that their lies could easily be turned into the truth. If he knew we were at the station, he could have

accused us of robbery and had us arrested. We would have had
no chance to plead our innocence and might have had to spend
the rest of our lives in jail. As long as the train stood at the station,
all we did was to pray and promise offerings to the Almighty if we
survived. We thanked God when the train moved, but we
continued to be full of fear till we reached Lahore. God had saved
us.

My accompanists arrived the same day with my luggage. They
told us that half an hour after we had left, the Maharaja himself
had stormed into our tent. When he did not find me there he
went to look for me in the other camps. He asked each woman
he saw if she knew where I was. Each swore that she had no idea.
He abused a few and slapped a few others to force them to admit
that they knew. The women wept and pleaded their ignorance
and innocence.

The soldiers were ordered to search the area. Half an hour
later they reported that I was not to be found. My accompanists
had been smart. Soon after we left, they took my stuff and joined
the accompanists of the other ladies. Their lives would have been
thrashed out of them had they been caught.

An hour and a half later, the Maharaja got into the car to look
for us. Because we had run so fast and because he did not think
we could reach that far, we managed to escape. He was convinced
that I was hiding or had been hidden in Bahadurgarh. That is why
after each foray he came back to Bahadurgarh. He was beside
himself with anger and constantly abused me, 'How dare she
disobey me!' When he would head back to the car he would hit a
few more women to make them tell him where I was. They all
reminded him that they were with him in the palace when I had
left. 'Lord knows where she has disappeared,' is all they could
say.

'This cannot be true,' he screamed. 'She cannot escape from
here.'

It was nothing but God's grace that he never imagined we could
reach the station on foot. If he had, we would have been caught
easily. When he had returned from his third search, his staff tried
to assure him that I would be found the next morning and that he

should now rest. It took a lot of convincing to make him go to bed.

Deep down I was convinced that he could not have harmed even a hair on my head because I had refused to prostrate myself before him. Running those twelve miles had not tired me out. Instead of a month, I had returned to Lahore in a week. For a few days the possible scenarios of what could have happened if we had been caught, kept re-playing themselves in my head. Who knows what he would have done to me in that fit of rage. If that furious man who kept looking for me all night on the road had caught me, what would he have done? I often had nightmares thinking about this and sometimes had to wake up my mother.

Shabbir was a magistrate at the District Collectorate. I sent a servant to tell him that I was back. Shabbir was at my home before the servant had returned. In a single breath he asked a dozen questions: 'Why are you back so early? Had you not gone for a month? Why this hasty return? Do you have to go back?' I told him everything and added, 'Be thankful that I escaped or we would never have met again.'

'If that had happened, I too would have died,' he said instantly. He later pretended to ignore what he had just said. A little while later he asked me, 'Did you miss me?'

'How could I have thought of anyone? Who could I have missed? There was so much to do that I did not have to think even of myself.'

He was not pleased with my answer. The joy disappeared from his face. He continued to respond to what I said but his mind was elsewhere. I wondered why he was this way because nothing had changed about me.

He was so simple and innocent that on returning from the station after seeing me off to Patiala he had told all his friends that I had written three words in a magazine and left them behind for him to see. He had asked them to guess what the words were. Shabbir also told them that the words were written on different pages. The rest of them were smart and quick and had immediately asked whether the words were in Urdu or English. When he told them that they were in English, in one voice, they said, 'I love you.' Shabbir had admitted that those were the words.

Shabbir left after spending an hour or two with me. A few hours later he was back. Almost in a whisper he asked me if I had written anything in the magazine.

'When? What?' I asked innocently. 'I don't know what you are talking about. What magazine?'

'Just as you were leaving for Patiala, you took the magazine from my hand. You returned it when the train began to move,' he said, trying to jog my memory.

'I do not remember writing anything,' I lied.

'But those words have changed my life,' he confessed, 'I have not slept a moment since you left. And now you deny that you wrote anything at all!'

'You are my friend,' I reassured him, 'how could I ever have written anything to hurt you? At least tell me the words that I am supposed to have written.'

'Are you really telling me the truth?' he wanted to be sure.

'You are a strange man,' I now said in mock anger, 'why would I need to lie? I am not a crude person and I am confident that I would not write anything that is so inappropriate as to hurt you.'

By the time I was finished saying all this, he had begun to sob loudly. In fact, he cried for so long that I began to worry. I tried to calm him down.

'You know that I consider you my best friend. I have had no other friend till now. You are the only true friend that I have. Please tell me what I am supposed to have written that has caused you so much grief. If I unwittingly did something that hurt you, please forgive me. I swear I would not hurt you deliberately.'

My words did not help. He began to weep even more. In between his sobs he told me what the words were.

'This is too much!' I reacted angrily, 'First, I do not remember writing any such thing. And supposing I did write them, is it the end of the world? You know I practise my English by writing down words. And if I did write those words, you decided that they were meant for you? Is it not true that you are a close and dear friend of mine? If I say I love you, why does it hurt you? In any case they were not written for you nor meant to convey anything. It would be a coincidence if I wrote those words. Anyway, I love you and you will always be my friend.'

Actually, I had been very angry about him having told the entire group about it. Salamatuallah had already told me about this. To him too, I had denied any knowledge of the matter. Why did Shabbir have to tell everyone about this? Had it been necessary for him to advertise it? I was angry at his lack of discretion and that he had been so foolish. That I had admitted that I loved him had raised Shabbir's hopes. For effect, I told him a story.

I had been nine or ten when I was walking through Kanak Mandi in Jammu with a girl friend. I was trying to tell her how much I loved her. In the kingdom they would buy cows and bulls and set them free to roam the streets. Since there was grain piled up everywhere in Kanak Mandi, the cattle preferred to hang around this area and they roamed around freely. Whenever they got the chance, they would eat some trader's grain.

Sometimes two bulls would get into a fight. In their fury they would take a few steps back and charge at each other. They hit each other so hard that the sound was like a cannon shot. People would run and find safety inside shops.

While I was trying to reassure my friend of my love for her, I saw a bull charging straight at me. In a flash I caught my friend by both her arms and put her between the bull and myself and hid behind her!

Shabbir was not amused. He had lost his sense of humour. He now appeared lost. Now, I began to get angry with myself. Why had I done this? Shabbir was very restless and wanted to spend all his time with me. However, he would sit silently. I too began to lose interest in him. I was no longer happy to see him when he dropped in. Time dragged when he was around. I was tired of seeing him sad, desolate and silent.

49. Rai Sahib

Every weekend, a teary-eyed Rai Sahib continued to recite Shakespeare to me as though I understood every word of it. He was
also very scared of me. To please me he gave me expensive gifts
including very beautiful earrings with my name written on them
in diamonds and emeralds. He often gave me gold jewellery for
my neck. He was a miser but behaved to the contrary as far as I
was concerned.

Once I was going to Rawalpindi. He told me of the attractions
of Head Rasool where he was posted—the canal, the gardens, his
bungalow and asked me stop there for a night. He assured me
that I would love the place. I accepted the invitation.

It was really a beautiful place and he was extremely hospitable.
He served all kinds of food. One call from him brought five servants
running in response. He was very rude when he spoke to them.
The labourers and the gardeners were paid by the government
but spent the day working for him.

I had to leave for Lahore the next morning. He ordered a servant
to get a canister of ghee for me. The servant did so. The moment
he returned, Rai Sahib immediately wanted to know whether he
had taken an empty canister with him to exchange and save money
on buying a new container. The servant had not.

'Why not?' an angry Rai Sahib wanted to know.

'I did not think of it,' the servant admitted fearfully.

'*Hai Hai*,' exclaimed Rai Sahib, 'do you have no brains? Did
you not know that it would save money if you took the empty
canister with you? All of you are bent on ruining me. You are
wasting all that I sweat so much to earn. You bastard, you idiot,
you mad man—you and the rest are all squandering my money.'
He was so angry that he forgot that I was sitting right there,
watching all this in amazement. I was stunned. On the one hand

there was this tight fistedness and meanness. On the other, there was the jewellery and the weekly canister of ghee that he gifted me. Here he was ready to kill for two annas, for that was what an empty canister of ghee cost in those days.

Yet, he never had the guts to ask me if we really consumed the whole canister of ghee that he presented me every week. He did not ask if we were running a house or a confectionery shop. This was the first time I had been exposed to the low and base side of him. He had tried to impress me by showing how he could terrorise people and they held him in great awe. I had never liked him in any case. Now, I did not even want to look at him. He treated his servants as if they were not even human. I had looked at all his actions and his recitations as a theatrical spoof and enjoyed them for that. After that trip to Head Rasool, I never wanted to see him again. Each word and each action of his began to annoy me and I began to behave rudely to him. He, however, was so insensitive that he was there every Saturday. He would listen to me sing or he would recite Shakespeare till midnight. Unlike earlier times when I listened to him earnestly, I now paid no attention but this made no difference to him. Falling in love in old age is a dangerous thing. You lose your reason and your senses. When a man falls in love after he is sixty, he usually ends up being humiliated. Rai Sahib was totally insensitive to how I was insulting him.

We had now been in Lahore for over two years. During this period I had come across some men that I liked and considered marrying. However, invariably, within four months or so, I ended up more conscious of their shortcomings than their attractions. I could not imagine having to spend even a month with them. I realized that wealth and good looks were not the only things that mattered. What really mattered was loyalty.

In the society of those days a woman associated with singing became a millstone around a man's neck and was the reason for constant taunting. If they married, the man's parents would not accept her. Or if they relented because of their feelings for their son, the others in the family still refused to accept the wife. They would humiliate the husband in so many ways that it became difficult for the man to keep his self-respect intact. His resolve would crumble and he would often end up losing respect for the woman. He would start regretting his actions and start worrying about his image in society. Since it was impossible for him to leave his city and his family, he would become ill-tempered and irritable and start quarrelling with his wife.

And then, there was the poor woman who had also defied her own family to marry him, and in the process had left behind everything to run away with him. She now found herself totally helpless, friendless and with no moral support. She would be tortured and humiliated in all sorts of ways in her new home. And this was made worse by the fact of her husband turning against her. In fact, his sisters and sisters-in-law would incite him to the point where he became violent. She would be left with no option but to return home.

Not that the decision helped her for the woman carried her misfortune with her. Everyone at home continuously taunted her and she lacked respect even in her own home. It was a difficult lesson for her to learn. This one act of hers turned her from a woman into a dangerous proposition, and often it would make her turn against all men for they would now appear the same to her and she would never be able to trust another man again. I knew of several women who had been through such experiences.

In Jammu I had had no diversions except reading magazines and novels. By fourteen I had read all sorts of novels. I would subscribe to all the magazines whether they were published in Lahore, Delhi, Lucknow or wherever else. I had become quite an expert in matters of love and of the heart. I was aware of the advantages and pitfalls of each situation. I never trusted anyone. Instead, I would first try and find out how far a man spoke the truth or if he lied. If it happened that I was attracted to the man who expressed his love for me, I would become even more alert. I would become suspicious of everything about him and distrust anything that he said. I would wonder about the things he claimed to be true. Was it possible that he could not sleep just because he was in love with me? How could someone stop eating or drinking because he had fallen in love? All these proclamations seemed very dubious to me.

Sometimes I would tell myself that since I could not find anyone suitable, should I still continue to look? Why should I bother about all this and make myself unhappy? Perhaps I was emotionally dead. The actual truth however, was that I had no problems about meeting people. I also knew that people chased those who were unavailable with more ardour than was usual.

Every year I would go up into the hills for five months in the summer. I particularly liked going to Shimla and Dalhousie. My mother, the Englishwoman whom I had employed, my mother's brother who drove our car, and a few others would come along with me. Shabbir and his friends would make fun of me by reciting the couplet, '*jadu barsaat di rut aawe, koyal ja pahad te ku kardi aye*'—the moment the monsoon arrives, the *koel* goes to the hills to sing. Wherever I went, Shabbir would visit me at least once or twice. He would spend the whole day writing short stories and then read them to us.

My good-looking suitor would also visit me three or four times in the hills. He would stay in a hotel for a couple of days. He would drop in to see me once or twice a day. My family would not even bother to be polite to him. I still liked him a great deal and often wished that I could spend my life with him. Yet I was afraid. Whenever he invited me to his home for dinner, there were always a few young women there. I do not know if they were there to impress me or to please him. I also did not know how much of him was real and how much false. He followed me everywhere and in summer he turned up wherever I was. Other friends also came to visit. Rai Sahib too would make a few trips. Those five months of summer passed wonderfully. It did not seem as if I had left Lahore at all. Salamatullah too always came for a few days. When summer ended, I returned to Lahore.

Whenever Shabbir went hunting he would come straight to my house on his return and leave behind what he had shot before he went home. One day he came to me in a panic, 'I have been posted to Wazirabad and I cannot stay away from you.' I tried to calm him down and explain that there was no place in the world for an unemployed man, and that no one respected such a man. He asked me if I would write if he went away.

'Why? So that you can show my letters to all your friends?' I asked, 'When I had written just three words, you showed them to the whole of Lahore. Do you now want to show them my letters?'

He was very embarrassed, 'I sincerely regret that. I have already suffered enough for what I did. If you want me to keep my job, promise that you will write.' I promised that I would.

He got Asghar a job as a manager of the dining car on trains. Shabbir would bring his letter to the station and Asghar would give the letter to Salamatullah in Lahore. Shabbir had a very beautiful handwriting and he always used green ink. Each letter was at least three or four pages long. If I had saved those letters, they would have made such a great book that people would have forgotten his novel *Jhok Syal* and his short stories. I was present in all the short stories in one form or the other. There was not a day on which he did not write to me. I used to tear up the letters after I had read them and I regret that now.

But this is the way I am. I have not kept any of my records or even the cassettes of my songs. Nor did I save any of the newspaper stories or photographs about myself.

But, when Shabbir died, I was glad I had made him complete *Jhok Syal*. I had it published after he died.

Wherever Shabbir was posted, he always came to Lahore for the weekend. Every time he came he said the same thing, 'I cannot live without you, marry me.'

'I will definitely marry you but you will have to wait for two years, provided you do not turn out to be fickle.' I had promised him this in the sentiment of the line of Ghalib's couplet *kaun jeeta hai teri zulf ke sar hone tak*—who is going to live to see the end of this.

'Do you swear on God that you mean what you say?' he asked.

'Absolutely. If I marry, it will be you,' I replied.

He was happy and at peace.

He told me about himself, 'I have been married. My father had died when I was very young. My wife is the daughter of my mother's brother to whom my mother was indebted for many things. We were three brothers and a sister. My second brother had incurable tuberculosis. His wife loved me as though I was her child and I reciprocated her love. All of them wanted that I marry my uncle's daughter. For years I had been putting off getting married. But at the insistence of my sister-in-law and my dying brother, I was married despite my protests. Every one made me feel guilty because I was not ready to fulfil the wish of a dying brother.'

I commented that when men fell in love they usually found some explanation or the other for their earlier marriages. Shabbir assured me that this was not so: 'My entire family knew how I felt. I never stay with her nor do I sleep in her room. In any case, she spends most of her time at her parent's home. When she comes to Lahore I move downstairs to the sitting room.' Shabbir changed the subject, 'My mother cooks very well. She has often asked me why I have never taken you to meet her.'

'When you come next weekend, I will come along,' I promised him.

The next weekend I went to Ahmadiya building where his family lived. He introduced me to his mother and sister-in-law. This was the same sister-in-law who was the widow of the brother who had insisted that Shabbir get married. She had three sons and Shabbir loved these boys very much. The youngest was three years old. Shabbir had often threatened me that if I did not marry him he would give away all his ancestral property to his nephews and go off to Africa to become a famous hunter!

His sister-in-law was genuinely beautiful and refined. His wife was very simple, fairly plump and ordinary to look at. She also looked as if she was not very intelligent. Shabbir introduced me to her as his good friend. This was the time when Shabbir insisted that my being a woman did not matter in our friendship. Shabbir's mother, however, did not believe this. She told Salamatullah who was a cousin of Shabbir; 'He is very much in love with her. Save him.'

Salamatullah was also my friend. He told me what she had said. He kept me informed about everything concerning Shabbir. He was the one who had told me about the affair of the three words I had written. When I heard what Shabbir's mother had said, I told Salamatullah, 'You should have told her to relax. That day will never come in Shabbir's life.'

Salamatullah laughed, 'I have already told her that you will never marry him.'

All of Shabbir's friends called him Shah ji and soon I began to call him that as well. After a year and a half he was transferred from Wazirabad to Lodhran. Shabbir said to me: 'Wazirabad is close to Lahore and Lodhran very far. A year and eight months have passed. Why do you not marry me a few months early?'

'No,' I was firm, 'Let the two years pass.'

Shabbir had imported a very beautiful black spaniel bitch from England. He was very fond of her. I asked him to give her to me. He brought the dog over the next day, and then he left for Lodhran. The bitch was called Bess. Before he left, he instructed me to write every day for I had not written to him even once while he was in Wazirabad. I told him that I saw him every week and could not think of anything to write. From Lodhran Asghar was given a letter every day, which he posted the moment he reached the station in Lahore and therefore it reached me the same day. Asghar had now started travelling as far as Multan as manager of the dining cars. In every letter Shabbir complained about me not responding to his letters. I had always been lazy about letter writing. I would think of writing every day but never ended up completing even one letter. It would take months for me to finish a letter. I am still the same about writing letters.

It was difficult for Shabbir to come from Lodhran every week. Yet, he managed to find an excuse to come after every ten or fifteen days. He invited me to Lodhran many times. I kept ignoring the invitation for months. He would tell me to come and watch him hunt crocodiles and promised that I would have a good time. I tried to convince mother to accept his invitation, and when she did, she, her male cousin and I went to Lodhran.

Part II

Part II

50. Lodhran and After

Shabbir lived in a few spacious mud rooms. There was also a large courtyard and a couple of thatched huts. The courtyard was unpaved and servants sprinkled water on it twice a day. When we arrived there, Shabbir's happiness had to be seen to be believed. It was as if he were walking on air.

He had cooked for us himself. There was partridge, quail, fowl and fish, meat and all kinds of fruit. Everything was in great abundance and he spent his entire day looking after us. He was a good cook and one of his specialties was Pulao. All he wanted to do was to cook all day and he wanted me to eat all the time. Afraid that his cook might ruin something, he had the stoves carried into the courtyard and cooked the food himself. Everything was delicious and there were at least half a dozen things to choose from.

He showed us a baby crocodile he had kept in a small enclosure. We went to see him hunt crocodiles. It is said that you can only crocodiles them by shooting them right between the eyes. Shah ji was a good shot and on the very first day he shot three crocodiles. Then we went on a partridge hunt. He could shoot down partridges as they rose into the air on both sides of him. He managed to bring in a bag of nearly thirty birds from just a few fields. Game was in great abundance in those days. In fact there were so many quails that they cost two *paise* each in the market. There used to be five or six kinds of meats at the table as well as different kind of *halwas*. Shabbir was so concerned that there be nothing wanting in his hospitality that he thought of little else. In the end, I got so fed up of meat that I announced that I was going to eat only *dal*.

Two or three days later Shabbir and I were talking after lunch. We sat facing each other leaning against the rolled up bedding on the servants' charpais in one of the thatched huts. Shah ji spoke of his love for me and tried to convince me that he could not carry on without me. He said that each day without me seemed as long as a year to him. He wanted me to think of his suffering.

He also talked about his life. He spoke of how, after he had lost his father at a young age, he had to go and live with his father's brother and how badly he was treated there. He told me of the comforts his family had been used to when his father was alive. I found what he was saying very interesting and was so engrossed in listening to him that I did not notice anything till my wretched mother actually entered the hut. The two of us fell silent as if we were confronted with a venomous cobra about to strike. It seemed as if we had been caught red-handed committing some huge crime and for no reason we felt we should be ashamed and repentant. Neither of us said a word to mother. She stood there silently for a few minutes and then left without saying a word.

We asked ourselves what had just happened. Were we committing a crime that we had not dared to even look mother in the eye?

Mother became Shabbir's implacable foe from now on. She did not want us to meet. The more Shabbir tried to be hospitable, the more haughty and disdainful she became. I have already mentioned how severe mother was. She was also easily enraged and suspicious by nature. Because she prayed and fasted regularly, she considered herself very pious. She loved me with a passion, yet had never even embraced me. As a result, later in life, I never embraced my children either. If I ever felt like doing so, I felt so ashamed that I could not bring myself to take that step. However, I have always been friendly to my children.

We had planned to stay in Lodhran for a week but after this incident mother was ready to leave immediately. Shabbir pleaded with her to stay on but she very rudely brushed him aside. We returned to Lahore two days early.

From then on, things became very difficult for Shabbir. He would come to Lahore every fortnight and come straight to me. Like a good watchman, mother did not leave us alone for a minute. He would speak to me in English and I would twist my Punjabi around to convey my answer to ensure that mother did not understand what we were talking about. Interstingly, the fact that

I became increasingly hostile to mother, suited Shabbir. I did not miss Shabbir nor was I particularly attached to him. I considered him a friend, thought I knew him well and was sympathetic to his feelings. I liked him.

Now, however, I began to like him much more. I was constantly asking myself the same questions over and over again. Why should anyone watch over me? Did anyone have the right to do so? Did they consider me their slave that I could only meet the people they wanted me to and not the ones I wanted? I was angry at the way they were behaving. When Shabbir came, no one spoke to him. In fact, they did not even acknowledge his greetings. Mother treated him with contempt. It was not as though my world would have become desolate if Shabbir had not come to visit me. But the situation at home was intolerable.

I was supposed to only do those things, good or bad, which my family wanted me to do. Very often I felt like asking them what harm Shabbir's visits did to them. I wanted to ask them what their objections to him were. I also wanted to warn them to stop behaving the way they were doing. Yet, they had held such power and terror over me since I was a child, that I could not say a word.

Things did change in little ways. Every time Shabbir came, I would welcome him warmly and serve him tea. The two years that I had asked Shabbir to wait were now over. He pressed home the advantage and said that I should have no reasons to hesitate any longer. He asked if I still did not trust him.

I told him that I trusted him completely but there was still some unfinished business that I had to attend to, and asked if he could wait for another year.

* * *

He continued to write to me every day while he was away from Lahore, each letter was at least three or four pages long. I managed to write one or two a year. However, every third or fourth day, I would send him a telegram asking for money, sometimes for three hundred rupees, sometimes four. In those days, I think, the salary of a *tehsildar* started at two hundred rupees a month. He would borrow money from his friends and send it to me. Not once in his letters did he remark on the fact that I, who could barely manage to write a letter in six months, was able to send a telegram every four days! In fact, he would not even mention the matter when we met in Lahore. We had been friends for nearly four years now. I was now sure that he was not like the others and I respected him. I enjoyed talking to him a great deal and I felt sorry for him. Yet, we could talk for hours and I was never tired. But the thought of marrying him never entered my mind. When I saw how honest and stable he was and how much he loved me, I would berate myself for having led him on. Why had I not told him that I would love to have him as friend, to stay with him, love him but not in the way married couples did? He had been fine until I wrote those three words, and turned his life upside down. I had turned a happy man into a tortured soul. Now, I could neither refuse him nor marry him.

I kept extending my deadline a year at a time. I hoped he would get disgusted and give up the idea of marriage. Then an idea struck me. It involved the spaniel bitch that I had taken from Shabbir.

Rai Sahib from Head Rasool continued to visit me every weekend. I told him I was going to the hills and it would be very difficult for me take Bess with me and asked him to look after her while I was away. I firmly instructed him to look after her well and carefully. He was delighted and said that for him looking after Bess was like 'love me, love my dog.' He promised to treat her like a princess.

He came every Saturday. One Saturday, Shabbir was also there when he came. I handed over the dog to Rai Sahib right there in front of Shabbir. I even told him to carry her out. You had to see Shabbir's face to believe it: anger, sorrow, helplessness writ large, his face the colour of blazing copper. He was a brave, fearless man and if he had slapped someone in anger, the victim would have fainted. I felt he was about to knock Rai Sahib down. Somehow he managed to regain control and stood there silently, afraid that his actions might lead to the end of everything. When Rai Sahib had left, he said: 'If you hated the bitch so much, you could have given her back to me. She was such a beautiful bitch and I was very fond of her.'

I tried to sound matter of fact. 'Since you had given her to me, what I do with her now is my business. In any case, I have not given her to him for good. He will only keep her while I am away. I have sent her to Head Rasool because the house and the grounds are large. It is also cool there because of the canal.'

'You have hurt me like you have never hurt me before,' Shabbir said.

Indifferently I replied, 'What am I supposed to do now? You always start a weeping-fuss over everything.' We spoke a little longer after that and soon, on the point of tears, he left. While leaving, he said, 'Perhaps you do not like me coming here anymore.'

'Maybe,' was my casual response.

'Then, if God is willing, I will never trouble you again. I have just found out that you are bored of me.'

'No, I am neither bored of you nor will I ever be,' I said. 'However I do not like you finding fault with everything. It is up to you to decide what you want to do. Think about it.'

* * *

He did not come back for four months. Nor did he write. The dozen or so of his friends chided him, 'We always told you that she would never marry you. You continue to be a fool. Wake up. Do not waste any more of your life—you've already given up the best four years of your life for her. Use your brain in the future. If she had wanted to marry you, she would have married you long ago. You had better accept she is not going to marry you no matter what happens.'

What could he have said? He kept silent and listened to what they said. His friend from Gujarat, the one who had faucets instead of eyes, came to me. He was a decent, sober man and had been a classfellow and an old friend of Shah ji. Their families too, had been friends for generations. He loved Shabbir like a brother. The gentleman said to me: 'Shabbir is in a bad state. He weeps incessantly whenever he mentions you. There was a time I too loved you a great deal but in no way as much as Shabbir loves you. He is truly in love with you. What a pity that you do not appreciate him for you will not find a man like him no matter how hard you look. I have known him since we were children. He is innocent and a pure-hearted man. There is no one else who has a clearer conscience than he does. If you lose a man like him, you will regret it for the rest of your life.'

'How am I to blame for his state?' I asked him, 'He is the one who got himself into this situation.'

'Why do you not write a few lines asking him to come and see you in Lahore?' he pleaded.

'I never stopped him from coming,' I clarified, 'Nor will I now write to invite him.'

'You are a hard-hearted woman,' he said, 'People are right in what they say about you.'

'What are they saying about me?' I wanted to know.

'It is well-known that people think that you are devoid of any emotions, insensitive and hard as nails,' he told me.

'God knows whether that is true or not,' was all I said.

Two days later I was returning after shopping at Anarkali. The car was crawling because of the crowds. I suddenly saw Shabbir coming from the opposite direction with a large bag in his hand. Our eyes met. He forgot that he was angry with me and ran towards me. He threw the bag of clothes into the car on top of me. Panting, he hurriedly asked, 'How are you?'

'Are you coming over?' I asked from the moving car.

'Yes,' he said.

He was there within half an hour. I had liked Shabbir's spontaneous reaction in Anarkali. Mother too, had by now relaxed and had stopped worrying about him. She greeted him warmly. Yet she continued her watch over us. I was very happy. My respect for him continued to grow by the day. After meeting him that day in Anarkali, I was convinced that he loved me without any reservation. I was forced to reconsider my decision about not marrying him. As for how I felt, that had not changed even though we had known each other for four years. Shabbir kept telling me that he had a lot he wanted to say to me and that I should find a way of meeting him so that we could talk freely.

One day he told me that his mother had invited me for lunch the next day. I told mother that I wanted to go to Shabbir's house for lunch. The next day mother and I went there for lunch. When

I went to wash my hands, his mother came to me and said, 'Shabbir says that you will marry him?'

I was thrown off balance by this unexpected query. I wondered what I should say. For a second I also wondered if she would beg me as they did in the movies, 'For God's sake, leave my son alone. Have pity on me. Let my home be happy again.' Instead, she said firmly, 'If you want to marry him then why don't you? What are you waiting for? Sometimes you tell him to wait for two years and then for another. When that year passes, you add another. He is restless in the day and disturbed at night. Do you want him to fall ill? On Eid, when everyone else celebrates, my unfortunate son prefers to lie with his face covered. I have already suffered a great deal. I have seen many tragedies and have had only few occasions for happiness. We are all very happy that you are here today.'

Shabbir's mother had said all this while she washed her hands. All I could say in response was that I would try. Shabbir's mother was old but pretty and healthy. Her complexion was pink, she had an impressive personality, was mature, kind and loving, and an excellent cook! Throughout the meal I kept thinking about how, for the sake of her son, she was forgetting about her brother's daughter's marriage, and asking me to marry him. After lunch we stayed for a little while and then came home.

*   *   *

I had always wanted to learn to play the piano and now decided to do so. I found a governess who agreed to tutor me at two hundred rupees a month. She lived in Qila Gujar Singh and everyone in her family was a superb musician. The husband, the wife, the brothers, the sisters and their children were all masters at playing various western instruments. Even the children played some instrument or the other. They all played from notations. The had a complete orchestra of sixteen or seventeen people in the family.

I arranged to go for lessons between two and three in the afternoon. I told Shabbir to come there at three if he wanted to talk to me. I also warned him that my driver, who was also mother's cousin, should not see him. If he did, he would surely report it to mother. The next day, Shabbir was there before three. He had the same old thing to say: 'Marry me.'

I told him frankly, 'Look, you have a wife. Why should I do this injustice to her? If you did not like her, you should never have married her.'

He repeated the same old story. His brother had been dying; he was helpless because he could not deny him his dying wish.

'And now by marrying me you want to please the soul of your brother?' I asked.

'I have my own life,' he responded, 'I too want to live. If you want I will divorce her. I am prepared to do that for you.'

'That would be worse,' I reacted instantly, 'I do not wish that fate on anyone.' In those days the life of a divorced woman was a living hell. Nothing could be worse for a woman's reputation than a divorce. It was not like today when divorce is something people go in for over the smallest of matters. At that time, the woman would be branded for life, the news of her misfortune would spread and as people go to condole at times of death, people would visit the parents, brothers and sisters of the woman to commiserate. I told Shabbir clearly, 'At this point I am not in a position to leave my family. Nor do I have the courage to do so.'

'You will have to leave them whenever you get married. I promise you that you can ask whoever you want from your family to come and live with us. My home will be your home and you will have all the freedom you want—to go where you want, invite whom you want and do what you want.'

'Just wait for a little while more,' I said.

'This has been going on for four years now, and the time you had asked for is over.' Shabbir added, 'Thank God the atmosphere here is not suffocating as it is in your home. There your mother does not let me out of her sight for a minute.' He left for Lodhran the next day.

His letters began arriving regularly again. He returned in a week and turned up at the piano teacher's house without any warning. I was very angry for it would have been disastrous if word of our meetings had got out. He told me that it was necessary for him to come. 'I have decided that I am going to bring a *maulvi* here tomorrow. Please agree to go through a *nikah* with me. I swear on the Quran that I will tell no one about it unless you permit me. You can stay with your family for as long as you want. I want nothing more than the assurance that you are mine. I trust you fully. You can live wherever you choose. I will bring the maulvi and the nikah can be registered.'

'No,' I said. 'Just be patient for a little more time. When I get married, I will not live at home.'

I had heard from his friends that he was becoming irregular at work. I tried to convince him to take his work seriously or else his record would be ruined. His answer was, 'For whom shall I make the effort? Come to me and I will not take a single day off work. I cannot live without you. I can get nothing done without you.'

I was firm with him, 'If you come back to Lahore in a hurry, I will not meet you.' But, he found an excuse to come back. Shabbir's mother sent us a message that she wished to see us and asked us to drop by. Shabbir was in Lodhran so mother accepted the invitation without hesitation. There, Shabbir's widowed sister-in-law took mother into a room to either show her something or to introduce her to some one. She left mother in the room and hurried back to me to say this, 'Shabbir is as dear to me as my own child. I beg you to marry him immediately. Every festival turns into an occasion of mourning for him. Shabbir does not leave his bed during festivals. On Eid everyone wore new clothes but this unfortunate one spent the day crying. Have mercy on us. We can no longer bear to see him suffer. Promise me that you will marry him soon. He loves you blindly.'

'Yes,' I said, 'I will definitely marry him.'

I did not know what to do. I was repentant for what I had done. I was to blame for everything that was happening. If he lost his job, I would never be able to forgive myself. I had reached the stage where even if I could discard the blanket of guilt, the blanket wasn't going to let go of me that easily.

During this period there had been many others whom I had considered as husbands. It took just a few months to make me conscious of their weaknesses. As I began to hate people like these, my respect for Shabbir grew. I finally reached the decision that if there was anyone who would stick by my side all my life, it would only be Shabbir. Over five years I had not noticed even the minutest indication that his love for me had decreased in any way. On the contrary, I had seen it grow by the day. He had not missed writing to me even for a day. He refused me nothing. He did exactly as I wanted.

His friends had also abandoned him. Every one had the same thing to say: 'You have lost your mind. You are an idiot. Even after five years you have not found out that she is not going to marry you. She is making a fool of you. Unlike you, she is too smart to marry you. If she does marry, she is going to marry a rich man. Why would she marry a pauper like you? Forget about her.' Shabbir hated having to listen all this and had started avoiding his friends.

He was coming from Lodhran to meet me at my piano teacher's one day. I left home earlier than usual. Shabbir was getting out of the tonga when my car reached there. My uncle had a good look at him. To make things worse, Shabbir tried to hide. If he had been clever, instead of trying to hide he could have thought of some explanation. He could have said that he was only passing this way. But he was caught in such a flap that he looked this way and that as if he was looking for a place to hide. Without acknowledging us, he told the tonga driver to move away fast.

I was furious but what could I have done? Mother's cousin, who was driving the car, watched everything intently. He said nothing to me but I was afraid that he would tell mother about it. Lord knows what she would do to me. I prayed all the way back home that he would say nothing to her. I even thought of asking him not to tell but I was sure that he would pay no heed to my request. It was pointless saying anything to him.

No one at home said anything to me. Eight or ten days later a telegram arrived from Jammu informing us that Nana was very ill and if we wanted to see him alive, we should go there immediately. We started making preparations to travel. When we got to Jammu I saw Nana hale and hearty. I was surprised but it did not take me long to figure out what had happened. This was the result of my uncle spotting Shabbir that day. Mother was convinced that I was planning to elope with him. She wrote to Jammu and had them send a telegram—and now here we were in Jammu.

* * *

This was the limit. I found the situation intolerable. I decided that I was going to do something about it. This was no way to live. Everything had to be the way the family wanted it to be. I was supposed to dance to their tune. I had been in Jammu for five or six days when Ghulam Haider, a mason who sang well and from whom I had learnt pahari songs, told me at the first opportunity that he got, that Shabbir was in Jammu and staying at the Dak Bungalow. He had sent a letter to me and was eager to meet me.

I sent back word that it would be impossible for us to meet since I was under surveillance round the clock. I sent word asking him to be patient because we would have to return to Lahore soon and asked him to go back. Shabbir however, was not going to be patient anymore. He sent word to mother that he wanted to meet me. Mother firmly refused saying that we had no desire to meet him. I pleaded with my ustad who had taught me how to read and write, with his wife, and my aunt, to carry a letter for me to the dak Bungalow. My ustad's wife dropped in on the pretext of seeing us and told me that she had a letter from Shabbir. I told her to take it back with her and that I would come to her place to fetch it. When she was leaving, I said that I was going to go with her. I read the letter at her house. He had written, 'I have been staying at the dak bungalow for a few days and have sent one letter through Ghulam Haider and this one through aunt Ditto. Many people have approached your mother on my behalf asking her to meet me for I have something to say to her. Her answer has always been the same—that she wants to hear nothing from me. I have been hanging around here for five days. I have tried everything. If you can find a little courage, we can find a way out of this. You tell me what to do. Your family is insulting me harshly and I have to bear these humiliations. What crime have I committed? If you are willing to give me even the slightest support, leave alone your family I can take on the world for you. Why are you so afraid of them? Do you not have the courage to even say something as simple as 'I want to meet him.''

I wrote back, 'You just mind your own business. Go back. I will definitely come back to Lahore in a few days. What is most important now is that you pay attention to your job.' Two friends had accompanied Shabbir to Jammu. They too tried their best, but mother would listen to nobody. Defeated, they left for home.

He continued to write to me at aunt Ditto's address. She lived close by and whenever I got the chance, I would go over to her place. Sometimes I would bring back the letters of the past few days and hide them under the sofa. I would take them out one at a time and read them and then tear them up and then burn them so as to leave no trace of them.

One day mother was cleaning my room. She swept under the sofa too. Along with the dust came out a still sealed envelope—a letter that I had not even read. Perhaps I had pushed this envelope too far under the sofa when I was trying to hide it. The most awful part of this affair was that Shabbir had written to me at aunt Ditto's address.

I was summoned immediately. The moment I appeared I was asked what address I had been using to get my mail. I did not have the faintest suspicion that she would have found one of those letters. Fearlessly I told her I used nobody's address. Mother took off her slipper and hit me countless times with it. She continued to ask which address I was using while she hit me. I again denied everything and got a slap across my face and had the letter thrown at me. 'Is this why you go running to her place all the time?' she asked. 'And that Datti. I will deal with that vile piece of carrion later. Let me show you your place first.'

I was very sorry that this fury had to descend on aunt Ditto for no fault of hers. I had not even read the letter. Lord knows what he had written in it. Mother beat me till she had no breath left. Then she headed towards aunt Ditto's house.

There, she humiliated her as much as she could. She told her: 'You dare not come to our house again. You are supposed to be a well wisher as suggested by your name, but you are an enemy. I considered you my real sister. Instead, it turns out that it was a viper that I was nurturing.' She returned to tell me that if I ever went that way again, she would break my legs.

The result of the way they had behaved made me into a total rebel. I hated the deceitful way in which they had sent that telegram to make me to come to Jammu. I began to hate my family.

I was also amused at the irony of the situation. What if there was any basis to all that was happening? What if I had actually been in love with Shabbir? True, I had firmly arrived at the conclusion that he was different from all the others. He was sincere, and loved me a great deal. I knew he was firm of resolve and would never betray me. He was the person I should be marrying. If I wanted to avenge myself of my family, this was the way to do it—marry him immediately.

I was forbidden to leave the house and it was as if I was a prisoner. If ever I went visiting in the neighbourhood, someone from the family would soon start following me. Sometimes this would infuriate me so much that I would tell the person following me: 'Stop following me. Go, tell them that I have forbidden you to do so.' The entire family was terse towards me. Mother had stopped speaking to me completely. All I could think of were ways of teaching them a lesson. I now understood all that was going on.

I would ask myself: 'For what crime am I being punished? I have kept them in comfort and wealth since the age of nine. That uncle, the one who had reported to mother, was not even her real brother. He lived with us along with his wife, children and his two brothers, who also had their wives and children with them. One of them had nine children, the other seven. They all stayed with us. Every need of theirs was met. The children were brought up as princes. And that same uncle had gone and sneaked on me! Could he not have kept quiet?

I had always kept my distance from everything. I never asked anyone what they were up to and what they were not. Instead, I followed every order that was issued. I told myself that I needed to be courageous now. Yet, my upbringing had been such that I could not find the courage. Often I thought of quietly getting to the station and going to Lahore. There I would take them on. I would then confront them and ask them why they had treated me like a slave that they had bought. However, all these scenarios were confined to my head. I never had the guts to even step out of the house.

It had been a month since we had come to Jammu. Any outsider, man or woman, who came to visit, was watched carefully.

Aunt Ditto was completely boycotted. She no longer came over nor did anyone from our house visit her.

Shabbir's friend, the one whom I had convinced to think of me as his sister, came to visit me. He told me, 'Shabbir is in a bad state. He is not at peace for a moment. He has sworn that if you do not return to Lahore in ten days, he will come to Jammu, come to your house to meet you and confront your family. He is convinced that there is nothing that your family can do.' He also carried a letter from Shabbir. I read it and found he'd said that matters had crossed all limits and that he could no longer bear to go on this way. He also wrote that he would be coming to Jammu in ten days.

I went to the bathroom and wrote him a letter. 'Do not even think of coming to Jammu, for it will be of no use,' I discouraged him firmly, 'Swear by me that you will not come. If you do, then I will never see you again.'

Fortunately my family did not suspect my guest to be a messenger for they assumed he was a suitor as he had come to visit me in Lahore as well. I had told no one that I had convinced him to look upon me and love me as a sister.

He was very concerned about Shabbir and he tried to convince me that I would never find another man like him, and that Shabbir truly loved me. 'For God's sake, where is your conscience? Learn to value him. He has forsaken everything for you and I know this because he is dearer to me than a real brother. He is a simple man. For God's sake, marry him as soon as you can.'

'Let us see what happens. Whatever is meant to happen will happen because Allah wants it that way,' was my repeated response to his pleas.

My real problem was that I never had been able to confide in anyone and, in the same way, I was unable to express any affection. Shabbir's friend left with my letter. He returned in a fortnight with another letter from Shabbir. Again I wrote back firmly telling him not to come. I told him he would not be able to deal with the abuse and taunts of my family. After all, had I not been caught red-handed?

* * *

We spent three months in Jammu. My family finally decided to return to Lahore. Perhaps they thought the danger was over. The moment Shabbir learnt of our return, he came over. He did not say a word to anyone nor did he acknowledge them when he came in. He came straight to me and sat down. We spoke to each other in English.

By this time I also wanted to get away from my family as quickly as I could. Yet I did not have the courage to get married. I respected, even honoured, Shabbir. I also valued his friendship and was sympathetic to his situation. But I could not bring myself to say yes to marriage.

I behaved badly with everyone who my family liked. Even if Shabbir was to sit for two hours, I would sit with him for the entire time. I would talk and laugh with him freely. I guess I wanted to convey to mother that I now felt as though I was mistress of my life. All mother could do was to timidly reprimand me, 'Bad manners and pride are not good for you.'

To this, and with my new-found courage, I told her, 'Why do you not make a list of all the things that I should do and say? I will memorize them and when someone visits, I will behave accordingly.'

My reply made it clear to mother that I was no longer the same person that I used to be. Shabbir dropped by whenever he wanted. Whenever he would be ready to leave, I would talk him into staying longer. No one in the house spoke to him out of fear of mother. Mother however, no longer dared to reprimand me for if she ever said, 'Why are you so hospitable to him?' my immediate response was, 'Because you are hospitable to so many others.' Mother now was sure that I was a rebel. She well understood this change. I had become indifferent to everything.

Summer arrived and we had to go into the hills for five months. All Shabbir's friends and relatives that I ran into said the same thing, 'Marry him immediately or he will lose his job.' Shabbir was always in Lahore without sanctioned leave. More and more people were beginning to ask if I was getting married. This I would deny outright. Irritated, I asked Shabbir why he was telling people that we were planning to get married.

Shabbir denied this, 'Absolutely not. I do not do that.'

'Then everyone must be imagining the same thing,' I retorted, 'I have told you never to talk about me to anyone. Why then are your friends, your family and all the others saying the same thing?'

He then admitted that he had talked about it to his family. 'They all ask me why we are still not married. Whenever you postpone the decision, I tell them about it only to convince them that I believe you will marry me, since they are all convinced that you are just giving me a merry chase. I have to reassure them for I have my dignity too. Shall I now go and tell them that you will not marry me?'

I too was tired of many things. My fantasies—that there would a man who would express his love in a unique way, how he would pine for me in his own exclusive way, gaze at me in a special way; the way he would look and move; how he would express his inner turmoil either through Ghalib's poetry or Waris Shah's *Heer*—had begun to bore me.

Instead I had to face those dark, small-eyed faces, the eyes that glistened while they spoke. Others recited entire monologues about their love with their faces looking as though all the blood in their body had gathered there. They no longer amused me. I felt as if I had suddenly grown old emotionally. Strange thoughts started coming to me. Sometimes I thought of renouncing the world and becoming a *faqir*. This idea I would reject immediately because I could not think of living alone and because I might have to live without a proper bathroom. Pointless questions arose within me. I was distracted by nothing. There was no one in the family I could speak to about what was going on.

When Shabbir came, I spoke to him for hours. He too had now begun to believe that I would never marry him so these conversations were always depressing. Fun and joy had disappeared from my life.

Then, something happened that changed the direction in which my life was headed. One evening I was playing solitaire. Sitting close-by was Rahima *Pehalwan*, a good, though poor, man. Pehalwan was only a title for he was not a real wrestler. He was a friend of Shabbir, Khurshid Anwar and the rest of the group. He followed all their orders. Since he was built like a wrestler, everyone added Pehalwan to his name. He was very fond of listening to music and turned up every evening.

I was concentrating on the cards when I suddenly noticed two polished pointed black boots. I had heard nothing and was totally unconscious of the presence of another man. Above the boots I saw two thin legs encased in khaki breeches. Over them was a short black riding jacket. The man carried a small riding crop. He was dark and with very thin moustaches which had been curled into upward pointing tips with the help of wax. He wore a coloured turban, the starched end of which was half a yard long. He was built like a skeleton. I looked at him, and the way he was dressed, and burst out laughing.

I laughed so much that I had to double up in amusement. He must have felt terribly humiliated and angry, for he stepped forward to attack me. I was still laughing and did not notice him move.

Rahima saw what was about to happen, that the man was about to hit me. As the man took a step forward, Rahima caught his leg and gave him such a jerk that he fell down flat. Rahima lifted him by the collar and threw him out of the house. He then threw the turban that had been knocked off, after him. Rahima told me that he was a police official and had been recently dismissed. I thanked Rahima profusely and came to my room. I was still in shock. What if the man had hit me? If Rahima had not been there, would I have had any respect left? The whole night I lay thinking about what could have happened. That night I decided what I had to do.

The next morning I told mother, 'From now on, I will sing for nobody. In fact, I will not sing at all. You already have enough to live comfortably. Just the rent from the houses and the shops is enough to ensure that. Damn this situation where a two-bit person can walk into the house. If Rahima had not been there the man would have actually disgraced me. Damn the car, the horse carriage, the jewellery, the clothes and the money. Damn everything!'

Mother was silent. She knew that once I had made up my mind, I could not be budged. I might have taken days thinking about the most insignificant of things. However, I took decisions within seconds. All mother said was, 'Do as you wish.'

I told her to pack up our stuff for we were leaving for Jammu for the moment. There I would decide what to do next.

Within a week we were ready to leave. If there was anything that I was unhappy about, it was my musicians. They pleaded so seriously that I change my mind that I wanted to weep. We had spent the last fifteen or sixteen years together. They bemoaned their fate for they wondered what was going to happen to them now. The *sarangi-wallah* who was addicted to opium, had been with me since I was four and a half years old. Both the sarangi-wallahs were from Jammu while the *tabla-wallah* was from Gujarat. Fifteen years is a long time in one's life. They wept and said that they were not going to leave me. 'We want nothing other than be allowed to stay with you. We have never worked for anyone else,' they cried as though they were children. I wish I had been rich enough to take on the responsibility of bringing up their children. I swear to God that if I could, I would never have let them go. However, there was nothing I could do because there was nothing to my name.

I explained the situation to them: 'I have given up singing and therefore there will be no more opportunities for you to earn if you stay with me. How then will you look after your families? You know well that I am not replacing you with any other musicians. You can come and visit me whenever you want. If you wish to, you can stay with us. As for singing, I will never sing for anyone again.'

When Shabbir found out that I was leaving, he was very upset. 'You are moving away even further now. At least in Lahore I could see you whenever I wanted to. In Jammu, I will be at the mercy of your family again.'

I did not tell him the truth about why I had stopped singing. Instead, I reassured him that my quitting singing would make it easier for us to get married. My family too had begun to behave a little more cordially towards him.

Shabbir began to come to Jammu every month for a couple of days. Sometimes some friends of his would come along with him. Since he was a habitual *huqqa* smoker, he used to bring a servant along to tend to the huqqa. When he was there, for a few days, things would cheer up because of his jokes and his laughter.

Sometimes I wished that he would not leave for there was nothing else for me to do in Jammu.

On one trip Shabbir told me that he had been transferred to Jhang. He invited me to come and visit the saint's tomb there which was visited by people from all over. I promised him I would. On his next visit he again insisted that I come to Jhang. I told mother I wanted to go. At first she refused to let me go. However, when she saw how persistent I was, she gave up and kept silent. I told Shabbir the day and time when he should meet us at the station.

I left for Jhang with my aunt. We both wore burqas. Shabbir was at the station with a couple of servants. In those days a senior tehsildar was a very coveted posting. At the station there were also a number of helpers to take care of our luggage and us. We got into a tonga and went to his house. It was built in the old style with very high ceilings and set in an acre of land. There was a large unpaved courtyard. The house had thick mud walls, which were plastered on the inside to keep the rooms cool in the summer. On one side of the courtyard there were rooms for the servants and on the other a kitchen. The courtyard had been sprinkled well with water and there was no dust. In the grounds there were sheds for three buffaloes and two horses.

There was no grass and no trees in the courtyard. The mud was sand-like and our feet sank deep every time we stepped onto it. It had to be sprinkled twice a day to keep it firm. Outside, in the grounds were *Shisham* and acacia trees. There was no sign of any grass or flowers. There were a few houses for various government functionaries like the Session's Judge and others. All the houses were built along a similar plan.

The rooms in Shabbir's house were empty. There were about a dozen chairs and another half a dozen disproportionate tables. All the furniture was dragged out into the open in the evening. There were also innumerable beds and a lot of bedding, for Shabbir always had uninvited guests staying with him. And these were not the regular guests who just came for a few days. Once they arrived, they forgot about leaving. God had been kind to many of his friends that they had nothing to do except indulge in their obsession for hunting.

Shabbir's trunks were always left open. When a guest needed something, he would, without even asking, take whatever he wanted out of the boxes and wear it. Those who could fit into his boots, also wore those. Each of the guests came with practically nothing except the clothes they were wearing and would stay for at least six months. For meals there was always partridge, quail and chicken as well as pulau and desserts. All visitors would give orders to the cook as if they were living in a hotel.

If they left, they were usually back in ten days or so. All of Shabbir's servants had been with him for a long time—they were old family retainers who had come as children and had spent their entire lives working for Shabbir's family. I mentioned to one of his servants that given the situation in Shabbir's home, his wife should come and live there and take charge. He told me that he had never sent for his wife. When I said that she should have thought of coming on her own, I was told that she had done so a couple of times, but on all occasions, Shah Sahib himself had gone away from the house for as long as she was there. He would return only after she had left.

Shah ji was not interested in too many things. He bought only books and spent his time writing short stories. He hunted whenever he could. He did not care what people took away or left behind.

While I was there, Shabbir would go to the Collectorate for a few hours, finish his work for the day, and come home. When he returned, he brought with him such cheer that you could feel it in every corner of the house. On his return, he would first look for me. He would spend some time with me and then head for the kitchen to check on the progress of the meals. He would start cooking if things were still not ready. He joked with the servants while he was in the kitchen.

For the first time I realized how much I liked Shabbir. I also realized what it meant to have a home of your own. For the first time in my life, I was completely comfortable and at ease. I was tasting freedom. All my life I had worried about each step I took and whether mother would approve of it. If there was anything that I wanted to do, I thought about it for hours wondering if I would be permitted to go ahead with it. I now fully realized the difference between freedom and bondage.

Shabbir was an extremely concerned host. The first thing that was decided in the morning was the menu for the day. Everything I asked for, was provided. It seemed as if I had shifted into another universe. There was nothing to worry about and nothing to fear. I was master of myself and empress of my own world for there was no one to set any restrictions.

We had come for a week but ten days passed in a flash. I did not want to go back but was afraid that mother would turn against Shabbir and me again. So I had to return. When Shabbir heard of my plans, his laughter and joy vanished and he fell completely silent. This was also the first time that I was sad about leaving him. I told him, 'I do not want to go back but what am I to do? I am helpless. I am extremely weak as far as this situation is concerned.' I was slightly embarrassed about admitting this to Shabbir.

Shabbir had his answer ready, 'Let us send for a maulvi and go through with the nikah. Then let us see who has the courage to take you away from here.'

'I know all that,' I said. 'Yet I cannot do that. Mother will die.'

Shabbir dismissed my fears, 'Nothing of the sort will happen. No one is going to die nor will anyone fall ill. All it will take is a few months for the whole matter to settle down.'

'I just cannot do this. I do not have the courage,' I admitted again.

He wept. He held on to my feet. He called on God and other holy things to make me change my mind. 'Please do not go. Have courage. Marry me and then, go and live there for a year if you want.'

I told him there was no point in trying to convince me. For the two days before I left, we spoke about nothing else. I was unhappy at the prospect of leaving but he was devastated and always on the point of tears. The day I was to leave, he pleaded with me again to postpone my departure, 'I will send a telegram that you have missed your train and that you will be arriving tomorrow.' He cajoled my aunt into agreeing. My aunt was a kind woman.

She agreed without much fuss even though she too was terrified of mother. The next day we returned to Jammu.

Back in Jammu, all I could think of was the house in Jhang. I remembered the fragrance of wet earth that filled the air when the courtyard was watered; the beds covered with colourful bedcovers made in Jhang; those empty high-ceilinged rooms and the slightly dirty muddy walls. Those visions of Jhang never left me. I had now realized that I wanted to have a home where Shabbir was with me. I thought of how I would rule my own house, how the servants would refer to me as '*Bibi ji, Bibi ji*', all the time and dance to my tune. No one would ever defy me over the smallest matter. It would be as different from this house as the earth is from the sky. That seemed like heaven and I felt as though my own house had turned into hell. To be honest, I did not think of Shabbir as often as I did of his house in Jhang. Jammu began to suffocate me and I was convinced that I could not go on living there. I was also convinced that mother would die if I did anything to drastically change our situation.

I was caught in a dilemma. I spent all my time feeling every single strand that was woven into my person and I still could not find an answer. One important fact I had to keep in mind was that I had lived all my life with mother and had not spent ten minutes without her around. I never went anywhere without her. But then, the ten days that I had spent in Jhang were the first days of real freedom that I had had. I had gone wild at the very idea of being free. I knew by now that Allah mian had made only one man that I could marry and that man was Shabbir.

I had always been unable to trust anybody. Suspicion was something I had received as an inheritance. I had seen enough instances of men who were meek and sad when in love. But after a few months or years when the passion declined, they could only find fault with the woman they had pined for. In time, they could find nothing about her that they liked.

I had known Shabbir for some time now. I had not seen him change in any way. I made up my mind that I should marry him. I had also seen his love for me increase. Shabbir was not very handsome nor was he very rich. However, he had all the qualities that a man should have: bravery, courage, generosity and decency.

He was also a simple and innocent man. I had often deliberately behaved as meanly as I could, but he had not complained even once.

Before going to Jhang, I had never believed I would end up marrying Shabbir. I liked him as a friend and enjoyed talking to him. I wished him well in life and had never wanted to be the one who harmed his career. He was a wonderful man and in the six years that I had known him I had never see him do anything superficial or shrewd. I did not want to cause any harm to such a man.

Lord knows what had happened to me on my return from Jhang. I started listing all the sacrifices he had made for me. I even dreamt about them. That is when I decided to write to Shabbir asking him to take leave and come to Jammu for a few days. I also told him that I was sad.

I do not know if he took permission to leave, but he left the moment he read my letter. It seemed as if he had found the treasure of Korah, the mythical miser. I had never written a letter like this to him before. The moment he arrived, he pressed my hand so hard that I screamed in pain. But he seemed not to care that he had almost broken my hand. Nor did it matter to him that my entire family was around for he seemed to be in another world. He said to me: 'I went crazy when I read your letter. You sent for me and here I am!'

The moment I got the opportunity, I told him, 'What a strange man you are! Did you have to announce to every one that I had asked you to come?'

He said what he had been saying all along, 'I have gone crazy. I care for nothing but your life. This is the first sign that my efforts over the last six years have had some effect. Damn everything, just tell me that honestly whether you were unhappy without me or not?'

'Yes, a bit,' I admitted

'So you wanted me to come?' he pressed home the point. 'For me too, Jhang became devoid of joy and light the moment you left. I read all night. The house seemed haunted. I felt like crying when I looked at the places where you would sit and the place where you slept. Did you also find it difficult to sleep?'

'Yes, it usually took me about ten minutes to fall asleep,' I said.

He did not stop asking questions like a child. He said, 'I am so happy today. If I were to die this moment, I would die a happy man. Allah has finally heard my prayers. All I wanted was for you to love me. And this is what I have prayed for since the day you came into my life. My friends and relatives told me that you were deceiving me, that it was impossible that you would ever become mine. I always believed that was exactly what was going to happen. In six years you have not admitted to anything like this. Now that you have said it, I have what I wanted. How can I describe how hard the last few years have been; the taunts I have had to put up with; the nights that I could not sleep? Now, I am surprised that I had it within me go through all that. I had become so bitter that once I went up and sat waiting on a hill in Simla for days. I wanted to shoot you if you passed that way and then kill myself. Often, there were nights when I wanted to put an end to my life.'

What he said and the way he said it left me dumbstruck. Just one letter asking him to come over had had such an effect! It seemed he wanted nothing more from me. What a simple and naïve man he was!

He returned to Jhang after a few days. A few days later I wrote to him that I was going to Lahore and that he should come there. I had been away from Lahore for nearly six months. Life had become very boring since I had stopped singing. I had nothing to do with myself and was constantly depressed. Maybe, that is why I went back to thinking about Shabbir so often again.

Mother had bought a small house in Lahore and we moved into it. I was very fond of movies. In Jammu there had been one dilapidated movie hall which usually ran old movies. In any case, the equipment was so bad that you could never tell what was happening on the screen.

In my letter to Shabbir I had written and stressed he should not tell people that I had asked him to come to Lahore. I wrote to him that I would go and see Salamatullah and he could come there and we could meet as though it was a coincidence. After that we could continue to meet as before.

I told mother that Shabbir's mother had invited us to come over whenever we returned to Lahore. So we went to call on her.

Shabbir was there to greet us. He was very welcoming and told us that he had just arrived from Jhang. He also told his mother not to let us leave without having dinner. I left the decision to mother.

After dinner Shabbir came to drop us home. The next day he came again. I told him I was in Lahore for a fortnight or so and asked how long he was going to be there.

'That is of no consequence,' he said, 'I'll get my leave extended on medical grounds. How can I go back to Jhang when you are in Lahore?'

Shabbir's friends had told me all about how badly he had been behaving at work. He had stopped bothering to find out if his leave had been approved or not before he took off. There had already been a few official complaints against him about this.

I spoke to him. 'You will end up losing your job if you continue to take unauthorised leave as you have been doing. Your friends tell me that is exactly what will happen if there are a couple more complaints against you. Do you not realize how wrong that is? Please stick to the leave rules and go back.'

'That is out of the question,' he said dismissing my concern, 'Let the job go to hell. Tell me what have you planned for tomorrow?'

'Come over tomorrow and we will go the cinema,' I told him.

The next evening Shabbir, mother and I went to see a movie. I was wearing a burqa. The film began but I could not concentrate on what was happening on the screen. Instead, I was convincing myself that if I had to get married, I should do so immediately for if I postponed it any longer, he would lose his job. If that happened, marrying him would be out of the question. Would I be able to forgive myself then? Would I ever find peace after that? Would I be able to forget all the sacrifices Shabbir had made? He had catered to every whim of mine for the last six years. I knew that if I did not marry him now, I would regret it forever.

Here was a man who loved me with every emotion there was in his heart. He had been ready to take on the world for me. I knew that it was easy to get married but very difficult to make a marriage work. If there was anyone who could make it work, it was Shabbir. I knew I should not let this opportunity go by. I decided that if I had to get married, it would have to be that very day.

Till today I cannot recall the name of the film we were watching. Nor do I recollect what the plot was for it seemed as if huge hammers were pounding inside my head. My ears buzzed and I was unaware of everything around me. I had always been like this. I was mortified of anything that I was not sure about. But once I made up my mind, I would take on the most difficult of challenges.

At that moment I was obsessed by just this one thought, that I had to do what I had decided, and without delay. The film ended. I deliberately took my time as I fussed over my burqa. Mother had moved on a little ahead. Shabbir was standing next to me.

'Do you want to marry me?' I asked.

'Yes,' he said.

'Then bring a car at two at night. Park it close to my room and honk five times. I will come down to the road to meet you.'

* * *

The cinema hall had many steps. Shabbir's legs had begun to wobble in total panic. I had spent the last three hours during the film thinking about all this and had made up my mind. But poor Shabbir now looked as if he was walking through an earthquake. His feet were no longer falling where they were meant to. Once or twice he had to make a great effort to keep himself upright.

We got into the car. Mother was with us and we came straight home. Shabbir walked us to the door. Before I stepped into the house I turned to Shabbir and said, 'The film was good. It was the perfect film.' Then without exchanging another word I went in.

It was ten o'clock at night when Shabbir left us. He went to straight to a friend's home. 'Help me arrange for a taxi immediately. She has said that she will be ready to leave at two.'

'Come on, forget it,' his friend said, trying to dissuade Shabbir, 'she is playing another prank on you.' The friend who said this had two wives and he had invited me to dinner just a couple of days ago. One of his wives was a relative of his and the second one he'd chosen. Both of them, in their supposed concern for

Shabbir, had said to me, 'The poor guy is ready to die for you. So many years have gone by. Marry him.'

I hate people like these—people who incite matters or interfere in other people's business.

'How can I marry him when I have not even thought about it?' I had asked them curtly.

'What?' they exclaimed, 'what is this that you are saying? The poor soul has been waiting for six years.'

'You better ask for God's forgiveness,' I said rudely, 'if I do get married, it will definitely not be to Shabbir.'

These people were indebted to Shabbir for many things. He had stood by them through thick and thin. His friend now tried to convince Shabbir that he was being a fool because all I was doing was to mock him. Shabbir however was firm in his resolve, 'I believe her. This is no prank for she has never said these words before. I am definitely going to arrange for a car and be there at two.'

His friend too, did not have any money to help. At that time in the night, he went to a friend of his and borrowed two hundred rupees. They rented a taxi from Anarkali and brought it and parked it in front of my window at midnight. At two, he honked five times, softly.

I was already in a state. After the film I had not slept a wink. All I had done was to pray, 'Oh Allah! Please do not let me falter in the step I am about to take. I have not taken this decision on impulse or because I am consumed with passion. I have thought about what I am about to do. If I do not do this now, both of us will be destroyed forever. Give me the strength. Give me courage. Let my future steps be firm. May Shabbir and I never be separated.'

I heard the five-horn signal. I put on my slippers but in the dark I could not find my dupatta. The car was parked close by. I saw Shabbir sitting in it. I saw his friend Mir Asghar Hussain in the front seat. The engine was already running. I got into the car and asked where we were going. Shabbir told us we were heading towards Sialkot.

All three of us were lost in our own worlds. Shabbir, because he could not decide whether he was dreaming or awake. His friend, because only two days ago both his wives had convinced

him that if I did marry, it would be someone other than Shabbir. I,
because I was marvelling at my courage. I had never done anything
without mother's permission. Where had I found the courage to
do this? I was also thinking of what mother would do in the
morning when she found me missing. She would cry and beat
her breast and drive herself into a hysterical state. Would I ever
be able to face her again?

In about ten minutes, even though it was not winter, I began
to shiver. The shivering was so strong that my teeth chattered and
I could not speak. It lasted for more than an hour. I asked why we
were not going to Jhang. Shabbir said he had relatives in Sialkot
where we would get married and then we would go to Jhang.
'Your mother will definitely report this to the police, therefore we
have to go through the nikah as soon as possible.'

We reached Sialkot. Mir Asghar left immediately saying that
the first place mother would go looking would be to his house
and that he better be there before break of day.

The people whose house we went to in Sialkot were distant
cousins of Shabbir. The host's name was Ashiq and he was very
surprised to see us. Shabbir asked him to immediately arrange for
a maulvi who could perform the nikah and give us the necessary
certification. Ashiq asked us to rest for a while. Tea was served
and we talked a bit and soon it was eight o'clock. Ashiq left to get
a maulvi. The maulvi sahib soon came and married us. The maulvi
asked what the amount of *mehr* would be.

'Everything I own,' Shabbir said.

'No,' I objected, 'It has to be thirty-two rupees.' This was the
sum traditionally agreed upon.

We left for Jhang the next day by train. We hired a tonga at
the station and reached home. Once there, I told Shabbir, 'Now,
you better get down to taking your work seriously. Get promoted.
This is the one thing on which everything else rests.'

I had no clothes except the shalwar and qameez that I had left
home in. I had a few suits of clothes stitched in Jhang but they
were so awful that I did not want to wear them. Instead, I started
wearing Shabbir's kurtas and tahmads.

Shah ji would leave for the Collectorate every morning. The
moment he returned he'd call out to me. I do not know what it

was about him, but that moment immediately cheered up the house. When he entered the house he was always laughing and this was a habit that stayed with him forever. Even if I was alone in the house his presence made it seem as if it was full of people. When he was around he did not sit quietly for a moment.

Often friends or neighbours would drop by in the evening and they would stay to dinner. Shah ji would introduce me to them and I would feel ashamed of the way I was dressed. I had to make up a story of how my trunk had been left in the train and I would have to wait till I got back to Lahore to get new clothes made. I also complained about how bad the local tailors were.

* * *

I had been in Jhang for about ten days when suddenly, one day, my aunt appeared. I was delighted to see her and after some time she said, 'Your mother is very unhappy because you have run away from home like a thief. If you wanted to get married, you could have said so because she would have been happy to arrange it. When you decided to stop singing, did anyone oppose that? If you had told her your wishes, what would she not have done for you?'

'Come on *Khalajan*,' I said, 'Have you forgotten how you got married? Did they not oppose your marriage? If you had told them what you were planning to do, mother would have beaten you as though you were a swine.'

My aunt went on nevertheless, 'Your mother has sent me with the message that if you return, she herself will arrange a grand wedding for you. The way you have run away has caused a great deal of scandal and dishonour.'

'Khala,' I said to my aunt, 'I am now legally married. A nikah has been performed. Forget about how all this happened, the fact is that I am now a married woman. I will definitely come home but only after I have spent a few months here.'

My aunt continued to insist. She was obviously following mother's instructions and she seemed certain that she could convince me to do what she was asking me to do. My aunt was a simple, innocent woman and she took any job assigned to her seriously. I told her that whatever had to happen had happened, that I did not want a grand wedding and that I was not ready to go back to mother.

My aunt persisted for nearly a week and her last gambit was, 'This is a matter of honour for me. I had assured them that you would definitely return with me. Why do you not come back, even if it is for two days? I will bring you back myself.' I continued to refuse and my aunt was upset and started getting ready to leave. I tried hard to dissuade her, and convince her to stay on for a few more days. 'I can wait for a fortnight,' said my aunt, 'provided you promise to return with me.' How could I have given in to my aunt's request? She was angry and left in a week.

Eight or ten days later I looked out of the window to see a tonga drive up and stop in the porch. Mother was in it. Shah ji was at work. Fazluddin, who had been with Shah ji for a very long time, was in the kitchen, cooking. The peons were in their quarters at the back. My legs went weak at the sight of mother. I ran to where Fazluddin was and said to him, 'Send a peon to the office and ask him to tell Shah ji that mother has arrived and that he should drop everything and come home. Tell him to tell Shah ji that I am in trouble for I do not know how to face mother.'

I came back to my room and looked out of the window again. Mother was talking to somebody. I ran to Fazluddin and ordered him not to leave me alone with her till Shah ji had returned. I told him to leave the cooking to some peon and come into the house.

I was dressed in strange, shabby clothes. I thought it best to pretend that I was ill. I immediately got into the bed and covered myself with a sheet. Mother asked someone something before she knocked on the door. The door was latched. She knocked softly at first and then started banging on it. Fazluddin opened the door for her. Seeing me in bed, she said, 'Get up and come with me.'

It was Fazluddin who answered her, '*Bibi ji*, this is not possible. Let Shah ji return, then you can take her with you. In his absence, she cannot leave.'

Mother was furious and charged at me. Fazluddin immediately came between us. Mother quickly stepped back and picked up something to hit me on the head with. Fazluddin jumped and grabbed it from her. She lifted something else and again Fazluddin snatched it away from her. She kept on finding things to hit me with and Fazluddin kept protecting me. Mother was out of control and I watched all this silently. I was bewildered and my throat had gone dry.

Mother noticed the typewriter. She ran and grabbed it and came towards me to hit me with it. I saw the large iron machine and had visions of my head splitting open and screamed, 'No, no.' Fazluddin, in the meantime had rid her of the machine. Mother now commented, 'You have not said a word all this time and now your heart bleeds! You are worried that the typewriter might get damaged. You who did not think of me!'

She was absolutely wrong but I did not say a word. All I did was to pray that Shah ji return. Mercifully he arrived and wished her. Mother did not acknowledge his greeting. Instead she told him, 'I have come to take her away.'

With great respect, Shah ji answered her. 'She cannot go right now. Later, when we find the time, we will surely come.'

Mother was livid, 'I am talking to her and she is leaving with me right now.'

'Absolutely not,' Shah ji was firm, 'She is my wife. No one can take her anywhere without my permission.'

Mother turned to me, 'Tell me. Are you coming with me or not?'

I kept quiet but Shah ji said, 'She is not going with you.'

Mother looked at me again, 'Are you coming with me?'

Seeing me unresponsive, she started banging her head against the wall. Shah ji caught hold of her and made her sit in a chair. He told her, 'Look, there is no point in behaving this way. You are also my mother now. If you want, you can come and spend the rest of your life with us for this is your home too.'

To this, mother's answer was, 'I will die right here but I will not return without her.'

Shah ji again tried to placate her, 'At the moment that is impossible. Why do you not have some rest and some tea or *lassi*?'

There was a change in mother's temper. She got up and said, 'All right, I am leaving. From now on consider me dead as I will consider you dead.'

Shah ji pleaded with folded hands that she not leave in these conditions. He asked her to have lunch before she left but mother was having none of it. She opened the door and walked out. Shah ji followed her and continued to request her to stay. The tonga was summoned and mother did not even look back. Shabbir came back into the house.

I was really troubled by all this. He calmed me down, 'Do not worry. This will only last for a short time and soon everything will quieten down.'

*   *   *

After a few days we came to Lahore to get some clothes stitched for me. Shah ji's mother welcomed us very warmly. His mother was called 'Bebe' by everyone. She was a simple and good woman. Since Shabbir was her youngest son, she loved him blindly while he constantly played minor pranks on her. She used to have a small cash-box, which she kept beside her when she prayed. Shabbir would pick it up and start rattling it. Bebe could not interrupt her prayers and all she could do was to make '*ooonnnhhh hooonnnhhh*' sounds with her breath. After she had finished her prayer, Shah ji would tease her, 'What sort of worship is this? Even while you are praying, your mind is constantly on your cash box!' When she opened her cash box, he would try and take money out of it while she scolded him and tried to ward him off. He teased her all day and though she pretended to be angry, she secretly enjoyed every moment of it. Those days passed very pleasantly.

Shabbir was a hero to all the young men and women in his family. Every relative wanted to spend time with him. They all soon found that Shabbir himself had no time for anyone except me. He did not leave me for a minute if he could help it, and I was never away from his thoughts. If I called out for a servant, he would immediately call out even louder to make the servant come more quickly. If the servant was delayed, he would get up do the job I had called the servant to do. A couple of times Bebe even commented on this, 'Just have a bit of patience,' she would say, 'the servant will come.' That had no effect on him and he went ahead with the task. He never thought about what people would make of this behaviour of his. He was not in the least bit self-conscious about doing anything that I wanted done. All that mattered was that my comfort not be disturbed in the least.

Every morning Bebe would ask him, 'What do you feel like eating today? What shall I order?' Instead of answering her, Shah ji would turn to me and ask, 'What would you like?' Finally, after a few days, Bebe once said, 'Why do you not, for a change, tell me what you would like to eat?' To this, Shabbir's answer was, 'From now on, I only like the things she likes.' His mother laughed a bit and then fell silent.

We returned to Jhang. Soon it began to get warm. A long time ago, some of Shabbir's relatives had bought a house (from an Englishman) at Kashmir Point in Murree. A large hill was a part of the estate. Shabbir too had a share in the property. As soon as summer began, all the relatives who had built themselves houses close to each other, moved there. The whole place buzzed with holiday activity. We were also there and then Shah ji left after spending ten days.

Every day he wrote a five or six page long letter to me. Each letter said the same thing—that he was very lonely. I too was missing him—his chatter, the noise, the joy and laughter. I was still not close to the women of his family. I decided that the next time Shabbir came, I would go back with him. I would rather bear that heat than put up with this cold. Time seemed to drag. Ten days later Shah ji was back on leave though I am not sure if his leave had actually been granted. As far as I was concerned, I knew he lied easily about such things.

With Shah ji back, things came back to life. Days merged with nights and time passed seamlessly. In the day, he had stoves placed in the verandah and would cook himself. He always found something to do. I told him that I would not stay there by myself and that I wanted to go back with him. He tried to make me change my mind and told me how much I would suffer in the heat. He knew that I always spent the five summer months in the hills and that I was not used to summer in the plains. But I was adamant and came back to Jhang with him.

* * *

Three years later we were transferred to the sub-collectorate of Samundari. It was a small village where most of the residents were Sikhs. There was no electricity so we had to use lanterns and gas lamps. All those friends of Shah ji who used to come and stay with him for months, now gradually dispersed. Only one friend, who had nothing else to do with his life, continued to stay with us. All he was interested in was hunting and his hunting dogs. His main concern in life seemed to be to get up at five in the morning when the servants brought in ten or twelve seers of fresh milk. He skimmed off two or three seers of this froth from the buckets and fed it to his dogs. Then he would have breakfast and leave with his dogs to hunt rabbits.

I would get very angry with him for taking away the froth, (which was what turned into cream,) and feeding it to his dogs. I even told him off once, 'Cream comes from the froth and from that comes butter and ghee. Why do you not feed your dogs milk instead of the froth?'

His answer was, 'The foam is best for dogs. You have no idea about the pedigree of these dogs that I have imported from England. People would rather give away their daughters than these dogs.'

He would return from his hunt around one. Back at home, he would immediately start pestering the cook for lunch saying that he was dying of hunger. The cook was called Khadim and like the other two servants, had been with Shabbir's family for generations. The servants too were very irritated with this guest but they dared not say anything. Instead they would constantly complain to me about him.

Khadim used to occasionally use *bhang*. An idea struck me. I told Khadim: 'Why do you not make some kababs and add bhang to them. When he comes home shouting "hunger, hunger," just feed them to him. Go and get two or three annas worth of bhang.'

I had no idea, about what the effects of the kababs would be. Lord knows how much bhang you could get for two or three annas then. Khadim later told me that a faqir had shown up just then. Khadim had asked him for some bhang and the faqir had generously given him two or three large fistfuls of the stuff. Khadim added the bhang along with extra spices to the kababs that day.

The moment our guest returned screaming about being hungry, Khadim placed the kababs and bread before him.

People who know, say that using bhang makes you laugh at everything. Pretending as if he was only tasting them, our guest had quite a few of the kababs. Shah ji had two and another guest who was there and I, had one each. Except Khadim and me, no one else knew what was going on.

When he had been transferred to Samundari, Shah ji had made a new friend. He was Shambhu, a nephew of Prithviraj Kapoor. A pretty Muslim woman lived with him for nine years and later she married a High Court Judge. Shambhu was a rich man and he had a well in his courtyard. However, the well was not used for drawing water but to dump empty bottles of liquor that Shambhu had consumed. Lord knows how long this had been going on. When his friends came to visit, he would show them this well and point out that it needed just a few more bottles to fill it up!

Once when I had just come back from Jammu, Shambhu had come to the station with Shah ji to receive me. Shambhu bought a few bottles of liquor on this trip since liquor was not available in Samundari. He had forgotten to take the bottles home when he had left our house.

When I told Shah ji about the bhang, he immediately opened one of the bottles of liquor. He knew that alcohol was the antidote for bhang. He diluted it with water and made us all drink a dose and drank one himself. The guest with the dogs, whose name I do not want to mention, had started throwing up within half an hour of lunch. He then passed out, for after all, he had eaten four or five kababs. Except for Khadim, there was no one in the house who was sober. I told him to fetch a doctor immediately. Shah ji tried unsuccessfully to pour some liquor down the throat of the unconscious guest too.

By now it was ten or eleven at night. Khadim woke up a few of the neighbours and some of them agreed to go with him to get a doctor. Khadim told them all that we had all been poisoned by something we ate in the food. They ran in haste and soon fetched the doctor. With great difficulty, and with everyone's help, we managed to get the medicine down our guest's throat. The doctor gave us all medicine too. Allah had been very kind for the guest

survived. The whole room was covered with vomit. We told the
doctor that it must have been the tinned fruit we ate.

For the next few days we all would wake up for brief periods
before going back to sleep again. Except for Khadim, everyone
slept continuously for four days.

Fifteen or twenty days later something happened that gave us
a rude shock. We were suddenly rendered destitute and helpless.

*   *   *

In Jhang there was a Sikh landowner who had not paid revenue
for years. Shah ji too, had been trying to make him pay for over a
year. The Sikh had dismissed all of Shah ji's attempts. One day, in
the grounds of the house Shah ji told the Sikh very politely, '*Sardar
ji*, it would be best if you would pay up.'

The Sikh replied, 'Shah, you have no idea who I am. No other
tehsildar till now has even dared to ask me to pay . You are new
so you do not know what you are doing.' The Sikh was a big,
strong man and had a fierce reputation.

It took a lot to make Shah ji angry, but once he was angry, he
was uncontrollable. Since the conversation was taking place near
the servants' quarters, the servants of the house were present along
with the peons, and the village revenue official.

'Go to hell!' a furious Shah ji said, 'Let the legal process takes
its course but let me tell you something about what tehsildars are
all about.' He held him by the hair and slapped him so hard that
the Sikh fell to the ground. Shah ji continued to thrash him and
the Sikh was soon shouting, 'Shah ji, you are mightier than me,
forgive me; I am sorry, my father is sorry.' The others had to try
hard to drag Shah ji away. He ordered that the Sikh be taken into
custody and only be released once he had paid his dues. The
very next day the money was deposited.

The Sikh paid up the money but he filed a case against Shah ji.
I don't remember what the case was about specifically, whether it
was a case of assault or something else. Shah ji and the Sikh had
to appear before the Sessions Judge and they were questioned.
The Sikh either abused Shah ji or said something so vile that Shah
ji flew into a rage again. Once again he slapped the man and

added a few punches too. He had such strong arms that he could have knocked down the strongest of men.

Hitting the man in court now became a full-blown case against Shah ji, which went on for some time. I was pregnant then and Shah ji was shuttling between Lahore and Murree. He paid no attention to the case while on the other hand the Sikh was doing everything he could. Within two or three months, Shah ji was suspended from his job.

For the first time in my life I felt crushed by all that was happening around me. We had no idea where we were going to live or what we were going to eat. We had no house to live in and no other means of income. Shah ji's elder brother looked after the lands that Shah ji had inherited. Shah ji had never interfered in this matter matter in any way. In fact, he did not even know if there was any income from the land or not. For the first time I realised the importance of money. The few days that we took to pack up our things, I wept constantly. The only person who wept more was our guest with the dogs. We had lost our appetites for we had no idea what lay ahead.

Shah ji's mother lived in Lahore because of her orphaned grandsons. The house belonged to the grandsons. Her brother had built Shah ji a house but soon after the house was ready, Shah ji's older brother had said, 'You will not be needing this house because you are going be posted elsewhere because of your job. Since all my children study in Lahore. I need a house in Lahore.' Without a moment's hesitation, Shah ji gave the house to his brother.

We ended up staying with Shah ji's mother. Though I had visited my family a few times after my marriage, I did not want to go there in these circumstances.

We had lived in Samundari for almost seven months. The Sikhs of Samundari had grown so fond of Shah ji that they would drive down in a delegation at their own expense to see Sundar Singh Majithia. They lobbied hard to get Shah ji reinstated as soon as possible. Most of the population of Samundari was Sikh and they were all very rich and owned large estates. A few of the families there were also related to Sundar Singh Majithia who was a very influential man at that time. When the news reached them, two friends from Jhang came to see us. They said, 'Till now we were two brothers. From now on we will consider that we are three.' They had brought the relevant papers transferring one third of their lands to Shah ji. I remember their names—Qasim Mallah and Muhammad Hussain Shah. Their land holdings were enormous.

In those days, friends were loving and true. For friends, neither caste nor religion mattered. In spite of the fact that a Sikh was opposing him, the Sikhs of Samundari did all they could for Shah ji. They came to lobby for him in Lahore at least three times a month. They would come and see us in Muslim Town, where we lived, before they went back.

Shah ji's mother helped us as much as she could. She also prayed a lot for us for she loved Shah ji more than any one else. She lived off the pension of her late husband and her grandchildren's share of the ancestral property.

Shah ji wrote to his older brother, 'Till now I have been asking you for money only when I needed it. Now I need a steady income urgently. Please let me know what my share of the income from the property has been.' This was the first time that Shah ji had written something like this to his brother. He was so respectful of him that he did not smoke in front of him even though he was a heavy smoker. All of Shah ji's jacket pockets were full of holes because that was where he would put his cigarettes if his brother chanced upon him smoking. He was forced to write this letter because he had no other option. He sent a servant and got five or seven thousand rupees immediately. In those days, that was a lot of money.

Despite all that had befallen us, Shah ji's attitude towards life had not changed. The banter and the jokes continued as before. Even the most worrisome of things did not faze him. In fact he did his best to make others forget their troubles.

He would take me along when he went to Auction Mart in the evening. There, with friends, we would listen to poetry or music. The newest jokes emerged from the Auction Mart. Because of Shah ji those difficult days were made very easy and I soon stopped worrying as much as I used to.

In fact, it was this time which was among the most interesting periods of our life. If I ever panicked and asked what would happen if he did not get his job back, he would casually point his finger upwards and say, 'The power holding up that blue canopy will take care of everything.' He looked so peaceful that even I would automatically calm down. All kinds of food was still cooked and he would invite friends as before. Many Khan Sahibs would come and we would have music sessions. Every day he found new things to amuse us. Every evening we went to Auction Mart or the group would come to our house in Muslim Town. Time passed easily with daily sessions of music, poetry and jokes. The evenings lasted till ten or eleven. Akhtar Shirazi, Hafiz Jallundhari, Faiz Ahmad Faiz and Sufi Tabassum were all part of these gatherings.

The attitude of my family in Jammu had already changed for the better. Mother sent the car for us to Lahore—petrol used to cost two annas a gallon in those days. Life became easier. Shah ji started paying attention to his property and our financial situation improved considerably.

* * *

It was also during this period that I did something that I had always wanted to do—act in films. I had always been very fond of films and they affected me so much that after watching a film I would think of the hero's helplessness for a long time afterwards and want to cry for him.

When I had first moved from Jammu to Lahore, the owners of a few film companies came from Bombay to Lahore and tried to get me to agree to work in their films. Mother hated the idea. I argued hard to be allowed to work in films but mother would have none of it. I tried to convince her by telling her about how big Bombay was and how much I wanted to live there. I assured her that we would have a lot of fun, but the arguments fell on deaf ears. At that time I was already friendly with Shah ji and mother then had held Shah ji and Salamatullah in great respect. I asked them to intercede on my behalf. Mother would not listen to them either and my desires had to be buried within me. I dreamt about Bombay for a long time afterwards.

The manager of Regal Cinema in Lahore was a Parsi and his wife was European. They lived in a lovely flat above the Regal cinema house. The flat was beautifully furnished and they lived in great style. Before I was married, I used to go to Mrs Kanga to learn English and we had become good friends.

For some reason Mr Kanga lost his job. I had not met Mrs Kanga for a long time so one day I told Shah ji that I wanted to go and see her. Shah ji and I went to the Regal building only to find that Mr Kanga had been fired. We got their new address and went to see them. We found them in enormous trouble and very worried. They needed seven thousand rupees immediately. If Mr. Kanga did not pay that money soon, he would be arrested. Perhaps there had been some trouble with accounting in his office.

A worried Mrs Kanga said to us, 'We are outsiders here. If we were in Bombay, we could have asked some relative of Kanga's for the money. If we do not find the money by day after tomorrow, Kanga will be arrested. We have neither the money nor any jewellery nor is there anyone who will come to our help. We are helpless and without hope.'

Shah ji and I looked at each other. We had seen in what style they used to live. Now, they were without home or hope, and even facing imprisonment. Shah ji assured them, 'Be strong, keep faith in God. I also will do my best. Pray that I succeed.'

Shah ji borrowed a thousand from one friend and two thousand from another. We had three thousand with us. In this way, we got the seven thousand together and gave it to Mr Kanga and he was able to avoid going to prison.

One day, the owner of the Sagar Film Company came from Bombay to see Mr Kanga. The seth who owned the company wanted Mr Kanga to convince me to agree to work for his company. Mrs Kanga immediately came to see me in Muslim Town and told me about this offer. She said Sagar was a reputed company and that I would be well paid.

Shah ji had never denied any wish of mine. I am sure than in the thirty-six years of our marriage, he refused me nothing. Anything that I wanted, was done. He knew how much I had wanted to work in films. Therefore, despite not wanting to live without me for a moment, he did not try and stop me. All he said was, 'Do as you please. But Bombay is so far.'

The agreement was signed within two days. Mr and Mrs Kanga were also moving back to Bombay and Shah ji instructed them to find me a flat close to theirs and to take good care of me. The agreement was for five years. I was to be paid two thousand a month for the first year and then there would be an increment of a thousand every year. They also made me agree that even if the company changed its name, the agreement would be binding.

In those days the heroes and heroines in films sang their own songs. The owner of Sagar Film Company was convinced that I would be a great success and that is why he wanted to tie me down for five years so that I worked exclusively for him.

From Bombay, Mr Kanga sent a telegram that he had found flats both for themselves as well as for me. He had taken an advance from the seth and furnished the flat with all the essentials. I left for Bombay in a week with three servants. The flat had everything that I could need. I could see the sea from my window, and our building had a lift.

I rang up the seth and told him that I had arrived and asked him what I was expected to do. He told me that till they started a film with me, I should go the studio every day to watch the others work. He felt that this would help me to get a proper orientation.

However, I was finding it difficult to manage without a car. I had known Rasheed Kardar and Prithviraj Kapoor for a long time. Since the seth had assured me in Lahore that he would advance me money for a car, I requested these two to go with me and help me buy one. We went to quite a few showrooms and all that I wanted to know was about the petrol consumption of the various cars. I remember Prithviraj getting very irritated and saying to me, 'Why do you not buy a motor cycle instead of a car?' Actually I wanted a smaller car because I wanted to learn how to drive. The driver had come with me from Lahore. Finally, I bought a Vauxhall Ten and had it driven home the same day from the garage. The car cost me eighteen hundred rupees.

The next day I was at the studio at ten. They were getting ready to shoot a film. The studio was huge and around it, at the height of two hundred and fifty or three hundred feet, ran a wooden gallery, which was about three feet wide. Lights were fixed at various places in this gallery. The entire ceiling was also covered with lights. The cameraman was constantly instructing people to shut off some light and switch on another. A few actors, all made up, sat in chairs waiting. Every ten minutes, tea in small glasses would come round, perhaps to kill time. This went on for over an hour. When the cameraman was satisfied with the arrangements, the director appeared holding some papers in his hands. The actors were summoned to take their places. The director looked into the camera and moved the actors around for some time. He then went up to them to give them instructions and then the shooting began. It must have lasted a minute before all the lights went off and the cameraman began to rearrange the lights all over again. I was really disappointed. Watching a film being shot was no fun. Bored, I returned home at noon.

I had always been fascinated by the costume jewellery that they used in films. I went out looking for some and visited a few shops. In real life the jewellery looked completely fake, totally unlike what it appeared on the screen. I spent some ten days going around shops of clothes and jewellery. Soon, this curiosity too, was satisfied. For the first few days, I went to the studio regularly. I found that there people only talked about films. Soon I was fed up with this talk and I started to leave early. On the fourth day, I went to the seth and told him that I didn't feel the need to come to the studio every day, and that he could inform me whenever he needed me for work.

However, going to the studio had one beneficial fallout for me. One day I saw a plain looking simply dressed man walk in. He was limping for he had a sprain in his ankle. Even as he limped, his steps fell with the grace of a dancer. I asked who he was and was told he was Lachchu Maharaj. Lachchu and Shambhu were acknowledged as famous ustads of the Lucknow style of dance. They had no match in the whole of India.

I went straight to the seth and asked if Lachchu Maharaj worked for him. When he said yes, I asked him if he would ask Lachchu to teach me to dance. The seth called Lachchu immediately and asked him. Lachchu agreed. I asked for his address and told him I would rather come to his house to learn because there were always too many people in the studio and I would not be able to concentrate. Lachchu lived in Mahim, which was fifteen or twenty miles from where I lived. Out in the wilderness, there were these poorly built dwellings which were cheap to rent. Lachchu lived in one of these with his wife and daughter. A boy who used to learn the tabla also lived with them. The boy would play the tabla as well as do house work. Lachchu's wife and daughter danced too. Everything about their home indicated their poverty which in no way affected Lachchu Maharaj's natural pride and self-confidence.

I later found out that the girl I'd seen in their home was not Lachchu's daughter. His wife had married him because she wanted to dance and the girl was her daughter. When the girl grew up she worked in a few films under the screen-name Kaushalya. She was not very successful because she was very plain looking.

They lived in the midst of a crowd of people, next to dangerous traffic and in surroundings that were not very salubrious. Their living quarters were small and ill-ventilated and that is where I used to practice. In my eagerness to learn, I arrived on time every day. I had spent my entire childhood in learning, and till today I jump at the idea of learning something new if I get the chance. Lachhu Maharaj's wife and daughter would make me practice to the *ta thai thai tat* beat. They would make me dance to rhythms at double and treble the normal tempos. With them I would learn how to move from one tempo to another. For the first time I realized what a complicated art dance was, and that it could not be mastered even in a lifetime. So far I had thought that all it took was to memorize the syllables and then repeat them with your feet. I had also believed that all it took to be a dancer was courage and stamina.

Learning from Lachchu I understood that there was more to dance than recreating the syllables of the *todas* of the tabla and that dance was a discipline by itself. Because I was so enthusiastic, Lachchu took a great deal of interest in teaching me. I had already learnt how to control my limbs, therefore I learnt in weeks what would have normally taken months. I had already mastered the control of the neck, the eyebrows and the chest, which is not easy to do but which I used regularly in my *nritya bhav*. Learning was enjoyable and Lachchu was very happy. He repeatedly told me that within a year there would be no one else to match me. 'God has made you to dance,' he encouraged me. He would even put his wife and stepdaughter to shame using me as an example, 'Look at her! You two have been learning for years and you are still nowhere near as good as she is.'

If I had stayed in Bombay for the whole year I might well have mastered the art. The truth was that within two or three weeks of being in Bombay, the charms of the city had begun to wear thin and it seemed impossible that I would be able to stay there for long. I had also lost interest in the studio and films, I had done all the touristy things and now I began to feel depressed a lot of the time.

I would go to a German woman for a massage every evening. All the other actresses went to her. In the clinic there were about a dozen large boxes, which were heated by electric bulbs. The lady would make me sit in one and slowly raise the temperature and within half an hour I would be sweating profusely. First the massage, then the sweating and then finally she would sit me down in a tub of warm water. She used to charge a lot of money for this but the company paid for it for they wanted to keep their actresses in good shape.

About a month later, the seth called me and told me that I had to start working the next day. He told me it was an outdoor shoot and that the car would come and fetch me at eight to take me to the location at Petite Hall. At eight the next morning, a Station Wagon arrived. It had already picked up some of the actors and actresses and we all reached the location. The house belonged to some very rich Parsi. There were a few acres of garden with a fountain in it.

The moment we arrived, we all got busy with our make up. I had absolutely no clue about how to do up my face. The make-up man started working on me. He applied various creams and lotions and began patting them—*thup thup*—into my face. He curled my eyelashes with a brush and made them as stiff as wood. When I touched my face, my fingers seemed to stick to my skin. Apart from face cream and lipstick, I had never used any other cosmetic. The whole process was very annoying because it took more than an hour to complete. I then put on my sari. I felt totally stiff and could not touch my eyes, face or my neck. I felt filthy.

There was a marble wall around the fountain in the garden and the scene was to be shot there. The dialogues for the scene were given to me. The director told me how I was to deliver them, from which direction I was to enter the frame and from which I had to exit. The director did not seem to be very good but I did my best to follow his instructions. After a few rehearsals, I was ready.

About fifteen or twenty people were watching the shoot. In the evening when I had finished working, four of those who had been watching all day, came up to me. They asked me if I was who I was, and I confirmed it for them. They then told me that they had recognized me immediately because they also were from Jammu. They were two sets of cousins who worked as drivers at the Petite Hall. 'Your sisters-in-law are here in Bombay with us. They live in those quarters out there. They have sent us with firm instructions to bring you home. Why do you not come with us and have a meal or tea with us?' they asked me. I told them it was very kind of them but I could not accept their invitation. They kept on persisting and it was with some difficulty that I rid myself of them.

The next day the car again arrived at eight and it brought us to Petite Hall. The shooting began and I noticed that all four of the men were watching the shoot again. They were staring at me in particular and their eyes did not seem to leave me for a minute. I did not like this. I was not a shy person but I felt self-conscious with them around because they knew who I was. I felt like leaving the location and running away. Instead of concentrating on my work, I was preoccupied in looking at them and I always found them staring at me. I prayed that they would go away somewhere. But they were there till pack-up was called. Again, they started to pester me to go with them because their wives were waiting for me. This time I refused these invitations rather curtly. Their love and hospitality had become a nuisance for me.

The third day we had to shoot at Petite Hall again. All the way there I prayed that the cousins not be there, but they were there as usual. And they continued to stare at me. I could not pay attention to my work because I was conscious that they were watching every move of mine. At home, I began to dread the idea of seeing them again the next day. After about seven or eight days of work, when the car arrived in the morning to fetch me, I sent word that I had a severe ache in my stomach. They agreed to do without me for a day. The next day when the car arrived, I again sent word that I was not well enough to work that day.

The company was losing a lot of money because of me. Fed up, they eventually replaced me with a woman called Prabha. I was not in the least bit sorry about this. For one, the fascination of working in films had worn off by now. Secondly, I did not think much of the director. Finally, I was free of being constantly stared at by those men. I wished I could fly back to Lahore immediately. In Bombay, except for the dance lessons with Lachchu, I spent the whole day at home with nothing to do. Finally, I wrote to Shah ji that I was very unhappy and asked him if he could come to Bombay.

The next day I got a lengthy telegram from him telling me that he had been reinstated at his job and had been paid his salary for the last two years. He also wrote that he had been transferred to Okara and that he had been granted ten days of joining time. The next day he flew down to Bombay.

Rafiq Ghazanwi was a friend of Shah ji's. He was a cultured man. He called us over for dinner and there I met Khursheed Tansenwali. Rafiq began visiting us every day with Khursheed. The week passed in a flash. When there were only two days left for Shah ji to leave, I told him that I did not want to stay on in Bombay and asked if I could come back with him.

'Thank God,' Shah ji said. 'At least you have got over your craze for acting. I never wanted you to leave me but then, whatever pleases you, makes me happy. I have decided that throughout our lives we will do exactly what you want. This is why, even when I did not want you to come to Bombay, I agreed,'

I reminded him of the five-year agreement that I had signed. He assured me that there would be no problems over that. The next day he arranged for the servants and the car to return to Lahore. I rang up the seth who was not at home. I left a message saying that some urgent business was taking me to Lahore and that whenever they needed me, he could inform me and I would return immediately. So, without so much as his permission, I left with Shah ji for Lahore.

* * *

I left all the furniture with Mrs Kanga and told her that she could keep it in case I did not return to Bombay. We spent two days at Lahore and then went to Okara where Shah ji took charge of his new responsibilities. Our house was very close to the Collectorate. Sometimes, Shah ji would hold court in the verandah of the house instead of going to office. There was a very large garden in front of the house and the litigants would wait there and come forward when their names were called.

Often I would sit behind the reed curtains to listen to the cases being tried. The most interesting were the kidnapping ones. Young women, extremely unhappy with their old husbands, would tearfully plead, 'Kill me if you have to, push me into a well, but please do not send me back with that old man again. I would rather kill myself than go back with him.' Lawyers of both the parties would present witnesses and there would be endless arguments. The witnesses were all coached in advance, yet some would forget what their lawyers had instructed them to say and the lawyer would go wild with fury at his own witnesses.

Soon the director of the Lahore Radio Station found out that I was in Okara. Many people working with radio were good friends of Shah ji and they all tried their best to get me to broadcast on the radio. Lahore was only 80 miles from Okara and when I had to record, I would come to Lahore the night before. I would reach the radio station at seven the next morning. I would finish at eleven at night and then leave for Okara straight from the radio station. In Okara, Shah ji would listen to my broadcast on the radio and then leave for Lahore himself. We would meet somewhere near Pattoki. I was soon recording six or seven times on the radio every month. On every occasion Shah ji met me halfway on the way back home. It took two or three hours to travel from Okara to Lahore and therefore we would travel back together for only about an hour of the journey.

Often I asked him why he had to do this. He would smile in response. '*Begum*, you would not know the feeling. When I meet you on the way, it seems to me that I have run into you after ages.' On the drive back he would tell me all that had happened that day. At home we would talk for hours.

In Okara we made another very good friend. This was Syed Ali Raza, a lawyer. We visited each other frequently. He was well educated and very interested in poetry and music. He declared that he considered me his sister and I came to love him a lot too. I would often go to his house and his wife and children would visit us. Another friend we made was Maula Baksh. He was very influential and owned a great deal of land, which was very close to the town. In fact the house that we lived in belonged to his brother.

My fame was growing day by day. Every song that was broadcast became popular. Radio stations in other cities started receiving mail praising my songs. Now, every month I also had to go Delhi and Lucknow and sometimes even to Calcutta and Hyderabad in the Deccan, to record. Shah ji would put pressure on me to go to Delhi and Lucknow and sometimes he even took leave and accompanied me. He wanted me to become famous all over the world and to be respected by everyone. If someone said something good about me to him, his face would glow with pride. He would not let me miss a single programme.

People liked my songs and the very first broadcast brought in nearly a hundred and fifty fan letters and many telegrams to the various radio stations. When I visited Delhi after 45 years, I met the then former Station Director of radio and he reminded me of the response to my first broadcast. He also showed me some wonderful pictures.

The amusing thing is that till today I do not have any of my own pictures, or records or newspaper and magazine articles. I have even misplaced some of the awards. I have never been interested in collecting any of these.

Our life was contented and full of cheer. Every year there was an annual ten-day vacation for Christmas. Shah ji would take another twenty days off and arrange a shikar party to go to Amanpur and Kanashpur. The group would eventually add up to fifty people including the servants and friends . All kinds of people were included. Some friends would be in shalwar-qameez and other in jackets and trousers and yet others in tahmads. Some friends could not afford to join the expedition, so Shah ji would pay for their train fares, only to make sure that that they could join in. A couple of friends came from Gujarat and others from Lahore, Jhang, Okara and Mian Channu. He sought out all his friends and convinced them to join us.

Every one of these hunting trips was memorable. Each trip had its unique adventures, which we talked about for months afterwards. When the train that we had to take pulled into Lahore station, the first thing that we did was to capture a large third class compartment. Then the big wooden chests, which had been built specifically for these trips, were loaded into the compartment and were placed between the berths in the train. Over these we spread a few thick mattresses. A comfortable, five-foot wide bed would thus be ready. Our third class compartment was more comfortable than a first class one!

All the provisions, the gaslights, the flour, the rice, ghee, spices and utensils were packed in these chests. A basket of live fowl, which would be needed for meals during the trip, was hidden in the bathroom. The cook made tea and cooked meals on a kerosene stove in the compartment as though we were at home. We spent our time playing cards. If some unfortunate soul tried to board our compartment, he would be in trouble for the guests and the servants would put the fear of God into him. At every station where the train stopped, there were fights with travellers who wanted to get into our compartment.

The month that we spent on these shikar trips, was spent as though we were royalty. There was nothing that we wanted or that was not available, for preparation for these trips would begin three months in advance. All sorts of fruit and dry fruits and all kinds of halwas were arranged for. Shah ji was so fond of hunting that he would have hunted every day if it had been possible. Those days things were so cheap that he was able to import a large double-roofed residential tent. It had a drawing, dining and a bedroom as well as a bathroom and a verandah. Thick wooden poles held up the whole structure. For the servants, there were ordinary tents.

I rarely ate the meat of jungle fowl or deer. So, for my sake, every second or third day, a goat was slaughtered even though there was such abundance of blue bulls, deer and buffalo calf. They could have shot twenty animals a day if they had wanted to. There were countless people to work as beaters to surround the larger game. They were even willing to work for free if they could take away a few wild boars at the end of the day. For this free meat they would work the whole day rounding up tigers and cheetahs. Even though there was so much game, no hunter killed more than was necessary. Every third or fourth day they would shoot an animal for food though they did shoot partridges and jungle fowl every day. They had to make no effort to find these because they were to be found everywhere. I would sometimes eat the partridge meat, otherwise it was only mutton for me. One night the servants had tied a goat and then spread their cots around it. Yet, while they slept, a cheetah managed to carry the goat away without them being aware of it!

Shah ji was extremely well versed in how to prepare for shikars for he thought of everything. There was a huge box containing medicines for almost all illnesses and if anything ever went wrong with someone, there was always medicine for that malady. They would hunt for four or five hours in the morning and in the evening they would spend their time chatting and getting into arguments. Sometimes it seemed that these arguments would degenerate into scuffles. There were a couple of people in the group who were very good shots while four or five were not so good. The rest of the friends would come along just for the fun.

I remember the sarcastic conversations between Ali Raza and Salamatullah over the way Mian Maula Baksh spoke Urdu. Ali Raza and Mian Maula Baksh both lived in Okara. Ali Raza was a graduate and also had a degree in law. He was a refined and cultured man who was fond of poetry and had an excellent command over Persian. Mian Maula Baksh was a graduate from Aligarh. When Maula Baksh spoke his strange mongrel mixture of Urdu and Punjabi, Ali Raza would react immediately. 'O Mian, have some fear of God! Who on earth has awarded you a

Bachelor's degree from Aligarh College? If I find out who was responsible, I will have him driven out of Aligarh.' Ali Raza and Salamatullah found Mian Maula Baksh's Urdu so grating that everyone was very amused at their reactions. Actually Mian Maula Baksh's Urdu was amazing in the way he would plant a Punjabi word in the middle of Urdu sentences.

The dream of every shikari was to bag a tiger. If even one tiger was shot during the month, there would be a great deal of celebration. Every night, two hunters would take turns to tie the bait and keep watch from the machan through the night. In the morning, others would go and replace them.

The beaters too were very amusing in the way they spoke and told stories. They usually dealt in the hides of cows and buffaloes. According to them, when they came across a tiger which had just killed a cow and was feeding on it, they would creep up to it and say, 'O, our great benefactor! we are here.' The tiger would then just walk away into the jungle leaving them to skin the animal! Even though it is said that a tiger is ready to kill if disturbed while feeding, these people talked as if the tigers were close relatives of theirs.

However, the trip back home was far from comfortable. In Lahore the train we normally took used to pull into the station empty and all it took was for fifteen or twenty of our men to occupy a compartment and place our luggage in it. They would then make sure that no one else entered the compartment. On the way back, the train arrived almost full and stopped for only a few minutes. We would have to book our luggage separately and except for the servants we had to buy first and second class tickets. We all had to arrive at the station hours in advance. There was no waiting-room, nor any benches or chairs to sit on at this small station. Since it was impossible to stand and wait for so long, we would sit on the wooden chests. Our luggage consisted of these large chests, gas lamps, stoves, bedding rolls, black steel trunks, and the skins of tigers and cheetahs that had been shot on the trip.

Shah ji was a bit overweight and looked quite plump in his corduroy trousers. Ali Raza and Salamatullah would be in trousers and bush shirts. Asghar and Mian Maula Baksh would be in their shalwar-qameez and Peshawari slippers. Those who had joined us from Mian Channu would be in tahmads, long kurtas and local shoes. A couple of servants were very fond of wearing breeches so they would be wearing those.

During one such trip I had to leave for a performance to Calcutta and had joined the party on the way back. I was in a sari and my eldest daughter, who is now Mrs S.M. Zafar, was then about four or five years old. Since it was winter, she was wearing long woollen stockings along with a skirt and blouse. There was no form of dress that was not represented in our group.

There was a man at the railway station who looked like a dandy. He wore a white pyjama, an achkan, and a white linen cap on his head and Salim Shahi shoes. His hair was oiled and his eyes were lined with kohl. He kept walking around us observing us all. He must have noticed the tent, the gaslights, and the large chests and automatically presumed that we were a circus troupe on our way to perform somewhere. He must have also thought I was an acrobat and that my daughter was surely the one who would be dancing on a tightrope.

Shah ji was running around trying to get the luggage booked. He must have taken Shah ji to be the ringmaster. He approached him and asked, 'Sir, where are you going to be putting on your next show?' I had already complained to Shah ji about how the man was constantly watching me. I had also told him about my hunch that he had mistaken us to be a group of circus performers. So Shah ji did not respond to him but, looked at him angrily and moved away without saying a word.

The man was persistent and was not ready to abandon his interest in us. When he saw Shah ji heading towards me from the booking office, he began to follow him and again, very respectfully, asked, 'Sir, where is the next show going to be?' We all heard this and broke out into laughter leaving Shah ji feeling sheepish. All he said was, 'I will leave you to find that out for yourself.' For months afterwards we spoke about the incident and had a good laugh.

* * *

Whether it was a shikar or official tours, Shah ji would not go anywhere without me. Sometimes the car broke down or something else happend and we'd arrive at the place we were supposed to stay, very late. On such occasions, even if it was midnight, he would send the local watchman to the some large landowner or village official informing him that we had just arrived, and that since the children were with us, we needed something to eat.

By the time the gas lamps were lit and the beds laid out, a full meal would arrive. Shah ji had a fantastic memory and remembered the stature, the lineage and even the names of the landlords of each village. He remembered their family histories and into which families their children were married. Wherever we travelled we were very comfortable. The three years we spent in Okara were wonderful.

There was no Imambara in Okara. The few Shias who lived there would cordon off a street with charpais and hold their majlis there. Inside the city there was a disputed piece of land over which there had been a conflict for two years. The Hindus wanted to construct a wedding hall there while the Shias wanted to build an Imambara. Shah ji decided in favour of the Imambara.

Ali Raza came to me and said: 'Sister, God gave Shah ji the privilege of making this decision. I want you to get the Imambara built. In this way, God's work will be done entirely by the two of you and God will take care of you for the rest of your lives. I will build a mosque next to it.'

I agreed readily. 'I will consider this a stroke of great luck.' With Allah's blessing, the Imambara was built and Allah gave me an opportunity to do something for him. Otherwise, I could not even have dreamt that I would get a chance of doing something so virtuous.

Three years later we were transferred to Montgomery. During this period I had become better known because of my gramophone recordings. Indeed, every song I recorded was a sell-out and the gramophone company was constantly pleading with me to record more. Both the young and the old liked my renditions and my records were played in every restaurant and hotel. Every day I received countless letters from all over via various radio stations. The monthly magazine that the radio station published always carried a couple of my pictures. With the publication of these pictures, love letters usually followed.

People would say that I was the last word as far as diction was concerned. They began to refer to me as the 'reciter' of the ghazal in the same way as they referred to the 'reciters' of the Quran. Some said that if there was ever any controversy about the pronunciation of a word, all they had to do to settle it was to listen to a record of mine! People also praised my voice a great deal and said it was unique. And yet, the honest truth is that I did not find anything special about myself. Yes, I was always in tune but the rest of my good fortune was all due to Allah's kindness.

Shah ji wanted to move to the Food Department. Not only was the salary three times what he had been earning, but the move would mean that we would be able to live permanently in Lahore. General Bird, who was in charge of the department, was a fine man and a good officer. Shah ji got a letter inviting him for an interview, and when he went for it General Bird was very happy with him. He told Shah ji that he was just the sort of person he had been looking for and that he would be appointed soon.

Within a month Shah ji had received orders to take up the new job. We moved to Lahore and a new life began for us. Shah ji was earning much more and he was lucky to have an officer like General Bird and within a month, Shah ji had become his favourite subordinate. He would summon him frequently and entrust all difficult tasks to him. Shah ji wrote very good English and the General praised him to others for that. He also invited us to his home to eat. His wife was very nice and they treated us like friends. Inevitably, other people in the office did not like this friendshp and they tried their best to make General Bird stop trusting Shah ji. But then if Allah is kind, people cannot easily harm you. The more jealous his colleagues became the better Shah ji did at work.

General Bird was also a close friend of the Resident, Thomson. Both came from good families, they were principled, hard-working and brave men. The Resident looked after the affairs of eighty kingdoms which included those of Jammu and Kashmir, Nabha, Patiala, Faridkot, Loharu, Dojana, Shimla, Dalhousie, Kapurthala and Chamba. He controlled the fate of these kingdoms. Not even a mustard seed could enter or leave these kingdoms without his permission. No one could interfere in his work and he ruled over the Rajas and the Nawabs.

Thomson and Bird often dined together. Thomson told Bird that he was on the lookout for a bright and capable man because he just did not like Rai Bahadur Izzat Rai, the Deputy Commissioner who worked with him as his GLO (Government License Officer). Rai was diabetic and his illness meant that he needed to go to the bathroom every ten minutes. He therefore kept a piss pot under his chair. One of the duties of the GLO was to tour the princely kingdoms for eighteen days a month and to spend the remaining twelve days in Lahore. The GLO thus had to have an impressive personality. Thomson was very dissatisfied with Izzat Rai.

General Bird told Thomson that he had a dynamic and capable officer working for him. The General knew of Shah ji's passion for hunting, and all the physical activity that it entailed. Thomson asked Bird to send Shah ji over to meet him.

The next day Bird told Shah ji that the Resident needed a GLO and that he had recommended him for the job and advised him to go and see the Resident the very next day. The Resident was very happy to meet Shah ji. He later told Bird that Shah ji was just the sort of man he was looking for for the job. Shah ji was asked to join the Resident's office within a week. All the people in the Food Department congratulated him though some also wrote anonymous letters against Shah ji to the Resident.

Izzat Rai protested to Sir Srivastava about the injustice done to him. He said it was unprecedented that an ordinary tehsildar should be given a higher position than that of a Deputy Commissioner. Srivastava was an influential man who worked with the Viceroy. He spoke to the Viceroy and the Viceroy's office refused to approve Shah ji's appointment. This created a very difficult situation. After all those congratulations, it would have been very difficult for Shah ji to return to his job in the Food Department. His self-respect would not have allowed him to work with the same people again.

When Shah ji went to the Resident's office the next day, he was told not to worry about anything and to carry on with his work and leave the problem of his appointment to the Resident. Subsequently, every file that Shah ji sent up to him came back with the endorsement, 'excellent.' There were two Englishmen working along with Shah ji and often their files were returned with 'very bad' scribbled on them. It was well-known that Thomson was a difficult man to please and was rarely satisfied. However, he was so pleased with Shah ji that he entrusted the most difficult tasks to him.

As I have mentioned earlier, Shah ji wrote very well in English. This was because he read a great deal. Everyone used to comment on how well Shah ji wrote and often people said that he wrote better English than an educated Englishman. God had blessed Shah ji with a very fine mind.

Within a month the Resident began to rely on him so much that he sought his advice on all matters. The Viceroy's office had still not approved Shah ji's appointment. Without this, his salary could not be paid. At the end of the month, Thomson offered to pay Shah ji from his own pocket while the matter was being sorted out. Every few days the Resident would make him an offer to loan him some spending money. General Bird told us that Thomson had told him how grateful he was to him for having recommended Shah ji for the job.

Shah ji worked at great speed. He would go through three or four hundred files a day and would leave no file pending. For the first month he went to the office at seven in the morning and returned at six in the evening. The next month he arranged matters so that even though he still left at seven he was back home for lunch with ten or twelve sacks full of files. He would work on them at home and take them back to the office the next morning. Every day there would be three or four hundred telegrams from the various kingdoms and Shah ji would prepare responses to them. The Resident never found any occasion to complain.

The Viceroy's office issued an order that till Shah ji's appointment was approved, he should not sign as the GLO. Thomson sent a terse response saying that as long as he was the Resident, Shah ji would continue to sign as his GLO.

Soon, the Resident suggested that Shah ji start touring the various princely kingdoms. The year before we had purchased a second hand station wagon for eighteen hundred rupees. The wagon could easily accommodate eight or nine people along with their luggage. The Resident telephoned the authorities at Nabha and informed them that his GLO would be arriving for a visit. The next day, with two or three servants and the children, we set off for Nabha. The moment our car pulled up at the guest house, fifteen or twenty men came towards us. There were also a dozen soldiers in uniform from the Nabha army and they offered us a formal salute.

We did not have a driver so Shah ji had driven the car himself. He got out and the various ministers, the diwan and the secretary introduced themselves. We had no clue that this was the sort of reception that awaited us. Since we were meant to be travelling I was dressed rather shabbily and the children were very untidy by now. A few ministers approached me and opened the car door for me to get out. Bashfully, I did. They showed me the way to the guest house. They opened the door of the guest house and when the children and I had entered, they returned to where Shah ji was.

To flatter the Resident, the officials of the kingdom had decided to put us in the Viceroy's suite. The guest house had been done up by some famous decorator from England who had charged a few lakhs of rupees for the job. She had done a great job of decorating the drawing and dining rooms. The table lamps and the electrical fittings were very tasteful. The chairs and sofas were so soft that they sank almost to the ground when you sat on them. The children started jumping on these sofas the moment they entered the drawing room. I managed to get them under control with the help of the servants. Everything was a novelty for them for they had never seen such soft sofas or wall to wall carpeting before. It was like letting little dogs into a palace of mirrors. Their boots were caked with mud and I had to tell the servants to watch over them carefully. I went to take a look at the bedrooms, which I found were done up in pink and blue. The beds were covered with floral printed bedcovers. The bathrooms had be seen to be believed. The tiles were light pink with dark pink flowers on them. There was a beautiful tub and superb fittings. Of all the rooms, the Viceroy's suite was, of course, the most well-appointed and elegant.

Shah ji's old servant Khadim was with us. I firmly asked him
not to let the children out of his sight for a minute for it would be
very embarrassing if they broke anything. I told him to watch
them extra carefully and not to let them wander about. The suite
was extremely tasteful as were all the things in it, and it was
luxurious. But the children were going so crazy over everything—
leaping on the beds, dancing on the chairs, tugging at the curtains
and I was quite concerned. It was as if they had turned into
footballs because they were all over and were making a complete
nuisance of themselves.

Soon Shah ji came in and when he saw the suite, his jaw
dropped. I had seen a lot of splendour but this was Shah ji's first
exposure to such grandeur even though there was nothing unique
in the room. He went around the rooms and the bathrooms and
was stunned. A bed, which was very high to look at, sank down
four feet when he sat on it. He enjoyed sitting on it so much that
soon he, like the children, was jumping on it. I quickly shut the
door and sarcastically asked how I could stop the children from
doing what the grown-up child was now doing. I told him how
badly the children had been behaving; how when I stopped them
from pulling the curtains or dancing on the sofas, they would go
and find refuge in the tub. I asked him to finish whatever he was
here for so that we could leave as soon as we could, 'I will go
crazy otherwise,' I told him.

Shah ji replied casually, 'Begum, for God's sake, sit down and
relax. Thank God for everything and let the curtains and everything
else go to hell. If they want to pull the curtains, let them. If they
want to jump on the beds, let them. Nothing will happen. I want
you to be happy and to have a good time. Just pay no attention to
any of these things. Think how much fun it will be to sleep on
these beds tonight. Does it not seem that we are in legendary
pleasure palace on Mount Caucasus? Why are you letting such
minor things make you unhappy?'

'Yes,' I said, 'let the children do what they like and let these
people wonder what sort of people we are? Let them know that
we are unused to things such as these?'

'Let them think and say what they want. How will anything
they say affect us? Set your mind at rest,' Shah ji told me.

Soon it was time for lunch. A servant knocked gently on the door. I quickly gathered all that was lying scattered around and asked him to come in. With great politeness the bearer said, 'Your honours, lunch is ready. Please honour us with your presence.'

We told him we would be there in ten minutes. I instructed the servants to be extra watchful of the children during the meal. We went into the dining room which was equally well done up. The black dining table could have easily seated a hundred people. It was so well polished that you could see your face reflected in it. Around the table were chairs upholstered in burgundy velvet. Three large chandeliers hung over the table. The combination of black and burgundy was very striking. The meal was elaborate: *biryani, qorma*, roasted meat, fish, chicken, partridge, vegetables, dal—almost everything you could think of. The children immediately began to fight over the chairs. Once seated, each one demanded this or that dish. They were not used to using cutlery so they dropped as much food as they put in their mouths. I wonder what the bearers must have thought! Perhaps they said, 'Look at God's greatness that he has given rustics such as these such a high status.'

After lunch we came back to our room. Some people came to call on Shah ji and the meeting lasted for a couple of hours. At tea time the bearer informed us that tea was served. I asked him to bring it to our room as I was afraid that the children would start misbehaving again in the dining room. Along with the tea, there were many things to eat. In the evening the Maharaja had invited us for dinner and he discussed matters with Shah ji for a long time. When we returned from the palace we went to our rooms to sleep. We happily rolled around in the beds and extolled the softness of the mattresses. But no matter how hard we tried, we could not sleep. When I was tired of tossing and turning, I turned to Shah ji and found that he too was having difficulty sleeping.

It was summer. At home we used to sleep on the terrace with a table fan. We were also used to sleeping on tightly strung charpais. I told Shah ji to ask them to spread some charpais for us in the open or I would have to spend the night sitting up in bed. The servant was called but he said that he would first have to make a call to the Secretary. Whe he reached him the Secretary said he was sending over a truckload of charpais. Within half an hour our beds had been made out in the open and pedestal fans placed next to them, and we were able to sleep!

The Resident used to move to Shimla for the summer. In Shimla, tons of potatoes were produced and it was very important that they be strictly inspected. The GLO therefore had to be in Shimla as well. The British were very considerate of those who worked for them and the Resident told Shah ji to go to Lahore every fortnight or so, so that his travel allowances etc., were protected. The Maharaja of Faridkot had sent a message saying that he had a house in Shimla and we should make use of it while we were there. The house was very close to the Mall Road, where all the tourists spent their time.

The arrangements for food at the house were very good too. The cook was excellent and we had all sorts of dishes at each meal. Sometimes the Maharaja of Faridkot would also come to visit. He was a man who had no airs. All he was interested in was business. Whenever he came over, he talked about business for hours. He was constantly asking Shah ji for this or that contract. After meeting him a few times, I could not help myself and said, 'Maharaja ji, in spite of being a Maharaja you do not look like one.'

'What do I look like then?' he asked.

'A *bania*,' I told him truthfully.

After a fortnight we came to Lahore for three days. On the way back to Lahore we stopped at the Dak Bungalow in Solan. We called the Resident and told him that one of our children was very unwell and we might have to stay in Solan for a few days. The Resident was so kind that within three hours a doctor had arrived from Shimla as a safeguard in case adequate medical help was not available in Solan.

The next day we heard about the wrestling tournament that was to be held in Solan. Shah ji was appointed as the judge for the bouts. I had never seen wrestling before. Both the wrestlers would enter the arena draped in sheets while the drummers beat their drums very hard. The wrestlers then rubbed mud all over themselves, shook hands and then the bout began. For about an hour they would wrestle and show their manoeuvres. The supporters of the winner lifted him high on their shoulders and Shah ji then garlanded him after which singing and dancing began. The wrestlers would then leave the arena making way for the next bout. I watched for over two hours and it was really memorable. It was more fun than any other sport that I had seen so far. There was a great deal of excitement amongst the spectators during each bout and it almost seemed as if the wrestlers were related to the audience. It was really sad to look at the face of the loser.

* * *

We would spend eighteen days in each month touring the various kingdoms, and we came across some very interesting things. The palace at Dojana, for example, was a little like a mohalla of interior Lahore. It was an old large house whose walls had not been white washed for years. The once-green moss, which now covered the walls, had turned black and the house looked like it was haunted. We were put up at the palace.

The inside walls were also black with dirt and age. Even if you lit ten bulbs, the place would not lighten up. Luckily we were on the first floor which was a little better. But the conditions of the palace made vs realize that we lived better than these rulers. The Diwan of the state was very solicitous and often asked if there was anything we needed and if we were comfortable. The food was very good and they were hospitable in every way. Shah ji met the Nawab of this very small state. There would have been about a hundred or so dwellings in the state. Or perhaps there were more but surely not more than five hundred.

Shah ji told me that the Nawab also lived in a similar palace, and I felt a strange depression seting in when I looked at it. Loharu, like Dojana was also a very small kingdom. But there were others, like Chamba, which were famous. Shah ji decided to visit Chamba and I decided to tag along. I had heard many beautiful hill songs and loved their tunes. Chamba was mentioned in many of these songs and I had a great desire to see it.

Our friend Ali Raza would often visit us in Lahore with his wife and children. I liked him a great deal because he was cheerful, amusing, and someone who recited poetry at every opportunity.

I asked him to come along to Chamba and he was happy to do so. The officials of the kingdom had been informed of our visit. When we reached Dalhousie, two of the children came down with measles and high fever. The Chamba officials had sent some *dandis* and horses to Dalhousie to take us to Chamba. I wrapped my sick children and laid them in the dandis and instructed the men who carried these dandis on their shoulders to move fast. Halfway to Chamba there was a bungalow at Khajiyar and we had planned to spend a night there. Everyone insisted that I sit in a dandi too but I felt awkward about being carried around by others like an ill person. Ali Raza suggested that I get onto a horse although he said that he preferred to walk. I thought it was a good idea to walk with him—we could talk and the distance would be easily covered. Ali Raza, the servants, the men leading the horses, those carrying the dandis and I set out as a caravan at a slow pace. We suggested to the servants that they get on to the horses but they said that they would not dare ride when we were walking. Shah ji was with the dandis carrying the children and was way ahead of us. The men carrying the dandis did not walk, they ran.

After some time it started raining and the dandi carriers started walking faster. I was very worried for I did not want the children to catch a cold too. Shah ji and a servant who had accompanied the children were no longer even visible.

The route was very beautiful. On the way whenever we passed a beautiful woman, Ali Raza would recite a couplet. Chamba was famous for its beautiful women. I think it was God's decision to make the men of Chamba very ugly and the women extremely beautiful. Their complexions were clear and glowing and they were tall and beautifully built. We did not see a single woman who could have been described as plain. The women also worked twice as hard as the men did. Every woman carried a basketload on her back and they would climb the slopes at a slow measured pace. What's more they never seemed to tire or get out of breath. I could not understand how they could carry such weights up a mountain. We, who had nothing to carry, were already panting.

When we were close to Khajiyar we saw men and women planting paddy and singing a pahari. They bent to plant the seedlings and then straightened up to the same beat. The women would sing one line and the men would respond in song. The melody was so beautiful that I was speechless. Ali Raza and I decided to stop and listen to them sing. Our paharis from Jammu had the same beat as all paharis but these songs had a charm of their own. We sat and listened to them till sunset. I decided I was only going to leave Khajiyar for Chamba after I had learnt some of these paharis.

We walked fast to get to the bungalow at Khajiyar. Shah ji had already put the children to bed and a doctor was expected from Chamba. There was a huge grassy lawn around the bungalow where cattle and horses were roaming freely. There were so many mosquitoes that it seemed impossible that anything could protect us from them. Because of the children's illness, we had to spend a few days here. We asked that the grounds be cleaned and within a day a hundred or more men had spruced up everything. I had already told Shah ji about the pahari that I had heard, and that I did not want to leave till I had learnt a few of the paharis myself.

Shah ji told the officials of the kingdom that we loved the paharis of their region and asked if pahari singers could come to the bungalow in the evenings. That same evening a group of men and women arrived. I heard them sing ten or twelve paharis. I wrote down the words of some three or four and made them sing these over and over again till I had learnt their tunes. When they were leaving, I tipped them generously and asked if they would come every evening. They came regularly for the next four or five days and I was able to memorise the paharis well. The children too were much better by then.

We informed the Chamba officials that we were now ready to come to Chamba. They sent a few armed dandi carriers and some men with horses. We were told that there were many bears on the way and that there had been several accidents because of them and the route was thus dangerous. Luckily, we reached Chamba before sunset.

The bungalow that we were to stay in was right on the bank of the river. The view from the windows was stunning. In the evenings the women came to fetch water from the river and Ali Raza would sit and watch them till sunset. They carried two or three brass pots on their heads and walked with infinite grace. Their waists were thin and there was a swing to their gait. Their features were sharp and once you had seen them, it was difficult to forget their beauty. Such beauty as I saw in Chamba, I had never seen elsewhere.

The *choghan* of Chamba that was mentioned in so many of the paharis turned out to be a market with a lot of small shops. People from the small surrounding villages came to shop here. The women bought clothes, jewellery, and colourful braids for their plaits, drawstrings and all sorts of odds and ends as well. This was the centre of all commerce in the kingdom. There was nothing else that was special about this choghan of Chamba.

We had been away for nearly ten or twelve days when we decided to return to Lahore. I will never forget three things about Chamba. First, the rays of the setting sun on the clear sparkling blue water of the river, second, the way the women carried the pots on their heads and finally, their beauty. The cook at the bungalow was also very good. He was particularly good at cooking *maash dal*, which he prepared in a number of ways.

When we left, all sorts of food was packed for us and loaded on to the horses and the dandis. We found a nice place in the jungle and spread out a carpet where we had our lunch, which included *rotis* made of maize and the maash dal. We eventually reached Lahore safely.

The Resident was to meet the Viceroy in Delhi. I went along with Shah ji to Delhi. At the meeting the Viceroy complimented the Resident on the potato yield which was many tons more than usual. He said he was grateful to the Resident because such a yield was unprecedented. The Resident spoke after the Viceroy and said that he could not take any credit for the year's high yield. He pointed to Shah ji and said the credit was all due to this hardworking man, a man whose salary has not been sanctioned till this day. This was very embarrassing for Sir Srivastava.

On our return from Delhi we went on a tour to Sarmaur. On the way there were a few rivulets and it was difficult to get the car across them. Otherwise too, the road was very bad. There were beautiful grounds in front of the rest house where we stayed and there were a few well-known spots near it. Shah ji and I went out for a walk and before we knew it, we had walked quite far. I had left the children at home and when we returned I found that the youngest child had eaten his way through a whole bottle of Milk of Magnesia tablets thinking them to be candies! We always carried a box of essential medicines with us and the bottle had been carelessly left around because we thought it was harmless. I started crying in panic and sent for a doctor. He reassured us that nothing would happen and if it did, we should send word to him immediately. The amazing thing is that nothing did happen to the child. He carried on playing as if nothing was the matter. We went to Naahan and Tehri Garhwal too, before we returned to Lahore. Over time, I toured all the eighty kingdoms that fell within the jurisdiction of the Resident. We also went to Patiala, Faridkot and Nabha several times.

The maharajas were rulers of one kingdom but Shah ji ended up being master of eighty kingdoms. God was kind to us and we got a great deal of respect from different people. At times, the maharajas would even open car doors for us! Wherever we went, the ministers and the Diwan would wait for hours to welcome us and they never tire of calling Shah ji 'Sir.'

I had worked for a maharaja for nine years and had seen a lot and had lacked nothing. Yet, I was an employee then and the comfort and honour I had seen then seemed meaningless when compared with all of this. Even Jammu and Kashmir now came under Shah ji's control.

* * *

I have mentioned Rahima the wrestler before. Rahima had been good friends with Babu Sadiq, a film director, whom he had known since they were children. One day Rahima brought Babu along with him and introduced him to me as a very good director. He had directed a film called *Baharon Phool Barsao* and had just finished another film for Liaqat Hayat. He was paid Rs 5000 a month for directing films and he was supposed to be very good. He was also known to complete his films quickly. Rahima spoke very highly of him. When Baba came to se me, he brought along a film idea and story—a good one—with him.

Rahima suggested that I produce the film, and said he was sure it would do well. Rahima also convinced me of Babu's abilities and vouched for his honesty and asked me to go through the story. He added that Babu had been unable to find work in Bombay because he was a Muslim.

I read the story and it was a powerful one, and so I decided to produce it. I told Babu about my decision the next day and told him that he would have to work with me not as an employee but as a partner though he would continue to get the salary he'd been getting till now. We would share the profits from the film equally.

Babu reacted very strangely to this. He put his head on my feet and wept. At that moment, Babu was a pauper and had been forced to leave Bombay. I told him that the only condition that I would impose on him was that he swear by the Quran that he would never defraud me in any way. I then suggested he leave for Bombay and start work immediately. I bought furniture for an office and began to set things in motion. As it happened, we also had to go to Bombay for the *mahurat* of another film, *Kajal*. We stayed with the film director, Sunny. In Bombay, Khurshid Anwar, a music director, Babu Sadiq, Khurshid Nazir, who ran a journal called *Mussawir*, Om Prakash, Saadat Hasan Manto , Nakshad and various others would get together in the evenings and would talk and joke till midnight.

Babu selected Suraiya and Wasti as the leads for our film. We spent ten or fifteen days in Bombay because we were having such a good time meeting friends and then we came back to Lahore. Babu Sadiq wrote to me every week. He said the same thing in all his letters: that he was not the sort of man who bit the hand that fed him; that no one would have done what I had done for him; that he would be indebted to me forever. Three months later I heard that Babu had fallen in love with Suraiya. Some time later, the film was finally finished and I went alone to Bombay for the opening. From there, I would speak to Shah ji for hours every night on the phone. All Shah ji had to do was to pick up the phone and tell the operator that the call was 'On behalf of the Resident' and we were immediately connected.

Rahima told me that Babu had gone crazy in his love for Suraiya. Others told me about this too, but I did not tell Babu that I had any idea what was going on. A well-known composer called D.N. Madhok had composed the music and written the lyrics. He was at the peak of his popularity at the time and every song of his was a hit. People often had to wait for him for a year to work in their films. He composed the tunes of the songs by playing the rhythm on the lid of a box and when he wrote the lyrics, he would use a matchbox to play the beat on. His songs were so simple that every one would begin to hum them immediately after hearing them. I recovered the money that I had invested in *Kajal*.

Later, one day we were sitting out in the lawn in Karachi when a man came to see us. He was wearing a wide bottomed shalwar of long-cloth, a small black coat and ugly Peshawari slippers. A *karakul* cap was placed sideways on his head. I looked him up and down. After formal greetings had been exchanged he said he had brought me a letter from Babu Sadiq. The letter introduced the man as Agha Gul and said he wanted to buy the distribution rights of *Kajal* for the Punjab. Babu Sadiq wanted me to sign the contract. I told Shah ji later that for some reason my instinct told me not to trust the man. Shah ji reassured me that if Babu Sadiq had recommended him, I should go ahead and sign the contract.

The trailer of the film was to be screened in a fortnight. Agha Gul was lucky and soon he was making a lot of money. However, except for the money he had paid me at the time of signing, he did not give me another paisa. A few years later I filed a case against him. Agha Gul, who always carried prayer beads in his hand, presented himself before the judge. I went and took my place in the witness box. The judge asked Agha Gul if he knew me and Agha denied it. I was furious.

'You liar, you deny that you know me! Can you swear that you do not know me? Did you not have a meal with me day before yesterday? Place your hand on the Quran and say you do not know me.'

'I swear by God that I do not know you,' Agha lied blatantly. 'I swear by Him that I have never set eyes on you before.'

This was about a fortnight before the Partition. Babu Sadiq had come from Bombay for he wanted to announce the next film called *Char Din*. He told me that the profits from *Kajal* would be enough to produce the next film. I told him to go ahead but that I wanted the film to be made in Pakistan, not in Bombay. Sadiq argued that Partition was going to make no difference and that it would be much more beneficial to make the film in Bombay. I did not agree with this and asked him to hand over my share of the profits to me. If he wanted to make the film in Bombay, he could go ahead and do so by himself. Sadiq hung around in Karachi for ten days. He kept trying to convince me that since *Kajal* had been a hit, the new film would be sold even before it was completed and we would recover twice the amount we would invest.

Shah ji did not agree with me and managed to cajole me into accepting Sadiq's suggestion. We began the production of *Char Din*. We went to Bombay for the mahurat. Again we had a wonderful time there with friends. All the friends would collect around six. I remember one incident about a friend, Nakshab, from this trip. Nakshab was very fond of Anwar Agrewali, a young, dark and very beautiful woman. She also sang very well and her songs were often broadcast on the radio. Anwar went to Delhi for a recording and from there eloped with Asad Khan who was neither a good singer nor much to look at. We were very informal with Nakshab so I asked him if he loved Anwar a lot. He admitted she had been his first love and that he had fallen in love with her even before he had finished his studies. I then asked him if she had loved him in return and he said that she loved him a lot. He said that he had no money when they met but she would find ways of meeting him without her family finding out. So I asked him why she had then chosen to run away with Asad who was just a *mirasi*. Nakshab was silent for a few minutes and then he said, enigmatically, 'She was a very generous woman.'

Because of the success of *Kajal*, we got a good deal on the sale of *Char Din*. Babu Sadiq wrote saying that he had Rs 150,000 that belonged to me and that I could come and take the money anytime I wanted. It was two months before I could manage to go to Bombay again.

One day, Shah ji decided to go Kapurthala for a visit. Twenty or thirty miles short of the place, we saw thousands of people heading towards Kapurthala. There were truckloads of men and women, cars full of people, the young and the old, men and women, all heading in the same direction. We stopped the car and asked people what the matter was. We were told that the Agha Khan was coming and they were going there to look at him. I had met him in Kashmir once but had no idea that people actually worshipped him.

We reached Kapurthala and the Maharaja's Secretary told us that we were expected to dine with the Maharaja that night. Sir Agha Khan was also going to be there. We went for dinner at eight-thirty. The Agha Khan and his beautiful French wife were already there. I was wearing a French brocade sari, which the Agha Khan's wife liked very much, and in her broken English she complimented me on it. Sir Agha Khan said that he thought we had already met in Kashmir, I confirmed that we had done so. I was amazed at his memory. He must have had to meet hundreds of people every day and yet he remembered someone from so many years ago. After a pleasant evening everyone got up to go to bed and we left. Outside the palace, the crowds were still waiting on the street and it seems they sat there all night hoping that the Agha Khan would come out of the palace and they could greet him. I had never seen such a celebration. Whole families had left their homes and were out sitting on the streets hoping to be lucky enough to just get just a glimpse of him. We returned to Lahore in a couple of days.

*   *   *

When Partition took place, all the princely kingdoms were abolished. Many flourishing homes were destroyed. People with homes suddenly found themselves homeless. Those who had never even had a hut to live in, now occupied mansions. Raja Ghazanfar Ali was appointed Minister for Rehabilitation and Shah ji was appointed his Secretary. A huge refugee camp was set up in Lahore and huge caravans of thousands of people began arriving every day. The people of Lahore did all they could to help the refugees. Every day they sent large quantities of food, and also clothes, and bedding.

The cleverer refugees immediately occupied large houses, while others who were not so quick had to live on the streets. Camps were ill-equipped to deal with the thousands of infants

who were brought there. When I saw this, I suggested to Shah ji
that since God had been so kind to us by giving us all we needed,
perhaps we could think of adopting two children from the camp.
I went to the camp the next day and told them what I wanted and
asked to see some children. I had thought I would pick up nice,
good looking and healthy children. On one charpai I noticed a
dirty mattress which was half on the bed while the other half hung
over the side sweeping the floor. We lifted the mattresses to find
a thin child of about six or seven months lying there. You could
see her head and swollen stomach and under her stomach dangled
two rope-like thin legs. Her fist was tightly curled around a small
piece of bread. With great difficulty she opened her eyes and
looked at me. There were dark circles around her eyes.

I do not know what I saw in those eyes but I thought to myself
that if this child had to die, she might as well die in comfort and I
asked them if I could take her away. Another child I chose was
four or five years old and I brought these two home. Raja Ghazanfar
Ali was leaving for Karachi in two days and we were also moving
there because of Shah ji's new job. In those days there were special
trains for ministers and their staff, and we were travelling in one
of these with him. We boarded the train with our family, luggage
and servants. Many people had come to see Raja Sahib off, and it
took him quite a while to say his farewells and board the train.
The windows of the train were such that if you were inside, you
could see what was happening outside but the people outside
coundn't look in. A few minutes after he'd got on, Raja Sahib
opened the door and again got off the train. When I looked out of
the window I saw him talking to a woman dressed in a shimmering
sari. I looked carefully and recognised her as the famous Mukhtar
Begum. Showing no signs of any urgency, Raja Sahib took his
time talking to her and got back onto the train after fifteen or
twenty minutes.

I had heard from many people that Raja Sahib had a colourful
temperament and was very fond of song and dance. I knew
nothing else about him for this was the first time I had met him. I
was surprised that Raja Sahib had the train stopped only to get off
to see Mukhtar and without caring what the onlookers would say,
and then had chatted with her for so long.

At every stop people came to meet him. At Multan, someone served us a very delicious and elaborate meal. The journey passed very comfortably. But on the way, the younger child from the camp developed a fever, perhaps due to the air-conditioning in the train. I got a doctor to examine her when we reached Karachi. I had known the doctor, Dr Hashmi, since I had met him in Delhi. He diagnosed her condition as double pneumonia and advised that I change the plaster every three hours and suggested that I trust in God. Mercifully she became well very soon, and grew into a healthy, fair child who was loved by everyone.

At the time, Hindus were running away from Karachi. The Hindu brokers were chasing people so that their houses and lands could be sold for they wanted to salvage whatever they could. The going rate was only Rs 60,000 for a huge house in the upmarket Clifton area. A broker came to me too. He told me about two properties. One was a four-part house in a housing society and another a building on Clayton Road, which was owned by a single owner though the building was still incomplete. The owner had built it as a hotel. The deal was struck and I kept all the four flats in the housing society with myself. Mother had already migrated from Jammu and we all settled down comfortably in them.

The biggest mistake I made was to acquire property at that time by paying for it. I was a refugee, so were mother and my brother. We had left behind property worth lakhs but we did not have a single house or any land allotted to us. I had been so disgusted at the way others were behaving that I felt like giving away whatever I had rather than claiming anything new. Shah ji was the person in charge of allotment and it would have taken no effort to get compensatory property.

The ones who really benefited were those who thought only of themselves. There are many people in Karachi whose family fortunes were made at that time. Since I had bought the property with cash, I faced major problems later and all I could do was to pray to God for relief. I could not complete the building work because I had no money to do so. I had thought I would use some money that I had in Bombay so Shah ji took ten days off and we went to Bombay. We stayed with Nazir Musawwir and Khurshid Anwar and went to see Babu Sadiq the next day and reminded him of the Rs 150,000 that he owed me. Babu began to look for excuses to avoid paying me my money. He admitted that he had it but began to lie and invent all sorts of stories about what had happened to it. I do not even remember the lies he told us. But he refused to pay up and we did not get a paisa from him. When we were leaving he tried to make up by offering his car to drop us off. This was the same car that I had sent from Lahore! I told him that we never licked what we had once spat out and that we would take a taxi. I also told him to remember one thing— that his behaviour was going to cost him dear and that he would have to pay ten times over for it. I reminded him of all the things he had written to me in his letters and said that I trusted in God's justice. I impressed upon him the fact that it was I who had given him freedom to do what he wanted as long as he did not cheat me and that he had placed his hand on the Quran and promised never to do so. I asked him to think of me when he faced final justice. Once I'd given vent to my feelings, we left and came home and the next day, we left for Karachi.

In Karachi another broker approached me and asked if I wanted to rent out the building on Clayton Road. I told him the building was still incomplete and asked who would want to rent it. The next day the broker returned and said that I should meet a man called Sydney Cotton at eleven the day after. We had heard some rumours about Sydney Cotton. It was said that he piloted his own plane and that he was a courageous man who, during the war, would successfully dodge all the planes that followed him. Lord knows what he ferried in those planes of his. One of the rumours was that he brought gold and arms from Hyderabad in the Deccan. The next day we went to the designated meeting place in a hotel. Cotton's secretary informed him of our arrival and he immediately came to receive us. It was difficult to guess how old he was but he was certainly more than six feet tall. He was handsome and had a strong and attractive physique. I had never seen wrists as wide as his! He was full-bodied but he did not seem to have an extra ounce of flesh on him. Just one look at him and one knew that here was a courageous, brave and fearless man. He greeted us very warmly. For some reason, he seemed to like our building very much. We agreed that he would advance us money with which we would complete the building in a month. Babu had cheated us but God found this new way out for us. In a month Sydney Cotton had moved into the building.

He furnished all the rooms with Persian carpets. There were about twenty-five rooms and they were all redone. His entire staff, including the cooks, were foreigners—though where they were from I don't know. All I know is that there was no Pakistani employed in the building.

* * *

Whenever Raja Sahib went to Lahore, Shah ji accompanied him. Sometimes I would also go along with Shah ji and we'd spend hours with Raja Sahib, talking to him in the train. Raja Sahib was a great conversationalist and he had a sense of humour. You never wanted conversations with him to end. He was well informed on practically everything: religion, *hadith*, politics, poetry and music. There was no subject that he did not know and on which he could not talk for hours. He made even the most ordinary incidents sound interesting. He had a great memory too and remembered works ranging from the *Heer* of Waris Shah to the poetry of Ghalib and the *Diwan* of Hafiz. He was also a well-mannered man. I never saw him being rude to anyone—indeed he was both modest and humble to the core.

Raja Sahib was dark, very tall and very plain to look at. He always wore a dark coloured achkan, shalwars of long-cloth and a dark turban, with a short end hanging loose. This made him look even taller. Since Shah ji had to accompany him, I went along to Lahore as well. The next day we went from Lahore to Sambli. Raja Sahib's wife had suffered from consumption for a few years and now she was in Sambli for treatment. He went to see her the moment he arrived in Sambli and after spending half an hour with her, he came out to meet other people who were waiting. His wife was very weak and feeble. She was excited about Raja Sahib's visit, and had dressed in shiny clothes and a stiff, bright dupatta. She had plastered so much rouge on her cheeks that they looked the colour of pomegranate seeds! She had also used so much powder that her face was covered with white blotches. She had turned herself into a strange looking creature. Six or seven village women attended on her. Next to the room were a few wooden crates full of mangoes. Some of these were rotting and the stench from these made it difficult to sit in the room.

The Raja Sahib's Personal Assistant came in and said that he had sent for some mangoes for his guests. She told one of the maids to put six mangoes on a plate. The PA timidly hinted that there were a lot of people outside. 'These are more than enough,' she told him.

Her speech was rustic. There was a lawn in front of the room, which was fenced off with canvas screens. There, on the clotheslines were clothes hung out to dry. At frequent intervals, two maids would change the Begum's shalwar. Begum Sahiba told me that she had asked for three girls from the camp and asked me if it was true that I had also taken two myself. I told her it was true and asked her where the girls whom she had adopted were. A maid told me they were outside and I went to see them. They were all seven or eight years old and it seemed as though they were still in the camp. I had heard that Raja Sahib had one daughter who had died of consumption at the age of sixteen or seventeen. This must have traumatised both of them because his friends said that they had both loved her to the point of madness. Raja Sahib however, continued to smile while he spoke to everyone, and gave no indication of his grief in any way. But people felt that his wife's illness perhaps was linked to this loss which had made her irritable and bad-tempered.

Raja Sahib came in again and spoke to her warmly. Then he asked for permission to leave and we all left. On the way back, we had a very good time in the train. Whenever the train stopped at a station, people would be waiting to talk to Raja Sahib. He'd greet everyone and would spend about half an hour with them and then come back into the train. He would tell us about many of the people he had just met. Raja Sahib often joked how once upon a time he used to pride himself on his knowledge of the family histories of people in the Punjab. Now, he admitted he had accepted defeat at the hands of Shah ji who seemed to know the family history of everyone he met!

We talked about the 'people of the house.' Raja Sahib's articulation were so sharp that even the best of the 'reciters' would not be able to match him. He recited sermons and *marsiyas* in Urdu and Persian. He talked in a manner that made it clear that he was well aware of history when he spoke about any subject. One never tired of hearing him speak; in fact, often you just wanted him to carry on speaking. He was a great individual. The more I got to know him, the more I came to respect him.

When we were preparing to go to Lahore next, he gave me a shopping list of things the Begum Sahiba wanted. In Sambli she had already instructed me that I should personally choose the things she wanted. I looked at her list. It included brocade suits, sequins and silver embroidery, lace, suits and dupattas of *Banarsi* silk and satin shalwars. The colours she wanted were red, crimson and orange. I assumed that she wanted these to give to someone who was getting married. I bought everything she had asked for. When we went to Sambli next, she went through the shopping in front of me. I was happy she liked the things I had selected. She then told me to go with her husband whenever he went to buy things for her.

Every month she prepared a similar list. Just before we were to go to Lahore, Raja Sahib would give it to me. We would get everything she wanted. She would look at them, then send for a large steel trunk. She would unlock the trunk and count everything before she put it into the trunk. As long as we stayed with Raja Sahib, this became a monthly ritual. Raja Sahib did not even once ask her why she needed all these things when she had been confined to bed for six years. I had never seen such a generous, magnanimous man till now. God had gifted him with the qualities of simplicity, decency, and humility. He always thought the best of every one. I never saw any signs of greed or anything else that suggested that he was ever capable of stabbing any one in the back. I think it was two years later that he was appointed Ambassador to Iran. He wanted Shah ji to go along with him but it was impossible for us to leave, for something unexpected had happened.

* * *

The Pakistan government had ordered Sydney Cotton to leave the country within twenty-four hours. I have no idea why they did this. The rumour was that the bill for the services that he had rendered for the government of Pakistan had become so large that it was difficult to pay it and this seemed to be the only way to get rid of this problem. Sydney Cotton called us to the hotel and said that he was handing back the building to us along with the furnishing and the carpets. He handed over charge to an employee who was either a Memon or a Bohra and left the country. The building had thirty or thirty-two rooms, all with attached bathrooms. All the furniture—tables, chairs, beds—that Sydney Cotton had bought for his use, now belonged to us.

There was a relative of Shah ji's who had been living with us for three years. He had tried his hand at doing various small jobs but had not had any success. He was in a hurry to make quick money. We appointed him manager of the hotel and made him swear innumerable times that he would not cheat us. After much thought we decided to name it the Green Hotel. The food there was very good. Gradually the rooms began to be occupied. Shah ji would find some time to check affairs at the hotel and we earned about Rs 5000–6000 a month from it.

Those were days when things were cheap. The most expensive car cost twenty thousand rupees. Our family then consisted of the children, mother, the two children that I had adopted from the camps, my aunt and the family of my brother who were with us because of the Partition.

We could not leave all this and go off to Iran, though we were very sorry to see Raja Sahib go. Whenever he came back to Pakistan, even if it was for a week, he would first come to Karachi. He would come to our house straight from the airport. He would eat with us and would always want rice cooked with jaggery. I loved turquoise and had asked him to bring me a stone. He promised that he would get me one the next time he came. When he came next, he brought three stones. One was for Fatima Jinnah, one for me and one for his wife. Fatima Jinnah was going to get the first choice but since her brother, the Qaid i-Azam, had just died, he could not present her with one right away. He showed me all three stones and I got to choose one first.

Some time later, Shah ji resigned his job and he spent some time looking after the affairs of the hotel, and doing a little hunting.

He also spent time with Chachu, the little infant I had brought
from the refugee camp. She was a delightful child and Shah ji
loved her. In fact everyone loved Chachu. Even our neighbours
would call out to her a few times a day. She was nice and healthy,
never threw tantrums, nor did she weep. All day she would run
around and at night when I put her into the crib she would play
with a ball or a doll till she fell asleep. She never cried or asked to
be taken out of the crib. It almost seemed as though she thought
she had no right to make demands on us. She never refused to do
anything we asked her to do.

I remember an incident, which still makes me want to weep
whenever I think of it. One day Chachu told mother, who also
loved her very much, that she was hungry. When the food was
ready, the cook would bring it and place it before mother who
served everyone. That day she told the cook to hurry up. There
were about thirty or thirty-five people who had to be served.
Chachu sat on one side, waiting. All the other children ran around
getting mother, whom they called Bebe, to serve them various
things. Some wanted more meat, others, more rice. Chachu sat in
the corner and kept watching all this. Mother was so busy serving
food that she forgot that the child for whose sake she had asked
that lunch be served early, had still not been given any food to
eat. When she had finished serving even the adults, she suddenly
noticed Chachu sitting there. Bebe beat herself on the chest and
said 'Hai, may I die. You are still sitting there without food! Why
did you not come and get some?'

Chachu smiled and came to her and took the food. I was sad
when I saw this resignation of hers. There were times when she
would be playing with a toy that belonged to one of the other
children and if anyone asked her why she was playing with
someone else's toy she would immediately take it and lovingly
cajole its owner to take it back. She was only three years old and
yet her patience and her desire to please were amazing. No wonder
everyone in the house loved her so much.

Our friend, Nazir Musawwir had been visiting us from Bombay
and we had to go the airport to drop him off. We returned at
about five and I saw Chachu coming down the stairs from the
upper floor. Water was dripping from her hair and her wet frock

was clinging to her body. Water was also flowing down the staircase as in a flood. I rushed in and saw that the tap in the bathroom had been left open and the water gushing from it had spread into the rooms. I asked Chachu what she had done and in her childish lisp she said she had been bathing. I dried her up with a towel, dressed her and brought her down. The other children—including the twelve or thirteen year old girl I had brought from Lahore to look after Chachu—were playing. She bore the brunt of my anger. 'Did I bring you here to play games? You are supposed to be taking care of Chachu and you do not know that she has been bathing for three hours,' I scolded her. Chachu played for a while and then fell asleep. The cook had spread a charpai out in the open. The charpai was so loosely strung that it would be impossible for anyone to roll off it so I laid Chachu on it.

We had to go out for dinner. I instructed the cook, who loved Chachu more than I did, to feed her in a little while and then put her in her cot. I also told him to stay upstairs with her till I returned. I came back at about eleven. Every night I would make Chachu sit on the commode before I put her to bed so that she would not wet herself at night. That day too I put her on the commode and she began to cry which was very unusual. Her limbs too had begun to shake in a strange manner. Alarmed, I called out to Shah ji. The first thing he said was, "Check her head and see if she has been hurt.' I felt her scalp carefully and found nothing. I finally found, behind her ears, marks of the small earrings that I had made her wear. Shah ji said that the shivering was a worrying symptom.

A doctor lived close by and we woke him up. He examined her and told us that the next twenty-fours were critical and if she survived those, she would be all right. I assured myself that the doctor had meant that everything would be all right in twenty-four hours. Chachu lay very still in her cot and stared at the ceiling. I thought that she looked very pale and I asked her how she felt. She looked at me and smiled. I had to go out for some work so I gave her an orange and a ball to play with. She gave me a long, intense look. Her eyes did not look too bright but I told myself that she was feeling sleepy so I told her to go to sleep. I turned her over and patted her.

Shah ji and I left the house. When we returned we were not yet out of the car when I heard someone say, 'Sister come, Chachu is dead.' I ran upstairs and saw that she was lying straight on her back with the ball and the orange on her chest. She looked as if she was sound asleep. Even today, I remember her last, forced laugh which had just been meant to please me and her drowsy eyes as she accepted the orange and the ball I gave her.

It was late at night. We called a carpenter who made a coffin for her. We bathed her and put her in the box. We arranged roses around her and she looked like a doll. Three days earlier Shah ji had bought a Landrover and we placed her in it and took her to the graveyard. I was sad but not devastated. I used to wonder if this was because she was not my own flesh and blood, for in that case I would have been destroyed. I went off to sleep and when I got up in the morning, the first thing I saw was the empty cot with no Chachu in it. Every morning she would lie silently in her cot staring at the book on her knees, and wait for me to wake up. This posture was exactly the same as Shah ji's when he read and she obviously tried to copy him. I would send for a bottle of milk for her and she would hold the bottle herself while she drank it. The maid would then take her to the bathroom. Chachu loved bathing. If she could have had her way, she would have bathed all day. I had to go to the bathroom a couple of times to tell her that she had bathed enough. She would look at me innocently and in her childish lisp tell me to wait a little longer and I'd leave her there. In fact, I had even put a few plastic toys in the tub for her because she loved to play in the water. Once she was dressed and ready, she would come to me and show me her clothes and say a dozen other things in her childish, lispy prattle, most of which I did not understand.

That day there was no bottle of milk nor did I call the maid. There were no sounds of water splashing in the bathroom. My room looked deserted without her. The shock of her loss hit me and memories of her came back in a rush and that is when I started crying. I wept so loudly that the whole house collected around me. Everyone tried to console me but I could not stop. That night again I cried for as long as I was awake. I was not at peace for a moment. I would look at my children, see them fighting, playing, laughing and I would immediately recall her ingratiating laugh. I often found myself wishing she had died the moment I had gotten her.

I had often told Shah ji that Chachu would one day be a great woman and that she would study a great deal. Now, I imagined I saw her in every corner of the house. I felt like doing nothing and I felt oppressed no matter which room I sat in. All I could do was wonder why this had to happen. If she had to die, why did she not die when she had lain there on the street hungry? Why did she not die while she was still at the camp? She had pneumonia and diarrhoea soon after I had brought her home, why did she survive those? Now when she was so healthy and robust, why did she have to die of no cause? It became increasingly difficult for me to stay on in Karachi.

* * *

Now that Shah ji was no longer employed our only source of income was the hotel. But it gave us enough to live in style. Shah ji would take an inventory of all the provisions in the hotel every day and go through the accounts. The hotel was becoming popular because of its good food. The rooms were always full and our income from it was constantly increasing.

A month after Chachu died, Shah ji said to me that if I wanted him to live, we would have to leave Karachi. He said he could no longer live in the house because he kept looking for Chachu in every corner. He kept asking himself why this had to happen. I was also in a similar state. Whenever I came back home, indeed, the moment the car turned into the drive, the hair on my body would stand up and I'd get gooseflesh, and it was only after I had been home for an hour or so that I managed to feel normal. I consulted with my doctor and he told me that something had gone wrong with my nervous system.

I argued with Shah ji that we were entirely dependent on the income from the hotel and if we left Karachi, we'd have nothing to live on. Shah ji reassured me that nothing would happen if we left. He would ask one of his relatives to manage the hotel—the person he had in mind had already learnt quite a bit about the job by then. Shah ji was confident that this man would be able to manage with the help of the clerk we had appointed, who was good with accounts. Shah ji said that monthly accounts would be sent to us in Lahore and that there was nothing to worry about. He was sure that they would not cheat us. I reminded him of our experience with Babu Sadiq but he dismissed my apprehensions and told me to have faith in God.

In truth, I was not too eager to continue living in Karachi. If I had insisted, I could have had my way, We took a few days to pack our belongings and then we moved back to Lahore. For the first few months, the accounts arrived regularly. Then the excuses began and every month there was a new one.

We had problems getting our boys admitted to Chief's College. Since commuting was a problem, I had them admitted as boarders. I constantly urged Shah ji to go to Karachi to check on the hotel. At the time of the Partition we had also bought a shop in Elphinistone Sadar for thirty thousand rupees from a Hindu. It was a specialised shop selling tinned food and tinned fruit. The Hindu had employed a Syed called Zaidi to work for him. We kept him on to work for us when we bought the shop.

We reached Karachi to discover that Shah ji's relative, who had been managing the hotel, was about to get married. We were told that he had told the parents of his prospective bride that he owned the hotel. What could we have done other than ask him to leave? He had nothing to his name and was a relative who had lived with us once. In any case, he had no money so there was no question of recovering anything from him.

In the hotel there was a guest, an Indian called Muzaffar, who had always wanted to manage a hotel. When he heard that there might be a job going, he began to hound us day and night. But we'd become wiser. We had decided not to appoint anyone since the person we had entrusted the job to had turned out to be a cheat. It seemed a much better idea to sub-let the hotel.

We also visited our shop in the Sadar. Zaidi told us that the shop was making no money because all the foreigners, who were the main consumers of tinned food, had left. Out of curiosity, Shah ji casually picked up a tin to see what it was and, to his surprise, found it empty. The next one that he picked up was empty too. We began picking up all the tins that we could reach and found that all were empty. We sent for a ladder and checked all shelves only to find more empty tins.

Shah ji said he was going to report the matter to the police and before we knew it, Zaidi was lying flat on the floor with his face more or less buried in Shah ji's feet. He then started switching between Shah ji's and my feet. He wailed loudly that he had eleven children and they would to starve if Shah ji reported him to the police. He was a brilliant actor and within two hours his wife and eleven children had also joined the cast. Zaidi kept repeating the same thing: 'Either forgive me or first poison my family.' He was smart enough to ensure that throughout this whole drama, he kept his face hidden at our feet so we actually did not see him crying. And then, there were the wife and the eleven children who stood to one side, also weeping.

We tried everything we could do to make him get up and talk to us but he refused to budge or to say anything other than what he had been repeating. We had no option but to forgive him. The shop was so well located that if we had not sold it in a hurry, we could have got a very good price for it. Today, just the deposit for renting the shop is twenty lakh rupees. At the time, though we sold it at the price we had paid for it. Today the shop houses the famous Ruby Jewellers.

I tried to talk Shah ji into getting involved with business. I argued that we not only had a home, but also a hotel, and a shop in Karachi, and since he was no longer working, he could make a lot of money if he paid attention to our business. I said that with the money we made, we could go on a trip to Europe and America. To this he would always reply, 'Begum, the pleasures of one's own *chaubara* are better than those of Balkh and Bukhara.'

I had been allotted a studio on the Mall Road in Lahore. This was the former Pancholi Studio. One Mr W.Z. Ahmad contested the allotment. Mr Ahmad was a shrewd man with such a smooth tongue that he could talk his way into or out of any situation. Only God could save you from that tongue of his. He did not have a good reputation in Bombay either. He submitted an application saying that the studio should rightfully be his, even though he had yet to make a film.

The two us got into a battle over the studio. Hearings were held before the board. With a great deal of effort we made our point and the Board decided in our favour and fixed the day when possession would be handed over to me. On that day when we reached the studio, we found a casual Mr Ahmad standing at the gate with an order from the court temporarily stopping any further action in the case. He greeted us warmly and handed over the court document to me. It was like winning the battle every time only to discover that victory was meaningless. He had us spinning.

We were so embarrassed by this latest setback that we did not feel like facing anyone. This went on for months. When Ahmad failed in every way to get the studio for himself, he went to the minister, Sardar Amir Azam in Karachi. We heard about this and went to Karachi too. The Minister's secretary was a friend of Shah ji's and he told us that the Minister's wife was well known to Ahmad's wife and that Ahmad's wife had been spending a lot of time at the minister's house. Shah ji's family too had known the Minister's family for generations. Shah ji asked for an appointment and we went to see the Minister. We explained our case, showed him the title deeds of the property that I had left behind in Jammu. We told him that we had nothing allotted to us till then and had bought a house to live in, in Karachi, even though I, mother, my aunt and uncle, were all refugees. Shah ji himself had been in charge of allotments but he firmly believed that properties should be allotted to those who had absolutely nothing.

We also told the Minister how good Mr Ahmad was at inventing stories, that he had not made a single film while I had already produced a film in Bombay. Mr Ahmad had spent his entire life in Bombay and there no one had ever heard of any film that he had produced.

Sardar Sahib, the Minister, was a gentleman and he listened attentively to the entire story. His secretary had told us that Ahmad's wife had already warned the Minister that if he did not rule in her husband's favour, she would kill herself by throwing herself under his car. Yet, Sardar Sahib decided in our favour.

We rented out the studio to Choudhary Eid Muhammad. I do not remember what happened but it seems his son got involved in a murder case and the studio was returned to us. Then Hafiz

Agha Hussain showed great keenness to rent the studio and even began making a film there. He paid the rent for the first few months then he too turned out to be untrustworthy. He had lived as an aristocrat since he had migrated and before long, he ran out of money. Yet he continued to maintain the same lifestyle. He was an amusing and cultured man and whenever we went to him to ask for the rent, he told us jokes instead. He made many promises but did not keep even a single one. Every time we decided that on the next visit we would settle matters once and for all, Agha Hussain would be so affectionate and so convincing in his promises that nothing changed. Instead, he began boasting that he had bought the studio. He did not pay rent for a year and a half. We finally got him to vacate the studio though we were not able to recover any of the rent arrears from him.

Shah ji was the kind of man who could only work at a job and had no aptitude for business where you cannot afford to be considerate of others. He was a very considerate and a careless man. He should have taken over the running of the studio himself but he preferred to rent it instead. Here too, he should have thrown out the tenants the moment they defaulted on the rent. We were not successful at any business venture that we attempted.

We had no equipment of our own so the studio was shut down. Now we just had the hotel to provide us an income. After much thought we decided we would rent the hotel to Muzaffar. The sight of Zaidi's eleven weeping children was still vivid in my mind so I insisted that he hire Zaidi as well.

I had become good friends with the cameraman and the sound recordist of the film I had produced in Bombay. The recordist was called Beg and he advised us to buy our own sound truck and camera for that would generate a lot of money. At that time a sound truck cost ninety thousand rupees of which thirty thousand had to be paid in advance and the rest could be paid in instalments. With the thirty thousand we had got from the sale of the shop in Karachi, we acquired our own sound truck and camera.

In Karachi there was a man called Bukhari who had set up a studio-cum office in Gandhi Garden, his five or six rooms looked like hutments, and there he began producing a film. At that time, in Gandhi Garden, there were just these few rooms and the rest was five or six acres of garden with coconut trees and a tubewell. The pathways were well laid out and in this huge area, there were just those ordinary rooms that Bukhari occupied. Soon, Bukhari came to Lahore and asked to rent the sound truck and the camera and take it with him to Karachi. We settled the terms, which stipulated that Beg go along with the equipment.

It had been nearly a year since we had rented out the hotel and Shah ji had been planning a trip to Karachi which he kept postponing. Finally he did go. The day after he left, the postman delivered a letter written by one of the waiters at the hotel. We had hired this man when we had run the hotel ourselves and we had stayed friends. In the letter the waiter asked why we were being so indifferent and ignoring the many letters he had written to us. He was surprised that we had not yet gone to Karachi to take stock of the trouble at the hotel. He also informed us that he had now heard that Muzaffar was trying to get the hotel allotted to himself.

The ground beneath my feet seemed to give way as I read this letter. It also now became clear that this had been going on for some months and the Shah ji had kept the matter secret. A detailed letter from Shah ji arrived a few days later. In it he mentioned that by some devious means, Muzaffar had managed to get the ownership of the hotel transferred to his own name. Shah ji wrote that he had complained to the custodian about this but the matter would take some months to sort out. This meant staying in Karachi for a few months. He asked me not to worry about anything.

He returned after a few days and I decided that we all had to move to Karachi. I had been saving money and had managed to collect thirty thousand, which I had placed in a jewellery box in my bank locker. This reassured me for there was something to fall back upon. In those days this was a lot of money. I went to the locker and opened the jewellery box and found that there was not even a paisa in it! I remembered that I'd recently had the ownership of the locker changed to a joint one.

Furious, I rushed home. Shah ji was there when I arrived. In my anger I hit him hard on the chest and asked him to explain where my money had gone. Shah ji told me that for the last few months the rent from the hotel had stopped arriving and he had not felt up to going to Karachi to deal with the matter. He had hoped that things would sort themselves out and, wanting not to worry me, he had taken out five thousand rupees from the locker every month and handed them to me pretending that this was the rent money from Karachi.

My anger did not go away. 'You did not want me to get worried? Instead you have not only crushed but buried me under more worries. And all this to keep me happy! How many times have you deceived me earlier?' I was calmer after I had let off steam.

At the time, three of our boys were boarders at Aitchison College. My eldest son was about eight. We left him in the school and withdrew the younger ones. We packed up and sent some essential stuff with the servants on the train and we left for Karachi by road. We had a Mercedes-Benz which ran on diesel. I remember it cost us eighteen rupees to get to Karachi.

The problem was finding a place big enough for all of us to stay in Karachi. The four flats we had in the same building were all rented out. Muzaffar now controlled the hotel. Shah ji had already spoken to Bukhari, the man who had rented our camera and sound equipment. We drove straight to the Gandhi Gardens. Beg lived with his family in one brick-built room which was more or less the size of a charpai. He insisted that we use it to rest in the afternoons and he shifted into one of the hutments. We rented four proper though small residential tents and two ordinary tents for the servants and about twenty-five simple charpais. The rent for all these was eight *annas* a day but they were cheaper if rented by the month, which is what we did. We converted the garage into a kitchen.

The road in front of the rooms had large coconut trees on both sides. For water there was the huge tubewell, next to which there was a shady neem tree. The gates of the garden were constantly locked and at night we slept on charpais laid out on the roads in the garden. There were often strong winds at night. During the day, we'd put a few charpais in the shade of the neem tree. The food was brought there and we would eat under the tree.

Bukhari too, was in dire financial straits. When we first arrived, there would sometimes be a music director or a singer sitting around in his office but that was about it. The sound truck and the camera had never been used. Now neither Bukhari, nor anyone else came to the office. The time for which he had paid rent in advance was fast running out and we were all very worried.

Every day Shah ji would write to the Custodian on my behalf. He repeatedly told him that the hotel was our main source of income, that we had had to withdraw our children from the Chief's College and now had no place to live in, in Karachi. He requested him to settle the matter as urgently as possible.

Beg and the cameraman who was called Fazil told us that someone who was planning a film wanted to rent the sound truck and the camera. We told Bukhari about this. He also wanted the equipment off his hands since he had still to use it. We agreed to rent out the equipment on condition that it would be taken only when they needed it and that it be returned the moment they finished work. No one ever made a film using the equipment but as soon as we were about to run out of money, someone would come forward and pay us the rent for it, in advance.

One day I was sitting under the neem tree. The hot wind that was blowing scorched my face and there was nowhere I could go to escape from it. I looked at the sky and prayed. 'O Allah! You know that we do not have a roof over our heads. For the sake of Prophet and his family, please give me some relief. I know I am a sinner but you are beneficent and control the world. If you want, you can flood this place with rain.'

Half an hour later, suddenly, the rain came down in a downpour so severe that it was difficult even to walk back to the tent. It was still raining at nightfall and it was impossible to sleep in the tents. We removed the tables and chairs from Bukhari's room and put our beds there. It rained all night.

We got up early the next morning and removed the beds and put back the tables and chairs, just in case Bukhari came in. It could not have been more than half an hour later when the roof of two of the rooms caved in. I thanked God, for helping us to get out in time. Had we delayed even a short while we would all have been buried alive.

Through all this, Shah ji continued to be the same and always stayed in good humour. Every time he came home, he would bring back fruit, eight or ten fowl or some fish. In short, he was spending money as usual. If I ever reminded him of our situation he would say immediately: 'That power holding up the blue canopy—trust Him. If you trust Him, you will stay happy.'

Ali Raza from Okara, who treated me like a sister, came to visit us with his family. We had a great deal of fun while they were there. We used the guests as an excuse to treat ourselves to roasted meat, seekh kababs, pulau and sweet rice. Sometimes even I would forget that we were in serious trouble. With our guests there, there would be twenty or twenty-five charpais spread out on the roads of Gandhi Garden at night. We talked for hours, recited poetry and joked and laughed till we fell asleep.

During the day, we had our breakfast and lunch under the shady tree over the tubewell. Ali Raza's wife and children frequently commented that life at our home seemed like an endless picnic. A couple of times Muzaffar sent messages that we could have the hotel back if we paid him fifty thousand rupees. I sent back word that Allah willing, I would drive him out of the hotel while I beat him with my shoe. The irony was that it was Zaidi who was behind all this trouble—the same Zaidi whom we had forgiven and for the sake of whose children, we had found him a job with Muzaffar. Muzaffar was a naïve man and it was Zaidi's brain that had cooked up all the mischief.

Every day Shah ji tried to get the matter placed before the Custodian but it was difficult to get an appointment for this. Finally the day arrived when both the parties had to present themselves before the Custodian. Shah ji explained everything in detail. Muzaffar's lawyer could counter none of this. The Custodian reserved his judgement.

Shah ji continued writing on my behalf and requesting an early decision. Finally, two months later, the decision went in my favour. Shah ji found out and came back with the good news. He also said, 'Pack up our stuff, load the car for we have to immediately move into the Green Hotel. If we rely on the legal process to take its course, it will take another two years. This is our chance to repossess the hotel.'

We drove to Green Hotel. We were lucky that room no 21 on the third floor was vacant. We moved in and Muzaffar and Zaidi had no clue what was going on. I then went down to the office and took off my shoe and hit Zaidi at least ten times on the head. Remember, I had vowed that I would drive them out of the hotel with my shoe.

A few hours later, Muzaffar had managed to hire a dozen ruffians. We called the police and told them that we owned the building and that we were living in room 21 which was constantly reserved for us. We complained that the men were there to create trouble and harass us. The police questioned the men, all of whom claimed to be guests of the hotel. The guest register was checked and none of their names was there, so their lie was exposed. The police took back nine of these men with them. The next few times that Muzaffar came back to the hotel, I saw him being carried up the stairs by two people. We presumed he was ill only to discover later that nothing was wrong with him. I think he had lost his mind. The real culprit was Zaidi who had made a lot of money out of the hotel and had disappeared immediately. After two days we never saw Muzaffar again.

I was tired of the hotel by now. Someone suggested that we convert it into six flats and rent them out. In those days the flats would have rented for two hundred and fifty or three hundred rupees a month. We were suffering a huge financial loss because we had chosen to live in Lahore. If someone else had had the property we had, they would have made a great deal of money from it. I sold the beds, chairs, tables and all the furniture. Some I gave away to people I knew. We converted the hotel into six flats, rented them out and returned to Lahore.

* * *

A long time ago I had bought eight acres of land in Garden Town. It had not been easy to put these eight acres together. I had to buy land from about twenty or twenty-five different people. I ended up paying much more than the going price. At that time a 'canal' of land cost six or seven hundred rupees and I often had to pay a thousand to some people.

The land however was close to the city and consisted mostly of cultivated fields. The only habitation close by was Jiyunnana, which had about twenty dwellings where *mazaras* lived. Jiyunnana was a village and all the people were either cultivators or gujars who bred livestock. For years it had my dream to live in Lahore, but to live as though I was living in a village. I wanted a garden with fruit trees; I wanted to keep cows, buffaloes, sheep, goats, deer and other animals. I wanted peafowl to live in my garden.

A very good offer of marriage came up for my eldest daughter. She was eighteen and had finished her Senior Cambridge exam and had become engaged. A few months before the wedding I was in a strange state of mind. I loved her dearly and I would cry a few times a day, in secret, so that no one realized how much I loved her. She was also very attached to me and never used to leave my side for which she was teased by everyone as 'mummy's flea.' I could not imagine life without her.

After my daughter got married, we regularly visited each other. Soon she had a child and since both the parents were inexperienced, the child stayed with me most of the time and that in a way filled the vacuum created by my daughter leaving.

In the eight acres that I had, I started planting fruit trees. I had already acquired cows, buffaloes, sheep and turkeys, all of the best breeds. I also had a tubewell installed. The feed for the animals and birds, the milk, butter and vegetables were now all produced on our land. I collected fruit trees from far and wide. I got mango saplings from Bulandshahar in India. I wanted to grow every possible kind of fruit on my land. People said that it was impossible to grow *chikoo*s in Lahore. I looked after the chikoo plant so carefully that it soon grew into a huge tree with abundant fruit. I planted grapefruit, oranges, sweet lemon, custard apples, mango, lichi, *falsa*, *jamun* and every other fruit that I could think of. The land was stony so I had six feet deep pits dug before I planted each tree. Everything I planted survived. I loved gardening and often spent the entire day at it. The tubewell ran the whole day and the sound of gushing water, the tinkle of bells tied around the necks of bullocks, the green fields all around, made me wish that I could stay there always and not have to return home to Muslim Town.

* * *

In the last seven or eight years, Shah ji had developed diabetes. This caused gangrene to develop in one of his toes. I had him admitted to the United Christian Hospital and they amputated the toe. Very often we had to get the medicinal cream that he needed from America. Every day the doctor would undo the bandage and dress the wound. Shah ji and I stayed in the hospital for three months. The American doctor was very kind and capable and would spend hours talking to Shah ji. One day, during a conversation he casually mentioned that even if a foot had to be amputated, there were good artificial feet available and so it made little difference for the amputee. It was clear from his conversation that he was preparing Shah ji mentally for the possible amputation of his foot.

Everyone in the hospital had become a friend by now. Watching the patients in the hospital I often felt that I should abandon everything and devote my life to caring for the sick in the hospital. I sat through many nights with different women who needed moral support and courage. There was a Memon woman from Karachi who had brought her husband to the hospital. When her husband was troublesome and would not listen to her she would head straight to our room. 'Sister, your brother will not listen to me. Will you please come and convince him?' she would tell me. I would go to their room and tell the man, 'Bhai Sahib, why do you not do this?' His immediate reaction would be. 'All right, if that is what will please you.' There were other patients too with whom I had got very friendly. Having lived in the hospital for three months, I had lost all touch with the outside world. Property, money, a grand life style—all this meant nothing to me in there.

On the tree outside the window, a black piece of cloth was tied to one of the branches. That was the first thing I saw when I got up in the mornings. I would stare at it for hours till other patients distracted me. Our house was very close by but I did not want to leave Shah ji alone for a minute. Our food was sent over from home twice a day and we were very comfortable, However, the world of a hospital is a world in itself. Everyone inside looks worried, fearful or helpless. Shah ji was a courageous man and he was constantly reassuring others around him and making them laugh. When anyone came to see him, he would banter on as though nothing was wrong with him.

Even though three months had passed since the amputation, there were no signs of the wound beginning to heal. One day the doctor called me aside and told me that perhaps they might have to amputate the foot for they were afraid that the gangrene would spread to the entire foot. The wound looked like a small hole on which cream was applied every day but that seemed to be doing no good. One day while I was lying down, it struck me that I should consult a *jarrah*, the traditional surgeons, about it. The next day without telling Shah ji anything, I left the hospital and went outside. There I asked a few elderly people where I would find a good jarrah. I was told a name and I found the man's house.

I told him all about the wound, that it was a small one but it had not healed for three months. The American medicine we were applying might have stopped the wound from growing larger but it definitely was not curing it. I asked him if he could help. He told me that Allah willing, the wound would heal. I reasoned to myself that since the doctors seemed to have no option but to suggest further amputation, where was the harm in trying what he suggested. I was also very afraid of the gangrene spreading to the entire leg and the possibility of Shah ji losing a limb. I was under a great deal of stress.

I went to the *Imambara* of Gamay Shah on the way back from there. This had become a habit with me. Every time I was in trouble I would go there and knock on the doors of the 'People of the family.' They always listened to me. I wept and entreated them again. 'The doctor says that they might have to amputate the foot. *Maula*, listen to me! Save his foot. Make the wound heal. If it does, I will offer a foot made of silver.' After I had prayed, I felt much calmer. I returned to the Hospital and told Shah ji that I had gone to see a jarrah who had assured me that there was a cure for the wound. I told him we should leave the hospital and instead of going home, we should go to Zafar's house.

Shah ji loved his daughter and grandchildren with a passion. I thought he would be happier staying with them for some time. Shah ji readily agreed to my suggestion. Even though he was an educated man and knew nearly as much about medicine as the doctors did, he behaved as though my word was a command. I told the American doctor that Shah ji was feeling very depressed and asked if I could take him home for a week or so. I told him I would bring him back for the operation. The doctor saw no harm in this and he agreed to my request.

The next day we moved to our daughter's house in Shah Jamal. We called the jarrah and he advised us to wrap some curd in a cloth and hang it till all the water had drained out and the curd had turned into *paneer*. He told us to apply the paneer to the wound and to bandage the foot. The first two days this had to be done twice a day. He told us that the first few dressings would make the wound smart. The application did hurt a bit the first time but when the wound was dressed again in the evening, the burning sensation was so strong that Shah ji said that it seemed as if I had placed a live coal on his wound. He could not sleep that night.

The next day when the jarrah came, he said that the burning sensation would last for six or seven days before it stopped. On the third day the pain was so severe that even a brave man like Shah ji who had not even let out a sigh of pain for fear of alarming me cried out, '*Pha ji*, I would rather die than have to go through this.' I reassured him that the jarrah had said that the paneer would eat away the dead flesh and the burning would soon stop.

The burning did stop in about eight days. Though the wound was just as it was, it now looked cleaner than before. We continued the treatment for a month and Shah ji began to feel much better. One day I convinced him to go out for a drive because he had been housebound for nearly four or five months. Shah ji must have been gone for half an hour when Raja Ghazanfar Ali dropped in. Raja Sahib himself had been having problems with his heart and his doctors had severely restricted his movements. Raja Sahib told me that he had to come to see Shabbir the moment he heard about his illness. He did not get out of the car which was parked in the porch, and I sat on the stairs close by. I explained how I had forced Shah ji to go out.

'So, you are his replacement?' Raja Sahib smiled.

'How so?' I asked.

Raja Sahib then told me the story of the blind beggar who sat at the same spot every day with a piece of cloth spread in front of him. People who felt charitable would throw some paisas on the cloth. A clerk who lived close by felt very sorry for the man and every morning on his way to work, he would drop some money on the cloth. One day the only change he found in his pocket was an eight-anna coin which he threw on the cloth. After he had walked a few steps ahead, it struck him that eight annas was no mean amount and he was afraid that some passerby might take it without the beggar knowing. He looked back only to see the man holding the coin, turning it over and examining it carefully. Surprised and angry he returned and asked the man if he was blind or not. The man said he was not, but then he was only a replacement. The clerk asked where the original beggar was and was told that he had gone to see a film. This is what he had in mind, Raja Sahib said, when he had called me Shah ji's replacement. He left after a little while.

Within twenty days Shah ji was able to walk on his bandaged foot. There was some work pending in Karachi so the two of us went there. A month and a half later when Shah ji was dressing the wound he noticed something white in it. We pulled it out with a pair of tweezers and discovered it was about an inch long piece of dry membrane. We applied paneer to the wound and dressed it again. A few days later we returned to Lahore.

In Lahore, we went to see the doctor who had been so kind to us at the hospital. He was the most qualified of all the doctors there, and he was the one who had operated on Shah ji's toe. Shah ji took off his socks and showed him his foot. The doctor was terribly excited. He sat on the floor and held the foot in his lap. He kept examining it and exclaiming: 'Wonderful! This is a miracle. I don't believe it.' He kept looking at it for a long time. We told him nothing about the treatment we had used. I was completely convinced that Shah ji had been cured because of the grace and a miracle performed by the 'People of the family.' The doctor had been convinced that the wound would not heal. Now that Shah ji was cured the doctor was delighted.

* * *

We built a house on our land in Garden Town and moved in. Apart from Shaikh Rasheed's house, there was no other house in the vicinity. The rest of the area consisted of green fields. The fruit trees that I had planted were now beginning to bear fruit. We even bought a small tractor which Shah ji would drive himself and he would supervise the planting of vegetables and fodder. Our days were busy and very pleasant.

We were both very fond of animals. Now we had black buck, blue bull, spotted deer that roamed around freely as did the peafowl. Right in front of the house the ground rose in a five foot high plateau. On this, we fed the peafowl a mixture of all sorts of grain twice a day. They would all collect there to feed and they roosted in a huge *shisam* tree at night. We only kept the pheasants in cages because it was said that they could not be domesticated. As an experiment I kept a pair of chicks outside the cages. I would hold them in my lap and keep them with me all the time. I stroked them when I fed them and they would make affectionate sounds in return. They got so attached to me that they came to me wherever I was and when I tickled them they would spread out their feathers and chirp with pleasure. At night they would sit on the parapet of the house. In spite of what they said about pheasants not making good pets, these two loved me so much that they were never quiet till I stroked them a few times a day.

Shah ji would often go out to hunt partridge. He would leave in the morning and come back in the evening. In those days many of our friends came to stay and some stayed for months and time passed wonderfully. Indeed, often our friends, did not want to leave. We produced our own grain, vegetables, milk, butter, and lassi. In fact, people living close by would come to ask for lassi and vegetables. Allah was very beneficent to us.

Our son-in-law was appointed the Law Minister. Since her marriage our daughter had always lived in Lahore. She was constantly in and out of the house. Her older son actually spent most of his time with us. Since he was their first child, even if he caught a cold, his parents would panic and bring him to us. Till now it had not sunk in that our daughter was now married and had moved out of our home. As Law Minister, her husband had to live permanently in Rawalpindi. My daughter whom we called

Saifi, was very unhappy about having to move. Some journalists asked her if she was happy now that she was the wife of the Law Minister. She truthfully answered that it was true that this was a happy development but she was unhappy because she would now have to live in Rawalpindi when her mother lived in Lahore. Within a week they had all moved out of Lahore, but we were happy that Pindi was not that far. We could meet whenever we wanted. Saifi and Zafar would manage to come once a week and sometimes Saifi came alone. We would go and see them whenever we could and thus we did not miss each other.

After three sons their fourth child was a daughter. Shah ji loved girls and now that he had his own granddaughter, he was in heaven. If he had been allowed to have his way, he would have brought her back with us to Lahore. But then, Saifi and Zafar doted on her too. Shah ji would send for her every so often and after a few days would send her back. However, he called a few times every day. Shah ji had loved Saifi a lot too, but now he loved her daughter Roshaneh more.

* * *

Roshaneh must have been two when one of the nails of Shah ji's foot turned black. Shah ji told me about it. I rang up Saifi and told her. 'Bring Daddy to Pindi immediately,' she said, 'I have spoke to Dr General Muhiuddin. Come so that the treatment can begin immediately.'

I immediately began to prepare to leave for Pindi so that I could get Shah ji into hospital. Meanwhile, Shah ji called Saifi and said, 'Send Roshaneh to Lahore for a day. I want to see her.'

'You are coming to Pindi the day after tomorrow,' she reminded him. 'What is the point of sending her now?'

'Yes, I know all that,' Shah ji insisted, 'but still, can you not send her to Lahore with a servant today?' I will send her back tomorrow.'

'This is very strange, Daddy,' Saifi said, 'I don't understand why I should send her in this heat for a day. How will a day make a difference? You will be here day after tomorrow in any case.'

'Please do as I say,' Shah ji pleaded, 'I know all that, yet I want to see her. Do not be so stubborn. Send her today.'

Saifi repeated herself and told him that he was behaving like a child. Shah ji gave up. 'All right Saifi, do as you please. What can I say? I was only asking for her to come for a day. Can you not send her?'

Saifi again refused. Disappointed, Shah ji put the phone down saying, 'I wish this was within my power. There is nothing left to be done. Do as you please.'

Shah ji had a slight temperature too. In the evening he had a table fan and a cot put out in the open and lay down. A close relative of his was getting married and Shah ji was insistent that I attend one of the ceremonies that evening. I did not want to go but agreed under pressure. I was in no mood to dress up for a wedding and I told him that if I were going, I would go just as I was.

There was a man who tutored my children in Mathematics when they were young. He dropped in just then. He was very interested in poetry but was always misquoting it. He recited a couplet of Ghalib, incorrectly as usual. Shah ji and he began arguing over it. Telling them that I was going to the wedding, and would be back in an hour or two, I left. There I met Shah ji's elder brother who had come from Khanpur for the wedding. We began to talk about Shah ji. I told him that one of his toenails had turned black and that I was taking him to Rawalpindi because Zafar had arranged for a good doctor to attend to him and that Shah ji would be admitted into hospital the day after tomorrow. Even though Sunday was a holiday, General Muhiuddin had said that we should go straight to the hospital and he would admit Shah ji. His brother Inayat agreed with my decision and instructed me that Shah ji be taken to hospital as soon as possible so that the gangrene did not spread. I came home a little while later

Shah ji was still outside talking to the tutor. I asked him if he had eaten anything. 'No, I do not feel hungry,' he said, 'God alone knows why I have lost my appetite.' Even though no troubling thoughts of what might happen to Shah ji had entered my mind, I did not feel like eating either. In fact, I was sure that nothing was going to happen to him. Yet, I do not know why, but there was a heaviness in my heart. I was not able to get rid of it.

We came into the house and went to sleep. I habitually woke at six in the morning. I sent for tea. Neither of us used to have any breakfast. Since Shah ji had not eaten the night before, I said: 'Shah ji, you had ordered *khichdi* for dinner. Why do you not eat some of it with curd?'

'I don't feel like eating anything right now,' he said.

'I will start packing for Pindi,' I said.

'Send for the suitcase and do it here, in front of me,' Shah ji requested.

I brought the suitcase into the room and asked him what he wanted to take along. 'Pack ten kurtas, ten vests, and tahmads— five of them.' There was one tahmad short.

'I am wearing one and there should be five more,' he said, 'Look for it.,

Shah ji preferred to wear kurtas and tahmads when at home. Like a child he insisted, 'Find the fifth tahmad and pack it.'

My eldest son was in charge of a factory at Renala. Every weekend he came with his family to visit me. Today was Saturday and his wife arrived alone. I told her how Shah ji's toe nail had gone black and that was why we were getting ready to leave for the hospital in Pindi. 'Saifi and Zafar insist that the hospital there is better than the ones here and that General Muhiuddin is a good and competent doctor. Because of Zafar we will get special attention. I am glad you have come for I have to go and get the air tickets.' I then turned to Shah ji. 'What else do you want me to pack?'

'Just that one tahmad that is missing. Just find that.'

I explained the problem to Manizeh, my daughter-in-law. We explained to Shah ji that perhaps the tahmad was with the washerman. After all there would be others going to Rawalpindi soon and they could bring it.

Having finished the packing I pleaded with Shah ji again to have something to eat since he had had no dinner the previous night. I also rang the doctor who had been treating Shah ji till now and told him that we were taking Shah ji to Pindi and asked him to please come over. Even though he would no longer be treating him, we had known the doctor for a long time. He was over in five minutes. He examined his heart, his blood pressure, his sugar level and said that it was safe for him to travel.

I served Shah ji some khichdi and curd. He ate some and left a few morsels remaining in the plate.

'Why not finish it?' I asked, 'Come on, eat all of it.'

Like an obedient child he did what I said. My youngest son offered to go and fetch the tickets so that I could stay with him.

'No,' said Shah ji, 'You go and get the tickets and on your way back pick up Tahira from the school. First get the tickets.'

It was eleven then. I left saying that I would return after picking up Tahira at one o'clock. The office of Pakistan International Airlines was on the Mall Road and there was a short cut through Gulberg. When I passed the United Christian Hospital, all the memories of our stay came rushing back: the small black cloth pennant flapping in the wind outside the window; my going to the nurses' room every morning at five and singing devotional songs. All this flashed before my eyes for a second. I prayed desperately: '*Ya maula*, I had prayed that his wound would heal, that we do not have to amputate it; that he never see the inside of a hospital again. I had promised a foot made of silver and I kept my word. Why is this now happening to me?'

I picked up the air tickets. Then I picked up Tahira from school. Remembering that the cook was on leave, I stopped at the *tandoor* and picked up some rotis. It was about a quarter past one when I reached home. A few servants and some others were standing outside. Someone opened the car door and I stepped out. They came up to me and one of them said softly: 'Something has happened to Shah ji.'

'Nothing has happened,' I dismissed the information, 'he will be all right soon,' I added as I headed towards the stairs to the verandah. There, a weeping Manizeh clung to me. I climbed the stairs on to the verandah and mother hugged me and said, 'Shah ji is dead.'

* * *

I went straight to our room. There I saw Shah ji lying turned on to one side. On his face was the familiar smile. There were no signs of pallor and there was no way you could tell that he was dead.

Instead, he looked as if he was in a deep sleep. There was serenity and peace on his face. Not a tear fell from my eyes. Our beds, which were separate, were next to each other and looked as though there was just one bed. I had had the beds made myself at Chiniot. I lay down on my bed and started staring at Shah ji's face. I was told that at one he had asked, 'Has she returned as yet?' Mother had told him that I was not back. He had then said: 'But it is time for her to be back.' He then turned on to his side. Mother noticed that as he turned over, his eyes rolled over. 'Shabbir, Shabbir,' mother had called out and had got no answer.

'Why are you waking him up?' Manizeh had told her, 'he obviously wants to sleep, so let him be.'

There had been no other signs. No hiccups and no gasping for breath. There were no signs of discomfort on his face as he quietly left the world. It was only my misfortune that I was late by ten minutes. Lord alone knows what he might have said to me. Even in his last minutes he had wanted to know if I was back.

Without shedding a tear, I lay there on the bed facing him for half an hour, looking at his face—his wide forehead, his half-smile. It seemed that he would speak any minute. He usually slept on his side, one hand under his cheek, the other hand on his hip. On his wrist was the Omega watch he had bought when we had gone to Hong Kong on the ocean liner named Asia. I took off the watch and put it on my wrist as a momento. Then I said, 'All right, *Khuda Hafiz*, may God protect you. Forgive me for all my mistakes, my rudeness and all the sorrows I caused you. I never asked for forgiveness while you were alive. Now, with folded hands, I ask to be forgiven. At times, I have been very cruel to you. For the sake of God and His Prophet, forgive me for those.' For a long time I kept sitting there with my hands folded. I did not shed a tear even then. I just sat there silently and stared at him. I was neither sad nor miserable. Nor was I in shock. Instead, I felt as if my strength and courage had doubled. What was surprising was that the realization of the extent of my loss had not begun to even sink in.

Choudhary Sultan, a Deputy Commissioner, had been a long time friend of Shah ji's. His younger brother was the Deputy Superintendent of Police. He arrived an hour later. He looked at

Shah ji and repeatedly told me: 'Sister, brother Shabbir is still alive. We should call a doctor. As a policeman I have seen countless corpses. Believe me, he is still alive.'

'The doctor has been to see him,' I told him.

It was the 15th of June and it was extremely hot. We arranged for blocks of ice and placed them around his bed. All of Shah ji's relatives had already arrived in Lahore for his niece's wedding. Saifi and Zafar had yet to arrive. There was also Shah ji's nephew whom he loved more than a son and who was out of Lahore. They had all been informed over the telephone. Some were driving in, others flying to Lahore.

Practically the whole of Lahore knew Shah ji. Both rich and poor had been his friends. As the news of his death spread, people began to leave work or close their shops and began arriving at our home. In those days, fields surrounded the house in Garden Town. The entire population of Muslim Town, including the children and women, was there and crying loudly. They were lamenting in one voice: 'Shah ji who will we now go to with our problems? Who will help us now? Oh God! Why did you not take us instead of him? Oh Shah ji, what is this calamity that has befallen us?'

I was sitting in the verandah listening to all this. There was such a crowd that the durries spread around the house were full. Many people were sitting on the ground talking to each other. People filed past me as they went into the room where Shah ji lay. Fifteen or twenty minutes later they would emerge saying the same thing—that he looked as if he was asleep, not dead. This went on the whole day. I sat and watched all this very calmly. I was not crying nor was I in shock. Saifi and Zafar also arrived.

Durries and mattresses were spread out on the terrace at night so that people who wanted to, could lie down. All the relatives stayed over. Throughout the night, Colonel Bashir, who was Shah ji's cousin, would come and sit by me for a few minutes and then he would get up and start pacing again. Two years ago he had lost his son, a pilot in the Air Force, in a crash. I had not seen him in such a state even at the death of that young man. Shah ji's older brother sat quietly leaning against a bolster. Every so often he would utter the same words: 'Shabbe, this was no time for you to leave. How has all this happened?' All the relatives sitting on the terrace were talking about him. I watched all this as a dispassionate observer. I heard what they said but felt nothing. Neither their words nor their mourning affected me. I was neither sorry nor worried.

Often I thought of going into the room and taking a look at Shah ji. But then I wondered, what if he had lost his colour, what if his face had lost its demeanour? I asked Saifi a few times if Shah ji's colour or expression had changed and she reassured me that nothing had changed. Yet I was so afraid that it might be so, that I did not dare go into the room. I wanted to remember him as I last saw him. The night passed.

The timing for the funeral had been advertised as ten in the morning newspapers. At eight they told me that they were taking him in for a bath and that I should come in and have a look at him. This was like a jolt. I went into the room silently and looked at Shah ji. I closed my eyes and quietly repeated. 'Forgive me for all my mistakes and for the sorrows I caused you. Forgive me.' I left the room before they carried him away. At ten they came and told me that he was ready and that I should come and take a last look. That is when I lost all my strength and courage. It seemed as if I had been hit on the head with a heavy hammer. For the first time I panicked. He was going away forever. We would never meet again. I began to shiver as my hands and feet went cold. I felt life draining away from me. Feeling like a corpse myself, I came and sat in the verandah.

Shah ji's body had been placed in the grounds of the house. There were so many people that all the surrounding fields were full. It seemed as if Lahore had emptied itself into these fields and that everyone from the city had come to join the funeral. All of them came and had a last look at him. This took two hours or so.

Shah ji's family burial ground was at Shah Jamal. The road between Garden Town and Shah Jamal was closed to vehicular traffic that day. When they lifted Shah ji to take him to the burial ground, I made no fuss nor did I plead with them not to take him away. Nor did I run after them wailing that they take me with them. I had seen women behaving like this at funerals. Other women had to hold such women back while they beat their breasts. Whenever I had watched a scene like this, I had wondered why they behaved in such a hysterical manner. If they had to weep and lament they might just as well stand or sit in one place and do so. It seemed so futile to run after a funeral procession.

They took Shah ji away and all the men left with him. Yet there were so many women left that the grounds below the verandah were full. All of them were talking about Shah ji. I was constantly asked about his last moments. What were his last words? How did everything happen so suddenly? I would answer the questions briefly and retreat into silence. I wished that no one would speak to me.

Those who had gone to bury Shah ji returned two hours later. A little while later food arrived for the nearly four hundred relatives who were there. White sheets were spread on durries and food was served in the verandah. Everyone insisted that I eat something for I had not eaten for nearly two days. With great difficulty I swallowed a few mouthfuls. Then they insisted that I go to my room and rest. When I went into the room, I felt as though I was in a wilderness. I felt frightened at being in the room.

What happened then was like what happens when a dam bursts and the water gushes out. I began to scream and cry and did so for so long that Manizeh got worried. 'That's enough. Stop crying Mummy.' She tried to help. For two days I had not shed a tear. Now the tears would not stop. Nor have they stopped since then. Neither my head nor my heart has accepted the fact that Shah ji is dead.

* * *

The whole house seemed deserted. I constantly worried about how I would manage without him. The possibility that something might happen to him, and I might be left alone, had never occurred to me. I began to wonder why I had teased him so much; why I had never told him that I loved him; why I insisted on having things my way and never gave in to his wishes. Everywhere that I looked, I only noticed his absence. My ears would long to hear the words, '*Pha ji*.' He would go on with his 'Pha ji, Pha ji' all day long. All I wanted to do was to lie in my room alone.

People came from near and far to offer their condolences. Everyone had similar stories to tell: how Shah ji had helped them out at some time or the other. One large landowner from a village near Okara came to call on us. He insisted that he would organise all the ceremonies for the 'tenth-day' rituals. He was told that that was out of the question. He replied that if we denied him his wish he would curse himself for the rest of his life. For two days he hung around and pleaded with folded hands that if not the 'tenth-day' rituals he should be allowed to organise the 'fortieth-day' ones. Finally the only way left for us was to try and convince him how difficult it would be for him to do so since he was not even from Lahore. He reassured us that he would bring all the things needed with him, and that he would also arrange for the cooks and helpers.

'Whatever I am worth today is because of Shah ji,' he told us, 'There was a time when an installment for my land was due and I did not have the money. None of my friends or relatives helped. They were not even sympathetic to my plight. I was very worried when Shah ji saw me sitting silently. He asked me, "Abbas, what is the matter? You look very worried." I told him everything.'

"Is that all?" Shah ji had said.

"Is this not something I should be worried about?" I had retorted. "If I lose my land, how will I live?"

"Do not worry, your land will stay with you," Shah ji had reassured me.

'God knows how but he managed to arrange the money and give it to me. When I went to return the money a couple of months later, Shah ji asked what the hurry was. He had stressed a few times that I did not have to get into debt in order to repay him. He was in no hurry to recover the money and had told me that I could return the money when I had nothing else to worry about.

'I had reassured him that I had no problems in repaying his debt at the moment. I never had the opportunity of doing anything for him. Now that he is no longer with us, please let me do this much for him. I will feel much better about it.' I accepted his offer to organise the 'fortieth day' ceremonies.

Every day, on every occasion, I missed Shah ji. I could not keep my mind away from thoughts of him. It had been ten or twelve days since he had passed away and yet it seemed I heard him calling 'Begum, Begum, Pha ji, Pha ji,' all the time. Sometimes the voices were so real that I would excitedly start looking around for him only to find that my mind had been playing tricks. My eyes longed for a sight of him. If I could, I would spend all the time in my room where I stared at a blank wall. I would think of him and of all the places we had been to together, the people we had met, the occasions when we had quarrelled and what had precipitated the quarrels. I thought of the times I had lost my temper and of the innumerable times when Shah ji went out of his way to humour and pamper me. It would seem as if all the memories were being projected on the wall like a movie. The memories also brought with them endless tears. This became an obsession with me. Whenever I got the chance I would retreat to my room, stare at the blank wall, think of him and cry inconsolably. I lay awake for hours at night. I longed to hear the words 'Begum' and 'Pha ji' once again.

I woke up every day to loneliness and desolation. When he was alive, even if he was alone in the verandah, the house seemed full of cheer and activity. He was always full of fun and nothing seemed to trouble him. He joked with everyone, called the servants by the names he had given them himself. He had so much energy that life had passed effortlessly.

Every so often I felt sorry that I had not appreciated him enough when he was alive. But then the thought of a life without him had never even crossed my mind. I had been sure that he would never leave me for he could not spend a moment away from me. Every wish of mine had been a command for him. Since we were married, he had not thought or cared for anyone else. On the other hand, I, even if I had to call out for a servant, would ask Shah ji to do it for me. He would call out to them and save me even that bit of trouble. When we travelled on one of his hunting or work trips, it was my comfort that he would arrange for first. When we out hunting he would have the gas lamps lit first and placed on either side of my bed for I was used to bright lights. He smoked the huqqa regularly but he only attended to that after he saw to it that I was comfortably settled. For him, my comfort, my happiness always came first. He loved me as much at the end of his life as when we had first met.

We used to have fights over the children and I would admonish him, 'Why do you behave like this?'

He would answer, 'Begum, you will come to regret this when I am dead for only then will you realize the difference between the children and me.'

Confidently, I would retort, 'After all these are my children. I have not produced pieces of stone from my womb. As for something happening to you! Well, I will weep and wail as all other women do and then get on with life.' Now, within just ten or twelve days, I found out what he really meant. I had been completely destroyed and each day brought more sadness with it. I wondered what I would do, where I would go, how I could bring those days back. I was completely shattered.

Within a fortnight I discovered that no one needed me any more. I longed to hear the words 'Darling,' 'Begum,' and 'Pha ji'—the sounds of words which once had begun annoying me. I had a constant sinking feeling for I was afraid I would not be able to survive without him. I wondered how all cheer, joy and happiness had disappeared so suddenly. These emotions were all associated with Shah ji and obviously they were not going to come back. He had been all that I had. Why had I not realized this when he was alive? Why did I not appreciate him then? How would I find any of this again? Feeling helpless and alone, I would weep constantly but that did not ease the pain. All of our life together I had behaved like a child and his pampering had spoilt me completely.

Before his death, when I used to go the bathroom at night, I would wake him up and tell him to keep talking to me while I was inside. If he fell back to sleep and stopped talking, I would come back and wake him to taunt him: 'Obviously your sleep is more precious to you than me.' Apologetically, he would say, 'Begum I am very sorry. I could not help it. I just fell asleep again.' He never retaliated with, "Begum, you are a mother of many children now. If I stopped shouting out to you, will a monster swallow you in there?'

Things changed dramatically with his death. I slept alone in our room. Tahira slept in a small room next to mine. I suddenly realized I was no longer afraid of death. Helplessness leads to resignation. There was no one to put up with my airs and whims now.

Days continued to pass. It is wrongly believed that time deadens pain. This is not so. In fact, as time passed, I missed him more and felt sadder. Every night I lay in bed, thought of the past and cried. My eyes began to cloud and my heart would begin to palpitate. I would try to calm it with my hands when I had to turn around in bed but that did not stop it from beating as fast as it did.

One day all the boys had gone out for a hunt. Tahira and I were alone at home. The house was huge and a servant and his wife slept at a distance from the room. The house was surrounded by eight acres of land without even a boundary wall around it. The past again flashed before my eyes—of how Shah ji took care of me in every way. For one he tried his best that I was with him wherever he went. If he had to go on official work for a week or so without me, he would invite some of his friends and leave them behind as guests with instructions not to leave till he had returned and also to see to it that I was never lonely. Sometimes my aunt would come from Sialkot to be with me but he was never fully reassured.

Now this had changed completely. Mother was in Sialkot. Tahira, who must have been eleven or twelve then, was asleep in her room. I thought of the past again and began to cry and might have cried myself to sleep though even till today, I am not sure whether I was asleep or awake when I saw Shah ji standing in front me that night. He was saying: 'You crazy one! Why are you crying? Why have you assumed that you are alone? Don't you know I will always be with you? Never again consider yourself alone. My crazy one, you know that I cannot live a moment without you.'

I sat up. I looked everywhere for him. I even went outside the house to see if he was there. Eventually I returned to my room and said loudly, 'Why have you left me alone? Please do not do so. I cannot live without you. I have no one except you. Only you were truly my own.' Like a mad woman I screamed to myself before I fell asleep.

I wept frequently for the next three months. My eyes now seemed to be clouded constantly and my heart palpitated all the time. I was also in serious financial trouble. The studio had been allotted to me, but all the claims that we had paid for turned out to be non-existent. This is a long story. In a nutshell, now along with facing personal loss, I had to deal with financial problems. I often wondered what would happen to me. One day, lying in my room it struck me that if all I did was to lie, think and weep about my problems, I would go mad, fall ill or go blind.

Now when the person who spent twenty hours a day with me had gone, there was no one in the family who cared to spend even an hour with me. In these three months, everything had become clear to me. It became clear that as far as others were concerned, my views did not matter any more; that no one needed me anymore. There had been a time when nothing in the house happened without my being consulted about it. Now I was deemed to be a foolish and incompetent woman. In those three months, no one called out to me even once.

I got up from the bed immediately and sent for the driver. I went straight to the office which dealt with claims. I met a few people and told them everything and they were very sympathetic. I made it a routine to go the office every day to get the prices of the claims reduced. The person who had the power to do this, soon became a friend. When the studio had been allotted the papers said that it contained equipment but there was none when we had taken possession. On this basis he reduced the price by eighty thousand rupees. This eased the pressure a bit. I kept myself busy. I hated being at home and therefore started visiting friends and relatives. However, wherever I went, I was ready to leave within ten minutes.

Saifi and Zafar would try and take me with them wherever they travelled. There is no place in Pakistan where they did not take me along. It pained me to travel and often I would start weeping. I missed him at every moment on these trips and I tried very hard to keep control over myself. I would be reminded of the things that he did for me when we travelled. I did my best to ensure that Saifi never found out that I had been crying. Saifi and Zafar tried to involve me in everything and tried to cheer me up and this would depress me further. I hated myself for having come with them and for ruining things for them, for in a group, it just takes one unhappy person to make the rest uneasy. The more attention they paid me, the more depressed I felt. I decided I would not go out with anyone anymore.

I had been fond of embroidery since I was a child. I began to embroider again. I did not leave a moment free. If I did nothing for ten minutes, memories would begin to flood in. I began to play the sitar and continued to play for some time till one of the strings broke. I did not get it fixed nor did I ever play again. Instead I filled my time with embroidery, and patchwork and started to make soft toys for children.

It was around this time that Reshma, the singer, had appeared on the music scene. I loved her voice, particularly her song *Hai yo rabba naiyun laga dil mera*—'O Lord, where do I find peace?' I wished I could listen to it all day. Reshma was then still very rustic, unaffected, naïve and meek. All she wanted was to find people who would listen to her and appreciate her. By nature she was simple and austere and she respected me a great deal. I said to her, 'Reshma, I wish you would come spend a week with me.'

'*Hai Baji!*' she exclaimed. 'How could I be more fortunate than this? But I have a small child.'

'That does not matter,' I reassured her.

The next day she arrived with her child and a man and stayed for a week. At least a dozen times a day I would request her, 'Reshma, please sing that song for me.'

Obediently, she would begin to sing. With no music, happy to beat the table with her fingers for rhythm. While she sang, I would cry my heart out and feel lighter. Often I asked her to sing at night. Before she began singing, she would always say, '*Na Bibi na*, please do not listen to this song anymore. Something might happen to you. Please stop this.'

'No,' I would insist, 'I like that song. It makes me feel better. Just sing it for me, please.'

The poor thing would begin to sing again. That whole week I kept listening to the song and weeping. I will forever be indebted to Reshma for this. Even though it has been fifteen or twenty years now, Shah ji continues to live within me. In fact the treachery and selfishness of those who were my own, makes me miss him more. I felt worse about how dismissive I had been of one who was Allah's boon to me. He was so unselfish, sincere and kind; ready to offer his life for each wish of mine; one who never stopped me from doing what I pleased. Now with him gone, I felt really alone.

* * *

I continued to live in Garden Town for another thirteen or fourteen years after he died. My family, even though they lived with me, never felt the need to consult me over any matter. And this, when everything legally belonged to me. Shah ji had ensured that I would never be in need and that legally, everything belonged to me.

Experience has taught me one basic truth. If a husband and wife love each other, there can be no stronger bond in life. I loved Shah ji dearly. However, the way he spoilt me, it would seem that the love was one-sided. I never acknowledged my love for him either in words or for that matter, even in my heart, even though I could not bear to be separated from him even for a moment. When he was away, I felt as if the house would swallow me up and I spent every moment waiting for him to return. Yet, I kept him ignorant of my feelings.

A few days before he died, he had been in a sad and dejected frame of mind. A few times I had asked him the reason. Finally he had said, 'I feel you do not love me anymore.'

To this I had retorted, 'When have I ever said that I did?'

He had looked even more sad after this. I had become increasingly angry over the whole matter. We were both getting on in years. Our children were adults and here he was thinking of love and romance! To show my indifference, I would start humming or doing something to show him that things were fine with me, and that I did not care how he felt.

Eventually he took his pen and paper and started writing a story. As time passed he appeared sadder and I was more irritable. I would laugh at the smallest matter when he was around. I ignored him and pretended that I was completely unaware of how he was feeling. He would sit with his pen and paper, think and write.

When I realized that by ignoring the matter, or treating it as a joke, the situation was deteriorating, I said: 'Shah ji I want to speak to you.'

He held the pen in his mouth and said, 'Go on, say it.'

'Just tell me,' I said, 'have you fallen in love with someone else?'

'No', he said

'Then what is your problem? Why are you being so silly? You sit and brood and imagine all sorts of silly things—that I no longer love you; that I no longer care for you. You feel I give the children more attention than you. None of this is true. I feel for you today just as I did at the beginning. Whether I loved you then or not is another matter, but the way I feel for you today has not changed. I had never made any claims of being in love even then. Nothing has changed. You are imagining all this because you have nothing to do. We do not talk and we do not fight anymore. So, you convince yourself that I no longer need you, or worse, that I have begun to dislike you. I am tired of listening to your monody so I have deliberately pretended to ignore you. I am still the same person and nothing has changed. You however, seem to have gone mad. At our age, it's a joke to think of these matters.'

Hearing this, his face went red with pleasure. 'Pha ji darling' he exclaimed. 'Even today I feel as though we have just met. You have no idea how often I prayed that you would accept me. You are the most precious thing in the world for me. Apart from you, I want nothing else from life.' He carried on saying things like this.

He was back to his normal self. The jokes, the humour, the teasing, returned. Nothing seemed to worry him any more and nor did he punish himself any longer. He forgot about the story he had started writing. If only I had not started that conversation, at least the story might have been completed! He had only written a page and half.

It was all over a month and a half after that. The world went dark on me. Suddenly, I had no friend left, not even someone who cared for me. I had lost my life companion. After his death I have kept myself busy from morning till night. And one of the reasons I keep myself so occupied is to stop myself from missing him. I move from one thing to another but my heart is really not in anything I do. I just try and keep memories far away. Now, I am even tired of trying to unburden myself. There is nothing that I feel like doing. I feel alienated from everything.

The selfish behaviour of someone for whom I stayed up nights has made me wary of the world. As the secrets were unveiled I was increasingly reminded of what Shah ji used to say. 'Begum, the ones to whom you are giving precedence over me will cause you regret one day.' Today, that memory embarrasses me.

What a fool I have been! Legally I owned everything. And I trusted someone very close to me so much that I closed my eyes to his deeds. The moment Shah ji died, he started thinking only of himself and I continued to trust him. Things only became clear when I came to my senses, but by then it was too late. Everything had been sold by then. I became embittered and missed Shah ji even more. After him, there was only one true well-wisher of mine left. Mother. She too passed away. She had given me back every paisa. She had handed over all the jewellery, money, clothes and had come to live with me.

In Lahore, Shah ji had lived in the house of his nephews. Mother had built us a house in Muslim Town and given us money for the land in Garden Town. She had kept nothing for herself. My aunt gave me money to build a house for my eldest son, and that paid for the building of the basic structure.

Mercifully I have a roof over my head but I continue to miss Shah ji at every step, a bit of me dies every time I think of him. I will miss him as long as I live.

I have six children. Thankfully, all except one, have been good children. My eldest son has an M A from Cambridge. He is obedient, honourable and considerate. He has a good job and is married into a well-known family. After him there is my daughter who is married to S M Zafar. We had my second son placed in a good company but he could only keep that job for a year and a half. My fourth child and third son is in the army. He is fearless and brave, afraid of nothing and no one but God. With some others he captured a fort in Chamb Jaurian and was decorated for his bravery with the *Sitara i-jurrat*. He was wounded in the war but thank God he recovered. My fourth son too is kind, obedient and brave. He was still studying when his father died. My youngest daughter was eleven and was at school at that time.

On the advice of S M Zafar I left the management of my affairs to one of my sons. I was advised to sell a few canals of the land to settle tax dues. S M Zafar also advised that all formalities be completed in his office; that I go there to sign the papers. He told my son to keep the accounts.

I remember well the time I signed the first documents. After that all deals were made without my knowledge. Nine acres of land were sold and my signatures forged on all the sale deeds. Even the house was sold without my knowledge.

There were so many memories associated with that house. I tried very hard to keep a few canals of that land for myself. Unfortunately I lost everything I continued to be under the illusion that he was doing all this for my benefit.

It was not as if I had not been warned. My third son who was in the army constantly advised me not to move out of the house under any circumstances. He was convinced that I was being cheated. 'He is cheating his own mother,' he had said. And even more categorically, 'He is appropriating everything you own.'

'God forbid,' I would scold him, 'he reads the Quran and says his prayers. He cannot be dishonest.' Instead, I had bought twenty canals of land along the canal that flows through Lahore and entrusted even the registration of that deal to the same son with firm instructions that the name of my youngest daughter be included in the registration papers. With the eighty thousand rupees that my aunt had given me for building a house for my eldest son, I had already begun construction on two and a quarter canals of the land.

When my son had sold the house I was living in, he started insisting that I shift as soon as possible into the house I was building next to the canal. He had the bathrooms, floors and the woodwork finished in a hurry. He wanted me to move into that house as soon as possible and pestered me every day about it.

My daughter and her husband Zafar said they too wanted seven canals of the land to build a house for themselves. I gave it to them at the same price at which I had bought it. My son, the one so regular with his prayers, told me that Zafar had taken eight instead of seven canals of land. I told him that since the matter involved my daughter, I would rather keep quiet about it. Even if he had taken more than he had paid for, after all, it ended up belonging to my daughter.

Since I had had a nine acre garden in Garden Town, I bought nine acres in Raiwind and had bamboo planted on it. I would go there every day. After a year of so I found out that that half the land had been purchased in my son's name. Later in connivance with the revenue official he had even the rest of my remaining land transferred to his own name. I stopped going there.

I feel sorry that I have to say all this about my son. But, since I have been honest about everything else, I have to write this too. Today I feel detached from everything.

I had always been attracted to plants. Now, I spend all my day caring for them. After Shah ji's death I started embroidering on canvas. I embroidered so many pictures that I exhibited them twice in Lahore and Islamabad. People said that they had seen no one else create such beauty on canvas using a needle. I embroidered a huge portrait of Baba Guru Nanak. I had his picture sent to me from Amritsar. I spent days on his eyes but failed to capture that special look in his eyes. I embroidered and undid them countless times. Finally, I prayed. 'Baba, it was only after I had looked into your eyes that I began this piece. Bless me that I can complete it the way I want to.'

The Lord accepted my prayer and I finished the portrait. A Sikh gentlemen from Toronto, a friend of Zafar, saw it. He was captivated and asked me to give it to him so that he could put it up in the Gurudwara in Toronto. Zafar pleaded his case and said, 'You can always do another piece for the Amritsar Gurudwara. Give this one to him.' I presented the piece to him and it now hangs in a Gurudwara in Toronto.

Select Glossary

Note: A large number of Urdu words appear in this book. However, much of the time, their meaning is clear from the context and therefore they have not been glossed. Below is a very short list of words with meanings/contexts that may need some explanation.

Bafta: A type of textile

Canals: A unit of measurement for land. One acre comprises nine canals

Dadra: A light classical genre of Hindustani music set to a six-beat rhythm

Doshala: A covering made up of a pair of shawls

Fasana-I-Azad: A well-known book

Fatiha: Prayers offered for saints or for dead people

Gujars: A caste, usually engaged in agriculture and cattle breeding

Imambara: A venerated place where the replicas of the shrines of Hasan and Hussain, the grandsons of the Prophet, are kept. Visited particularly during Muharram celebrations

Kafi: A raga. Also Punjabi lyric based compositions

Khayal: a vocal genre of Hindustani classical music

Majlis: Literally a gathering. Majlis' are a regular feature of Muharram celebrations

Masnad: A special seating place where people usually recline on bolsters

Marsiyas: A narration of the end of Hasan and Hussain, sung during Muharram.

Masaras: A caste of peasants

Noha: A lament

Qaaf: An Urdu letter (alphabet). The difference between qaaf and kaaf is considered crucial in Urdu diction)

Saif-ul-Mulk: A well-known book of history

Salim Shahi shoes: Shoes with pointed, curved tips

Sitara-i-jurrat: Literally, star of valour. Military Honour bestowed by the Government of Pakistan

Thumri: A light classical genre of Hindustani music

Toda: Rhythmic composition used in Kathak dance